Best of the California Coast

Ken McKowen
and
Dahlynn McKowen

Best of the California Coast

ISBN 978-0-9824654-2-4
Library of Congress Catalog Number 2014911841

Cover Design: Ken McKowen
Primary cover location: North Pebble Beach, Crescent City, CA

Great efforts have been made to make the information in this book as accurate as possible; however, over time trails are rerouted or closed and signs and landmarks may change. If you find a change has occurred to a trail or other destination site included in this book, please let us know so we can correct future editions.

A word of caution: Outdoors recreation by its nature is potentially hazardous. Those participating in such activities must assume all responsibility for their own actions and safety. The scope of this book does not cover all potential hazards and risks involved in outdoor recreation activities.

Published by
Publishing Syndicate LLC
PO Box 607
Orangevale, California 95662

Moonrise, Monterey Coast

This book is dedicated to Dahlynn's son— and Ken's stepson—Shawn.

Shawn: You have traveled with us since the age of three, and now you are in your last year of high school. Where has the time gone? Soon, you will venture out on your own, exploring more of the world and creating your own memories.

Thank you for sharing countless adventures throughout the U.S. with us, especially along the West Coast as we researched destinations for yet another travel book. The number of museums and parks and beaches and historic sites you have been to—and don't forget all those hotels—is exciting. Along the way, we both learned things from you we wouldn't have noticed, like trees are fun to climb and a great hotel has carpeting on its stairs. And don't forget the time we ordered room service on Thanksgiving Day—that was the best holiday meal, ever!

You'll notice there are many more photos of you in this book than here on these two pages; it was hard *not* to include you. We're sure they will bring back many special moments, as they have done for us.

We both love you so much and know you will go out into the world and make your mark. Be sure to send us a postcard or two along the way.

Love,
Mom and Dad

Dahlynn and Shawn, along California's coast; Ken and Shawn, goofing off on Enderts Beach, Crescent City. Shawn is four years old in both photos.

Shawn (age 14) and Dahlynn posing for a mother and son photo at a Northern California beach.

Shawn (age 5), who was too tired to hike any farther.

Shawn (age 10) and Dahlynn on the beach in Southern California

Grandpa Johnson (Dahlynn's dad) and Shawn (age 14) playing football

Shawn at Richardson Grove State Park: age 6 and age 16

Contents

The Northern Coast

Mendocino, Sonoma, and Marin Counties

San Francisco and San Mateo Counties

The Central Coast

The Southern Coast

Orange and San Diego Counties

SAN DIEGO COUNTY

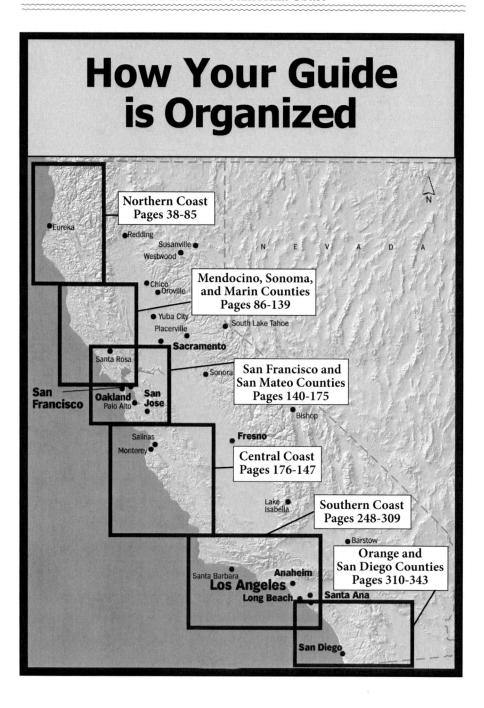

How Your Guide is Organized

Northern Coast
Pages 38-85

Mendocino, Sonoma, and Marin Counties
Pages 86-139

San Francisco and
San Mateo Counties
Pages 140-175

Central Coast
Pages 176-147

Southern Coast
Pages 248-309

Orange and
San Diego Counties
Pages 310-343

Using Your Guide

Best of the California Coast includes a wealth of detailed information on the best of what the coast has to offer, including hiking, camping, fishing, scenic driving, and historic sites. This guide also presents interesting information on the natural history, flora, and fauna of the coast, giving readers a starting point to learn more about what makes the Pacific Coast of California so special.

In this book, the coast itself is divided into six chapters, beginning north at the Oregon/California border and ending at the California/Mexican border. The book also includes two introductory chapters; one on the Golden State's natural history and the other, California's rich cultural history.

The maps in the book are intended to help both casual and expert coastal enthusiasts. Using a GPS for navigation is the best way to explore, but sometimes you will inadvertently end up in the wrong location due to no fault of your own—navigational tools can lead you astray, especially when traveling in mountains and dense forests. We suggest you double-check your destination on a more detailed map or visit the destination's website, most of which are provided in the contact listings within. Many of California's state and national parks offer detailed maps on their websites and have downloadable park brochures, trail maps, and additional information (www.parks.ca.gov and www.nps.gov).

A few words of caution: The ocean kills people in California every year. Coastal waters can be dangerous for swimming, fishing, and boating. California has powerful and frequently changing tides, rip currents, and dangerous sleeper waves. During winter, periodically and without warning, very large waves—sleeper waves—will crash ashore, knocking people over and carrying them out into deeper water as the wave recedes. Never turn your back on the ocean when you are on a beach, especially during winter when waves are much larger.

Bears, mountain lions, and coyotes are found throughout California, and seeing them can be exciting. But, wild animals can act in unexpected ways. If you encounter one on a trail, do not turn and run. That will invite the animal to chase you. Most often they will run away, but if they stand their ground, make noise and raise and wave your arms to look as big as possible. If you have small children, pull them in next to you or pick them up. If the animal doesn't run from you, back away slowly, continuing your arm waving and noise making.

Lastly, hiking trails change when they fall into disuse or disrepair, when landslides or fallen trees damage them, or when they are rerouted or closed. Serious hikers should carry a GPS unit or USGS or similarly detailed maps before setting out on long hikes. Carry plenty of water (or purifying systems or tablets) as safe drinking water often isn't available, and untreated water from streams may pose unforeseen health issues.

At all times, be aware of your surroundings and make safe decisions so all your memories are happy ones.

Introduction

Some say that California is as much a state of mind as it is a state of the Union. Perhaps. But no human mind could possibly have competed with the hand of nature to create all that is found here. Writing this book gave us a wonderful opportunity to revisit many of California's most breathtaking coastal treasures and to discover works of nature we'd somehow overlooked during more than 35 years of traveling the state's 1,100 miles of coast.

This book was also an interesting challenge. Having previously spent many years writing about California's coastal parks, we didn't wish to simply rehash old material. But instead, we wanted to take a new look at everything we could. And we did. Sometimes we traveled together, sometimes separately, walking on beaches we had never before seen and down trails we had never explored. We also wandered through our favorite old haunts in the northern redwoods, along the Big Sur coast, and in the Santa Monica Mountains.

Sometimes an old place turned out to be a new and wonderful experience. The only previous time we had hiked the trail to the Pygmy forest at Jug Handle State Natural Reserve, rain poured down and mushrooms were sprouting everywhere. This time, there was fog at the beach that opened to a bright blue sky by the time we made it to the top of the last ancient marine terrace, where the diminutive trees struggle for survival.

Hiking in the Sinkyone Wilderness one evening, Ken found himself standing alone between two bull elk, one with his harem peacefully grazing behind him and the second intent on having his way with the harem's cows. Rutting season makes bull elk kind of crazy. With his heart pounding from both trepidation and excitement, Ken took refuge of questionable worth behind the only nearby tree, hoping the loser wouldn't work out his frustration on him. He then enjoyed the sight and sounds of the bulls' challenges and counter challenges, unscathed.

At the southern end of the state, we hiked along a nearly deserted beach until coming face-to-face with a fence that ran from the adjacent hillsides out into the ocean. It was Border Field State Park and the fence marked the boundary between Mexico and the United States. And yes, there was a Border Patrol officer watching us from a nearby hill.

As our travels and writing for this project drew to a close, we wanted to be sure we had included the best of California's coast from thousands of choices. We believe we have succeeded on two levels. If you're new to California's coast, this book will prove to be an invaluable time-saving guide that can quickly lead you to the highlights of this magnificent, 1,100-mile coastline. And if you're a seasoned visitor, it's likely you've not seen everything. Even if you have, there may be an unexpected bull elk in your future travels.

Ken and Dahlynn McKowen

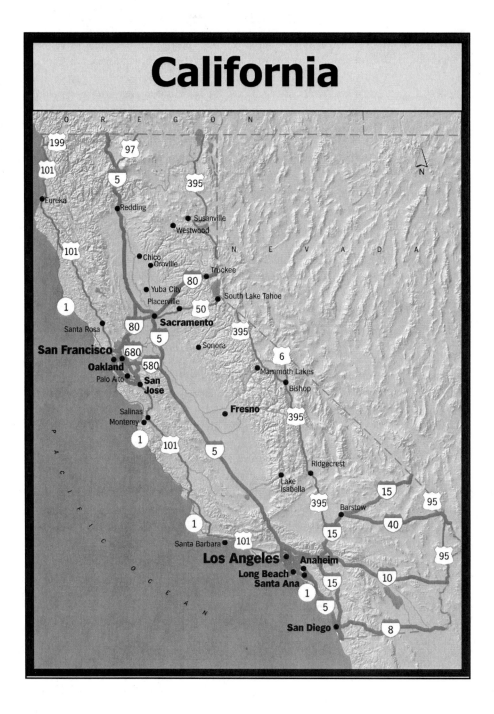

California

Natural History

California's Natural History

T he natural history of California is as varied and dynamic as the nearly 40 million people who call the Golden State their home. And California's borders are as varied as her citizens, with the forests of Oregon to the north, the deserts of Nevada to the east, and a foreign country to the south. But it's California's western boundary that holds most peoples' attention. The boundary is constantly changing as beach sands shift, cliffs collapse, and rivers deposit millions of tons of silt at their mouths every year. This constant geologic activity is coupled with the Pacific Ocean's pounding waves and changing currents to create 1,100 miles of sand-covered beaches and steep, jagged cliffs. Add the geologic changes that two battling tectonic plates have created, and the result is an extraordinarily rugged and beautiful coast.

The sometimes violent but most often subtle forces of nature have molded California's coast, and in turn have created plant communities that range from towering redwoods in the north to the low chaparral along the Central Coast and desert scrub in the south. Even though California experiences what is often described as a Mediterranean climate—mild, rainy winters and warm, dry summers—its rainy season can produce more than 100 inches of precipitation in Humboldt County while dropping less than 6 inches in San Diego County. These climatic differences help to support 54 of the West's 73 cone-bearing trees, with 21 found naturally only in California.

People have joked for years that one of California's infamous earthquakes might one day drop much of the state into the ocean. Several million years ago, much of California lay beneath the blue waters of an ancient sea. Look carefully at many of the coastal cliffs and at their skewed layers of ancient, metamorphosed ocean bottom mud, and you will discover the fossilized remains of small sea creatures. Come inland 100 miles or more, crossing the coastal mountains and the Central Valley, and once again these same fossils and their ancient sea floor home can be found in cliff faces of the uplifted lower Sierra Nevada foothills. But the joke about the catastrophic earthquake is not too far off. Although it won't happen in one sudden, giant jolt, geologists tell us that a large portion of California's coast will not remain with us forever. As the leading edge of the giant Pacific tectonic plate continues to dive beneath the North American plate, it is also moving north at the rate of about 1 inch each year, and it will continue to do so.

The Bixby Bridge and Big Sur coastline

GEOLOGIC HISTORY

What 17th century nautical map makers first noticed from the outlines of their crude maps, and 21st century scientists now believe through their use of modern technology, is that the earth is made up of a series of seven massive and numerous smaller plates. Study a map of Africa and Europe and compare their western coastlines with the eastern coasts of the American continents. The shape of their outlines, if pressed back together, match remarkably like correct puzzle pieces snapping into place. The widely separated modern continents also share many of the same types of rock, minerals, and fossils along the matching areas of their coasts.

These plates are essentially massive, broken pieces of the earth's crust that vary in thickness from 3 miles to 35 miles. They slip across the earth's surface on the underlying 1,800-mile-thick mantle, although at something much slower than a snail's pace. It is theorized that some 200 million years ago, there was but one continent. For reasons that may never be known, the original plates began pulling apart, gradually forming our modern continents and much of the California we know today. Return here following the passage of another 60 million years, and it's likely you'd not recognize a much changed California coast.

Two major plates—the North American plate and the Pacific plate—create most of the excitement for Californians. Through the eons, several smaller plates, such as the Farallon and the Juan de Fuca, have also contributed to this complex puzzle, pushing through and leaving behind minerals that don't always match those found in the two primary plates that we see today.

The heavy, basalt-laden (darker, iron- and magnesium-rich) Pacific plate, which covers much of the Pacific Ocean, moved east and dove into a subduction zone beneath the North American plate's much more complex geologic mix of lighter elements and minerals. What the disappearing Pacific plate left behind was the scraped and piled layers of ocean bottom, mostly the sedimentary mud that makes up much of today's coastal ranges.

About 25 million years ago, the Pacific plate began sliding in a more northerly direction. Over this time, the changed movement along the San Andreas fault has transported portions of what had originally been Baja, Mexico, to California's Central Coast. South of what appears to be a beak that juts into the Pacific Ocean from Santa Barbara, this northward moving landmass compressed part of the earth's crust into the 5-million-year-old Transverse Ranges, the only east-west aligned mountain range in the state. Curiously, because of where the two great plates meet along the edge of California, Los Angeles is built on the Pacific plate and San Francisco on the North American plate. At the Pacific plate's current rate of northerly movement, return here in 10 million years and Los Angeles will be directly west of San Francisco.

Coastal sedementary rock formed in horizontal layers beneath the ocean has been pushed and twisted in many directions by the movement of the San Andreas fault.

This phenomenon of plate tectonics creates several notable consequences for California. What comes to mind most often are the earthquakes that shake the state along the infamous 800-mile-long San Andreas fault and along several other less famous, but equally active and dangerous, faults. California experiences hundreds

Collapsed overpass, Highway 10, Los Angeles

of earthquakes every day, albeit most are very minor and seldom noticed. But periodically, much more destructive earthquakes strike, such as the temblor that destroyed San Francisco in 1906, the Loma Prieta quake that did a reasonable replay in the fall of 1989, and the Napa earthquake in 2014.

Researchers have come to better understand earthquakes and why they occur by studying the complex San Andreas Fault, as well as other fault systems. Unfortunately, scientists haven't yet learned to predict either earthquake frequency or intensity with any level of accuracy. For example, the 1994 Northridge earthquake that struck Los Angeles surprised seismologists when a previously unknown and deeply buried blind thrust fault gave way.

California's earthquakes are not going away. As the great plates continue to move and grind against one another, the rocks deep underground bend under the forces, occasionally giving slightly. Each day, these temporary stress reductions create dozens of barely perceptible small earthquakes throughout much of California. Problems arise when these small slippages don't occur as often as they should. After much longer build-ups of pressure, the faults release suddenly and with more power, producing temblors that knock food off grocery store shelves and occasionally level buildings and freeway overpasses.

Different types of earthquake faults create differing kinds of problems for California's cities and towns, freeways and roads, and even simple country fences and power lines. With a normal fault, also called a vertical dip-slip fault, one side drops anywhere from several inches to several feet in relation to its opposite side, which may actually be pushed upward. Equally descriptive names are given to other types of faults, including lateral left and right, oblique, and reverse faults. More important than their names is the fact that they all can, and do, cause earthquakes.

Earthquake aftermath

CLIMATE AND WEATHER

Those fortunate enough to live along California's northern and central coasts are often fond of quoting what Mark Twain supposedly mumbled: "The coldest winter I ever spent was a summer in San Francisco." Summer tourists escaping 100-plus degree Fahrenheit interior valley temperatures often encounter this weather phenomenon when, clad only in T-shirts and shorts, they stream to coastal resorts and are greeted by bone-chilling 55-degree fog-shrouded days.

Fog rolls in to San Diego Bay, chasing sailboats back to port.

Summer fog extends along much of California's coast, although as one nears Los Angeles and San Diego and their warmer ocean water temperatures, summer's gray blanket of morning moisture, when it forms, tends to be thinner and burns off more quickly.

A combination of inland air temperature differences, changing ocean currents and water temperatures, jutting landmasses, and landform orientations—along with numerous other factors—is responsible for where coastal summer fog forms. During summer when warm, moisture-laden air crosses the cold, upwelled ocean waters offshore, it condenses into fog. It's then drawn inland by a pressure difference created by the air rising from the heated landmass. Generally each day's rising sun evaporates or "burns off" the fog. On good weather days, the fog remains well offshore and the winds that bring it over coastal landmasses never develop. But more often summer fog does arrive, and it settles in for the night, dropping anything from a light veil of translucent white to a shroud of nearly impenetrable gray over the landscape.

Not every summer day or every location along California's coast experiences the same degree of fog. For example, on a particularly gray day along the shores of Monterey Bay in the city of Monterey, where the temperature struggles to reach

Snow in the Sierra Nevada

65 degrees Fahrenheit, Santa Cruz (just across the bay) may be 75 degrees and sunny with no fog. And while Monterey may be foggy in the early morning and evening and 75 degrees in midafternoon, a thick, drippy fog may engulf adjacent Pacific Grove all day, and the temperature may never reach 60 degrees.

Certainly, the Pacific Ocean plays the key role in California's climate. The coldest winter storms begin in the Pacific, usually near the Aleutian Islands, and track southeastward, bringing with them varying amounts of rain. Tropical storms form in the western Pacific then sweep in from near the Hawaiian Islands or even from farther south. These storms tend to be warmer and bring with them significant amounts of precipitation. While these rains initially may cause some local flooding along the coastal lowlands, most of the damage is usually done in the higher Sierra and Central Valley as the warm, spring rains quickly melt the winter snowpack, which raises river levels to flood stages.

OCEAN CURRENTS

California's climate is the result of numerous worldwide, ongoing natural events, and understanding ocean currents is key to gaining a better understanding of the state's entire climatic picture. Wade into the warm waters splashing ashore along one of San Diego's beaches and you will be standing in water that months earlier was probably passing offshore near Alaska and before that, Japan. Worldwide, ocean currents—and in the case of California, several linked currents—move water in giant circular patterns called "gyres." A Pacific Ocean gyre circulates huge amounts of surface water that help regulate California's climate. The southward moving California Current moves warm water into the westward moving North Equatorial Current, which in turn pushes the surface water northward into the Kurishio Current that flows along the east coast of Japan. From there, the North Pacific Current picks up this now cooled water and, moving eastward, further cools its huge mass, where it is captured by the California current and warmed as it moves south to begin the cycle anew.

It's these southern-flowing cold waters that make California's north coast beaches much too chilly to swim in, at least without a wetsuit. They also help to moderate much of California's coastal temperatures so that the beach at Malibu may be a comfortable 75 degrees Fahrenheit on an August afternoon. Same day, same time, but directly inland 30 miles, the temperature is 90 degrees, while inland another 80 miles, the temperature hovers at a sweltering 110-plus degrees.

A second and equally important type of ocean water movement is the thermohaline current. This is a deep water current, primarily driven by temperature and salinity differences, friction, and the forces of gravity. The current acts as a continuously moving conveyor belt, transporting and mixing deep, cold waters from the poles with waters from the warmer equatorial zones and from ocean to ocean. This constant movement is vital to moderating worldwide water temperature extremes.

This dock washed up on a beach in Oregon in June 2013—the 188-ton dock is part of the aftermath from Japan's March 2011 earthquake and tsunami.

Other factors affect not just California's coastal weather, but weather around the world. A slight increase or decrease in the earth's current 23.5-degree tilt on its axis in relationship to its orbit around the sun can have dramatic effects on weather. Increases or decreases in the makeup of the earth's atmospheric gasses—especially carbon dioxide—can impact weather. Many of these factors, such as the earth's tilt or orbit, change only over tens of thousands of years. Others, such as levels of carbon dioxide, can change within a century or less.

EL NIÑO AND LA NIÑA

There is no doubt about the dramatic effects that El Niño and La Niña have on weather, not only in California, but also around the world. Although cycles and intensities vary, every two to seven years El Niño brings extended periods of heavy rain to Northern California and tends to leave normally dry Southern California even drier. Central California gets caught in the middle, with either a very dry winter or with heavy rains that begin in November and don't slow until late spring, inundating roads, homes, and farmlands and causing massive landslides along the coast. El Niño provided California with warm, water-driven weather during the winters of 1985-86, 1991-92, 1993-94, and 2004.

California drought years

During the 1997-98 El Niño, scientists recorded the warmest winter ocean water temperatures ever along parts of Northern California's coast. While anglers in Central California that winter enjoyed catching fish species generally found no farther north than San Diego, two years later many areas of the state were still repairing damage from the record-setting rains.

During non-El Niño conditions, the trade winds blowing west across the tropical Pacific Ocean push warm water toward Indonesia and leave nutrient-rich, cooler waters off Ecuador, greatly enhancing the fishing success of that country's fishermen. As the trade winds begin to slow, as happens during El Niño years, the situation changes. Ecuadorian water temperatures warm, the upwelling of nutrient-rich colder water slows, and the ocean's surface temperature rises 14 degrees Fahrenheit or more. This, in turn, triggers rainfall as the air rises over the warming waters. It's when these warmer Pacific waters push northward that they begin to interfere with California's normally moderate weather patterns.

Fishermen trying their luck

It is thought that fishermen off the coast of South America coined the term "El Niño" because of the warming of the ocean waters that periodically occurred in late December. El Niño is Spanish for "Little Boy" or "Christ Child." La Niña, or "Little Girl," creates the opposite effect.

Natural Processes

Beyond the inevitable changes that the earth's restless tectonic plates bring, including the earthquakes that occasionally send quivers through portions of California, numerous other forces of nature have greatly assisted in molding the look and feel of the coast. These forces place their individual footprints on the land, whether that land lies 1,500 feet above sea level or 2 miles below the ocean's surface.

WATER AND EROSION

Water serves as one of the greatest forces of change. By freezing and thawing, it can break large rocks into smaller stones and ultimately grind stones into sand. Water can very quickly transport massive amounts of soil and sand from inland valleys and mountains to coastal river mouths. Ultimately, most of California's winter rain and snowfall that doesn't sink into underground aquifers or evaporate into the atmosphere cascades over vertical cliff faces, tumbles down steep mountain canyons, and meanders through wide valleys, ceaselessly moving small pieces of the earth with it.

Cliffs are constantly eroding at Torrey Pines State Beach.

While it may take eons for water to reduce big rocks to smaller rocks, once the sand is light enough for water transport, it tends to accumulate at the mouths of rivers, thus creating bars and dams. During the slow flows of summer, these dams can effectively prevent the stream's water from flowing directly into the ocean. Increased water flows during winter generally break through the sand dams, allowing fish and other wildlife to once again move freely from fresh water to salt water.

Fast-running rivers are not the only vehicles of erosion. Ocean waves have a tremendous impact on the changing shape of California's coastal zone. The size of waves is related directly to the strength of the winds that drive them and the distance they are pushed. Waves work untiringly, whether it's summer's gentle rollers or the spectacular and dangerous giants that a winter storm front can smash

11

against coastal rocks, sending plumes of white water dozens of feet into the air. While waves serve a good purpose in aiding the mixing of the ocean's warm and cold surface waters, when combined with high tides, powerful winter waves can be especially damaging, washing dozens of feet of coastal cliffs into the ocean over short periods of time.

UPLIFT AND MARINE TERRACES

Over the past several million years, California's coast, like many of the world's coastlines, has seen relatively dramatic rises and falls in the level of the ocean. As with manmade inland reservoirs where fluctuating water levels create small terraces around the shoreline, several Ice Ages and weather changes, along with tectonic plate movements, have created expansive marine terraces along California's coast. Often they are difficult or impossible to distinguish, having been eroded or filled or covered by vegetation. But there are a few areas along the coast where such geologic formations are relatively easy to identify.

One of the easiest places to explore an ancient marine terrace is along the Mendocino Coast, where the land pushed upward approximately 100 feet every 100,000 years. If it were possible to create a side view of the rising mountain be-ginning at the ocean's edge and moving inland about 3 miles, there would be five distinct terraces, each about 100 feet higher in elevation than the last. Each terrace is composed of a deep base of graywacke sandstone, which is covered with up to 20 feet of ancient beach deposits. Above the beach sand and gravel lies 1 to 3 feet of more recently deposited soil

Jug Handle State Natural Reserve

of varying compositions. In Southern California's Los Angeles County, the Palos Verdes Hills exhibit 13 terraces that rise a total of about 1,300 feet above sea level.

California's coast also offers a firsthand look at the past 60 million years of the state's complex and very confusing geological history. Study a geologic map of California and the profusion of colors representing rock types is phenomenal. The abrupt changes in rock types found along the coast generally coincide with the presence of the numerous parallel faults. Most coastal alluvial deposits are marine sedimentary in nature. They are the scrapings of marine soils from the top of the Pacific plate as it dives beneath the North American plate along the coastal subduction zone. As a result, few continental (North American plate) sedimentary rocks and alluvial deposits are present along the surface of California's coast.

Near Cape Mendocino, where a relatively short, 50-mile-long fault exists, late Mesozoic rocks of the Franciscan Formation lie adjacent to Cenozoic marine sedimentary rocks, and fronting those are Cenozoic nonmarine (North American plate) sedimentary rocks and alluvial deposits. And while Cenozoic volcanic rocks are extremely common in northeast California and in the Mojave Desert in the southeast, they are rare along the coast, except in a small area north of Los Angeles, on Santa Cruz Island, and in the coastal mountains of Sonoma County.

While marine sedimentary rocks dominate the coast, occasional intrusive igneous rocks are present, primarily Mesozoic age granitic rocks similar to those that make up much of the Sierra Nevada and Southern California's Peninsular Ranges. These granitic rocks are a result of the remaking of the Pacific plate. As the continental shelf forces the Pacific plate's heavy basalt deeper toward the earth's mantle, it is heated to a state of magma, becoming lighter and more buoyant. The magma then rises toward the surface, melting lighter North American plate minerals as it rises. Where it reaches the surface, its silicon- and aluminum-rich content, mixed with other minerals, solidifies as granitic rock.

TIDES, CURRENTS, AND LITTORAL SAND MOVEMENT

The littoral zone, that narrow band of land that lies between the low and high tides, is an area of constant change. Over time, rivers transport millions of cubic yards of sand from mountains, hills, and valleys to river mouths where it is washed into the ocean. Ocean currents moving laterally along the shore spread sand onto beaches and into tide pools. Winter's strong wave actions erode bluffs and further add to the growing collection of transportable sand. It's generally summer's gentler wave action that rebuilds the sandy beaches, replenishing sand lost to wind, tide, and storm actions. The result is that much of California's coast experiences wide and sandy beaches during summer where during winter, only beaches of cobbles existed. But even the cobbles have their own special attraction as they clatter up and down the beach to the rhythm of winter's crashing waves.

The Pacific Ocean's tides have created their own unique worlds in and near the coastal littoral zones. The plants and animals that cling tenuously to life in this hostile environment have spent eons evolving so they can survive alternating periods of wet and dry, pounding surf, and desiccating sun. They experience two high tides and two low tides each 24

Sunflower starfish

hours and 50 minutes, with sea levels varying widely, driven by the gravitational pulls of the moon and the sun.

To better understand tides is to understand the synchronized movements of the sun and the moon and the changing power of their respective gravitational pulls on the earth's oceans as the three heavenly bodies pass around one another. The moon's diminutive size is more than compensated for by its nearness to earth in its battle for gravitational control of the oceans. It closeness gives it about twice the gravitational pull as the sun.

The sun and moon's gravitational pulls, along with centrifugal force created by the earth's rotation, simultaneously stretch and contract portions of our oceans' elastic and contiguous surface. Place the moon and sun in alignment—either with the moon between the earth and sun as during a new moon or with the earth between the moon and sun as during a full moon—and together they stretch the ocean's surfaces nearest them, creating the highest tides. When the moon lies at a right angle to the alignment of the earth and sun—as during the first quarter and third quarter moons—the high tides, called "neap tides," are much lower. Each day's two high

tides are offset by two low tides where the moon and sun's gravitational pulls are at their minimums.

Tide levels and their corresponding times are significantly different in the northern and southern parts of the state. Since tides change with the earth's rotation—and considering that San Diego lies well east of Crescent City (and east of Reno, Nevada)—the result is widely varying high and low tides for the two cities. For example, on the same day, the high tides in Crescent City will crest at 1:30 A.M. and again at 3:07 P.M. The two high tides in San Diego will occur at 12:30 P.M. and again at 11:30 P.M. And while the highest of those high tides in Crescent City will be 6.46 feet, the higher of the two high tides in San Diego will be only 5.2 feet. Printed tide tables are good for giving general predictions for the tides in specific areas of California's coast. What tide tables can't accurately predict are the local changes that winter storm surges or local coastal geography can cause.

14

Natural Communities

The orientation of California's shoreline in relation to the south-trending ocean currents has also helped define the look of the state's seashore. From the Oregon border south about two-thirds of the way to the Mexican border, the coast tends to follow a gentle southeast line. But as it nears Point Conception—not far from Santa Barbara—it abruptly turns more easterly, swinging inward as though a giant bite has been removed, and not moving back to its more gentle southeast line until nearly reaching San Diego. This change in orientation to the prevailing ocean currents, combined with a different angle that faces attacking winter storms whose fury is further blunted by eight large offshore islands, has helped to create and maintain Southern California's many broad sandy beaches.

Within or near California's generally rocky north and central coasts and the sandy beaches of the south coast are several other important terrain features: streams and rivers and their sometimes accompanying wetlands, coastal dunes, bluffs and headlands, marine terraces, coastal mountains, rocky intertidal zones, near-shore waters, offshore islands, and open ocean. Each zone supports unique and fascinating species of plants and animals, and each has specific attributes that allow for survival and propagation in very hostile environments.

OPEN WATERS

Unlike that of the Gulf and Atlantic states, California's coast tends to drop off into very deep water quickly, which helps explain why California's many rivers have never built the broad flat deltas found at the mouths of such rivers as the Mississippi. The continental shelf that runs the length of the state and lies about 25 miles from the coast at San Francisco has moved to within 10 miles of shore in Monterey Bay. Deep underwater valleys slash their way from the Pacific and into the shallow, but steep, continental shelf at several locations. The most famous of these underwater valleys is the Monterey Canyon. Within a few miles of Monterey's harbor and shoreline, the canyon's bottom has dropped 4,300 feet (about 8/10ths of a mile), the same distance as from the Grand Canyon's South Rim down to the Colorado River. The canyon's depth reaches 2 miles another few miles offshore.

These deep waters, with their strong currents and changing temperatures, bring an abundance of underwater life close to California's shoreline. The most obvious

Grand Canyon

15

to anyone who comes to the coast during January and February is the great southern migration of gray whales (*Eschrichtius robustus*). From numerous vantage points along shore—or better, standing on the deck of a charter whale-watching boat—it's possible to see dozens of these graceful creatures in a single day. Coming back from the brink of extinction, gray whales are now near their historic numbers before uncontrolled whaling began.

KELP FORESTS

A great forest lies just offshore along much of California's coast, a forest that supports incredibly rich and diverse underwater and surface worlds of life. Seen from the beaches and cliffs, the canopy of these great beds of giant kelp (*Macrocystis pyrifera*) rides upon the swell of waves outside the surf zone, held afloat on the water's surface by small hollow float structures that grow among the kelp's leaf-like blades. Bull kelp (*Nereocystis luetkeana*) is also common within or near the giant kelp forests.

Both are forms of algae and both are prolific growers. During summer's long sunny days, kelp can grow up to 18 inches every 24 hours. Beneath the surface, these long stalks of kelp may reach 100 feet or more in length, rising from the bottom where they are secured to rocks with a holdfast structure rather than a root system. Winter storms often tear free holdfasts that aren't well secured to solid bottom structures and toss piles of kelp onto the beaches.

On the surface, the long fronds create a dense forest that serves as both shelter and a food source for numerous species. Sea otters (*Enhydra lutris nereis*) frolic on the floating beds of yellow-brown kelp fronds that undulate slowly with the rhythm of the waves. Between their near constant preening sessions, the otters dive for aba-

Giant kelp

lone or other food. Then, floating casually on their backs on the water's surface, the otters use small stones to pound the succulent meat free from its shell, as gulls swarm nearby hoping to glean small bits of leftovers. Many other species depend on the kelp forests, including blue rockfish (*Sebastes mystinus*), brown turban snails (*Tegula brunnea*), Pacific sardines (Sardinops sagax), and leopard sharks (*Triakis semifasciata*). Most of the kelp's different inhabitants feed on one another. Few actually feed on the kelp, with the exception of sea urchins (*Strongylocentrotus* spp.) and abalone (*Haliotis* spp.), both of which can consume large quantities. Fortunately, sea otters enjoy eating both urchins and abalone, helping to maintain the delicate balance between plant and animal.

THE SEASHORE

Washed by tides, dried by the sun, and pounded by waves, California's seashore is a place of contradictions. Within its boundaries, much of the life that's present and dependent upon the ocean's waters for survival are left dry twice each day as the tides reach their lowest points. Other creatures, such as bacteria and diatoms, survive on the higher rocks, those splashed with life-giving ocean waters only during the highest of tides or when storm-driven waves splash well above the mean high tide level. Scattered across these rocks, acorn barnacles (*Chthamalus* and *Balanus* spp.) open their trap-like doors to feed and reproduce when life-giving seawater splashes across them.

A few feet lower into the splash zone, powerful winter waves unmercifully pound the animals and small plants that cling tenaciously to the rocky shore. Many animals that inhabit the shoreline, including California sea lions (*Zalophus californianus*), sea otters (*Enhydra lutris*), harbor seals (*Phoca vitulina*), and dozens of species of birds, are able to move to more agreeable surroundings when water conditions no longer meet their needs.

Those animals that are less mobile have developed their own mechanisms for surviving in their dangerous homes. One of the most common of those seashore creatures is the mussel (*Mytilus* spp.). Mussels thrive in one of the most hostile of environments—the splash zone. They survive the force of tons of crashing water by attaching themselves to rocks in tight bunches with the sharp edges of their shells pointed outward so as to divert the water's force. Tough, fibrous, byssal threads of glue bind each mussel's shell to the rocks, helping to keep them in place.

Mussels and acorn barnacles

The best time to explore the shoreline is at low tide when the ocean recedes, revealing the secrets of the tide pools. Animals scramble about, either coming out to secure food in the absence of crashing waves or to follow the receding waters where food and safety from predators are most easily found. Small fish, such as sculpins (*Clinocottus* spp.), search for food and lay their eggs in the shallow tide pools. Black shelled turban snails (*Tegula funebralis*) scrape algae from the rocks, while others such as dog-winkle snails (*Nucella* spp.) eat any creature not too big that meanders into their territories.

Anenomes are found in different colors and sizes

Probe a little deeper and more of a tide pool's magic comes to life. Coralline algae, which looks like tiny reddish fingers of coral, bend at their numerous joints as water moves over them. Sea stars, such as the ochre star (*Pisaster ochraceus*), can release a telltale scent in the water as they travel about searching for food, allowing the quicker animals to escape their deadly grasp. Sea stars use their powerful sucking action to peel less mobile creatures—such as mussels—from their safe and secure rock perches. Even when one of its own arms becomes lunch for a passing sea otter, the unlucky sea star simply finds a safe haven where it can stay until its missing arm regrows.

Anemones (*Anthopleura elegantissima*)—soft, puffy-looking creatures with short tentacles—shrink themselves in size to reveal sticky little bumps that help keep them from drying out when tides recede. Often, the many individuals in a colony of anemones appear identical. This occurs because they reproduce by splitting in half, then the twins do the same, and so on. Other animals, such as hermit crabs (*Pagurus* spp.), take up residence inside the shells of dead turban snails, discarding smaller shells for larger ones as they grow. Since hermit crabs can live up to three decades, they can go through numerous stolen houses. Mixed into these tide-pool menageries are spiny sea urchins (*Strongylocentrotus* spp.) that are able to grasp and hold onto tide-pool rocks with their hundreds of tube-like feet. They then use their upper tentacles to grab food that is constantly moving past them in the water currents.

While healthy tide pools are rich with life, even richer are the areas that lie slightly farther offshore, which can only be revealed to the drying air by the lowest of tides. Hundreds of species of plants and animals inhabit this rich zone, among them slimy waves of green surfgrass (*Phyllospadix* spp.). The thick blankets of surf grass serve as both homes and food for sea stars and other creatures, such as seaweed limpets (*Discurria insessa*). Surfgrass is a true flowering plant—not an algae as are so many of its neighbors. It clings to the rocks and boulders where the sea keeps it wet. Blades of surfgrass serve as homes for crustose coralline algae (*Melobesia mediocris*) and food for bat stars (*Asterina* spp.). Near-by, different species of sponges, each sporting its own brilliant color, along with surfgrass limpets (*Tectura paleacea*), thrive in this oxygen-rich environment. This same coastal area also serves as a crucial transition zone for animals that must move between the open ocean and the estuaries

Surfgrass matted over rocks at low tide

and wetlands where they feed and reproduce.

SANDY BEACHES

Most of the sand that accumulates on California's shoreline begins its journey from the interior mountains, washed to the sea by rivers and streams. Significantly smaller amounts of sand come from coastal cliff and rock erosion and from sand washed ashore from ancient and submerged near-shore dunes. All of this sand is caught in a series of conveyer belt-like littoral currents that slide down California's coast. As this natural conveyer belt removes old sand from a beach, it drops newer sand as a replacement, maintaining a delicate balance. Only during winter storms is more sand removed than is replaced, but mostly in Northern and Central California. Sand is also lost along its way down the coast, dropped off the conveyer belts into the dozens of marine canyons that cut laterally into the coastal shelf. Once in these marine canyons, the sand is swept downward and lost to the deeper parts of the ocean, often well offshore.

Well-meaning efforts to improve some of California's harbors have often resulted in costly and unforeseen circumstances. In the 1920s, Santa Barbara built a breakwater to create a protected harbor. The breakwater caused huge amounts of sand to accumulate on one side, while on the harbor side, there suddenly was no beach sand available to replace that which continued to be removed by ocean currents. A series of heavy winter storms cut away up to 150 feet of shoreline from some beaches. Santa Barbara is not the only community to make such a mistake. Those cities that followed Santa Barbara's breakwater construction actions often continue to spend millions of dollars every few years to keep their harbors dredged free of sand and their beaches replenished with sand.

Andrew Molera beach: no sand during winter

WETLANDS: ESTUARIES AND SLOUGHS

Wetlands are wedged into the few areas of California's coast not already covered by steep cliffs or broad expanses of open sand or cobbles. Within the broad category of wetlands lie the coastal sloughs. These narrow and winding waterways can be filled with salt water or fresh water, seasonally or year-round, and their shorelines are primarily mud and marshy soils. They may or may not have a year-round connection to the open ocean.

A different kind of wetland is the estuary, which lies inland beyond the reach of the ocean's waves, but within the influence of the tides and the ocean's salt water. It depends on a flow of fresh water to mix with the salt water. The flow of fresh water may be a continual flow, such as where the Sacramento and San Joaquin rivers create permanent estuaries around San Francisco Bay, or a seasonal, rain-fed steam such as that which flows into the estuary at Elkhorn Slough on the edge of Monterey Bay.

Salt marshes are those areas within the estuaries or sloughs where high tides inundate large flats, creating extremely hostile conditions for all but the most specialized plants. Yet, in spite of such an apparently inhospitable environment, salt marshes are amazingly productive, their plants creating much more oxygen and carbohydrates per acre than a wheat field. Such a rich food source also creates an equally rich and diverse food chain.

In those areas of California where wetlands still remain, they are most often made up of broad mud flats and estuarine salt marshes. San Francisco Bay, itself significantly reduced in size following more than a century of being filled and developed, contains nearly 90 percent of California's remaining salt marshes. There are only about two dozen other smaller salt marshes along California's coast. Most of the marshes were drained, filled, and developed during those early years before their true importance was fully recognized and protective legislation enacted.

The brackish waters of California's remaining coastal wetlands support an incredibly rich palette of life. In this natural community that experiences flooding from daily tides and from seasonal rises in rivers and creeks that drain nearby hills and mountains, aquatic and terrestrial life find refuge. The Pacific Flyway also brings an autumn rush of not only ducks and geese, but also many dozens of other species of smaller birds escaping the cold northern winters for the temperate climate of coastal California. Then there's the spring rush north again as they return to their nesting grounds.

The many plants that live in these estuarine wetlands have developed special morphological and physiological traits for surviving in a world that would be deadly for any normal terrestrial plant. Some plant species, such as saltwort (*Batis maritima*) and pickleweed (*Salicornia bigelovii*), are highly tolerant to these hypersaline conditions. Some, like cordgrass (*Spartina foliosa*), have specialized their

Los Peñasquitos Marsh Natural Preserve and Lagoon is a coastal marsh in San Diego County, adjacent to Torrey Pines State Beach.

Sea otters in Monterey Bay

adaptations so much that they can grow only where tidal flows come regularly year-round. Cordgrass is not found farther inland or where fresh water flows are more prevalent. One of the critical adaptations that these salt-tolerant plants have developed is a mechanism for excreting the excessive amounts of salt that they absorb as they take life-giving water into their stems and leaves. Many of these plants excrete the salt to the surface of their leaves and stems where it forms as tiny crystals and finally falls or is washed away by wind or rain.

The most obvious residents and visitors to California's wetlands are birds that come to feed on the rich bounty of food that thrives in this diverse habitat. In the deeper waters, birds that share their time between the sloughs and the open ocean waters are able to rest and feed. Cormorants (*Phalacrocorax* spp.) and loons (*Gavia* spp.) dive for fish, while the once nearly extinct brown pelicans (*Pelecanus occidentalis*) cruise inches above the water's surface or circle above and dive headfirst into the water, hoping to return to the surface with lunch. The great Pacific Flyway brings a winter flood of waterfowl, including mallards (*Anas platyrhynchos*), American widgeons (*Anas americana*), and numerous other species of ducks into the calm waters. And while birds such as great blue herons (*Ardea herodias*), snowy egrets (*Egretta thula*), and common

Common egrets have yellow bills and black legs.

egrets (*Ardea alba*) wade in shallow water mud flats hunting small fish, a marsh hawk (*Circus cyaneus*) glides low over the nearby drier grasslands searching for unsuspecting birds and mice. Sea otters (*Enhydra lutris*), harbor seals (*Phoca vitulina*), and sea lions (*Zalophus californianus*) enter the canals and waterways, while songbirds add their own touch of color and melodies to the constant movement of estuary life.

COASTAL DUNES

Rivers, streams, ocean currents, and wave action deposit sand onto open beaches, but it takes wind to constantly move and mold the tons of tiny sand grains into dunes. It is rare for enough of those ingredients to exist in the right amounts in the same place, so dunes occupy only a few small areas of California's coast. Where dunes exist, their shifting sands—devoid of nutrients and unable to retain moisture—are inhospitable to most plant and animal life. Yet, there are a few hardy pioneering plants and animals that are capable of existing in this hostile and changing environment and provide the first footholds in the long road to dune stabilization.

Dunes begin life as sand that blows freely across a beach until a protrusion—such as a rocky outcropping or a changing shoreline orientation, driftwood, clumps of kelp, or existing plants—blocks its

Dune trail at Marina State Beach

passage. The sand accumulates to a point above the water's surface where small dune plants are able to establish footholds—the beginning of dune stabilization. As the life cycle of dunes continues, the more recently built foredunes afford protection for the older dunes behind them, enabling the older dunes to support larger forms of vegetation, which act to further stabilize the sand.

Some of California's coastal dunes were formed more than 18,000 years ago. These ancient dunes are found inland, often a mile or more from the shoreline, but are difficult to identify because they are often covered by houses or forests. The plants that are able to establish a tenuous toehold in the shifting dune sands are generally low growing in order to escape the wind. They are deep-rooted to reach as much life-giving water as possible—water that very quickly percolates down through the porous sand. Plants such as beach strawberry (*Fragaria chiloensis*), yellow sand verbena (*Abronia latifolia*), Menzies wallflower (*Erysimum menziesii*), and beach primrose (*Oenothera cheiranthifolia*), in addition to being able to establish themselves on bare dunes, also provide food and cover for a variety of insects and small animals.

COASTAL MOUNTAINS

California's nearly 1,100-mile long stretch of coastal mountains is comprised of many major ranges, each of which includes several small mountain ranges within them. The Klamath Mountains parallel the coast in the far northwest corner of the state, but they also include the Siskiyou Mountains, the Marble Mountains, the Scott Mountains, the Trinity Mountains, and farther inland, the Yolla Bolly Mountains. Running south from the Klamath Mountains along the coast, with about 80 miles of overlap with the Klamath Mountains, is the Coast Range, which extends 600 miles from Humboldt County south to Santa Barbara County near Point Conception where the coastline turns suddenly eastward. The Coast Range is separated at its midpoint by San Francisco Bay.

The Transverse Ranges are one of North America's few primarily east-west oriented mountain ranges. They start near Santa Barbara and extend east 320 miles to near Joshua Tree National Monument in the Mojave Desert. The San Andreas Fault serves as its northern boundary. The Transverse Ranges include the San Rafael Mountains and Sierra Madre Mountains in Santa Barbara County and reach from Ventura County into Los Angeles County with the Topatopa Mountains and Santa Susana Mountains. Within L.A. County are the Simi Hills, the Santa Monica Mountains behind Malibu, and the Hollywood Hills. The Transverse Ranges include several additional mountain ranges as they head east, including the San Gabriel Mountains, Puente Hills, Chino Hills, and the San Bernardino Mountains.

Southern California's Transverse Ranges, located mostly north of Los Angeles, connect with the Peninsular Ranges that extend 930 miles south to the tip of Mexico's Baja California. They include the Santa Ana, Temescal Mountains, and the San Jacinto Mountains, primarily inland in Riverside County, and the Viejas Mountains, which are located near San Diego.

For the most part, the mountains of all these ranges reach the seashore. In many areas along the coast, Highway 1 offers breathtaking views over precipitous drops of 600 feet or more to the ocean on the west side of its often narrow ribbon of asphalt, and equally precipitous mountain rises on the east side. One of the most dramatic stretches of Highway 1 is in the southern portion of the Coastal Ranges through the Santa Lucia Mountains. Here, some of the steepest mountain rises are found. Just 4 miles inland, Cone Peak rises 5,155 feet. But it's the northern coastal mountains that hold the highest peaks. Solomon Peak in the Trinity Mountains rises 7,581 feet above sea level.

California Coastal Mountain Ranges

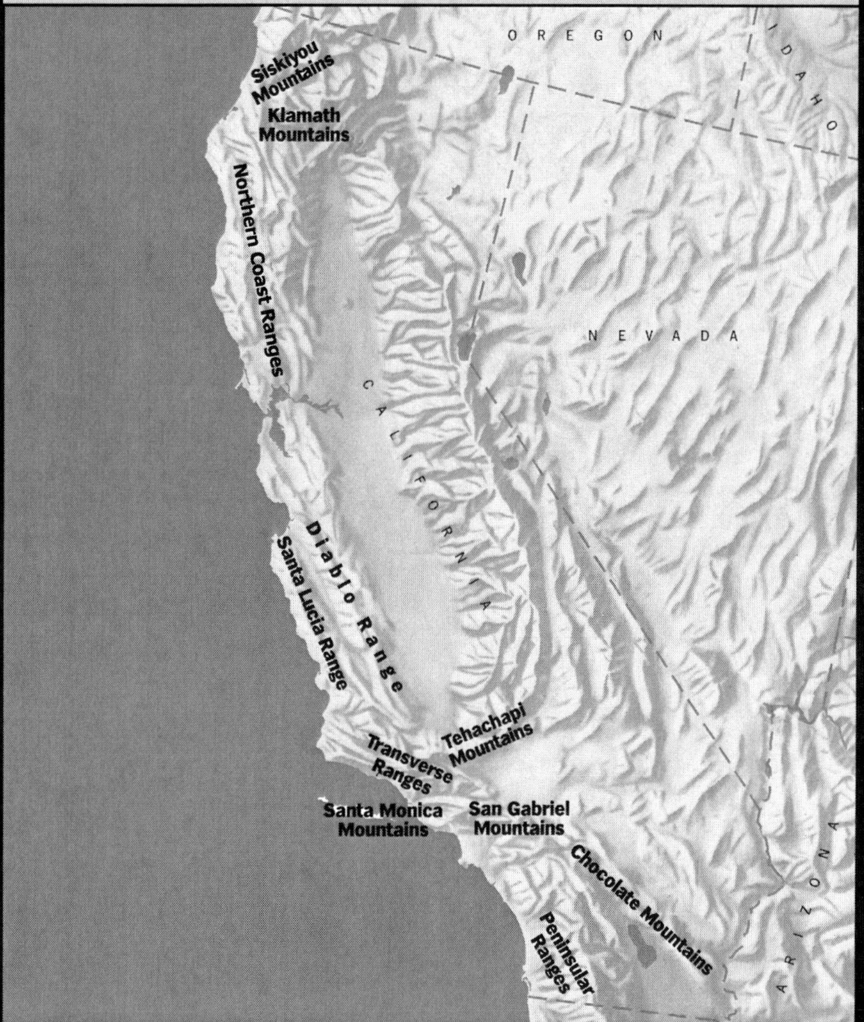

Siskiyou Mountains

Klamath Mountains

Northern Coast Ranges

OREGON

IDAHO

NEVADA

CALIFORNIA

Diablo Range

Santa Lucia Range

Transverse Ranges

Tehachapi Mountains

Santa Monica Mountains

San Gabriel Mountains

Chocolate Mountains

Peninsular Ranges

ARIZONA

Co-author's son strolling through the redwoods.

Besides differences in the types of rocks found, what is most obvious to anyone traveling the length of California's coast is the mosaic of vegetation found in the coastal mountains. The wet northern reaches of the coastal mountains support large stands of coast redwoods (*Sequoia sempervirens*), Douglas fir (*Pseudotsuga menziesii*), and understory plants such as California bay (*Umbellularia californica*) and madrone (*Arbutus menziesii*). Move farther south where the rains come slightly less often and the redwoods retreat to more isolated and protected canyons, while a different kind of conifer comes on the scene. Referred to as "fire pines," several trees, such as the generally twisted and picturesque Monterey pine (*Pinus radiata*) and knobcone pine (*Pinus attenuata*), grow in thick groves or stand in open spaces. Prevailing ocean winds often press and form the pines' crowns low and flat as they patiently await the heat of fire to release their seeds to the newly burned, bare mineral soil. Still farther south, scattered oaks (*Quercus spp.*) join sprawling sycamores (*Platanus racemosa*) in the canyons as coastal scrub covers much of the open hillsides.

COASTAL CLIFFS

Crashing waves have stamped their unique mark on California's varied geography, carving spectacular coastal bluffs from the steep mountain faces that have risen from the sea. Waves—especially powerful winter waves—that have already removed the buffering sand beaches can quickly, efficiently, and violently erode the relatively soft, steep mountain faces. Composed mostly of sedimentary rocks such as shale and sandstone, shoreline cliffs quickly succumb to wave action and are washed away, exposing more cliff face. Often, softer, unconsolidated alluvial soils lie on top of the crumbly sandstone, providing even less defense against the attacking ocean.

While such erosion is a normal part of nature, it causes great inconvenience for the people who try to contend with or choose to ignore its consequences. These erosion-prone soils are made up of small grains of quartz, mica, and feldspars. When saturated by wave action or rain, their structure tends to collapse. For most people, the consequence of building their homes on such geologically unstable ground does not come as a surprise. What is surprising is that so many coastal bluff property owners don't believe that their homes could possibly ever become floating ocean debris—some much sooner than others.

OFFSHORE ISLANDS

Lying offshore between Santa Barbara and San Pedro, the closer of the eight Channel Islands appear as faint, slightly dark mounds in the distance. The islands are remnant eroded peaks of the Santa Monica Mountains, which are part of the Transverse Ranges.

The geology of the Channel Islands is complex and not fully understood. Although the history of the rocks found on the islands goes back 100 million years, much of the original uplifting of the islands from beneath the sea began 5 million years ago. During the last Ice Age—which ended about 10,000 years ago—several of the islands became connected to one another as the ocean level dropped.

A variety of rock types exist on the islands. Mesozoic granite and late Jurassic and Cretaceous Franciscan formation rocks are found on Santa Catalina Island. San Clemente Island, located south of Santa Catalina Island, and Santa Cruz Island are made up of Cenozoic volcanic rocks. Cenozoic marine sedimentary rocks also cover parts of Santa Cruz Island.

A half million years of isolation from the mainland has done much to protect the rich variety of wildlife that inhabit the islands and the waters that surround them. More than a century of livestock grazing has significantly impacted the native grasses and other plants that Chumash Indians once wandered among. Introduced species, especially African ice plant, have further reduced or eliminated many native plants.

Five of the eight islands—San Miguel, Anacapa, Santa Barbara, Santa Rosa, and Santa Cruz—are part of the Channel Islands National Park, while San Nicolas, Santa Catalina, and San Clemente islands remain primarily in private hands. San Miguel Island serves as a seasonal home to more species of pinnipeds (seals) than any other equal-sized location in the world. Bulbous-nosed elephant seals (*Mirounga angustirostris*) and California sea lions (*Zalophus californicus*) are common along the islands' beaches where they haul out of the water for resting, mating, and birthing their young.

California's Cultural History

NATIVE AMERICANS

California's coast provided a rich and varied source of food for the Native Americans who lived here for thousands of years. With their primary need for sustenance so easily met, the dozens of different tribes that inhabited this land were able to develop rich and distinct cultures. Textiles, weapons, money, boats, woven and clay pottery, and even musical instruments were part of everyday life for California's Indians.

It is thought that California's first inhabitants arrived during the last Ice Age, probably 25,000 years ago or earlier. It's unknown how many of these early travelers crossed over the Bering Strait from Asia, but once in California, their numbers likely increased. Many experts have attempted to estimate the pre-European, Native American population of what we call California: their estimates have ranged from as many as 750,000 to as few as 125,000, with the real number lost forever. Few of California's Indians belonged to anything resembling the strong tribal political units that are so well known in the central and eastern United States. They spoke hundreds of dialects based on several families of languages. Some of those languages, such as Athabascan and Algonkin, were also spoken in one form or another in eastern North America. Some of the better known tribes, such as the

Photo above: Pomo feather basket

Tolowa, Hupa, Yana, Pomo, Costanoan, Modoc, Maidu, and Miwok, often had several subtribes. Within each of those tribes and subtribes there could be numerous villages, few of which maintained any political allegiance with their neighbors.

Like all Indians in the New World, California's natives had no natural immunities to introduced European diseases such as smallpox and measles. For thousands of Indians, the diseases were deadly, quickly decimating their populations. It is unfortunate that Native Americans had no formal written language, or that the Spanish padres had little desire or need to document aboriginal populations or their rich cultural heritages. What we know of them and their histories is generally derived from stories handed down verbally through the generations, late 18th and early 19th century studies by anthropologists, and from archeological research. By 1900, when many of the more serious researchers realized what was being rapidly lost, far too many of those Indians old enough to remember life before the Gold Rush had nothing left but faded childhood memories. Fortunately, there is a growing resurgence of interest in Indian history among the remaining ancestors of California's original settlers, as well as in the academic world, which is helping to increase an overall understanding of California's native cultures.

SPANISH AND MEXICAN PERIODS

In his book published in 1510, Garci Ordóñez de Montalvo wrote about the great riches in a mystical and mythical paradise he called "California." When Hernando Cortés began plundering Mexico's riches in the 16th century, his soldiers used the name "California" to describe what is today Baja California. Yet, in spite of the rumors of such great wealth, the Spanish were very slow in exploring and developing the lands that lay beyond their colonial empire in Mexico.

It wasn't until 1542 that Juan Rodríquez Cabrillo, a Portuguese navigator sailing under the flag of the Spanish Crown, discovered and claimed the lands from San Diego to Monterey. But without the obvious golden treasures like those being plundered from both Central America and Mexico, combined with long and difficult voyages against winds and currents along the Baja and Alta

Cabo San Lucas, part of Baja California

Cultural History

29

California coasts, Spain did nothing with the new lands that Cabrillo had claimed. Sixty years later, in 1602, Spaniard Sebastián Vizcaíno rediscovered both San Diego and Monterey bays and once again claimed these lands for Spain. And again, Spain ignored the lands that would become known as California.

Finally, in the late 1760s, Spain began taking serious interest in its claimed but unsettled lands in the wilds of California. Still, it wasn't the promise of easy riches to help fill the Spanish Crown's treasury that brought the change. It was the perceived need for a protective buffer between its established colonies in Mexico and the rapid expansion of Russian settlements and trading outposts spreading down the West Coast of North America.

While permanent Russian settlements came no further south than the Mendocino Coast at Fort Ross, Spain implemented a successful program that was designed to greatly expand its control of California. In March 1869, some 200 Spaniards began moving north from Mexico under the command of Gaspar de Portolá

Mission San Luis Rey in Oceanside

and stopped in what would become San Diego.

Spain charged Father Serra with the responsibility of building a series of missions to help establish Spain's control of these new lands. Already 56 years old, Serra established the first mission—San Diego de Alcalá—in today's San Diego. Each of Serra's settlements included three integral actions: 1) The mission or church would serve the religious needs of its small Spanish pueblo or village, 2) Elimination of the native culture and conversion of the Indians into Spanish-speaking,

Mission San Juan Capistrano

tax-paying citizens, and 3) creating a presidio or military fort near each mission and pueblo to serve as protection for the settlers and the missions and for keeping the Indians under control.

In only 53 years, the padres had built 21 missions, each placed roughly a day's walk apart, and spread some 600 miles from San Diego in the south to the Sonoma Mission in the north. Under the padres' direction, Indian labor built and operated the missions. California's natives also provided the labor that grew the grain and raised the cattle needed to support themselves and the accompanying civilians and military personnel who lived in the pueblos and manned the presidios.

The work of the missionaries, and particularly that of Father Serra, helped Spain expand its tenuous grip on California, but only temporarily. During the early 19th century, foreign wars in Europe consumed much of Spain's financial resources, reducing the Crown's already minimal support to its New World empire. As new generations of Spanish citizens were born in California, often of mixed Indian blood and never having visited the old country, their desire for independence developed. These "Californios," as they were called, tired quickly of Spain's arbitrary laws and of the officials sent to enforce the mother country's dictates. Those yearnings for freedom culminated with Spain's controlled portion of California, becoming the independent Republic of Mexico in 1824.

Mexico's independence from Spain did not end troubles in California. Internal conflicts between the missions, Mexican authorities, and the general populace led to secularization of the missions in 1835. The lands and the missions' Indian laborers were liberated from the missionaries, leaving the churches on their own. Under the new laws, Indians were supposed to receive back at least part of their lands. Unfortunately, the Californios and some of the early European and American settlers who were more educated and knowledgeable in the ways of markets, incentives, the law, and fraud were able to gain control of Indian lands.

It was during the ensuing years that California's newest land barons created their great ranchos. In addition to Indian lands, the Mexican government granted huge tracts of land to its governors, military leaders, and other prominent citizens. From the early 1820s until 1846, when United States citizens began entering Mexican California in force, the non-native population expanded relatively quickly, from about 3,700 people to nearly 8,000. But the pastoral setting where Californios raised cattle and traded hides and tallow with the growing numbers of trade ships that plied California's Pacific coast was being assaulted from several directions.

RUSSIANS AND THE FUR TRADE

In the late 1700s and early1800s, California's large population of sea otters offered opportunities for Americans, Russians, and the British to make huge profits in the fur trade. Trading ships brought in iron products, cloth, and other necessities, which were traded for otter pelts with trappers along the California and Pacific Northwest coasts. The pelts were then taken to China and traded for tea, spices, and silk. These and other highly prized trade goods were then shipped back to England, Europe, and to the East Coast of the United States, creating substantial profits for ship owners and their captains.

In defiance of powerless Spanish claims and threats, the Russians established Fort Ross on an ocean bluff along the Sonoma coast, north of the Russian River. It served as an outpost that supplied Russian pelt hunters who came down from the Aleutian Islands. The Russians finally abandoned Fort Ross when John Sutter purchased the outpost in 1841 from the Russian American Fur Company. Unfortantely for Sutter, he never

Fort Ross State Historic Park

Sutter's Fort State Historic Park

saw any substantial financial gain from his business dealings, even after acquiring a Mexican land grant and establishing New Helvetia (today's Sacramento). A poor head for business, coupled with the onslaught of the tumultuous Gold Rush in 1849, led to Sutter's economic downfall and the subsequent loss of his land holdings at Fort Ross and at Sutter's Fort in Sacramento.

THE EARLY AMERICANS

In 1846, no more than 700 Americans and a handful of British subjects lived in California. Some of the more ambitious foreigners assumed Mexican citizenship, married Mexican women, started businesses that prospered, and ultimately became leading citizens of their communities. Essentially isolated from Mexico by distance, politics, and economics, neither the old Californios' families nor many of the new Mexican citizens felt any particular loyalty to their mother government, its Alta California (Mexican-controlled California) appointees, or their policies.

The California Bear Flag Revolt was one of those anomalies of history that has been difficult to explain. It seems that a ragtag group of recent American immigrants, some of whom had also become Mexican citizens (but only for land acquisition purposes), feared that the Mexican government was planning to take their property and expel them from California. As a questionable preventative measure, they stole a small herd of horses that a Mexican military officer was moving from Sonoma to Monterey. Probably under the influence of too much brandy, and attempting to better justify their

Inside look at the Sonoma Barracks building

33

actions, they proclaimed their horse-thieving as the beginning of a revolution. On June 14, 1846, they marched on Sonoma where General Mariano Guadalupe Vallejo immediately surrendered his command and welcomed the conquerors into his home. Vallejo soon found himself under arrest and jailed at Sutter's Fort (future site of Sacramento) and the Bear Flaggers created a flag for their newfound republic. It featured the words "California Republic" proudly emblazoned below a crudely drawn grizzly bear that more resembled a pig. While the original design remains on the state flag, albeit with a more honorable appearing grizzly bear, the new republic lasted only three weeks.

The war between Mexico and the United States had already broken out earlier that spring, but the initial and heaviest fighting was along the Texas-Mexico border. The U.S. Navy was under standing orders to take and occupy California as soon as war was declared. This was done as much to firmly eliminate Mexico's control of the western side of the continent as to keep the English and Russians at bay, each very much aware of the riches in furs and timber that California held. Finally, on July 7, 1846, with his U.S. Pacific fleet anchored in Monterey Bay, Commodore John D. Sloat came ashore, peacefully lowered the Mexican flag from beside the Custom House, and raised the Stars and Stripes, declaring California under U.S. control. Two days later, the Stars and Stripes was raised over Sonoma, thus ending the Bear Flag Revolt. While Monterey and Sonoma surrendered immediately and peacefully, U.S. military forces in California soon fought several battles with Californios, not always emerging victorious.

With the signing of the Treaty of Guadalupe Hidalgo on February 2, 1848, California, along with most of the land that would become the other western states, now belonged to the United States. And, unknown to most everyone, just nine days earlier James Marshall had discovered gold in the Sierra Nevada's American River, about 200 miles northeast of Monterey.

Marshall Gold Discovery State Historic Park in Coloma

THE ENVIRONMENTAL MOVEMENT

The environmental movement in the United States has many of its roots buried deeply in the West. In California, there was an early group of visionaries who pushed the original idea that not all federal lands should be given away for people to develop and exploit, but that special areas should instead be protected. Yosemite Valley and California's coast redwoods served as catalysts for many of these early environmentalists and the organizations that they created. Frederick Law Olmsted, a well-known writer and the principal designer of New York's Central Park, became one of the pioneers of the movement, especially after he moved to California. Once here, Olmstead helped to push the Yosemite park idea, becoming an early lobbyist who enlisted the support of architects and artists, photographers, and others who could help promote the importance of saving Yosemite. John Muir was another of those whose articulate and persuasive writings about the wonders of nature, and of Yosemite in particular, helped to create a public awareness for the need to protect such national treasures.

Finally, in 1864, as the Civil War raged, President Lincoln signed a bill that set aside Yosemite Valley as California's first state park, although Yosemite ultimately reverted to federal control. With the vision firmly in place and a single

Yosemite Valley, Yosemite National Park

victory under their collective belts, a number of individuals continued the fight.

While there were some limited efforts to protect the Sierra's giant sequoias (*Sequoiadendron giganteum*), little was being done for the coast redwoods (*Sequoia*

Cultural History

sempervirens). That began to change in 1899, after Andrew Hill brought back photos of a private grove of coast redwoods that a European magazine had commissioned him to take. The following year, Hill brought a group of prominent politicians and community leaders to the redwood groves in Big Basin (Santa Cruz Mountains) where they decided to create an organization that could help preserve these grand trees. Collecting a total of $32 from among themselves, they chose officers for the newly formed Sempervirens Club.

Following numerous uphill battles that broadened public, political, and academic support, the state finally introduced and passed legislation that provided funding for acquisition of redwood lands. The first acquisition became Big Basin Redwoods State Park. As lumbermen eyed other prime old growth redwood groves, California's citizens heightened their efforts to purchase and protect them, but successes were few and slow in coming. Another organization, Save the Redwoods League, was also actively raising money and purchasing redwood property, but it wasn't until 1921 when the organization began its memorial grove program that significant amounts of acreage began to be secured.

Co-author hiking in Big Basin Redwoods State Park 20-plus years ago.

With timber interests and conservationists now vying for redwood lands and the California legislature taking little positive action to help save groves of 2,000-year-old trees, additional people—including William Crocker, president of Crocker National Bank in San Francisco, and John D. Rockefeller Jr.—got involved. In 1927, the California legislature approved a ballot measure for the sale of $6 million in bonds for park acquisition. The following year, in November 1928, voters passed what had been dubbed Proposition 4 by a nearly three-to-one majority. The modern California State Park System was born. Today, there are 280 state parks encompassing more than 339 miles of coastline as part of its 1.59 million acres.

Santa Monica State Beach

<u>CITIZENS AND THE COASTAL ACT</u>

With 85 percent of Californians living within 30 miles of the ocean, the demand for control of and access to coastal property has been increasing each year. For too many years, the result of this insatiable demand was that much of the coastline was being turned into private havens for the rich at the exclusion of everyone else. Hotels and other structures began blocking public views of the ocean and bays, and wetlands were being filled and dammed in alarming numbers. Finally, in 1972, the people of California, tired of inaction by their state legislators to protect one of their state's greatest assets, and reminiscent of struggles earlier in the century, took things into their own hands. Through the initiative process, which allows private citizens to bypass do-nothing state lawmakers, Proposition 20—The Coastal Conservation Initiative—was placed on the statewide ballot.

Proposition 20 passed, and with its passage came the establishment of the California Coastal Commission. With extensive public input, the commission developed a coastal plan designed to ensure the protection of critical coastal resources, and, just as importantly, the plan guaranteed continued public access to the coast.

Today, the Coastal Commission continues its watchdog role. Coastal development is still allowed, but on a more limited and much more sane basis. Continued public access to beaches and protection for wetlands and endangered plant communities are more often the primary considerations.

The Northern Coast

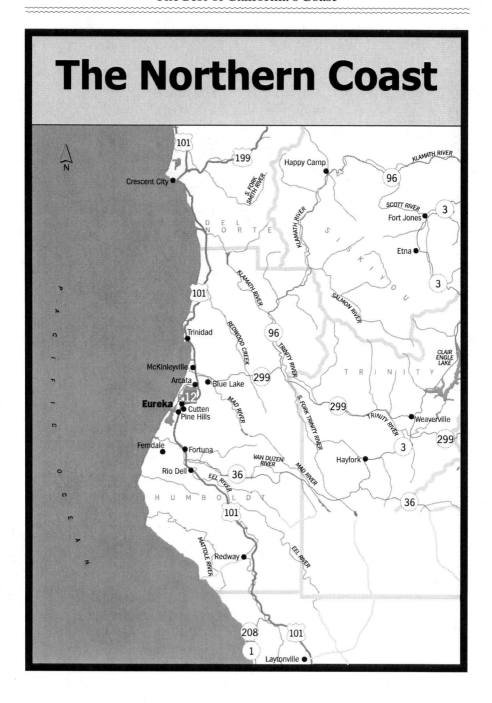

The Northern Coast

R ain is a staple for California's northern coast. The forests that grow the world's tallest trees, along with lush green meadows, fern-covered forest floors, and rivers filled with migrating salmon and steelhead, all depend on the 60 to 100 inches or more of annual rainfall. These rain-enriched resources allowed California's Indians to live full lives and to develop exceptionally rich cultures. And these were the same resources that attracted the first Europeans, the Russians, and finally the Americans. While each had specific economic interests, often based on which commodity from nature was most profitable at the time, few countries had any problems crossing vague and rarely defended colonial boundaries during California's 18th and 19th centuries. Within Spain's claimed lands of Alta, or upper California, the English hunted whales, the Russians trapped furs, and the Americans came for it all.

Within 150 years following the Americanization of California, most of the old-growth redwood forests had been logged and the salmon and steelhead runs were significantly reduced. But with new, more enlightened attitudes, many of California's North Coast natural resources are returning. State and national parks protect most of the remaining old-growth redwoods, and now, more than 150 years after the first redwood and Douglas fir forests were harvested, second-growth trees have created replacement forests that, in some areas, are approaching the

Northern Coast

habitat values of their parent groves. Legislated protections have allowed California otters, hunted to near extinction in the 19th century, to return to near their historic population levels. The same types of protections, along with help from scientists and their ongoing monitoring programs, are helping restore salmon and steelhead runs to many rivers and creeks where they once were found in unimaginable numbers.

Co-author with her children (atop the fallen tree) in an old-growth redwood forest

Major rivers in this region—such as the Klamath, Mad, Eel, and Smith, along with their numerous forks and the hundreds of small creeks that feed them—add to the appeal of the North Coast for visitors. Each year, kayaks become more numerous on many of the rivers, and drift boats carrying fishing enthusiasts have always been popular. Other people enjoy the great opportunities for bird watching that the rivers afford, swimming or wading in some of the calmer pools, or simply walking along their shorelines.

Much of Northern California's breathtaking coastal lands remain as private property holdovers from the 19th century when lumber barons, farmers, and cattlemen gained control of thousands of acres of Indian lands. Today, pockets of public property—mostly state and national parks acquired through purchases or gifts—punctuate the private lands, protecting old-growth redwoods and providing access to ocean beaches. But whether publicly or privately held, even today, most of Del Norte and Humboldt counties remain wild, with steep mountain trails, dense forests, and meandering rivers always worth exploring.

Del Norte County

CRESCENT CITY

The quiet coastal community of Crescent City is famous for many things, but mostly as a victim of tsunamis. The city's crescent-shaped bay and harbor is home to fish processing plants, public boat slips, a launch ramp, and the 87-foot United States Coast Guard cutter *Dorado*. A relatively small town, Crescent City boasts a great beach at its southern end, directly adjacent to U.S. Route 101. When the surf is decent, you can watch wetsuit-clad surfers riding the breaking waves.

As trade increased significantly along California's rugged coast, especially during the Gold Rush, maritime safety became a significant issue. Dangerous winds and currents drove numerous wooden sailing ships onto the rocky shoreline, often with

Crescent City's Battery Point Lighthouse at low tide

significant loss of life in the cold waters. In response to these growing tragedies, the United States began building lighthouses, first near some of the busier and more difficult-to-access harbors, and later along the most dangerous stretches of the coast.

Battery Point Lighthouse (707.464.3089 or www.delnortehistory.org) was constructed in 1856 near the mouth of the bay. The lighthouse is accessible to the public, generally Wednesday through Sunday, from April through September, and when tides are low enough to walk across the rocks from the mainland. The lighthouse contains a museum that is devoted to early maritime history and holds a collection of Tolowa Indian artifacts.

Northern Coast

St. George Reef Light is located 6 miles off the coast of Crescent City. On clear days, and with good eyes or a pair of binoculars, the structure is visible. First lit in 1892, construction costs totaled $752,000, thus making it the most expensive lighthouse ever built in the U.S. It was erected on what Sir Francis Drake coined the "Dragon Rocks," due to the fact that many maritime catastrophes occurred here, including the famed shipwreck of the *Brother Johnathan* in 1865.

The 90-foot tall structure—actually 144-feet tall if adding the protruding rock and added foundation—was simply referred to as a "light" when it was built. It was decommissioned in 1975 when a floating lighthouse buoy was established there instead. Today, you can see the lighthouse's first-order Fresnel lens and learn more about St. George and the *Brother Johnathan* at the **Del Norte County Historical Museum** in Crescent City (707.464.3922 or www.delnortehistory.org).

Pebble Beach Drive connects with Fifth Street in downtown then parallels the coast as it heads north along the bluffs overlooking the Pacific. There are several pull-outs along the road and stairways to the beach area below.

Preston Island lies on the north end of Crescent City and really isn't an island, but a spit. There's a paved road off Pebble Beach Drive that leads to the island-spit, where great views and picnic tables await.

Pelican State Beach (707.465.2145 or www.parks.ca.gov) is situated on the California and Oregon border, about 21 miles north of Crescent City and just off U.S. 101. It is a secluded, 5-acre park that sits on a bluff overlooking the Pacific

---

Tsunamis

When giant, unpredictable waves strike coastal areas, far too often the media mistakenly describe them as tidal waves. "Tsunami" is a Japanese word that much more accurately describes this great underwater disturbance: a series of higher than normal waves caused by sudden movements of the ocean floor. Earthquakes are the most common cause of the largest tsunamis, but underwater volcanic eruptions can also trigger this destructive phenomenon.

The waves, generally several hundred miles long and as much as 75 feet high, are hardly noticeable in the open ocean, but as they approach the shallow coastal waters, they begin to rise rapidly. The 1964 Anchorage, Alaska earthquake (9.2 on the Richter scale) generated a tsunami that struck Crescent City with a wave 12 feet high. The wave surged inland 1,600 feet, destroyed most of the city's central business district, and killed 12 people.

Even though high, destructive tsunamis are rare, warning sirens have been installed along some of the populated, low-lying areas of the far Northern California and Oregon coasts. The sirens sound when a tsunami threatens the area, hopefully giving people time to reach higher ground before waves strike.

Surfers and co-author's son enjoying the beaches in Crescent City

Ocean. Surf fishing from the beach can be quite good, especially considering that only about 5,000 people visit the park each year and most come to enjoy the views or walk the beach, not to fish.

Tolowa Dunes State Park (707.465.7335 or www.parks.ca.gov), located not far from California's Pelican Bay State Prison, is a large wetland that provides refuge for tens of thousands of waterfowl and other birds, especially during the fall migration. **Lake Earl** and **Lake Tolowa** are found in this wetland, and scattered ponds and dunes surround both lakes. There are only a few access points, and they can be a challenge to find, since there are not many directional signs to the lakes. The area parallels U.S. 101, north of Crescent City. Take Lake Earl Drive then turn west on Lower Lake Road and enter the park by turning west on Kellogg Road or Pala Road.

Crescent City's Harbor

The masts of boats in the **Crescent City Harbor** are visible from U.S. 101. The public wharf portion of the harbor was originally constructed in 1950. In 2014, the harbor was redone and is now the only 50-year tsunami-safe harbor on the West Coast. During fogless evenings, the wharf is a great place to enjoy beautiful sunsets.

Info: Crescent City/Del Norte Chamber of Commerce, 1001 Front Street, Crescent City, CA 95531, 800.343.8300 or www.delnorte.org

Northern Coast

The Smith River

JEDEDIAH SMITH REDWOODS STATE PARK

Giant, ancient redwoods, a lazy flowing river, and trails that wind through waist-tall forests of ferns make this park extremely popular. It's a combination of isolation, good fishing, and the opportunity to be well away from civilization that attracts most people. Many families have been coming here annually, some for generations.

This most northern of California's major redwood state parks was named after a famous early American explorer who traveled through this area. In 1822, a time when America's frontier West began at the banks of the Missouri River, Jedediah Strong Smith was 23 years old and embarking on his fur-trapping career that would soon bring him to California. Five years later, Smith and 19 other men were herding 250 horses from Red Bluff in the northern Sacramento Valley over the mountains to the coast near Crescent City, and then on to Oregon. By this time, Smith had experience surviving violent encounters with Indians. On this trip, several weeks after the group had camped on **Elk Creek** (now a part of Jedediah Smith State Park), Smith's party moved north and soon clashed with the Kelawatset Indians near Oregon's Umpqua River. Only Smith and three of his men survived. In 1831, he was killed near the Santa Fe Trail in Kansas by Comanche hunters.

During his short lifetime, Jedediah Smith was credited with being the first Euro-American to visit the redwood coast. He also rediscovered South Pass, one of the easier and more popular routes over the Rockies, and he was the first to reach the Mexican settlements in California via the Great Salt Lake. That was a trip that

Redwood National and State Parks

The dense redwood and Douglas fir forests of the North Coast thrive on 60, 70, or more inches of rain each year. But the North Coast, like most of California, is a land of rainy winters and dry summers. Swirling clouds of heavy, summer fog often envelope the great forests of the north coast and provide critical moisture and humidity to the shallow-rooted trees, which helps them to survive until the winter rains return. But today, it takes more than nature's hand for the remaining old-growth redwoods to survive.

When Redwood National Park was established in 1968, it marked a renewed commitment to an ongoing land acquisition program. Added to the long-established redwood state parks, the new land was designed to save the relatively few old-growth trees that still remained on private lands and to implement conservation efforts to better protect the previously logged upland watersheds. That protection included purchasing logged-over mountains and replanting the areas in order to reduce flooding, erosion, and the resulting mud that clogged the spawning gravels of salmon and steelhead.

When Congress established Redwood National Park, it included three, long-established California State Parks within its boundary, although the state parks continued to be managed by the California Department of Parks and Recreation. As the national park expanded with additional land acquisitions, it became evident that having two separate public landowners managing adjacent lands with policies that could potentially impact one another was not an efficient way to operate. Today, staff from Redwood National Park and the three contiguous state parks—Jedediah Smith Redwoods, Del Norte Coast Redwoods, and Prairie Creek Redwoods—work together on planning for such things as maintenance, resource management, and interpretive programs.

One of the joint visitor centers can be found just across from the entrance to Jedediah Smith Redwoods State Park. Open during the summer only, the Jedediah Smith Visitor Center offers park information and is the headquarters for ranger-led activities and Junior Ranger programs. Info: 707.458.3496

Coastal redwood cones

got him tossed in jail for having entered the country (Mexico) illegally. Smith was the first to cross the Sierra Nevada and to travel the length of California, and the first to reach the Pacific Ocean from the upper Sacramento Valley.

While the history attributed to Jedediah Smith is certainly fascinating, it's his namesake river and redwood state park that attract most people to this secluded corner of California. The **Smith River** begins life in the Siskiyou Mountains to the east and flows freely all the way to the ocean, bisecting the park. It is the largest California river to run its entire natural course without at least one man-made diversion dam used either for water storage, flood control, or hydroelectric power.

To see where the Smith River empties into the ocean, take Highway 101 north to Oregon. When you get to the small town of Smith River, watch for a sign to your left that states "**Mouth Smith River Road.**" It's directly across the street from the **Lucky 7 Casino.** Follow the road until it dead-ends, and then carefully make your way down to the beach. The sand spit on the other side of the river mouth's opening is a favorite spot for harbor seals (*Phoca vitulina*), cormorants (*Phalacrocorax* spp.), and many species of gulls.

The mouth of the Smith River

For the geological origins of the Smith River, wander back in time some 200 million years to when erosion was washing sediments into the Pacific Ocean that settled on what was known as the Gorda plate. The Gorda plate, like the much larger Pacific plate, slid under the North American plate. The North American plate scraped the thick, ancient sediments off the top of the diving Gorda plate, leaving them back on shore once again as mountains to be eroded and carried back to the sea. The **Smith River Basin** resulted from all of this tectonic activity.

As the Smith River drops down through the Klamath Mountains, it enters what is called the Franciscan Assemblage, an area made up of those ancient, softer, ocean sediment scrapings. It's within these more easily erodible rocks that the river channel widens into the alluvial flats that support the park's giant redwoods.

The gravel bars at the river's edges are great places to begin a relaxing float on inner tubes or to wet a fishing line. The Smith River also supports fall runs of steelhead (*Oncorhynchus mykiss*) and salmon (*Oncorhynchus* sp.), while Mill Creek, a

Banana slug and the co-author's fingers—the slugs are big!

major tributary, provides valuable gravel spawning beds for both species.

The Smith River's riparian zone is home for willows (*Silex* sp.) that grow quickly and profusely. Big leaf maples (*Acer macrophyllum*) and red alders (Alnus ruba) thrive in the shade created by the redwood forest. In addition to the extensive groves of old-growth redwoods, the park's 10,000 acres also support sitka spruce (*Picea sitchensis*), Port Orford cedar (*Chamaecyparis lawsoniana*), Douglas fir (*Pseudotsuga menziesii*), and western hemlock (*Tsuga heterophylla*).

While wandering through the forest and along the river, it's always exciting to spot some of the less commonly seen birds such as the bald eagle, pileated woodpecker (*Dryocopus pileatus*), endangered spotted owl (*Strix occidentalis*), and marbled murrelet (*Brachyramphus marmoratus*), the last two being small birds that have brought huge changes to the timber harvesting industry throughout the Pacific Northwest. There's also a chance of running into black bears (*Ursus americanus*), coyotes (*Canis latrans*), black-tailed deer (*Odocoileus hemionius columbianus*), and the ever-present banana slug (*Ariolimax californicus*).

Activities: Fishing, camping, hiking, swimming (no lifeguard)
Facilities: Campground, picnic facilities, group campground
Dates: Open year-round
Fees: There are camping and day-use fees.
Closest town: Crescent City
Info: Jedediah Smith Redwoods State Park, 1440 U.S. 199, Crescent City, CA 95531, 707.465.7335 or www.parks.ca.gov

Northern Coast

47

TRAILS

There are too many trails in this park to list them all. The most popular is the **Simpson-Reed Trail**, right off Highway 199. The 1-mile loop is level and easy to hike. The **Hatton Trail** is across from Simpson-Reed; this .03-mile trail connects to the **Hatton-Hiouchi Trail**, which is 1.2 miles long.

Along **Howland Hill Road**, you'll find three more popular trails. This road is not the best after it rains, so be prepared for unknown conditions, and RVs and trailers are not recommended. The first trailhead is for **Mill Creek Trail**. This is actually the west trailhead—the east trailhead is found at the **Jedediah Smith Campground** and is only accessible via a seasonal footbridge. The 2.5-mile-long trail is moderate and perfect for those wanting to enjoy the best the coastal redwoods have to offer.

Back on Howland Hill Road, across from the east Mill Creek trailhead, you'll find the **Boy Scout Tree Trail**. This trail, which is 2.8 miles long, ends at **Fern Falls**. At the 2.5-mile point, watch for an unmarked, but obviously well used, trail that leads to a double redwood. This redwood is called the "**Boy Scout Tree**" and was named in honor of a local troop leader who discovered it.

Last is the **Stout Memorial Grove Trail**. This trail can be accessed either via Howland Hill Road or from the Jedediah Smith campground, but only during the dry season. The 0.5-mile loop is easy and flat after the initial descent from the Howland Hill trailhead. In 1929, wanting to honor her late husband—lumber baron Frank D. Stout—and also to save old-growth trees from logging, Clara Stout donated this 44-acre grove to the Save the Redwoods League.

Info: http://www.nps.gov/redw/planyourvisit/hiking-trails-north.htm

Co-author setting up camp at Mill Creek

DEL NORTE COAST REDWOODS STATE PARK

Del Norte Coast Redwoods State Park is fairly typical of most of California's North Coast redwood parks. Hike the trails beneath the redwoods and where there are breaks in the stands—especially in that half of the park's 6,400 acres that was logged before it could be protected—and a woodland of madrone (*Arbutus menziesii*), red alder (*Alnus rubra*), bigleaf maple (*Acer macrophyllum*), and the ever-present tanoak (*Lithocarpus densiflora*) grows profusely. But the redwoods will ultimately win the battle. Near the second-growth redwoods that are slowly reclaiming their original boundaries, the woodland forest struggles for what little light escapes through the spread of the overstory redwood branches.

Mill Creek carves its way through a portion of the park, where forest land ranges in elevation from the ocean shore to 1,277 feet above sea level. Mill Creek serves as an important spawning stream for both salmon and steelhead. The creek also is home to dippers (*Cinclus mexicanus*), curious little birds that hop along the stream banks and among the rocks then disappear for several seconds underwater as they swim after insects. Great blue herons (*Ardea herodias*) also search the shallow waters looking for fish and crustaceans, while the more terrestrial birds—varied thrushes (*Ixoreus naevius*), Steller's jays (*Cyanocitta stelleri*), and a variety of hawks—are found throughout much of the park.

Great blue heron

Much of the coast within the park is extremely mountainous and generally too steep to explore safely. The 0.5-mile-long **Wilson Beach** and **False Klamath Cove** allow access to tide pools during low tides. The beach is steep, the water very cold, and currents much too dangerous for swimming.

> **Activities:** Hiking, camping, fishing, beachcombing
> **Facilities:** Campground
> **Dates:** Open year-round; campground mid-May through September
> **Fees:** There are camping and day-use fees.
> **Closest town:** Crescent City
> **Info**: Jedediah Smith Redwoods State Park, 1440 U.S. 199, Crescent City, CA 95531, 707.465.7335 or www.parks.ca.gov

THE KLAMATH RIVER

The Klamath River is California's second largest river and drains much of the state's northwest corner, which includes some of its most rain-drenched mountains. The river's lower portion, below the **Iron Gate Dam**, was designated

Northern Coast

a Wild and Scenic River in 1981. When some of the Klamath's tributaries are included, such as portions of the **Salmon River** and **Wooley Creek**, there are 12 miles of river classified as wild, 24 miles that are scenic, and another 250 miles that are classified as recreational. When visitors drive across the Klamath River bridge on U.S. 101, most prominent are the two **golden grizzly bear statues** (pictured

to the right) that stand guard at each end. The Klamath River is a major salmon fishery for coho (*Oncorhynchus kisutch*) and chinook (*Oncorhynchus tshawytscha*) salmon that migrate upriver annually, heading to their spawning grounds.

The river's mouth can change each winter as the large sand and gravel bar is eroded, moved, and redeposited. Roads off U.S. 101 parallel both the north and south sides of the river. On each side, there are places where boats can be launched. During summer, the relatively calm river area that lies inland from the mouth becomes a popular kayaking destination. There's plenty of shoreline to explore and it's a great place to see numerous kinds of birds, including raptors.

Klamath River Overlook view

MORE TO EXPLORE

Cal-Barrel Road is a very narrow dirt road not recommended for RVs or trailers. Some drive the road, but most walk. The road is about 0.5 mile north of the Prairie Creek Redwoods State Park headquarters entrance and on the east side of the Newton B. Drury Scenic Parkway. Spring is the best time to hike up the 1.5-mile road because scattered among the towering redwoods are colorful clusters of wild rhododendrons (*Rhododendron macrophyllum*). Their pink and white blossoms beautifully accent the deep, red bark of the redwoods, especially on those days when sunlight filters softly through light fog or cloud cover.

On the south side of the Klamath River, take Klamath Beach Road to **Coastal**

Drive. (**NOTE:** This road may be closed because of slides or floods.) This dirt and gravel road offers a great view of the mouth of the Klamath River and wonderful ocean views along much of its 9.5-mile length. Along the road, which takes about 45 minutes to drive and connects with Newton B. Drury Scenic Parkway, watch for a structure that resembles an old farmhouse and barn; it was actually a World War II radar station. Its farmhouse appearance was a disguise to protect it from a possible Japanese attack.

From U.S. 101, cross to the north side of the Klamath River and turn west onto Requa Road, which winds upward to the **Klamath River Overlook**. On warm, sunny days, this is a great place to sit at one of the picnic tables and enjoy a little wine and cheese and a spectacular view of the north coast. Look for whales, especially during winter when the gray whales are migrating south.

Humboldt County

PRAIRIE CREEK REDWOODS STATE PARK

Many years ago, a new freeway bypass diverted large trucks and fast-driving travelers off the original, narrow and twisting two-lane U.S. 101 that passed through the center of the park. Today, the old highway—renamed the **Newton B. Drury Scenic Parkway**—treats visitors to 8 miles of a much slower paced drive through the spectacular redwood forest.

Besides the redwood forest, there is one additional highlight that brings people here, many year after year—the large population of Roosevelt elk (*Cervus canadensis roosevelti*). One of the easiest places to view the elk is from the side of the parkway at the small coastal prairie (large meadow) near the park entrance to the campground and visitor center. There are almost always

A grazing Roosevelt bull elk

Northern Coast

elk, either bedded down or grazing in the open meadow or along the adjacent forest border.

As with many parks, the visitor center is generally a good place to begin your adventure. In addition to its small gift shop, which offers a great selection of publications, the **Prairie Creek Visitor Center** also features numerous natural history exhibits. Here, visitors can discover the names of the many wildflowers and birds seen in the park.

Prairie Creek Redwoods State Park has two campgrounds, the first of which is located at the south end of what is called "Elk Prairie." The second is the very popular campground on **Gold Bluffs Beach**. It requires a much more adventurous drive to find—after rejoining U.S. 101 and heading south past the park, watch

for Davison Road, which will be on the right (west). A meadow borders both sides of the road for the first 200 yards and is often a good place to find one of the park's elk herds. Soon afterward, Davidson Road turns to dirt and heads upward into the forest where it winds for several miles, finally dropping down and emerging at Gold Bluffs Beach. Be

Gold Bluffs Beach

warned, the road is narrow and many of the turns tight enough that vehicles more than 8 feet wide and 24 feet long are prohibited. The beach campground is another 2 miles down the road, which hugs the tall coastal bluff. Once again, elk can generally be seen, often in the low dunes between the road and the beach.

Gold Bluffs Beach was aptly named. In 1851, California's gold fever spilled over from the mines of the Sierra foothills' Mother Lode and the Trinity River area to these bluffs. Thousands of miners flooded the area and created a large camp along the base of the bluffs. There was, and remains, gold in the bluffs, but the early miners could never manage to extract large enough quantities to make the operation economically viable. While the name of the bluffs is a reminder of its history, most first-time visitors probably believe the name is for the gold color of the bluffs' crumbly rock.

Activities: Camping, backpacking, fishing, picnicking, hiking
Facilities: Campground, backcountry camps, visitor center

Dates: Open daily. Camping reservations are advised during summer.
Fees: There are camping and day-use fees.
Closest town: Orick
Info: Prairie Creek Redwoods State Park, 127011 Newton B. Drury Scenic Parkway, Orick, CA 95555, 707.465.7335 or www.parks.ca.gov

TRAILS

The **Revelation Trail**, which is near the visitor center, is a short, 0.3-mile, very level and easy trail that loops into the redwoods. As its name implies, the trail provides revelations about the nature of the redwood forest, not only for those able to see and hear normally, but also for those who may have physical impairments. The trail's many stopping points are designed to relate the same information to those who may be sight- or hearing-impaired.

At 6.1 miles the **West Ridge Trail** is the park's longest. It follows the ridgeline that lies about 500 to 600 feet above and about 2 miles east of the ocean. The trail is only moderately difficult, remaining relatively level. It begins near the park's visitor center and heads north, ending on Newton B. Drury Scenic Parkway. Many hikers head west just before the trail's end and take the **Butler Creek Trail** (1.8 miles) down to the beach.

The **Fern Canyon Trail** is one of the most popular destinations in Prairie Creek Redwoods State Park. It's an easy, 0.7-mile trail that begins at the north end of Gold Bluffs Beach. The short, level walk offers a look at the geologic history of this part of the North Coast. Following in the bed of the shallow creek, the trail meanders through a carved, sheer-walled canyon, revealing the nearby Klamath River's 4-million-year-old gravel deposits.

The narrow canyon walls rise 50 feet or more and are almost completely covered by thick mats of bright green ferns. Five-finger fern (*Adianthum pedatum*), lady

Fern Canyon Trail at Gold Bluffs Beach

Roosevelt Elk

Walking along a trail and suddenly coming upon a 1,200-pound bull Roosevelt elk (*Cervus canadensis roosevelti*) can be somewhat unsettling, especially during the fall rutting season when bulls are very aggressive. Fortunately, most of the time elk are relatively benign, as long as people keep a safe distance. During much of the year, the small herds of maybe a dozen or more cows are easily located as they lazily graze in the meadows, or lie resting in the tall grasses, often with only their heads visible. It's common most of the year to see the cows and bulls in their separate groups. The fall mating season usually finds bulls challenging other bulls with their loud snorting and bugling, and with short, false charges. Their occasional battles produce the loud sounds of colliding antlers that echo across meadows and through the forests. All this late summer and early autumn posturing, bluffing, and fighting determines which of the biggest and strongest bulls get the right to mate with the cows, which leads to calves being born in May and June.

WARNING!

These elk are wild animals and can be very dangerous. Do not be tempted to approach closely for that "perfect" photograph—or for any other reason.

Elk bedding down at Prairie Creek Redwoods State Park

fern (*Athyrium felix-femina*), and sword fern (*Polystichum munitum*) are the most common. Orange-colored salmon berries (*Rubus spectabilis*) ripen during June and July, and they're edible, but oenanthe (*Oenanthe sarmontosa*), which is related to carrots, is poisonous. Another berry popular with anyone hiking up the canyon is the thimbleberry (*Rubus parviflorus*), similar to the salmon berry. It has a very enjoyable flavor.

It seems nearly impossible that this small stream and its narrow canyon are home to so many animals, especially during late summer when the water is so shallow. Coastal cutthroat trout (*Salmo clarkii clarkii*) come upstream in early spring and spawn, and rare and endangered species, such as the red-legged frog (*Rana aurora*) and the Pacific giant salamander (*Dicamptodon ensatus*), also live in this moist refuge.

The trail heads upstream, then rises to the top of the bluff and loops back to the parking lot. It also connects with the **James Irving Trail** that leads back across the coastal hills to the visitor center (4.2 miles). The best time to visit the Fern Canyon Trail is during summer when the water is low and the small footbridges are in place, but be prepared to possibly get wet feet at any time.

Six noncontiguous sections comprise the **Coastal Trail** that leads hikers through Redwood National and State Parks. The Coastal Trail is an unfinished 1,200-mile-long series of trails that run the length of California's coastline passing through 15 counties. It meanders primarily along the coast, but occasionally detours inland, such as in Del Norte Coast Redwoods State Park. One of the gaps in the trail is at the mouth of the Klamath River. Hikers must turn inland to the U.S. 101 highway bridge to get across the river. This section of the trail begins near the end of Enderts Beach Road, just north of Del Norte Coast Redwoods State Park and ends in the south, about 1.5 miles north of Orick at U.S. 101. Camping is allowed in the established en route campsites on a first-come, first-served basis.

> **Info**: Redwood National and State Parks, 1111 Second Street, Crescent City, CA 95531, 707.465.7335, www.parks.ca.gov, www.nps.gov or www.CaliforniaCoastalTrail.info

REDWOOD NATIONAL PARK

Redwood National Park shares many stretches of its meandering boundary with three state parks—Prairie Creek Redwoods, Del Norte Coast Redwoods, and Jedediah Smith Redwoods. Together, the state and national parks form a World Heritage Site and International Biosphere Reserve, a worldwide recognition of their environmental significance.

Redwood National Park was created in 1968, several decades after the state parks were established to protect old-growth redwoods. Although much of the forest within the national park contains second-growth redwoods, the park plays

Northern Coast

a crucial role in protecting the old-growth trees that remain. The National Park Service is actively rehabilitating the logged lands, eliminating exotic plant species that have taken over many hillsides and planting native trees such as redwoods and Douglas fir. With thousands of acres of watershed now protected from the damage created by logging activities, especially during the early, unregulated years of the industry, flooding is much less prevalent. The ongoing efforts also help protect the stream and river gravels needed by spawning steelhead and salmon.

The coast portion of Redwood National Park is a relatively unspoiled meeting of land and sea that stretches from Stone Lagoon—directly parallel with U.S.

Look closely for the two whale spouts

101, just south of **Orick**—north to Crescent City. Most of it is accessible only by way of hiking trails, and there are several popular access points. One of the longest stretches of easily accessible beach, where you can park your vehicle and walk right up to the ocean's edge, is at **Fresh Water Lagoon**, south of Orick. The long pull-off between the highway and the beach is a very popular day-use area for RVers looking for a beautiful ocean beach view. It is also a great place to watch for whale spouts offshore, and maybe a glimpse of the whales coming to the surface.

A walk along the beach is likely to bring sightings of numerous shorebirds chasing the ebb and flow of the slapping waves searching the sand for insects, tiny crustaceans, and anything else that fills their bills. The rocky tide pools are a rich zone for exploration. Mussels, anemones, sea stars, and snails are among the dozens of very different animal species that are dependent upon the swirl of fresh, clean salt water for survival. Double-crested cormorants (*Phalacrocorax auritus*) and brown pelicans (*Pelecanus occidentalis*) glide low and elegantly above the water or rise high before diving below the surface to feed.

The **Thomas H. Kruchel Visitor Center,** located south of Orick, provides exhibits and a large assortment of publications about the area's cultural and natural history, as well as maps, permits for backcountry camping, and general information about both the state and national parks found in the area.

Activities: Hiking, backpacking, fishing, camping
Facilities: Campgrounds, visitor center, trails
Dates: Open daily except Thanksgiving, Christmas, and New Year's Day
Fees: Camping fees are charged in some areas.
Closest towns: Crescent City, Orick, and Trinidad
Info: Redwood National and State Parks, 1111 Second Street, Crescent City, CA, 95531, 707.465.7335 or www.nps.gov

TRAILS

Many of the trails in Redwood National Park, such as the Coastal Trail, connect with trails in the adjacent state parks. While hiking any of the trails, be aware that bears are occasionally sighted. If you come across a bear, make plenty of noise and back away from it slowly, and it shouldn't bother you.

DeMartin Section, Coastal Trail is a 10-mile round-trip hike that heads into the backcountry through forests of old-growth redwoods, western hemlock (*Tsuga heterophylla*), and Douglas fir (*Pseudotsuga menziesii*). While there are several grades, some relatively steep, this all-day hike is only moderately difficult. Pick up the trail south of Crescent City. Look for milepost marker 12.8 along U.S. 101 and the signpost marked "CT." Park off the road.

The **Dolason Prairie Trail** offers an opportunity to see elk up close, but not too close. This strenuous hike weaves through prairies and oaks as it switchbacks down to Redwood Creek. You can either hike back out on the same trail or connect with the Redwood Creek Trail that follows the canyon back toward Orick. Take Bald Hills Road, about 1.5 miles north of Orick, then drive 11 miles to the Dolason Prairie picnic area, which is located past the Thomas H. Kruchel Visitor Center picnic area.

Lady Bird Johnson Grove

The **Lady Bird Johnson Grove Trail** is an easy, 1-mile walk. It was named after former First Lady, Lady Bird Johnson who visited the grove for its dedication in 1968. To reach the grove's trailhead turn onto Baldwin Hills Road from U.S. 101, about 2 miles north of Orick. Drive about 3 miles up the mountain road to the trailhead. RVs and trailers are not advised, as there are tight turns heading up the steep road and there are no turnarounds until the grove parking area, and that can be unpredictable if the parking lot is full.

Redwood Creek Trail is a summer hike because seasonal bridges are removed during winter's high water. It's an 8-mile walk along the creek to **Tall Trees Grove**. It's another 6 miles to connect with the Dolason Prairie Trail. The hike is rated moderate, but the uphill hike to Dolason Prairie Trail is strenuous.

An 8-hour round-trip hike is required to reach the Tall Trees Grove. For those unable to hike the 8.5 miles up Redwood Creek to visit the Tall Trees Grove, a few permits are issued daily for vehicle access via Bald Hills Road, off U.S. 101 and Orick. From the drive-in trailhead, the Tall Trees Grove is only a 1.3-mile hike each way, with an 800-foot drop in elevation to the grove. Bald Hills Road is steep and winding. Trailers and motor homes are not allowed. Info: Redwood National and State Parks, 707.465.7335 or www.nps.gov

MORE TO EXPLORE

Humboldt Lagoons State Park is comprised of **Dry Lagoon**, **Big Lagoon**, and **Stone Lagoon**. Important resource management programs in all three lagoons have begun to reverse the adverse effects that pioneer farmers and dairy ranchers created by draining the wetlands. Today, the lagoons adjacent to U.S. 101, seven miles south of Orick, teem with wildlife, especially birds that thrive in the restored marshy areas. Adjacent to the highway, between Dry Lagoon and Big Lagoon, there is a small visitor center (open summer only) that once was a motel and restaurant. Boating, hiking, and fishing are popular in the park and there are some boat-in and undeveloped environmental campsites. Check tide tables before setting out. Info: 707.677.3570 or www.parks.ca.gov

Stone Lagoon

PATRICK'S POINT STATE PARK

Patrick's Point State Park has something for everyone. Be it beaches, animals, trees, Native American history, or gardens, this park is sure to please. Start your exploration of some of the park's more prominent features by visiting the **Patrick's Point Visitor Center**. Like most visitor centers, exhibits and information are available that will enhance your visit, including how to identify beach agates and the history behind the Yurok Indians.

Sumêg Village, a short walk from the visitor center, is a reconstruction of a Yurok Indian village. The Yurok's redwood shelters played critical roles in their lives. They believed that the redwood planks were spirits and that their shelters actually lived. The Yuroks gave their houses names, and each family's loyalty was to its home rather than to the tribe.

In 1990, local Yurok Indians reconstructed the village using traditional stone mauls and wedges to split the redwood planks. Inside the low-built homes, the Yuroks dug pits 4- to 5-feet deep to increase the living space. Today, the village is used for special Yurok ceremonies and events, but it is open daily for anyone to wander through.

Sumêg Village

The Yurok maintained a distinctive class system within the tribe. The aristocrats of a Yurok village, depending upon their level of wealth, maintained large collections of fine clothing. They would generally provide the special clothing or regalia worn by all the tribal dancers at many ceremonies. Displayed wealth included clothing adorned with various shells seen as valuable to the culture, such as olivella (*Olivella biplicata*), butter clam (various genera), cockles (various genera), dentalliam (*Dentallium* sp.), and red abalone (*Haliotis rufescens*). Even more rare and valuable were the dresses made from the skins of albino deer.

Like most public and private lands throughout northwest California, black bear and raccoons are always present, even though they are rarely seen. Exceptions to their natural shyness occur when they discover unsecured food left in campsites and quickly become campground scavengers. Sightings of black-tailed deer (*Odocoileus hemionius columbianus*) are common, especially along the bluff and in the open meadow near **Ceremonial Rock**, which is actually an ancient sea stack that was left high and dry following the rising of the land. It's located near the

Northern Coast

Western trillium

center of the park. Another ancient sea stack—**Lookout Rock**—is adjacent to the **Rim Trail**, near the hike- and bike-campground.

Along the park's rocky southern shoreline, tide pools are a cold, inviting haven for dozens of different animal species, from mussels and oysters to sea stars and anemones. California sea lions—once prey for Yurok hunters—bark their incessant calls from offshore rocks.

If you're interested in fishing, there's plenty of both rocky and sandy shoreline to be found within the park. During certain times of the year, various fish species migrate in close to shore toward their spawning areas, offering anglers the opportunity to regularly catch lingcod (*Ophiodon elongatus*), kelp greenlings (*Hexagrammos decagrammus*), sea trout or steelhead (*Oncorhynchus mykiss*), and cabezone (*Scorpaenichthys marmoratus*).

Douglas iris

The park's 65 inches of annual rain provides plenty of moisture for a tremendous variety of plants. Sword ferns and redwoods are common and easily identified, but spruce, hemlock, and Douglas fir are also prevalent within the park's boundaries. In the open meadows and along the forest trails, spring and summer bring a plethora of wildflowers, such as Western trillium (*Trillium ovatum*), Douglas iris (*Iris douglasiana*), rhododendrons (*Rhododendron macrophyllum*), false lilies-of-the-valley (*Maiantheumum dilatatum*), and the ever-present berries—blackberries (*Rubus ursinus*), salmon berries (*Rubus spectabilis*), thimbleberries (*Rubus parviflorus*), and huckleberries (*Vaccinium ovatum*).

Activities: Camping, hiking, fishing, beachcombing
Facilities: Campground, visitor center
Dates: Open year-round
Fees: There are camping and day-use fees.
Closest town: Trinidad
Info: Patrick's Point State Park, 4150 Patrick's Point Dr., Trinidad, CA 95570, 707.677.3570 or www.parks.ca.gov

TRAILS

Patrick's Point State Park has several miles of trails that connect the coastal beach on this small peninsula with inland areas, including park headquarters, the visitor center, **Ceremonial Rock**, and several campground loops.

Most of Patrick's Point State Park and its trails lie on a bluff 100 feet above the ocean beach. The **Rim Trail** leads around the park's coastal perimeter and has six steep, but negotiable, 0.25-mile side trails that lead to the water's edge. The coastal views are great nearly anywhere along the trail, which leads hikers to such special places as Wedding Rock, Patrick's Point, and Palmer's Point. Abalone Point—another side trail—is one of the more popular places to watch gray whales during winter. It's also a place to wander among the jagged coastal rocks and piles of driftwood that winter storms deposit along the shore. The Rim Trail begins near Palmer's Point on the south end of the park and after about 2 miles, ends at the Agate Beach parking lot on the north end of the park.

At the end of Agate Beach parking lot, a 0.25-mile-long trail, with its last portion being a steep stairway, leads to very popular **Agate Beach**. The beach is long and wide and is a great place to explore and look for small agates. The ocean waves constantly move the semiprecious gems on and off the sandy beaches, polishing the stones and making them wonderful finds. As always, use caution whenever exploring near the surf line, especially if there are high waves. The water is cold and

Agate Beach

the rip currents can be extremely strong. Sleeper waves have been known to sweep unsuspecting people off the rocks or from the beach.

The **Octopus Tree Trail** is a 0.25-mile loop that leads to a stand of sitka spruce (*Picea sitchensis*) where, over the years, many of the trees' roots have grown over fallen logs, most of which have since rotted and disappeared back into the soil. What's left are tentacle-like roots that loop away from their trunks.

TRINIDAD

The tiny community of Trinidad is a popular destination for many who visit Patrick's Point State Park. It's also a wonderful stopover for those traveling U.S. 101 and who are in need of a short diversion. Spanish mariner Captain Bruno de Heceta discovered the site and named it for the day that he landed here, Trinity Sunday, 1775. It was another 75 years before the town was actually founded, and then only because it offered a well-protected harbor where gold miners and their equipment and supplies could be unloaded. Mining operations first took place inland in the Trinity mines and later at Gold Bluffs Beach to the north.

Today, the tiny community provides a multitude of services, including a few shops, several B&B inns, small motels, and restaurants. About two blocks off the main road and through town, there is a well-marked turnoff to Trinidad State Beach. The beach parking lot sits about 120 feet above the ocean, so it's a short walk across the open meadow area and down through the trees to get to the beach. Two small streams empty into the Pacific here, making it a popular place to fish.

The Trinidad Memorial Lighthouse, overlooking Trinidad Bay and pier

The main street through town hooks around to a replica of the old lighthouse. The overlook offers a great view of Trinidad's small harbor and of gray whales during their winter migrations. The road continues down to the harbor and wharf where there's boat launching, a pier for fishing, fishing trips, and a restaurant. There's also a beach that's popular in summer.

Activities: Shopping, hiking, picnicking, fishing, boating
Facilities: The town of Trinidad offers groceries, gas stations, fishing, picnicking, restaurants
Dates: Open year-round. Fishing trips from the pier are available seasonally for a fee.
Fees: Trinidad State Beach is free
Closest town: Arcata
Info: Trinidad Chamber of Commerce, www.trinidadcalif.com. To reach Trinidad State Beach, contact Patrick's Point State Park, 4150 Patrick's Point Dr., Trinidad, CA 95570, 707.677.3570 or www.parks.ca.gov

ARCATA

North of Eureka is the city of Arcata. Arcata is home to Humboldt State University, which is well known for its marine biology and wildlife science programs. The school is perched on the hillsides overlooking Humboldt Bay, the perfect location for such programs. Inland, nearby redwood and Douglas fir forests thrive, and along the bay, wildlife-rich wetlands abound. Even though 90 percent of the original wetlands around **Humboldt Bay** have been filled, the remaining 10 percent play host to more than 425 bird species. While waterfowl are common, especially during the fall migration, it's equally reasonable to expect that a gray jay, ruffed grouse, rock sandpiper, or even a peregrine falcon (*Falco peregrinus*) might end up on the far side of a pair of binoculars or spotting scope.

Wandering around **Arcata Plaza**, especially on a sunny weekend, will confirm that Arcata is a college town. A third of the small town's population is between the ages of 18 and 24. The plaza, its centerpiece a statue of President William McKinley, was originally developed around 1850 as a place where supplies destined for Trinity County mines were loaded onto mules. Today, the grass-covered park square is surrounded by shops and restaurants, and it serves as a focal point for town celebrations and boasts the region's largest seasonal farmers' market.

ARCATA MARSH INTERPRETIVE CENTER

This is the perfect starting place to gather information about the surrounding wetlands, view numerous exhibits about the wildlife, learn about special efforts to restore the wetlands, or maybe join a guided nature walk. Outside the interpretive center, a trail meanders for 5.4 miles through 307 acres of restored marsh. This

Northern Coast

entire area was originally part of the wetland, but it was filled and turned into an industrial and timber processing area. Even today, old and rotted wood pilings mark the locations of buildings and warehouses from an earlier era. Much of the marsh has been restored in what began as a test project designed to naturally treat up to 5 million gallons of the city's raw sewage each day.

The incoming sewage circulates through a series of ponds, marshes, chlorinating facilities, and an aquaculture project, allowing algae, fungi, bacteria, and microorganisms attached to plant roots to filter and transform the solids. All this may sound pretty ugly, but thousands of birds have found new homes in this restored wetland including mallards (*Anus platyrhynchos*), cinnamon teal (*Anas cyanoptera*), American avocets (*Recurvirostra americana*), golden crowned sparrows (*Zonotrichia atricapilla*), palm warblers (*Dendroica palmarum*), and Thayer's gulls (*Larus thayeri*). Black-crowned night herons (*Nycticorax nycticorax*), great blue herons (*Ardea herodias*), American bitterns (*Botaurus lentiginosus*), and green herons (Butorides striatus) can be seen here, thus adding to your birder's list.

Besides being a birder's paradise, the Arcata Marsh is also a perfect place for the amateur or professional botanist. Trails lead past areas thick with shrubs

and trees such as bigleaf maples (*Acer macrophyllum*), coast willow (*Salix hookeriana*), transplanted Monterey pine (*Pinus radiata*), red alder (*Alnus rubra*), wax myrtle (*Myrica californica*), and coyote bush (*Baccharis pilularis*), one of the more com-

American avocet spotted at the marsh

mon shrubs found around the fringes of the marsh. Add bulrush (*Scirpus acutus*), broadleaf cattail (*Typha latifolia*), marsh pennywort (*Hydrocotyle ranunculoides*), and pickleweed (*Salicornia virginica*) to the list of plants that create this rich, biotic plant community.

Scattered around the trail that winds throughout the marsh are interpretive signs that help tell the story of this successful restoration. There are also bird blinds for anyone wishing to simply sit and wait for the birds to come to them.

Activities: Walks and information

Facilities: Exhibits, trails

Dates: Arcata Marsh is open daily from 4 A.M. to one hour past sunset. Visitor center is open 9 A.M. to 5 P.M. Tuesday-Sunday and 1 P.M. to 5 P.M. Monday

Fees: None, but there is a jar for donations.

Closest town: Arcata

Info: Arcata Marsh Interpretive Center, 600 South G Street, Arcata, CA 95521, 707.826.2359 or www.ArcataMarshFriends.org

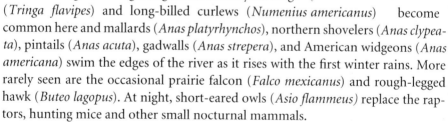

Long-billed curlew

MAD RIVER COUNTY PARK

This out-of-the-way park lies known as the Arcata and Mad River Bottoms. The lands that surround the mouth of the Mad River, where it empties into the Pacific Ocean north of Arcata, are primarily agricultural. The bottomlands host more bird species than anywhere else in the area, which is a significant number considering the rich habitat provided by Humboldt Bay. During winter, raptors and shorebirds are relatively common when the fields flood. In the fall, the skies and the fields fill with the sound and sights of migrating birds. Lesser yellowlegs (*Tringa flavipes*) and long-billed curlews (*Numenius americanus*) become common here and mallards (*Anas platyrhynchos*), northern shovelers (*Anas clypeata*), pintails (*Anas acuta*), gadwalls (*Anas strepera*), and American widgeons (*Anas americana*) swim the edges of the river as it rises with the first winter rains. More rarely seen are the occasional prairie falcon (*Falco mexicanus*) and rough-legged hawk (*Buteo lagopus*). At night, short-eared owls (*Asio flammeus*) replace the raptors, hunting mice and other small nocturnal mammals.

One of the best ways to enjoy the avian and water world is by boat, but only small boats can navigate the shallow river. Canoes and kayaks are common and considered the best way to slide silently along the shoreline habitat that many birds favor. When winter rains finally come, the river's flow can rise very quickly, making boating dangerous.

Activities: Bird watching, boating (small boats), kayaking, fishing

Closest town: Arcata

Info: Humboldt County Convention and Visitors Bureau, 1034 Second Street, Eureka, CA 95501, 800.346.3482 or www.redwoods.info

Northern Coast

EUREKA

It may be difficult to imagine how the rush for California's Sierra foothills gold in 1850 could possibly have created the town of Eureka, so far north and on the coast. As the prospectors spread out from the central Mother Lode in the Sierra foothills, they found gold in many places throughout California. One of those early discoveries was along the Trinity River, near what today is the small historic town of Shasta, located in the northern part of the Sacramento Valley. These early miners also discovered that getting supplies was much easier if they were hauled by ship up the coast, landed at Humboldt Bay, and then packed over the Trinity Alps, rather than being hauled by wagon or horseback up the often wet and swampy Sacramento Valley.

Eureka's prime location near the entrance to Humboldt Bay assured its continuing success even as the gold petered out. It was timber, giant redwoods, and Douglas fir that drove Eureka's continued growth and created millionaires of some of its citizens. One of those early lumber barons was William Carson. A grand and beautiful reminder of Carson's wealth remains today. The **Carson Mansion**—a whimsical, three-story Victorian—was constructed in the 1880s and includes elaborate scrollwork, gingerbread, and other embellishments that help make it one of the most photographed Victorians in the country. It's located near the waterfront, at Second and M streets in Old Town Eureka. Unfortunately, the mansion is a private club and cannot be toured, and photographed only from outside the fence along the street.

Clarke Memorial Museum

Old Town Eureka covers several blocks near the waterfront, bounded by C and G streets and Third and Front. Many of the old buildings, including several Victorians that have graced the waterfront area since the late 19th century, have been restored and are now filled with a wonderful and eclectic collection of shops, restaurants, and historic collections.

One such gem is the **Clarke Memorial Museum,** (707.443.1947 or www.clarkemuseum.org), located in the historic, Roman Renaissance-style Bank of Eureka building at Third and E streets. Among its treasures from Humboldt County's histories is one of the largest collections of Northwest Indian basketry, some 1,200 pieces.

Blue Ox Millworks Historic Park (800.248.4259 or www.blueoxmill.com), along with its small museum, is a wonderful place to watch modern-day craftsmen working with 19th and early 20th century woodworking hand and power tools to create all the beautiful and intricate gingerbread that adorns Victorian homes. Private builders and restorers of famous historic homes from around the country place orders here for replacement architectural millwork, from balustrades to turned porch columns. There's a fee to tour the complex, but it's well worth a visit to the millworks and museum. For those so inclined, Blue Ox also offers classes in woodworking, blacksmithing, and pottery.

Info: Humboldt County Convention & Visitors Bureau, 1034 2nd Street, Eureka, CA 95501, 800.346.3482 or www.redwoods.info

SAMOA COOKHOUSE AND HISTORIC LOGGING MUSEUM

The historic cookhouse is one of the more enjoyable places to eat. Established in 1890, this is the last surviving lumber mill cookhouse in all of California. Lumberjacks no longer eat here, but its long and fascinating history is captured in the old photos and the displayed artifacts, from the first chain saws to some of the cookhouse's first stoves.

This is a great place to bring those teenagers or other big eaters who never seem to get enough food. The cookhouse serves three meals each day in a family-style setting, and the cook determines what is being served. Breakfast generally

Samoa Cookhouse

Northern Coast

includes pancakes, scrambled eggs, bacon, sausage, juice, and coffee, and it's all you can eat, as are all the meals. Dinner generally offers two types of meat such as steak and ham. The prices are pre-set, and they are quite reasonable, considering that you get to enjoy your meal seated at long, picnic-style tables, passing bowls and plates of food among your tablemates, just like the lumberjacks of old. Info: Samoa Cookhouse, 908 Vance Avenue, Samoa, CA 95564, 707.442.1659 or www. samoacookhouse.net

FORT HUMBOLDT STATE HISTORIC PARK

Fort Humboldt was constructed in 1854, by Brevet Lt. Colonel Robert C. Buchanan and his troops after they arrived to quell the problems settlers were having with the Hoopa Indians. Indians had been killing white settlers who, since 1848, had been taking over Indian villages and hunting lands and killing all Native Americans who resisted. Buchanan constructed the fort on a bluff overlooking the bay, and included a large and open parade field surrounded by more than a dozen buildings. Everything needed to support his troops was built of wood, including the officers' quarters, which happened to house a young officer named Ulysses S. Grant.

While too many soldiers used alcohol to excess as a way of dealing with the boredom, Grant apparently wasn't so disposed. Yet he couldn't escape the never-ending, tedious days. He became so depressed with his assignment so far from civilization that after four months, he resigned his commission. He wrote to his wife, "Whoever hears of me in ten years will hear of a well-to-do old Missouri farmer."

The Indian Wars continued for another 10 years, although isolated skirmishes were much more common than major battles and campaigns. Often it was the settlers who took action when they weren't satisfied that the Army had done enough. In 1863, Governor Leland Stanford authorized establishment of the volunteer Mountain Battalion. It soon forced the Hoopa Indians

The restored fort is best known for its collection of working steam donkeys and other logging equipment.

68

into accepting lands in Hoopa Valley along the Trinity River. Within another half dozen years, the Army abandoned the fort and sold the property.

Fort Humboldt became a state historic park in 1955, and many of the original buildings that had long since disappeared were reconstructed. What's been added is equally interesting. Because the North Coast is known for its logging industry, a large collection of historic logging equipment is displayed in sheds and out in the open. Historic locomotives and steam donkeys, including a Washington slack-line steam donkey, are included in the collection. Loggers used this marvel of late 19th-century technology to haul huge redwood logs on overhead cables to the locomotive loading areas, sometimes as much as a half-mile away. There is a self-guided trail through the outdoor exhibit area.

Activities: Picnicking, exhibits
Facilities: Exhibits, visitor center
Dates: Open daily
Fees: There are day-use fees.
Closest town: Eureka
Info: Fort Humboldt State Historic Park, 3431 Fort Ave., Eureka, CA 95503, 707.445.6547 or www.parks.ca.gov

HUMBOLDT BAY NATIONAL WILDLIFE REFUGE

Humboldt Bay National Wildlife Refuge is critical habitat for hundreds of thousands of birds annually. More than 200 bird species either live or pass through the refuge during migration. For many of the winged visitors, the nutritious eelgrass that grows so prolifically in the shallow waters and the mud flats is the prime attraction. The diversity of habitat found in the tideland ecosystem also contributes to its attractiveness to birds, including several endangered species.

Humboldt Bay is a long and narrow body of water that lies between two towns—Arcata and Eureka. This large refuge covers 4,000 acres, and the U.S. Fish and Wildlife Service continues acquiring and restoring wetlands and related wildlife habitat areas including sand spits, brackish marsh, and other marsh areas.

A boardwalk gives visitors access into the wetlands.

Northern Coast

69

Ruddy turnstone (winter plummage)

The largest part of the refuge is around **South Humboldt Bay**, with several smaller parcels located in **North Humboldt Bay**. The habitat restoration program is designed to provide additional sites, not only for the winter visits by migratory geese and ducks, but also for endangered species like the peregrine falcon (*Falco peregrinus*), western snowy plover (*Charadrius alexandrinus nivosus*), Aleutian Canada goose (*Branta canadensis leucopareia*), and California brown pelican (*Pelicanus occidentalis*).

Because of the extensive eelgrass beds, the refuge is also a primary home for black brant (*Branta bernicla*). More than 30,000 of these small geese can be seen on the 14-mile-long Humboldt Bay during their fall migration. They use the bay as a staging area in spring for the trip to their northern nesting sites in Alaska, Russia, and Canada.

A good way to view the wildlife is from a boat. The most accessible boat launch is at the marina, below the **Samoa Bridge** in Eureka. There's a county boat ramp on the **Samoa Peninsula**, near the historic community of **Samoa**, west of Eureka. Winds and tides can be treacherous for small craft here, especially for kayaks and canoes, so always check weather forecasts and tide tables before heading out.

Activities: Bird-watching, fishing, hunting in season in specified areas, hiking, and boating

Facilities: Boat launch, visitor center, trails

Dates: Most of the refuge is open daily from sunrise to sunset. The visitor center is open daily from 8 A.M. to 5 P.M.

Fees: None, except in the hunting area during waterfowl hunting seasons

Closest town: Eureka

Info: Humboldt Bay National Wildlife Refuge, 1020 Ranch Road, Loleta, CA 95551, 707.733.5406 or www.fws.gov

TRAILS

The **Hookton Slough Trail** follows Hookton Slough for about 1.5 miles to where South Humboldt Bay begins to widen. The trail is open during daylight hours and passes through grasslands, freshwater marsh, open mud flats, and the open water of the bay. From U.S. 101 south of Eureka, take the Hookton Road exit and drive west for 1.2 miles, and follow the signs to the trailhead parking area.

The **Shorebird Loop Trail** is probably the best trail in the refuge for viewing shorebirds. This 1.7-mile loop is also relatively level, making it an easy walk. There's a short spur trail that leads to Long Pond, the largest of the refuge's freshwater ponds. Expect to see shorebirds and waterfowl, especially during winter, and the ever-present herons and egrets nearly any time of year. Look more closely to see tree frogs and river otters that live along the waterways. The trailhead parking area is reached via the Hookton Road exit from U.S. 101.The visitor center offers binoculars for check out.

FERNDALE

To get to Ferndale, one must cross over the Eel River by way of the historic **Fernbridge**, coined the "Queen of Bridges." Opened in 1911, at 1,320 feet, it remains the world's longest functional, poured-concrete bridge still in operation. The road then meanders southwest through open farm and dairy land to this intriguing historic Danish dairy town.

Ferndale's concentration of grand Victorians—many of them restored to their original colorful grandeur—were built by prosperous Danish dairy farmers who settled this rich bottomland in the 19th century. The farms remain prosperous, but today, it's the thousands of tourists who visit Ferndale each year who

Ferndale's Main Street

Northern Coast

71

have helped spur the restoration of the elegant old homes, which originally were referred to as "butterfat palaces."

The town's main street is a kaleidoscope of colorful buildings that have been transformed into a wonderful collection of gift shops and antique stores, restaurants and bakeries. The **Ferndale Museum** (www.ferndale-museum.org), located a block from Main Street at 515 Shaw Street, has exhibits of early farm machinery, logging tools, furniture, and clothing.

The **Kinetic Grand Championship Race** (www.kineticgrandchampionship. com), held each Memorial weekend, is one of Humboldt County's most popular single events. This annual three-day race was the first of its kind when started by two Ferndale artists in 1969. It requires individuals or teams to race their human-powered "sculptures" over land, sand, mud, and water from Arcata to Ferndale. Some of the devices look like contorted combinations of bikes, boats, and giant caterpillars.

For those with several more hours to kill and a willingness to drive a narrow, mostly one-lane road, Main Street through Ferndale turns into Mattole Road and heads west into the forested mountains. It ultimately emerges at the mouth of the Mattole River and Cape Mendocino, the northern end of an area called the Lost Coast and the westernmost point in California.

Activities: Shopping, walking, photography
Facilities: Museums, B&B inns, restaurants
Closest town: Fortuna
Info: Ferndale Chamber of Commerce, 240 Francis Street, Ferndale, CA 95536, 707.786.4477 or www.victorianferndale.com

HUMBOLDT REDWOODS STATE PARK

For two centuries, writers have attempted to adequately describe the ancient redwood forests. Most 19th century readers scoffed at the earliest writers' obviously exaggerated claims about the size and age of these trees, believing that nothing of such proportions could possibly exist. Even today, books, travel articles, and photographs fail to do justice to the old-growth forest in Humboldt Redwoods State Park.

Of the park's 51,000 acres of forest and rivers,

Giant redwood burl

17,000 acres are covered with old-growth forest. The trees must be experienced in person, even if only by driving through the **Avenue of the Giants**, the meandering, two-lane road that passes near some of the largest and oldest trees. Much better than driving is to

View along one section of the Avenue of the Giants

walk among trees that top 300 feet in height and range from 500 years to 2,000 years of age. Wandering among the ancient forests is like entering a magnificent, centuries-old cathedral.

Humboldt Redwoods State Park lies in the center of prime redwood country. Plenty of water and moderate temperatures are the keys to creating thriving redwood forests. The giant trees have very shallow root systems, requiring significant amounts of surface water, which comes primarily in the form of winter rains. The trees survive California's dry summers as banks of fog form along the coast, keeping the tree needles moist and the air humid.

The best place to start is at the **Avenue of the Giants Visitor Center** in **Weott**. Operated by the Humboldt Redwoods Interpretive Association, the visitor center and park headquarters provides exhibits, publications, and lots of great information about camping, hiking, and backpacking in the park. It is open year-round.

The first people to live here among the great trees and along the shores of the Eel River were the Sinkyone Indians. They used the redwoods for shelter, fashioning plank-like strips of the heavy, stringy bark into lodges for protection from the rain. Considering the massive size of a mature redwood, the tiny seeds found in its cones, which are not much larger than golf balls, did not serve as a food source. For that, the

"Mother tree" (single fallen tree that sprouted new trees)

73

Indians depended on the salmon and steelhead that seasonally migrated up the rivers and streams throughout the area. Redwood logs did provide the raw material for their canoes. Using fire and mostly stone and antler tools, the great logs were hollowed and formed into very serviceable boats.

It was California's gold that lured the first outsiders into the remote rivers and forests of the Humboldt region. In 1850, a group of miners chose the Eel River route from the Trinity gold fields when they headed back to San Francisco. The group's leader had the unfortunate experience of running into a grizzly bear. He barely survived the encounter, but when he finally reached civilization, he spread the word about the giant redwood forests to the north. It was another 25 years before the first settler—Tosaldo Johnson—homesteaded 160 acres near today's **Albee Creek Campground**.

Even the first few American settlers could do little to harm much of the great redwood forests. It took the expansion of roads and railroads to open the great forests to destructive exploitation. In 1914, a railroad was constructed into the area, and eight years later, the original **Redwood Highway** was completed. Thus began the era of large-scale commercial logging. It wasn't long before technology was clearing entire mountainsides of the ancient redwoods and shipping the trees to mills. While some of the more visionary lumber companies could see that there was indeed an end to the supply of old-growth trees and began replanting their harvested acres, other companies ignored warnings that they were courting ecological disaster and a certain end to their own livelihoods.

Northern Spotted Owl

Probably no single animal species has caused more court battles, demonstrations, or forced changes in human behavior than the northern spotted owl (*Strix occidentalis*). Its need to nest primarily in old-growth redwood and Douglas fir forests, and its use by scientists as an indicator species that is able to gauge the relative health of a forest environment, has stopped numerous major logging operations. The government recognizes the small owls as a threatened species, which generally makes the removal of their nesting habitat in the old-growth forests illegal, or, at best, extremely difficult to justify, even on private lands.

During the winters of 1955 and 1964, heavy rains washed untold tons of sand and gravel down bare hillsides, filling rivers and streams, flooding cities and highways, and toppling hundreds of ancient redwoods that once grew on the rich alluvial soils near the Eel River. The gravel beds that salmon and steelhead needed for spawning were clogged with silt, preventing the fish eggs from hatching and the fry from surviving and returning to the ocean. To this day, forest and streambed restoration continues to repair the damage caused by those floods, especially in the **Bull Creek** watershed that now lies within the park.

Redwood forests are often distinguished by the obvious absence of other trees and shrubs, especially in the largest groves found along the

Racoons are common here.

alluvial flats near rivers. The thick redwood canopy shades out competition, allowing only an occasional tall and spindly white alder (*Alnus rhombifolia*), tanoak (*Lithocarpus densiflorus*), or bigleaf maple (*Acer macrophyllum*) to grow. Periodic flooding deposits silt along the forest floor, causing the redwoods to develop new lateral root systems closer to the surface, thus discouraging understory plant competition. Wander along most of the forest trails beneath the great trees and sword ferns (*Polystichum* sp.) are generally the most conspicuous plant, but wildflowers also have their moments. The three white petals of Western trillium (*Trillium ovatum*) and the flower clusters of red clintonia (*Clintonia andrewsiana*) offer special surprises for hikers.

Avenue of the Giants is a U.S. 101 bypass road that provides an up-close look at the redwoods for those who may be unable to spend much time wandering on foot among the giants. Depending upon the starting location, the Avenue of the Giants is up to 32 miles long. It begins about 6 miles north of Garberville—there's a marked exit off U.S. 101. At the north end, the first exit is about 4 miles south of the old lumbering community of Scotia. The grandest portion of the drive is found between the towns of Myers Flat and Dyerville. As the Avenue of the Giants meanders through the forest and along the **South Fork Eel River**, there are numerous pullouts and short trails that lead into the trees or to the river.

Northern Coast

Rockefeller Forest is in the densely forested and less traveled northwestern portion of Humboldt Redwoods State Park. The dirt and gravel Mattole Road (at mile marker 20.6 along the Avenue of the Giants) passes through the forest,

which received its name from John D. Rockefeller, who, in 1930, provided the Save the Redwoods League with its largest donation up to that time. His gift of $2 million allowed the league and the State of California to purchase 10,000 acres along Bull Creek that Pacific Lumber Company had earmarked for harvesting. It was a major addition to the fledgling California State Park System. Rockefeller Forest holds some of the most magnificent of the park's old-growth trees.

You will find many named groves along the Avenue and most are identified by roadside signs and easy to find. The **Williams Grove** is located about 1 mile north of Myers Flat, adjacent to the Avenue of the Giants. The **Garden Club of America Grove** is

Rockefeller Forest

another mile farther north, and the **Federation Grove** is located near where Bull Creek enters the south fork of the Eel River. One of the most popular stops is the **Founders Grove**, located another mile north at the end of a short road off of the Avenue of the Giants. It has an easy 0.6-mile trail that is ADA accessible.

The Eel River and the South Fork Eel River combine their flows in the park, and generally, following the first rains in October, salmon and steelhead are the reasons most fall and winter visitors flock here. Drift boats by the dozens are found in the more popular areas of the river, while shore anglers often have equally good luck. Fishing success can be unpredictable on the Eel River as flows can change quickly, going from too little water for the salmon to high, unfishable, silt-laden waters to perfect flow-rates within a few days. During low water conditions that sometimes accompany California's periodic droughts, fishing may be prohibited temporarily. Before fishing, check the fishing regulations or call the California Department of Fish and Wildlife's north coast information center: 707.442.4502, 707.445.6493 (Eureka), or www.wildlife.ca.gov.

Most of the thousands of people who stay at Humboldt Redwoods State Park each year camp in one of the several campgrounds found in the park. **Burlington Campground** is the most popular—likely because of its central location in the park, its nearness to the visitor center, and the fact that it has only 35 campsites. **Hidden Springs Campground** is equally attractive. It's much larger, with 146 campsites. **Albee Creek Campground**, located on Mattole Road 5 miles west of U.S. 101 and the Avenue of the Giants, has 37 campsites. There are also hike and bike, group, and equestrian campsites, along with several trail camps in the park. During summer, reservations are generally needed.

> **Activities:** Hiking, mountain biking, horseback riding, fishing, camping, ranger-led hikes
> **Facilities:** Campgrounds, visitor center, picnic areas
> **Dates:** Park is open year-round. Some campgrounds closed during winter.
> **Fees:** There are moderate camping fees.
> **Closest town:** Garberville and Scotia
> **Info:** Humboldt Redwoods State Park, 17119 Avenue of the Giants, Weott, CA 95571, 707.946.2263 or www.HumboldtRedwoods.org

TRAILS

With more than 100 miles of trails in the park, there is something for everybody. Some trails, primarily those at least 5 feet wide, are open to mountain bike use, and many are also open for horseback riding. Stop in the visitor center or park office and get a copy of the park map to find out which trails are open for what kinds of uses.

The **Big Tree Trail** provides a bit more adventure for park visitors. The trail begins at Founders Grove and follows Bull Creek for 4.5 miles to the Big Tree area, which includes the **Giant Tree** and the **Flat Iron Tree**.

The **Grasshopper Trail** connects the Garden Club of America Grove, one of many redwood groves adjacent to the Avenue of

Wildflowers

Northern Coast

the Giants, with the **Grasshopper Trail Camp**. The camp is about 5 miles away, and the trail has a 3,000-foot elevation gain.

The **Burlington-Bull Creek Trail** offers a popular and relatively level hike that follows the south fork of the Eel River, connecting the heavily used Burlington Campground with **Decker Creek** to its north and **Canoe Creek** to the south. The trail is 4 miles long.

For those who are unable to enjoy long hikes, there are short trails that lead through several of the named redwood groves, many of which have small picnic areas and are located directly adjacent to the Avenue of the Giants.

THE LOST COAST

California's Lost Coast is appropriately named. Much is inaccessible except on foot, and there are only a few roads—some paved, some not—to those areas that have experienced any level of development. It includes the incredibly rugged King Mountains, isolated on a piece of coastline that bulges out into the Pacific west of **Garberville** and U.S. 101. Adding to the wildness, the San Andreas fault lies just offshore, marking the rift that separates the Pacific plate and the North American plate. The ancient and ongoing tectonic plate movements also make the Lost Coast's mountains some of the most geologically active in the country. The King Range has risen 66 feet during the past 6,000 years.

The Lost Coast

The mountains aren't the only things active here. The Lost Coast can receive 100 inches of rain during dry winters and twice that amount during wet winters. All this rain channeling its way down streams and rivers has severely carved the mountains, creating steep cliffs, lots of sliding slopes, and thick forests.

There is little private property, especially within the thousands of acres that stretch down the coast. The most notable nonpublic land is the small town of Shelter Cove, which effectively separates the King Range National Conservation Area on the north from Sinkyone Wilderness State Park and 3,800 acres of Trust for Public Land property on the south.

But even though the Lost Coast is a relatively wild area free of human inhabitants, this has not always been the case. In the 1850s, about 6,000 years after the first Indians arrived here, American settlers entered the mountains, bringing sheep and cattle to graze in the meadows and forests. They were soon followed by men looking for oil and who were successful in finding it. Although not a high-profit operation, they drilled California's first oil well here in 1865.

During this same period, the centers of industry required a continuous supply of leather belts needed to run steam-powered factory equipment. Harvesters came to the mountains of the Lost Coast to strip the bark from tanoaks, which was needed in the leather tanning process. Commercial fishing, based in Shelter Cove, followed, and then the loggers came. Even though logging continued in some areas of the Lost Coast as late as the 1960s, scattered forests of old-growth Douglas fir and redwoods remain.

For a few years, a railroad was operated from Bear Harbor, but the rugged mountains of the Lost Coast were not the best choice for such a venture. The Bear Harbor and Eel River Railroad was designed to transport logs from the coastal mountains to **Piercy**, which lies inland on the Eel River. The beginning portion of the route from Bear Harbor was so steep that a winch was required to raise and lower the locomotive and cars during the initial leg of the trip. A storm destroyed the harbor's pier in 1899, further hampering the rail operation. The railroad's owner died in an accident in 1905. One year later, the great San Francisco earthquake severely damaged trestles and stretches of track, ending the railroad's use. A few of the old rails remain today, rusting in the damp, salt air.

SHELTER COVE

The easiest and fastest route into the hamlet of Shelter Cove is to fly your private plane into the town's coastal airstrip. However, most people drive west out of Garberville, through Redway on paved, but narrow, Shelter Cove Road as it winds through the forest and over the coastal mountains. Dropping down from the summit into the aptly named community of Shelter Cove, the bluffs offer wonderful views of the rugged mountains and equally rugged coastline. There is a miniature maze of subdivision-like streets that wind around the area and a substantial number of mostly vacation homes scattered along the hillsides and across the flat meadows that once fed cattle and sheep and served as staging areas for harvested timber.

In the main cove at the end of Machi Road, there is a public beach with restrooms and a boat launch facility. **Little Black Sand Beach** is another popular spot and is located on the north side of the Shelter Cove community, off Beach Road. But many people who come to the Lost Coast are looking for more of a wilderness experience, and that's easy enough to find in both the King Range National Conservation Area and in the nearby Sinkyone Wilderness.

Activities: Hiking, camping, fishing, boating, backpacking, beach exploration
Facilities: Boat launch, marina, store, picnic area
Closest town: Garberville
Info: www.sheltercove-lostcoast.com

KING RANGE NATIONAL CONSERVATION AREA

Congress established the King Range National Conservation Area in 1970 and placed it under the control of the Bureau of Land Management. Within the conservation area's 60,000 acres, old-growth Douglas fir forest serves as home to Cooper's hawks (*Accipiter cooperii*), and bald eagles. Endangered spotted owls (*Strix occidentalis*) live in the canopy, and Roosevelt elk and black-tailed deer feed on the grasses and shrubs, as black bears and coyotes venture forth, searching for food.

The conservation area ranges in elevation from sea level to the top of King's Peak—at 4,087 feet it's the King Range's highest mountain. The conservation area stretches for 35 miles, from the mouth of the Mattole River in the north to Sinkyone

Coyote

Wilderness State Park in the south, and ranges inland about 4 miles at its widest point.

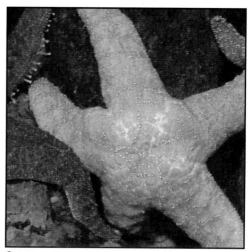
Sea stars

In an earlier time, Mattole and Sinkyone Indians lived throughout the area, but they were forced to give up much of their traditional way of life when American settlers began arriving in relatively large numbers. During the 1850s, white settlers first came to graze cattle and sheep and were soon followed by the commercial fishing industry and finally by the timber harvesters. The lands were logged for decades, with some of the most intense logging activity occurring during the 1950s and 1960s. When the steep and unstable mountainsides were clear-cut, they eroded easily, creating massive landslides that choked the Mattole River and other waterways in the area. Now, major restoration programs are beginning to return lush forests to the once clear-cut mountainsides.

The King Range offers an opportunity for both car camping and backpacking. There are 14 campsites (fees apply) at the **Mattole River Campground**, which are the only drive-in sites on or near the beach. **A.W. Way County Park**, which will accommodate 30 tents or trailers along the Mattole River, is located 8 miles north of Honeydew (www.redwoods.info). There are several smaller campgrounds including **Honeydew Creek**, which has five first-come, first-served creekside campsites for tents and trailers, and is located about 1 mile south of Honeydew.

Most of the camping done in the King Range National Conservation Area is in trail camps or in the coast camps, which are undesignated sites on or near the beach. Some of the more popular areas are near **Cooksie Creek, Randall Creek, Big Creek, Big Flat Creek, Buck Creek,** and **Gitchell Creek**. Each of the creeks crosses the Lost Coast Trail between the Mattole River in the north and Shelter Cove near the south end of the conservation area.

Activities: Hiking, camping, fishing, backpacking, beach exploration
Facilities: Some campsites with picnic tables and pit toilets, trails
Dates: Open daily
Fees: There are camping fees.
Closest town: Ferndale, Garberville, and Shelter Cove
Info: Bureau of Land Management, Arcata Field Office, 1695 Heindon Road, Arcata, CA 95521-4573, 707.825.2300, www.blm.gov or www.redwoods.info

Black Bears

Black bears (*Ursus americanus*) are common in California's forests, including redwood country. Their fur ranges in color from white to light brown to black. In many areas where people congregate, bears can become nuisances and more dangerous than normal.

Remember, all bears are wild and their primary goal is to eat and care for their young. They can smell food odors coming from ice chests, tents and even from inside cars. Do not make food available to bears or any wild animal. If camping, store food in airtight containers locked in your car's trunk. In many campgrounds where bears are present, bear-proof food lockers are often available. If backpacking, store food over tall tree branches out of a bear's reach. And always dispose of garbage in bear-proof trashcans.

If you find one or more cute little bear cubs, mom is not far away and she is very protective. Do not approach the cubs—move out of the area im-

mediately. Wildlife managers generally must destroy bears that make a habit of wandering into campgrounds, ripping open car doors and breaking apart ice chests for food.

Black bear

TRAILS

There are more than 70 miles of named trails lacing the mostly roadless Lost Coast. With so many interconnecting trails, it is critical to have a topographic trail map of the area.

The **King Crest Trail** is 11.4 miles long, with the top of King's Peak located at about the midway point. The trail begins in the north at the Smith Etter Jeep Road and North Slide Peak Trail. It passes the **Saddle Mountain Trailhead** near the south end, which leads back to Honeydew Creek tent camping area. The King Crest Trail's southernmost trailhead begins at the King Peak Road, which leads to Shelter Cove. There is a 2,000-foot elevation gain.

The **Lost Coast Trail** begins near the mouth of the Mattole River, then meanders inland and south for 3.2 miles, reaching the coast at the **Punta Gorda Lighthouse**. From Punta Gorda, the trail follows the beach, reaching **Spanish Flat** after 5.2 miles and **Big Flat** in 7.5 additional miles. It's another 14.1 miles before the conservation area portion of the trail connects with the Sinkyone Wilderness trail at Whale Gulch. No pets or mountain bikes are allowed.

SINKYONE WILDERNESS STATE PARK

One of only a few designated wilderness areas within California's State Park System, Sinkyone's nearly 7,400 acres, with an adjacent 3,000 acres owned by the Trust for Public Land, offer numerous trails, backpacking camp areas, and a wild coast accessible only on foot.

For thousands of years before the first Europeans arrived, the Sinkyone Indians lived on this part of the coast. They occupied permanent villages alongside streams and rivers and moved out in family groups to hunt and forage in the hills during summer. They spent time along the coast fishing, gathering seaweed and shellfish, hunting seals and sea lions, and harvesting the occasional dead whale that washed ashore. Fish were an important source of food during the winter. All kinds of fish were caught, but the seasonal salmon run was especially important, because once the fish were dried, they provided food for many months.

From the late 19th century and well into the 20th century, human activities stripped the land of natural resources. Grazing and logging were the two most common and popular practices. Game trails that once allowed elk and deer to reach fresh feeding areas were turned into rough roadways for horse-drawn wagons and pack mules, and later for logging trucks. Open marine terraces and inland meadows were filled with grazing sheep and cattle or turned into farmland. **Bear Harbor** became the main shipping transportation point.

Early logging operations had the most impact on the Lost Coast area. Well into the 20th century, narrow gauge railroads were constructed to reach the few accessible coastal bluffs where lumber schooners could safely anchor close to the shore. In 1875, timber companies developed the first steel cables or "wire chutes," block-and-tackle cables that stretched between the schooners and the bluffs to haul logs out to the ships. The wire chutes also

Roosevelt elk cows

were used at Needle Rock, Anderson's Landing, and Bear Harbor. Today, areas that appear to be modern jeep trails are actually abandoned railroad right-of-ways from a past era.

Needle Rock Visitor Center, which is located in a century-old ranch house, should be one of the first stops visitors make in the park. Actually, it's very near the end of the primary road into the area. The center is open only when volunteer camphosts are available. There are exhibits in the visitor center, along with related books and maps that are for sale. Since both staffing and supplies are limited here, you may want to bring your own toilet paper.

Camping is allowed only in the designated backcountry campsites. Some, such as the **Railroad Creek** (two campsites) and **Orchard Creek** (three camp-sites), can be reached by a short 0.25-mile walk from the roadside parking area. The **Bear Harbor Cove** sites, which are located near a meadow at the ocean's edge, are a 0.4-mile, relatively level walk away. The trail passes through an area frequented by elk, so watch for them, especially during the fall rutting season when some of the big bulls are a bit cantankerous—and dangerous if you're not paying attention.

For those not into backpacking, the only drive-in campground is at **Usal Beach**. The access road is narrow and rough—RVs and trailers are not advised.

Activities: Hiking, fishing, backpacking
Facilities: Visitor center, campsites with picnic tables, and pit toilets (but supply your own toilet paper)
Dates: Open daily
Fees: There are camping fees.
Closest town: Garberville
Info: Sinkyone Wilderness State Park, 1600 U.S. Highway 101 #8, Garberville, CA 95542, 707.986.7711 (recorded message)

TRAILS

The **Lost Coast Trail,** like many other trails within Sinkyone Wilderness State Park, runs north and south along the length of the park. This trail, which meanders from Usal at the south end of the wilderness area north to Bear Harbor, is not a trail for beginners. Even though the length is only 16.3 miles, it generally takes the better part of three days and two nights of difficult hiking to negotiate its mountain valleys and passes.

Taking a longer time to complete the trail is better than trying to rush along, because on those clear summer days when the fog remains far offshore, there is a plethora of incredible sights, including ocean views and redwood groves. Portions of the trail stay on the lower, western sides of the mountains, ranging up to about 1,000 feet above sea level, but much of it is along the coastal bluff, perhaps 250 to 500 feet above the pounding surf. The trail continues north from Bear Harbor another 5.3 miles through **Orchard Creek** and **Needle Rock** to **Whale Gulch**.

MORE PHOTOS FROM THE NORTH COAST

Co-author interviewing lightkeeper docent at Crescent City's Battery Point Lighthouse; the two are upstairs looking at the lens. The breakwater is in the background.

The town of Orick, found on Highway 101, is known for its many wood-carving artists.

Trees of Mystery, south of Crescent City, has a fun gift store and bounty of coastal redwoods (admission fee to tour the grove). And Paul Bunyon and Babe the Blue Ox will welcome you in the parking lot!

One of our favorite signs was found on a backroad along the North Coast.

Mendocino, Sonoma, and Marin Counties

Mendocino, Sonoma, and Marin Counties

The Mendocino coast is a favorite escape from the traffic, confusion, and the often frantic pace that most people face who live in California's urban areas. Most of Highway 1 along this portion of the coast is a twisting, two-lane road that requires sometimes agonizingly slow and careful driving, especially when stuck following a large RV or truck. But it's also not a highway that most people care to drive too quickly. The scenery and the special places hidden along many of the side roads make for great exploring.

Equally as rugged and beautiful as Mendocino's coastline, the Sonoma coast begins to show the subtle transition from the great redwood and Douglas fir forests of the far north that grow nearly to the ocean's edge, to the coastal scrub and mostly treeless exposed mountains of the Central Coast. California's coastal mountains are relatively low, at least by California's inland standards, yet they provide a distinct separation between the coast and the inland valleys. In spite of their lack of height, the mountains create vastly different climates within a short distance. On the ocean side, there can be up to 60 inches of winter rain annually, as well as cool, foggy summers. Thirty miles inland, half as much winter rain falls and thermometers often hover around the century mark in July and August.

By California standards, the Marin coast is not long, stretching from near the center of Bodega Bay to the Golden Gate. While much of the inland and especially the southern portion of the county is developed, nearly the entire coast remains in public ownership, most as part of several parks. Point Reyes National Seashore, Golden Gate National Recreation Area, and Mount Tamalpais State Park provide coastal access and inland trails, along with many recreational opportunities. As with its neighboring counties to the north, Marin County has a diverse coastline, with high cliffs and long sandy beaches, rich estuaries, and protected bays.

Travel across the coastal mountains and into the inland reaches of Mendocino and Sonoma counties, and coastal forests and scrub are replaced by rolling hills of vineyards that grow some of the world's finest wine grapes. Hundreds of wineries turn those crops into millions of bottles of wine each year, with hundreds of award-winning vintages being shipped to restaurants and retail outlets around the globe.

The vast majority of the Mendocino, Sonoma, and Marin county coastlines remain as wild and rugged as they were 200 years ago. Most of the tiny communities that managed to establish footholds along this stretch of coast were originally logging camps and have seen the boom and bust of the timber industry. Today, they depend on tourism—and with good reason.

Mendocino County

MENDOCINO

Redwood forests are what attracted the first settlers to Mendocino County. During the 19th century, shipwrecks were common along much of California's coast. Jerome B. Ford was with a search party looking for survivors of a China-bound trading ship when he reported the presence of the great redwood forests along the Mendocino coast to Henry Meiggs, the owner of a sawmill at Bodega Bay to the south.

Meiggs quickly established another mill on the Mendocino headland, placing Ford in charge. Two years later, in 1854, Ford sailed to Connecticut to marry 23-year-old Martha Hayes, leaving orders that a house be built in his absence for himself and his new

The town of Mendocino

wife. When the newlywed couple returned, Martha loved the beautiful views from the house's main and second floors, but disliked the kitchen and dining room—they had been placed in the basement. A remodeling effort was soon underway to correct the design flaw on their new home, which was only the second house that had been constructed in the town of Mendocino.

The Ford home survived and is now the **Ford House Museum and Visitor Center**. From its bluff-top perch on Main Street, the historic home overlooks Mendocino Bay. It is managed by state park volunteers and houses exhibits about historic Mendocino, a small bookstore, and art exhibits by local artists. The Ford House has limited hours, dependent upon volunteer availability. Info: 707.937.5397 or www.mendoparks.org

Historic Ford House

While the timber industry thrived long after Ford's time, it did begin to slow in the 1950s and 1960s. Fortunately, it was about this same time that artists and others came seeking the solitude and creative inspiration they couldn't find in the big cities. The new arrivals began repairing and caring for many of the old Victorians and other buildings that were strikingly reminiscent of a 19th century New England fishing village. Artists' studios, shops, restaurants, B&Bs, and museums slowly began to fill the 100-year-old-buildings along the quaint downtown area, which sits on an ancient coastal terrace above the Pacific Ocean. It's the collection of these historic structures, without the intrusion of modern-day fast food restaurants, chain bookstores, and hotels that has allowed the town of Mendocino to be named a National Preservation District.

The town of Mendocino consists of several square blocks that lie on part of a point of land that juts west from Highway 1. From there, the marine terrace merges into **Mendocino Headlands State Park** (707.937.5804 or www.parks.ca.gov). There are parking areas off Heeser Drive and a trail that meanders around most of the 2 miles of the spectacular coastal bluffs. Paths and a stairway allow access down the steep bluffs to the beach. Be cautious during and after winter storms when high surf and tides can make the beaches and the trails to them dangerous.

The **Kelley House Museum** (707.937.5791 or www.KelleyHouseMuseum. org) is another historic house that has become a museum. Originally built in 1861, today it houses photos related to the logging and shipping heydays of Mendocino.

Its hours of operation can be sporadic. Open Friday—Monday, 11 A.M. to 3 P.M.

The **Big River** enters Mendocino Bay and the Pacific Ocean on the south side of town. A wide sand beach is accessible from North Big River Road, which is located on the east side of Highway 1, between the Main Street turnoff into Mendocino and the bridge that crosses the Big River.

Activities: Picnicking, fishing, hiking, shopping

Facilities: The state park offers a visitor center in town. Mendocino has restaurants, shops, and overnight accommodations, mostly Victorian B&B inns.

Dates: Visitor center open periodically

Fees: None at Mendocino Headlands State Park. The visitor center asks for a donation. There is a small entrance fee at the Kelley House Museum.

Closest town: Fort Bragg

Info: Fort Bragg-Mendocino Coast Chamber of Commerce, 217 Main, Fort Bragg, CA 95437, 707.961.6300 or www.MendocinoCoast.com; Mendocino Headlands State Park, c/o Russian Gulch State Park, Hwy. 1, Mendocino, CA 95460, 707.937.5804 or www.parks.ca.gov

MACKERRICHER STATE PARK

The main entrance to the park is intriguing. Here, you'll find a skeleton of a moderately-sized gray whale. Inside the visitor center, several additional skeletons—including those of a sea otter and a sea lion—hang from the ceiling.

It is Scottish immigrant Duncan MacKerricher whose name is attached to the park. In 1868, he purchased 1,000 acres of what had been an Indian reservation for $1.25 per acre. MacKerricher and his heirs worked the former *El Rancho de la Laguna* until 1949, when they sold it to the state for a state park. Over the years, most of the area was heavily logged, especially the north end of the ranch near Ten Mile River. The remnants of an old railway that transported logs from Ten Mile River to the Union Lumber Company in Fort Bragg still remain. Today, a road passes between the ocean and **Lake Cleone**, once a tidal lagoon that was cut off from the ocean waters. The

American kestrel (once known as a "chicken hawk")

far north end of the park, which is about 5 miles from Lake Cleone, includes a long stretch of dunes.

Activities: Camping, fishing, hiking, picnicking, bird watching, beach and tide-pool exploration, coastal whale watching
Facilities: Visitor center with small gift shop, campground, day-use facilities
Dates: Open daily
Fees: There is a camping fee.
Closest town: Fort Bragg
Info: Russian River/Mendocino State Parks, PO Box 123, CA 95430, 707. 937.5804 or www.parks.ca.gov

FORT BRAGG

Elegant Victorian homes and early 20th century Craftsman-style buildings can easily recreate images of the old days. But in the old days, Fort Bragg went through many changes, not the least of which was complete destruction when the earthquake that destroyed most of San Francisco in 1906 also destroyed much of Fort Bragg.

The Pomo Indians had inhabited this land of ocean and redwoods for thousands of years by the time the United States acquired California in 1846. Four years later, American maritime traders discovered this area's potentially profitable redwood forests when *The*

Guest House Museum

Frolic crashed on the coastal rocks and scavengers came to salvage what they could. The Bureau of Indian Affairs soon arrived, and their goal was to place the Pomo Indians on a 25,000-acre reservation. In spite of the bureau's efforts, the Indians remained hostile to the American intruders. The Army was brought to the reservation in 1857 to establish a military post, which the first commander named "Fort Bragg," in honor of his former commanding officer Colonel Braxton Bragg. The garrisoned fort was meant to subdue the Indians and ensure peace in the area. The fort was abandoned in 1864, and the Indian reservation dissolved in 1866 when the land was opened to settlement.

After the fort was abandoned, the growing community depended heavily on logging redwoods to provide for their support. In 1889, C.R. Johnson was elected the first mayor of the newly incorporated city of Fort Bragg. Four years earlier, Johnson had founded the Redwood Lumber Company, which quickly dwarfed the other lumber companies in the region. In order to compete with the Redwood Lumber Company, many of the smaller mills joined forces in 1891, forming the Union Lumber Company. Even though the 1906 San Francisco earthquake destroyed most of the town's buildings, the mills produced much of the thousands of board feet of lumber needed to rebuild itself and San Francisco.

The **Guest House Museum** (707.964.4251 or www.fortbragghistory.org) offers a glimpse into Fort Bragg's logging history. C.R. Johnson had the Victorian constructed as his home in 1892. Union Lumber Company acquired the property, and in 1912, used it as a guesthouse for friends and customers. Georgia Pacific, another large lumber company, purchased the house in 1973 and donated it to the city in 1986.

The **Fort Building** is north of City Hall and is significant because it is the last remaining vestige of the original Fort Bragg. It served as the fort's storehouse and commissary. Today, it's a small museum, with photos, an old cannon, and a model of the original fort.

Noyo River and Harbor crosses under Highway 1, near the south end of Fort Bragg. Although tiny when compared with San Francisco, or even with many of California's other smaller port towns, it is extremely busy. Fort Bragg's commercial and sport fishing operations keep boats active on a regular basis. With its marina and boat ramp, a large number of anglers launch their own boats at the well-protected harbor. There are gift shops and restaurants, plus a great view from the adjacent road that passes beneath the Highway 1 bridge.

Striped skunk

In spite of its name, the **Skunk Train** (707.964.6371 or 707.459.5248 for the Willits Depot or www.skunktrain.com) draws thousands of people each year for the train ride from the coast to the valley. The train passes through redwood forests and over open meadows, offering a relaxing and different way to enjoy the coastal mountains. Mendocino Railway operates several locomotives, including steam-powered locomotives, more modern diesel-electric locomotives, and several real "skunks," which are quite rare gasoline motorcars.

Info: Fort Bragg-Mendocino Coast Chamber of Commerce, 217 Main Street, Fort Bragg, CA 95437, 707.961.6300 or www.mendocinocoast.com

JUG HANDLE STATE NATURAL RESERVE

When most people pull off Highway 1 and into the small parking lot located about halfway between Mendocino and Fort Bragg, their intent is often to take the short walk out to **Caspar Point** and view the craggy cliffs and pounding surf. During winter, this is a great place to watch for gray whales spouting as they pass close offshore. Visitors are often surprised by the small, secluded beach that is tucked into these same cliffs at the mouth of **Jug Handle Creek**. But the real treat here is the trail that ducks back under the highway bridge and heads up the forested hillsides to the east.

One of the most prominent, yet unrecognized, geological features along much of California's coast is the terracing that was created over the past 500,000 years. The combination of a rising land mass forced upward by the collision between the Pacific and North American plates, and the changing ocean level—caused by warming temperatures and melting ice caps—has created coastal shelves. Approximately 150 feet in height and 100,000 years separate the tops of each of the terraces. Jug Handle State Natural Reserve is one of those places where the terraces are easily identified, in spite of the covering forest and thousands of years of erosion.

The park's **Ecological Staircase** is a 2.5-mile trail (5 miles round-trip) that heads out from the parking lot, travels up five distinct terraces—which you'll feel as you hike—stopping finally at what is termed a "Pygmy Forest" because of the severely stunted trees that fight to survive in the poor, thin soils.

As the trail leads from the bottom of the canyon of Jug Handle Creek, it passes through thick walls of willows (*Salix* sp.), alders (*Alnus* sp.), thimbleberry (*Rubus parviflorus*), blackberry (*Rubus ursinus*), bracken fern (*Pteridium aquilinum*), and the unsuspecting hiker's nemesis—stinging nettles (*Urtica dioica*). Approaching the first terrace, the riparian habitat changes to bishop pine (*Pinus muricata*) and Monterey pine (*Pinus radiata*), the latter introduced here from its native Central California habitat.

When hiking between some of the terraces, many of the changes that the pioneer farmers made are difficult to identify, as nature has slowly reclaimed the cleared, tilled, and grazed land. By the second terrace, grand fir (*Abies grandis*), sitka spruce (*Picea sitchensis*), and western hemlock (*Tsuga heterophylla*) have

Stinging nettle in bloom

(side margin text) Mendocino / Sonoma / Marin

added their presence to the growing collection of conifers. This terrace is also a good place to begin noticing the soil. The grayish podsol—Russian for "ash soil"—has been leached of all its alkaline nutrients, making it highly acidic.

Still higher up the hillside, Douglas fir (*Pseudotsugo menziesii*) and redwoods are seen in growing numbers and many of the shrubs—such as rhododendron (*Rhododendron macrophyllum*) and tanoak (*Lithocarpus densiflora*)—begin to appear. But most people hike this trail to see the Pygmy Forest, which lies ahead. As the soil becomes poorer, the final stage of podsolization occurs when the leached acids mix with quartz below the surface and form into an impervious hardpan. The result is that plants are severely stunted because their roots are unable to reach the nutrients and water they need.

On the upper terrace, the reserve merges with the **Jackson Demonstration State Forest**, managed by the Department of Forestry and Fire Protection. The trail first connects with a wider road that quickly crosses another road serving as a fire break. Perhaps 100 yards past the fire-break road, there is a boardwalk trail that cuts into the Pygmy forest on the right. The boardwalk, along with interpretive panels, leads through a portion of the trees in a short loop trail. It's the perfect way to see these Bolander pines (*Pinus bolanderi* ssp.) and rare pygmy cypresses that may be 50 years old, but are only from 2- to 5-feet tall.

There is no other trail back to the parking lot, but the return hike provides a perfect opportunity to see some of the park's wildlife, such as yellow-bellied sapsuckers. And if it's been raining much, an incredible assortment of mushrooms can sprout seemingly overnight.

Activities: Hiking, bird watching, whale watching, fishing
Facilities: None
Dates: Open daily
Fees: None
Closest town: Fort Bragg
Info: Mendocino Coast State Parks, Hwy. 1, PO Box 440, Mendocino, CA 95460, 707.937.5804 or www.parks.ca.gov

TRAILS

Ten Mile River Beach Trail is just that—a 10-mile round-trip hike along Ten Mile Beach that follows an old logging road. The **Ten Mile River** got its name not because it's a 10-mile round-trip hike from Lake Cleone, but because it's located 10 miles south of the Noyo River in Fort Bragg. The trail passes dunes and two wet, marshy areas—**Sand Hill Lake** and **Inglenook Fen**—that are off limits to all but researchers. A "fen" is an ecological area that is a cross between a bog and a marsh. Both of these areas support rare plants such as marsh pennywort (*Hydrocotyle verticillata*) and bog orchid (*Platanthera leucostachys*). The trail heads inland as it nears the mouth of Ten Mile River. Seasonally there are wildflowers such as columbine (*Aquilegia* sp.) and larkspur (*Delphinium* sp.). Watch for belted kingfishers (*Megaceryle alcyon*) diving into the river for small minnows.

Laguna Point Trail begins near Lake Cleone on a coastal terrace, 20 to 30 feet above the ocean. The 0.3-mile boardwalk trail is located at the northwest corner of the parking lot, just a short distance past the lake. The level, wheelchair-accessible boardwalk trail leads through the woods and along the coast to **Laguna Point**, where there is a great view of the rocky coast.

POINT CABRILLO LIGHT STATION STATE HISTORIC PARK

Following the 1906 San Francisco earthquake, the high demand for lumber to rebuild the city spurred a significant increase in maritime trade up and down California's coast. That increase in ships braving the treacherous coastline prompted the government to build additional lighthouses, including Point Cabrillo Light Station.

Work on the light station and lighthouse began in 1908 and was completed in 1909. Other buildings were added, including three lightkeepers' residences. A third-order Fresnel lens was installed inside the lighthouse; what makes this lens special is that it was only one of three made in Britain (they were normally made

Point Cabrillo Light Station

in France). The other two are bigger and brighter first- and second-order lenses found at Heceta Head Lighthouse in Oregon and on Staten Island in New York. The Point Cabrillo lens, which has been restored and retrofitted with a single 1,000-watt electric filament, is still in active use today.

One interesting maritime story focuses on the clipper ship *Frolic*. In 1850, the 97-foot ship, which was assigned to run opium from India to China, struck a reef near Point Cabrillo on a trip from China to San Francisco. Needless to say, the ship sank in the cove north of the lighthouse and has never been removed. Now referred to as "**Frolic Cove**," the site has been designated a **California State Underwater Park**.

Located on a magnificent headland between Point Arena and Cape Mendocino, the park is easy to access. From the park's **Farm House Visitor Center**, it is a relatively flat .05-mile walk to the lighthouse. On the way, you will pass the three original lightkeepers' homes. Now beautifully restored, they serve as vacation rentals (800.262.7801 or www.mendocinovacations.com).

Activities: Bird watching, light hiking
Facilities: Visitor center, museum, gift shop, lighthouse
Dates: Visitor center open daily 11 A.M. to 4 P.M.
Fees: None
Nearest town: Mendocino
Info: 707.937.6122, www.pointcabrillo.org or www.parks.ca.gov

POINT ARENA LIGHTHOUSE

The stunning lighthouse was built in 1870, and its 2-ton Fresnel lens was a powerful beacon of safety along the rugged North Coast. Now, the old, hand-polished lens that served as a vital aid to navigation for the hundreds of ships that plied the coastal waters has been replaced by an electronic beacon maintained by the U.S. Coast Guard. While it may not be as romantic, the electronic beacon is certainly more dependable, at least in

Point Arena Lighthouse

the absence of the dedicated, onsite lighthouse keepers.

Marine algae

The 115-foot tower—the tallest on the Pacific Coast—sits near the end of a long and narrow point of ancient coastal terrace that someday will lose its battle against the crashing waves. Until then, the very windy promontory remains the closest point of the continental U.S. to Hawaii. The drive out to the lighthouse from Highway 1 takes only a few minutes as the two-lane country road leads out across open cattle country. Visitors must park outside the gate to the complex and walk the 0.5 mile to the lighthouse. Docents offer tours of the lighthouse and fog signal room.

Three of the former lighthouse keeper houses on the grounds are available as vacation rentals throughout the year, but reservations are required.

Activities: Sight-seeing, nighttime full moon tours

Facilities: Museum, vacation rental of historic houses

Dates: Open daily, with seasonal changes in hours

Fees: There is a fee for tours.

Closest town: Point Arena

Info: Point Arena Lighthouse, 45500 Lighthouse Road, Point Arena, CA 95468, 707.882.2809 or www.pointarenalighthouse.com

MORE TO EXPLORE

Driving on Highway 1 along the Mendocino County coast, it is impossible to travel more than a few miles without passing a sign that identifies a public coastal access, and generally those access points are state or regional parks and beaches. The only problem is that a planned short visit can stretch into hours.

Westport-Union Landing State Beach is located 19 miles north of Fort Bragg. The park offers campsites on a bluff above the ocean. This is a popular spot for surf fishing, abalone diving, and spearfishing. Info: Mendocino Coast State Parks, 707.937.5804 or www.parks.ca.gov

Caspar Headlands State Natural Reserve and State Beach, which covers only 75 acres, offers an opportunity to enjoy sculpted rocks, eroded fissures, and a sand beach. A permit, available at nearby Russian Gulch State Park (2 miles north), is required to enter the reserve. Casper State Beach has an RV campground. Info: Mendocino Coast State Parks, 707.937.5804 or www.parks.ca.gov

97

Coast Danger!

Sonoma Coast beaches are especially dangerous for swimming or wading. Be cautious about getting too close to the ocean when hiking along the beach, especially during winter. The beaches are fairly steep, and sleeper waves are common. Every year these large, periodic, and completely unpredictable waves sweep people from areas they thought were safe and into the cold Pacific waters. Many do not survive.

Mendocino Coast Botanical Gardens feature 3 miles of trails through 47 acres of wonderful gardens filled with hybrid rhododendrons, heathers, fuchsias, dwarf conifers, heritage roses, camellias, and dahlias. The gardens are ADA accessible, there is an admission fee, and well-mannered dogs on leashes are allowed. Info: 707.964.4352 or www.GardenByThe-Sea.org

Van Damme State Park, located 3 miles south of Mendocino, is one of the most popular abalone diving locations on the North Coast. The park is much larger than its coastal frontage, extending inland along the Little River about 4 miles. The park has developed campsites, along with trails that lead to a small bog with unique plants and to a Pygmy forest similar to the one in nearby Jug Handle State Natural Reserve. Info: Mendocino Coast State Parks, 707.937.5804 or www.parks.ca.gov

Hendy Woods State Park is an inland redwood park that is somewhat drier than its coastal neighbors. Prior to the property becoming a state park, a man known as the "Hendy Hermit"—sometimes called the "Boonville Hermit"—lived here for 18 years in a redwood hut. He died in 1981, but the hut remains. The Navarro River flows through the park and offers good steelhead fishing during the fall run, and swimming, kayaking, and canoeing during the warm summer months. The park offers 92 developed campsites. Info: Mendocino Coast State Parks, 707.937.5804 or www.parks.ca.gov

Schooner Gulch State Beach offers wonderful ocean sunset views and access to beaches for fishing, exploring, surfing, and diving. It's located 3 miles south of Point Arena, where Schooner Gulch Beach crosses Highway 1. Info: Mendocino Coast State Parks, 707.937.5804 or www.parks.ca.gov

Sonoma County

GUALALA POINT REGIONAL PARK

The combination of river, beach, and ocean make this the perfect place to spend a weekend or more. Highway 1 bisects the east and west sides of this park that surrounds the mouth of the Gualala River. The slow-flowing river is popular with kayakers and fishing enthusiasts, while the coastal beach offers sand and interesting driftwood to explore. A 2.9-mile coastal trail meanders along the bluff and through a meadow as it follows the 195-acre park's inland portion of the Gualala River. **Whale Watch Point** is a great promontory for whale watching during the winter gray whale migration. There is a visitor center located in the ocean-side parking lot, south of the river.

Beach driftwood

Activities: Camping, fishing, scuba diving, picnicking, hiking
Facilities: Campground, visitor center, picnic area
Dates: Open daily
Fees: There are camping and day-use fees.
Closest town: Gualala
Info: Gualala Point Regional Park, 42401 Coast Highway 1, Guala, CA, 707.785.2377 or http://parks.sonomacounty.ca.gov

SALT POINT STATE PARK

This park offers a little something for everyone. Vegetation ranges from coastal scrub on some of the more open hillsides to forests of Bishop pine (*Pinus muricata*), Douglas fir, second-growth redwoods, and scatterings of tanoak (*Lithocarpus densiflora*) and madrone (*Arbutus menziesii*). Hike up the mountain above the coast and there's a Pygmy forest where stunted versions of redwoods, cypress, and Bishop pine grow slowly in the nutrient-depleted hardpan soil.

The park's coastal bluffs and isolated beaches provide great fishing and diving. One of the most popular scuba diving spots is **Gerstle Cove**, a portion of which is an underwater reserve. Divers and fishermen aren't allowed to take or disturb any of the animal or plant life within the reserve's boundaries. But outside the underwater reserve, surf fishing and underwater spearfishing is allowed, within the bounds of California's fishing regulations. During the relatively short season, the parking lot near Gerstle Cove, as well as some of the other coastal access points in the park, serves as staging areas for abalone divers.

Highway 1 runs between the coast and the higher ridgeline of the park, and there is a campground on each side. The developed portions of the park, where the campgrounds and day-use picnic areas are located, are centered near the southern end of the park. From the campgrounds, several trails meander through the park, with the most popular hike leading through the prairie to the Pygmy forest. The hike is about 2 miles long, depending on the starting point.

Giant Pacific oyster

Activities: Camping, hiking, scuba diving, picnicking, fishing
Facilities: Campground and picnic area
Dates: Open daily
Fees: There are camping and day-use fees.
Closest town: Jenner
Info: Salt Point State Park, 25050 Coast Highway 1, Jenner, CA 95450, 707. 847.3221 or www.parks.ca.gov

FORT ROSS STATE HISTORIC PARK

The Spanish discovered that trying to keep other countries from intruding into lands that they had claimed for themselves was not an easy task. As early as the mid-18th century, Russian trappers had followed seal and sea otter populations down the West Coast from Alaska into the upper reaches of the Spanish-claimed California coast. Spain countered by pushing its mission settlements farther north into Alta, or Northern California. Unfortunately, Spain never settled much farther north than San Francisco and in numbers so small so as not to make any difference. Thus, it probably wasn't much of a surprise when California's Spanish government discovered that in March 1812, a large group of Russians and their Alaskan laborers had landed north of the Russian River and had begun building a very substantial wooden fort.

One of the Russians' first forays into this part of California's coast resulted in

Cannons at Fort Ross, with the chapel in the background

their returning to Mother Russia with more than 1,000 sea otter pelts. They soon returned with intentions of staying and farming the land, in addition to hunting sea otters. Within a short eight years, the Russians had hunted the sea otters to near extinction. Although they desired to trade both pelts and agricultural products with the Spanish settlements to the south, Spain remained nervous about her Russian neighbors, as well as the American ships also sailing California's coastal waters. Once the sea otters were gone, the Russian settlement began to fail; agriculture was not particularly successful on the cold and foggy North Coast.

Anxious to leave, in 1841 the Russians finally found an interested buyer named John Sutter, an immigrant who already had established Sutter's Fort in what would become Sacramento. Sutter's only real interest was in obtaining the livestock and supplies the Russians were leaving behind. The fort and surrounding land was largely abandoned until George Call acquired it as part of his 15,000 acre ranch in 1873. He used the somewhat sheltered anchorage below the coastal fort as a loading area for timber harvested from his land. The fort and its 3-acre site were given to the State of California in 1906, and since that time, more than 3, 270 acres have been added. Significant restoration work also has been completed on the fort.

A museum and visitor center serves as an introduction outside the entrance to the fort. Exhibits range from Native Americans to the Russian presence in the area. Exiting through the back door of the visitor center, you'll find a short trail that leads to the fort, passing a vegetable garden along the way. The fort's stout vertical timbers are impressive even today, as are the cannon muzzles that point out of the gun ports in the corner towers or blockhouses. The interior of the fort is largely open, with only four buildings, in addition to the two corner towers. The buildings include the chapel—reconstructed after the first chapel burned—the manager's house, the officials' quarters, and the Russian employee barracks. There is another short trail that provides access to the small beach at the base of the bluff.

Bald eagles can sometimes be spotted here.

For hikers who like to

102

wander, most of the park is located on the east side of Highway 1, which bisects the park. It consists of open meadows and redwood forests. Since there are no established trails, the area is open to meandering, mostly uphill. The mountains on the east side of Highway 1 rise to 1,400 feet above sea level. Since the Russians were the first people in California to do extensive logging of redwoods, the park has California's oldest second-growth redwood trees.

Activities: Hiking, beach exploration, whale watching
Facilities: Fort Ross Compound and Visitor Center (small gift shop—no food)
Dates: Open Thursday through Monday and most holidays, April—Sept.
Fees: There is a day-use and museum fee.
Closest town: Jenner
Info: Fort Ross State Historic Park, 19005 Coast Highway, Jenner, CA 95450, 707.847.3286, www.parks.ca.gov or www.fortross.org

JENNER

Tucked into the hillside above the Russian River, Jenner is a good place to stop along Highway 1 to view wildlife—mostly birds—and occasionally harbor seals (*Phoca vitulina*). Near the middle of the small, coastal community, a state park visitor center juts into the edge of the river. Even if the center is closed, it has interpretive panels outside that tell a little about the natural history of the area. There's a parking area on the ocean side of Highway 1 soon after the road begins to climb and head north out of town. This overlook provides a panoramic view of the Russian River and its mouth, Goat Rock, and the Pacific Ocean.

The town was originally known as Jenner Gulch and was settled primarily by workers from the nearby lumber mills. During the mid-19th century a ferry operated across the Russian River. It ran until the early 20th century, transporting passenger vehicles between the ends of the coast highway that stopped on either side of the river.

Like many of the Golden State's scenic coastal rivers, the river's mouth does not always flow into the ocean. During summer, large sand accumulations can block or severely restrict the river's ability to reach the Pacific. Winter storms generally

Harbor seals and gulls at the mouth of the Russian River

change that; high, crashing waves and significant increases in river runoff tend to scour out its mouth. During spring and early summer, this promontory is a great place to view harbor seals and their newly born pups that bask on the sandy beach and frolic in the water near the river's mouth.

This portion of the California coast is also free of the San Andreas fault, which lies offshore. The coast between Bodega Bay to the south and Fort Ross to the north is made up of nearly all Franciscan rocks scraping off the ocean's floor at the subduction zone. The relatively rare blueschist is found combined with serpentinites in road cuts south of Jenner. Blueschist is one of those rocks found only in subduction zones. It is created under high pressure, but at relatively cool temperatures, being expelled upward before its temperature can be raised to that of the adjoining minerals and its content metamorphosed into a different form.

SONOMA COAST STATE PARK

The park includes 16 miles of secluded, sandy beaches, dunes, rocky headlands, and natural bridges carved from ancient headlands. The public beach begins at **Russian Gulch**, a small creek located off Highway 1, about 2.5 miles north of Jenner and the mouth of the Russian River. There's a parking lot and a trail to the beach.

This entire stretch of coast is a great place to watch for migrating gray whales during winter and for several different species of gulls during the changing seasons of the year. Telling the difference between what most people simply call "sea gulls"

Herring gull (look for the pink legs)

can be challenging, even for experts. Gulls go through several color variations during the first few years of their lives, making immature birds especially difficult to identify. Heermann's gull (*Larus heermanni*), California gull (*Larus californicus*), ring billed gull (*Larus delawarensis*), herring gull (*Larus argentatus*), and the western gull (*Larus occidentalis*) are the species most commonly seen. Equally easy to view, but much easier to identify, are some of the other birds such as Pelagic cormorants (*Phalacrocorax pelagicus*) and the sleek-looking western grebes (*Aechmophorus occidentalis*), both of which are often seen swimming near shore. And common during summer is the brown pelican (*Pelecanus occidentalis*), a large, graceful flier that once teetered on the brink of extinction due primarily to the use of the insecticide DDT.

Goat Rock is a very prominent and popular stop for travelers along Highway 1, as well as for locals who like to fish the beaches in the area. Rather than hiking down long and steep trails from the highway, there's a road that winds down to

Goat Rock is on the right.

beach level, about 0.75 miles south of the Russian River bridge. The miniature peninsula has a parking area and restroom. There is a large harbor seal colony in the Goat Rock-Russian River mouth area, but you must stay back 50 feet. Dogs and pets are not allowed on the beach. Also, climbing Goat Rock is dangerous and not allowed.

Duncan's Landing is 1.5 miles north of Bodega Bay off Highway 1. It once served as a loading point for ships picking up lumber and other products produced along this area of the coast. Today it provides a great show during times of high waves, when the surf can actually crash up over the roadway that circles the area. And that makes getting too close to the lower cliffs very dangerous. During spring and early summer, the open coastal terrace is alive with wildflowers that contrast beautifully with the blue Pacific in the background.

Wright's Beach is probably the most popular part of Sonoma Coast State Park, primarily because of the 27-site campground that is situated on the beach at the base of the coastal bluff. A thick hedgerow of shrubbery around the campsites acts as a partial barrier against the ever-present winds that come off the water and can be quite cold most of the year, even during summer. The wide beach is a great place for exploring, fishing, or simply watching sunsets.

Bodega Dunes Campground is much more protected from ocean winds, although the summer fog that is common along all of California's coast can still leave tents and anything else left in the open very wet. Bodega Dunes has the advantage over Wright's Beach in offering both open coastline—where the Pacific's pounding surf can be experienced, especially during winter storms—and the more protected waters and

Ground squirrel

tidal flats of Bodega Bay. Although the 98-campsite campground isn't actually on the bay, it's a short walk from the campground and across Bay Flat Road to the water's edge.

Bodega Head overlooks the entrance into Bodega Bay Harbor. From the parking area, several short trails meander along the rocky bluff. It is often windy and cold on the exposed bluff, so dress adequately. There are a few steep trails that lead down to sand and gravel beaches at the water's edge along the head. Take Bay Flat Road from Highway 1, around Bodega Bay's harbor.

Bodega Dunes Horse Trail has its staging area off Bay Flat Road, behind the Bodega Dunes Campground. Horses are allowed on the beach for 5 miles. It's best to check at the Salmon Creek headquarters (1.25 miles north of Bodega Bay on Highway 1), for rules regarding restricted areas.

Facilities: Two family campgrounds—Wright's Beach and Bodega Dunes
Dates: Open year-round
Fees: Camping fees. Most day-use areas are free, with the exception of Wright's Beach and Bodega Dunes, which charge day-use fees.
Closest town: Bodega Bay on the south and Jenner to the north
Info: Sonoma Coast State Park, 3095 Highway 1, Bodega Bay, CA 95430, 707. 875.3483 or www.parks.ca.gov

Tide Pool Exploring

California's tide pools, especially along the lesser-visited North Coast, support a large and diverse group of plants and animals that are readily visible. Most of the animals are protected by fish and wildlife regulations, at least during certain times of the year. But they can be viewed during any month of the year by tide-pool explorers.

A few words of caution: Winter is generally not a good time for exploring tide pools because of the often dangerous high surf. Even summer can be dangerous when hopping on the sharp and slippery rocks above the cold and surging waters. Be careful and never turn your back to the ocean.

A most peculiar plant is the sea palm (*Postelsia palmaeformis*), which looks very much like a miniature palm tree clinging tenaciously to the rocks in the surf zone. It's actually an alga that is able to attach itself with holdfasts to the rocks and withstand the constant ebb and flow of the waves.

Perhaps the most commonly seen animal is a simple creature called the black turban snail (*Tegula funebralis*), so named because of the shape and color of its shell. The biggest are usually no larger than a walnut and are black or deep purple in color. A surprise comes when one of the shells suddenly sprouts longer legs—rather than its normal, boneless snail foot—and scrambles quickly across the bottom of a stranded pool of water during low tide. You are seeing a hermit crab (*Pagurus samuelis*). Hermit crabs are not true crabs, partly because they have no shell of their own, but instead, they take up residence inside abandoned black turban snail shells.

Hermit crab

While giant green anemones (*Anthopleura xanthogrammica*), ochre stars (*Pisaster ochraceous*)—often called starfish—and purple urchins (*Strongyloncentrotus purpuratus*) live well in the changing tides by seeking protective hiding places, the odd-looking goose-neck barnacle (*Pollicipes polymerus*) fights off the waves in a different manner. It produces a very strong natural glue to stick itself to rocks in the mid- to low-tide zones where the wave action is most powerful. As tons of water wash over them, they turn their plate-like, somewhat pointed heads toward the incoming wave then swivel around to strain plankton and absorb oxygen from the less powerful retreating wave. Goose-neck barnacles often live on rocks among colonies of California mussels (*Mytilus californianus*).

BODEGA BAY

While the Miwok and Pomo Indians were the first to settle this part of California's coast, the town of Bay was founded by Firmin Candelot in the late 1800s. In 1843, Captain Stephen Smith claimed much of the surrounding land, naming it Rancho Bodega, probably after Lt. Juan Francisco de la Bodega y Quadra who had sailed his ship *Sonoma* into the south end of the bay in 1775. Smith constructed the first steam-powered sawmill in California, and the bay served him well as a port for shipping his lumber products to distant markets. The area's name wasn't expanded to Bodega Bay until 1941.

> ## Historic Bodega
>
> People old enough to remember Alfred Hitchcock and his film *The Birds* still come to the nearby inland community of Bodega to see the old Potter School House and St. Theresa's Church where part of the filming was done. Bodega is located 5 miles southeast of Bodega Bay along Highway 1, then approximately 1 mile east on the Bodega Highway.

Even today, Bodega Bay remains relatively undeveloped along much of its shoreline. A few old houses, dilapidated fishing piers, and buildings long past their prime—especially along the southern portion of the bay—are the most visually intriguing. There are newer structures, and they increase in numbers and concentrations as Highway 1 continues south toward the harbor area.

Bodega Bay Harbor, with its small, picturesque community on its northeastern shore, has the largest and busiest harbor between San Francisco and Fort Bragg to the north. The community offers numerous hotels and restaurants and there are plenty of opportunities to try your hand at fishing. Besides the state campground at its north end, the bay is surrounded by mostly regional or county parklands including **Westside Regional Park** (707.875.2640) and **Doran Regional Park**

Bodega Bay Harbor

(707.875.3540), which lies at the end of the long spit marking the south shoreline of Bodega Harbor.

Info: Sonoma Coast Visitors Center, 850 Hwy. 1, Bodega Bay, CA 94923, 707.875.3866 or www.VisitBodegaBay-CA.com or www.SonomaCounty.com

SONOMA

The Franciscans came to Sonoma in 1823 and constructed the last and most northerly of their missions—**Mission San Francisco Solano de Sonoma**. This mission served the religious needs of the citizens, while the nearby **Sonoma Barracks** housed the troops of General Mariano Guadalupe Vallejo. There were varying efforts to establish a pueblo, but the local Indians weren't particularly cooperative in allowing a village of Mexican citizens on their land, at least any distance from the protection of the Mexican soldiers at the barracks. But things would soon change.

Mission San Francisco Solano de Sonoma

As the Americans continued to push their way into California during the 1840s, Mexican control was quickly slipping. Finally, a ragtag band of Americans stole a bunch of Mexican army horses and quickly decided they should escalate their actions to a full revolution. The Americans seized General Vallejo at his home, with the general not objecting or attempting to convince the Americans that what they were doing was a bad idea. The Bear Flag Revolt, as it became known, was short-lived, lasting only three weeks. It effectively ended on July 7, 1846, when U.S. naval forces, under Commodore John Drake Sloat, landed in Monterey and claimed Alta California during the Mexican-American War.

Today, **Sonoma State Historic Park** oversees the Mexican soldiers' barracks and several of other historic buildings in the once small town. **La Casa Grande**—General Vallejo's Sonoma home—and the **Blue Wing Inn**—the first building north of San Francisco constructed specifically as a hotel—are only a few pieces of the town's historic fabric. Within Sonoma Barracks, which is now a museum and visitor center, there are restored rooms and a small theater.

The center of Sonoma is a plaza park, surrounded by Sonoma Barracks, shops, and restaurants. For information about other regional destinations and the famous wine country in this region, visit the **Sonoma Valley Visitors Center**.

Activities: Picnicking, self-guided tours
Facilities: Museums, restaurants, hotels
Dates: Open year-round
Fees: There is a day-use fee.
Info: Sonoma State Historic Park, 707.938.9560 or www.parks.ca.gov, Sonoma Valley Visitors Bureau, 453 First Street E, Sonoma, CA 95476, 707.996.1090 or www.SonomaValley.com

JACK LONDON STATE HISTORIC PARK

Even if you have no interest in author Jack London's life or his work, wandering the trails among oaks and pines is a great way to spend a day exploring this 800-acre park. There's a 0.75 mile walk that leads to a dam, lake, and bathhouse built by London, and bicycling and horseback riding are permitted on some of the park's trails. But most people are lured here by a curiosity to visit the home of one of America's most prolific and best-loved writers.

Jack London's adventure novels, *Call of the Wild* (1903) and *The Sea Wolf* (1904), made him famous and provided the income for him to begin living life as he wanted. But his output did not stop there. London tried to write at least 1,000 words each day, a feat that allowed him to complete more than 50 fiction and nonfiction books from 1900 to 1916, along with hundreds of magazine articles and short stories. Some of his works have been translated into more than 70 different languages.

One of Jack London's dreams was to sail around the world in his custom-built sailing ship, the *Snark*. While he and his second wife, Charmian, made it only to Australia, the 1906-07 voyage provided background material for years to come. Another dream was to operate a modern farm. Seeking an escape from his home in Oakland, London purchased land outside the small community of **Glen Ellen**, near Sonoma. Here, living in a small ranch house on what he called his Beauty Ranch, he continued his writing to support himself and his wife. While managing his modern farm, London began construction of the couple's new home, which they called the "**Wolf House.**" He also managed to spend two tours as a

Jack London's home includes his office and a sleeping porch for those warm evenings.

war correspondent during World War I, travel extensively, and entertain a near constant stream of guests, all in addition to spending plenty of time in local bars, drinking and debating with other bar patrons.

The Wolf House— a mansion that cost more than $80,000 to build in 1913—burned to the ground a few days before London and Charmian were to move in. Stone and

Wolf House ruins

concrete walls are all that remained following the fire, and they are still standing today. Even after his depression eased over the loss of his house, London's health deteriorated. He worked longer hours writing, trying to make the money he needed to support his farm and other projects. Finally, on November 22, 1916, London's lifestyle caught up with him and he died at the age of 40 from gastrointestinal uremic poisoning. Jack London's ashes were scattered on a hill not far from Wolf House, next to the graves of two pioneer children.

Today, the famous ranch house where London did much of his writing has been restored and is open to the public. His widow, Charmian, had another house built in 1919-20, somewhat similar to the nearby Wolf House. Following her death in 1955 at age 84, the home became a visitor center and museum dedicated to her late husband. It showcases photographs and mementos of their world travels, as well as many of Jack London's personal possessions, including his roll-top desk and Dictaphone.

There are several miles of trails that lead to London's sherry barn, stone manure pit, the winery ruins, distillery building, the Pig Palace, the 40-foot tall concrete silos, and the 5-acre lake.

Activities: Hiking, picnicking
Facilities: Museum, visitor center, trails
Dates: Open year-round
Fees: There is a day-use fee.
Closest town: Glen Ellen
Info: Valley of the Moon Natural History Association, 2400 London Ranch Road, Glen Ellen, CA 95442, 707.938.5216, www.JackLondonPark.com or www.parks.ca.gov

Mendocino / Sonoma / Marin

POINT REYES NATIONAL SEASHORE

Miwok Indians were the first to inhabit this land, probably attracted by the abundant food supplies and moderate climate. In 1579, their idyllic life began to change when Sir Francis Drake, seeking new lands for England's Queen Elizabeth I, sailed his ship, the *Golden Hind,* into Drakes Estero. He stayed for more than a month, making repairs to his ship. The friendly Miwoks provided additional food to the English crew. During their stay, Drake's crew had opportunities to explore the area, discovering a rich land that certainly reminded some of them of home. Before continuing on his around-the-world journey, Drake named the land *Nova Albion,* or New England.

Although a few other maritime explorers passed by or landed near Point Reyes, including Don Sebastian Vizcaino in 1603, it took nearly 200 more years before there was any serious attempt to settle these lands. By the time the Americans had won Point Reyes and the rest of California from Mexico, who had taken it from Spain, the Miwok had disappeared. During Mexico's control, three men, collectively known as the Lords of Point Reyes, controlled the peninsula through land grants. Soon after it came under American control, a San Francisco law firm obtained the property and divided it into a series of ranches for beef and dairy cattle. Cattle continue to graze throughout the peninsula grasslands today.

For first-time visitors, the **Bear Valley Visitor Center** (415.464.5100 or www. nps.gov) is the best place to begin. It's located a few hundred yards down Bear Valley Road, off Highway 1 near the community of Olema. Besides offering maps,

camping permits, a museum, and book-shop, the center serves as a starting point for numerous trails that reach all parts of Point Reyes.

With so many working ranches still on the Point Reyes Peninsula, the historic **Pierce Point Ranch** offers visitors a glimpse at a turn-of-the-century ranch house and the outbuildings need-ed for a dairy opera-tion, including historic milking barns where

Point Reyes National Seashore

the cows were herded each day. Interpretive panels explain the dairy operation and the incredible attention that was paid to cleanliness. After all, the Pierce Point Ranch, established in 1858, produced some of the finest butter and other dairy products for markets in San Francisco and beyond.

As the park's Pierce Point Road nears the Pierce Point Ranch, it passes through the **Tule Elk Reserve**. Within the reserve, tule elk (*Cervus canadensis nannodes*) graze and bed down on the open grasslands. Before 19th century meat hunters decimated their population, thousands of elk once roamed these hills. Today, a program is in place to restore tule elk to the open lands of Point Reyes National Seashore, although they are being restricted to this small part of the park so they don't compete with the cattle ranches still operating here. **CAUTION:** Do not approach the elk for any reason. They are wild animals and can be very dangerous.

Tule elk

Activities: Hiking, camping, fishing, bird watching, beachcombing

Facilities: Visitor centers, historic buildings. Camping in the park is limited to four hike-in campgrounds. There is no car camping in the park. Permits are required to use the hike-in campgrounds and may be obtained at the Bear Valley Visitor Center. Reservations are suggested due to the popularity of camping at Point Reyes, 877.444.6777 or www.recreation.gov

Dates: The park is open daily. Hours vary for the visitor center and historic buildings.

Fees: There is a camping fee.

Closest town: Olema

Information: Point Reyes National Seashore, 7 Bear Valley Road, Point Reyes Station, CA 94956, 415.464.5100 or www.nps.gov

TRAILS

There are many miles of trails inside Point Reyes National Seashore. While they are well marked and well used, it's wise to pick up a map from the Bear Valley Visitor Center before hiking in the park. It's also important to go prepared for changeable weather. A warm, sunny afternoon can change to bone-chilling, wind-

driven fog, often within an hour or less. Winters can bring warm sunshine or heavy rain, along with extremely high and dangerous surf. But the surf can be extremely hazardous any time of the year, especially on the more northerly facing beaches and bluffs.

Beginning at the Bear Valley Visitor Center, the **Bear Valley Trail** is 4.1 miles of rolling hills on the way to **Arch Rock**. This popular rock formation landmark is located at the mouth of Coast Creek, which is at the north end of **Wildcat Beach**. Once at the beach, the trail connects with the Coast Trail.

The **Earthquake Trail** starts near the visitor center and leads to the nearby San Andreas fault. The 0.6-mile-long trail offers an opportunity to stand on one of the most unstable pieces of real estate in California.

The 0.8-mile-long **Kule Loklo Trail** also departs from the visitor center parking lot and heads up a short hill through a woodlands area, then a eucalyptus grove, and finally ends at an open meadow where current-day Native Americans and other volunteers have constructed a replica of a Coast Miwok Indian village.

The **Tomales Point Trail** consists of two trails that begin at the Pierce Point Ranch. The first is a quick 0.5-mile walk to the beach. The second is 3.7 miles long and follows the ridge—mostly on the Pacific Ocean side of the narrowing peninsula—out to Tomales Point. The hike offers great views of the ocean and of Tomales Bay to the east. It's a 40-minute drive to the trailhead from the visitor center.

The **Coast Trail** meanders about half the length of Drakes Bay, turning inland near Limantour Spit. To reach the south trailhead, from Highway 1 at the north end of Bolinas Lagoon, take Olema-Bolinas Road and turn right on Mesa Road. The trail begins at the **Palomarin Trailhead**, which is at the end of Mesa Road.

The 1.6-mile **Chimney Rock Trail** offers views of Drakes Bay and is known for its seasonal wildflower displays. There is no beach access, but it's a great place to whale-watch, especially during the gray whales' winter migration. The trailhead is located near the Point Reyes Historic Lighthouse, a 45-minute drive from the Bear Valley Visitor Center.

MORE TO EXPLORE

With so much shoreline, the beaches of Point Reyes attract thousands of people each year, but it's always important to be aware of the dangers that accompany high waves and cold water. The most popular beaches are those easily reached by car or by short walks.

Beach walking

Limantour Beach is one of the more popular beaches at Point Reyes because it can be reached by driving, it has a beautiful beach (but no lifeguard service), and it's near **Estero de Limantour**. There's a short trail that goes out onto **Limantour Spit**, providing a perfect place to view birds on Drakes Bay, on the open ocean, and in the Estero de Limantour wetlands.

Drakes Beach is home to the **Kenneth C. Patrick Visitor Center**. The destination offers one of the safer beaches for sunbathers, swimmers, and beachcombers. Even though the waves are smaller here than at other places around the park, it can still be dangerous. Lifeguards are not available, so use with caution.

Because **Point Reyes Beach (North and South)** face the Pacific Ocean, both are subject to dangerously heavy surf and strong rip currents. Of course the beaches are great to explore and, on the occasional sunny day, good for sunbathing, but entering the water here for any reason should be avoided. The beaches are located off Sir Francis Drake Boulevard, 13.2 and 15.7 miles respectively, from the Bear Valley Visitor Center.

POINT REYES HISTORIC LIGHTHOUSE

The drive out to the lighthouse is more like a drive back in history, when cattle ranches reigned over the open lands of the peninsula, producing beef and some of the finest dairy products available anywhere. Cattle still graze on the grasslands and are herded across the roads, stopping traffic. The ranch houses, barns, and corrals needed for ranching operations are still scattered throughout the low, rolling hills.

From the lighthouse parking lot, there is a 0.4-mile walk to the museum and visitor center. As you walk toward the light station facilities, check the road cut on the left. Several different plants color the shady, moist rock surfaces. The furry rock violet (*Alga trentephohlia,*) is an alga that contains green chlorophyll, but its red pigments are most visible. Pale green lichen also grows on the rocks. It is made up of both algae and fungi. The fungi secure the plant to the rock surface and absorb moisture, while the algae produce food for both.

A stairway leads down from the visitor center to the lighthouse, which sits near the end of the small point of land. It's 308 steps down, and for some, a very difficult 308 steps back up to the museum and visitor center. The stairs are closed when the winds exceed 40 mph. If the fog hasn't enveloped the point, there are excellent views down the coast and out across the open Pacific Ocean. It's a good viewpoint for watching gray whales during their winter migration. There is no fee to tour the lighthouse.

Activities: Hiking, bird watching, whale watching. Visitation can be heavy on weekends and holidays. Shuttle buses may be available.

Facilities: Visitor center, lighthouse

Dates: Open daily, Thursday through Monday, 10 A.M. to 4:30 P.M.

Fees: None

Closest town: Point Reyes Station

Info: Point Reyes National Seashore, 7 Bear Valley Road, Point Reyes Station, CA 94956, 415.464.5100, 415.669.1534 or www.nps.gov

Stairway to Point Reyes Historic Lighthouse

Marin County

TOMALES BAY STATE PARK

Long and narrow, Tomales Bay marks one of California's ongoing major geologic events. The San Andreas fault runs through the middle of the bay, effectively separating the westward-moving North American plate from the Pacific plate that is diving downward and moving slowly to the northeast as the two grind together. Each year, the land on the western side—primarily Point Reyes National Seashore—moves approximately 2 inches. During the 1906 San Francisco earthquake, which was centered near the park, the two plates shifted 20 feet within a few seconds. The combination of these movements over thousands of years has shifted the landmass of Point Reyes from its point of origin as part of the Tehachapi Mountains in Southern California to its current location more than 300 miles north.

Great horned owls hunt here at night

The fact that there are two colliding tectonic plates separated by a flooded valley provides an opportunity to compare the different rocks found on each side. On the east side of the lagoon, the outcroppings are mostly Franciscan rock, sandstones scraped from the top of the Pacific plate as it moves under the North American plate. Rocks on the west side of the bay are part of the Salinian block, with its granite outcroppings as evidence of its one-time connection to rock formations in Southern California. Much of the lower areas are buried under sedimentary rocks that were laid down when the granite was still beneath the sea, 10 to 20 million years ago.

Tomales Bay State Park spans a small portion of the land on both sides of the bay. The largest part of the park is on the western side, running into **Inverness Ridge**. The surrounding hills offer forests and woodlands to explore, while the main focus for many who visit is the park's beach access. There are a few short trails along its route. The park also has one of the last remaining virgin bishop pine (*Pinus muricata*) forests, located in the **Jepson Memorial Grove**.

Activities: Hiking, swimming, picnicking, fishing, beachcombing
Facilities: Picnic areas
Dates: Open daily

Fees: There is a day-use fee.
Closest town: Inverness
Info: Tomales Bay State Park, 1208 Pierce Point Road, Inverness, CA 94937, 415.669.1140 or www.parks.ca.gov

TRAILS

There are several trails in Tomales Bay State Park, the more popular leading to the park's four beaches—**Shell Beach, Pebble Beach, Heart's Desire Beach, and Indian Beach**. Follow the park access road (off Pierce Point Road) to the end where two parking lots are located. On busy weekends, the lots can fill by mid-morning, with no additional vehicle access allowed until people begin leaving. Trailheads are located at the two parking lots, and the two primary trails are interconnected, allowing hikes ranging from less than 1 mile to more than 5 miles.

From the parking lot, the **Jepson Trail** leads up a gentle slope through a forest of moss-covered twisted oaks. The trail dead-ends after about 1 mile into the Johnstone Trail.

The **Johnstone Trail** is the longest trail in the park, winding from the north at Indian Beach southward to Heart's Desire Beach then Pebble Beach before turning inland and connecting with the Jepson Trail (creates a loop trail). The Johnstone Trail continues south then east, back to **Tomales Bay** and Shell Beach at the southern end of the park.

MARTIN GRIFFIN PRESERVE

The Martin Griffin Preserve is part of the larger **Audubon Canyon Ranch**, which preserves more than 5,300 acres in Sonoma and Marin counties. Nature has created the perfect habitat for wildlife in the ranch's **Bolinas Lagoon Preserve**. With its open, protected waters and shallow tidelands, along with surrounding hillsides of grasses, chaparral, and woodlands, there is ample food and shelter for hundreds of animal species.

Great blue heron

The 1,000-acre preserve is home to one of California's largest great blue heron (*Ardea herodias*) rookeries, with at least 100 nesting pairs. There are generally a few pairs of snowy egrets joining in the nesting efforts each year. The herons arrive in January and, within a month or so, begin their very elaborate courtship activities, which are followed by nesting in the tops of the redwood trees in February. Together, the male and female herons incubate their two to five eggs for about 28 days until they hatch, and then share in feeding the chicks until they are able to fledge in 10 to 12 weeks.

Activities: Hiking, interpretive programs, picnicking
Facilities: Picnic area, bookstore, education hall, ranch yard
Dates: Open daily, if conditions allow, from spring through mid-December. On weekends, ranch guides are onsite to lead tours.
Fees: None, but a donation is requested to help support the preserve's operation.
Closest town: Stinson Beach
Info: Audubon Canyon Ranch Headquarters, 4900 Highway 1, Stinson Beach, CA 94970, 415.868.9244 or www.egret.org

TRAILS

The only way to really enjoy the full viewing benefits that the reserve has to offer is by spending time on some of the 8 miles of trails. Since most of the trails lead into the wooded hills above the lagoon, another benefit of walking is the opportunity to see some of the other wildlife. It's always exciting to catch a passing glimpse of black-tailed deer (*Odocoileus hemionus*), bobcats (*Felis rufus*), badgers (*Taxidea taxus*), raccoons (*Procyon lotor*), and brush rabbits (*Sylvilagus hachmani*).

It's a 0.5-mile climb up this popular trail to the **Henderson Overlook**. Here you get an unbeatable bird's-eye view of great blue herons and common egrets (*Ardea alba*) in their treetop homes. Audubon naturalists are often onsite to interpret the life cycles and needs of the breeding birds.

STINSON BEACH

The small seaside community of Stinson Beach is home to its namesake— Stinson Beach. The beach is operated by the National Park Service as part of Golden Gate National Recreation Area. Located south of **Bolinas Lagoon**, the town

is a curious collection of old and new homes, a few B&Bs, small cafés, and restaurants. In many ways, the town could be considered a holdover refuge for those who have never quite given up on the 1960s.

Runners heading toward Stinson Beach

It's fun, it's quaint, it's a quiet refuge—except on warm summer weekends when the beach portion of Stinson Beach fills with people. One of the more popular and car-accessible beaches for many miles, it's a quick drive for people living in Marin County. Also, the beach is one of only a few along the North Coast with summer lifeguard service. There's a small visitor center in the park.

Caution is advised as there have been shark attacks in the past, and dangerous rip currents are often present. Pets and glass containers are not allowed on the beach.

Info: Stinson Beach Ranger Station is operated during summer, 415.868.0942, 415.868.0734 or www.nps.gov

MOUNT TAMALPAIS STATE PARK

Commonly referred to as "Mount Tam," the 6,300-acre park rises from sea level to the top of the 2,571-foot-high peak that gives this meeting of coast and mountains its name. Spanish explorers originally named the mountain *La Sierra de Nuestro Padre de San Francisco*, which was later changed to "Tamalpais," the Coast Miwok Indians' name for the promontory.

This is an incredibly popular park with Bay Area hikers and anyone who simply wishes to go for a drive on the park's roads that wind along the coast and up to the mountain's majestic overlook. On clear days, you can see the Farallon Islands, 25 miles away, as well as have incredible views across the inland delta, San Francisco Bay, Mount Diablo, and occasionally even the snow-capped Sierra Nevada, nearly 200 miles east.

The mountain is part of the Coast Range and is therefore essentially the layer of ancient mud and other materials that were scraped off the ancient ocean floor as the Pacific plate plunged into the subduction zone along the eastern side of the San Andreas fault. The remnant scraped and uplifted layers of metamorphic rock—including sandstone, shale, greenstone, chert, and serpentine— are the most common on the mountain that has been rising higher for the past one million years.

The different mineral types, combined with a million years of

Cabins at Steep Ravine

weathering, have created a wide range of habitats and microclimates that today support more than 750 different plant species. Rolling grasslands, hillside chaparral, oak woodlands, and dense stands of Douglas fir and coast redwoods are found alongside the 50 miles of hiking trails inside the park. Spring is an absolutely glorious time to visit, as brightly colored wildflowers cover entire hillsides. California poppies (*Eschscholzia californica*), golden fields (*Lasthenia* sp.), white-spotted coral root (*Corrallorhiza maculata*), Calypso orchid, (*Calypso bulbosa*), Douglas iris (*Iris douglasiana*), and shooting stars (*Dodecatheon* sp.) join dozens of other species for their annual show.

With such plant diversity comes an equally diversified animal community. Bobcats (*Lynx rufus*), black-tailed deer (*Odocoileus hemionius columbianus*), raccoons (*Procyon lotor*), gray foxes (*Urocyon cinereoargenteus*), and even an occasional mountain lion (*Felis concolor*) call the park home. Ranchers and others who feared, misunderstood, or saw economic gain hunted some of the original wild inhabitants—including the bear and elk—into localized extinction.

Birds are especially prolific in the park. Red-tailed hawks (*Buteo jamaicensis*), turkey vultures (*Cathartes aura*), great horned owls (*Bubo virginianus*), screech owls (*Otus asio*), and pileated woodpeckers (*Dryocopus pileatus*) are relatively common, although none are seen as often as the some-

Turkey vulture

times obnoxious-acting Steller's jays (*Cyanocitta stelleri*) and ravens (*Corvus corax*).

A feature found here, and in no other state park in California, is an amphitheater that the Civilian Conservation Corps built during the Depression of the 1930s. The natural stone theater seats 3,750 people and often fills for its annual Mountain Play, which has been performed each spring since 1913. Pantoll Road, which will get you to the Mountain Theater, also intersects with Ridgecrest Boulevard, leading the remainder of the way to a parking lot and visitor center located near the 2,571-foot summit of Mount Tamalpais.

Camping is limited to 16 developed campsites at **Pantoll Campground**, and at the walk-in **Bootjack Campground**, both of which are available on a first-come, first-served basis. **Steep Ravine Environmental Campground** has six walk-in campsites that sit on a knoll overlooking the Pacific Ocean. In the same area, ten **rustic cabins**—each equipped with wooden bunks, a table, and a wood stove—occupy the opposite side of the same knoll, with gorgeous views that look north toward Stinson Beach. There is access to the rocky beach below the cabins. You must bring your own firewood, cooking equipment, and sleeping bags. Water is provided from outdoor faucets. Also found outside the cabins are shared primitive toilet facilities. The cabins are very popular and generally require reservations well in advance. Reservations: 800.444.7275 or www.ReserveAmerica.com

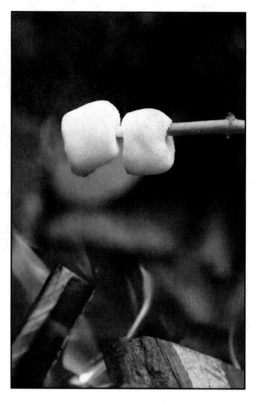

The reconstructed **Gravity Barn** is something not to miss. From 1896 to 1930, visitors to Mt. Tam came via a steam locomotive that traversed 8 miles of track (known as the **Crookedest Railroad in the World**) in order to reach the half-mile-high summit. There they had dinner, enjoyed the views, and when time came to depart, the bravest souls boarded the Gravity Car that would fly down the mountain, making 281 turns, finally reaching the Mill Valley Depot at the bottom. The Gravity Car no longer runs, but the barn and a replica of the car are on display at the top of the mountain. The barn is open on most weekends.

Activities: Hiking, fishing, picnicking, camping, and theater during spring and summer

Dates: Open daily—top of the mountain closes at sunset

Fees: There are camping and day-use fees.

Closest town: Stinson Beach

Info: Mount Tamalpais State Park, 801 Panoramic Highway, Mill Valley, CA 94941, 415.388.2070 or www.parks.ca.gov

TRAILS

There are more than 50 miles of extensively used trails within the park and some of them connect with 700 miles of surrounding trails on adjacent public lands. Many of the trails are short, but connect with so many other trails along the way that you can easily plan much longer hikes. The park's Pantoll Ranger Station is an excellent place to obtain maps and directions to trailheads. The nonprofit Friends of Mt. Tam (www.FiendsofMtTam.org) provides hike schedules.

The **Pantoll to Mountain Theater Trail** offers a 2-mile loop that begins at the Pantoll Ranger Station parking lot and winds up the ridge for 1 mile, with a 600-foot elevation gain to the CCC-era Mountain Theater. The trail provides excellent views of the Pacific Ocean toward Stinson Beach. The trail loops back down the **Old Mine Trail** to the parking lot, affording views of San Francisco Bay and Mount Tamalpais.

The **Pantoll to Old Mine Trail to Dipsea Trail to Steep Ravine to Pantoll** is a 3.5-mile loop that requires more of a workout, but also includes passages

through a redwood canyon. The trail, which departs from the Pantoll Ranger Station, offers many coastal viewpoints during its 1,000-foot elevation change.

The **Mount Tamalpais Peak Trail** is actually made up of a series of trails. It begins at the Pantoll Ranger Station and initially climbs 600 feet and 1 mile to the Mountain Theater. From here, take the **Rock Springs Trail** across the south-facing serpentine slope to hike the old right-of-way for the "The Crookedest Railroad in the World," which was an early 19th century tourist train route to the Mt. Tam summit. Follow the old track bed to the top of the 2,571-foot-high mountain. It's an 8.5-mile round-trip.

Hiking at Mount Tamalpais

John Muir

John Muir has been called many things, including "the father of National Parks" and "the patron saint of the American wilderness." Muir's first trip to California was in 1868—overwhelmed by this experience, this self-taught naturalist dedicated his life to exploring and protecting the Sierra Nevada.

A philosopher, scientist, and author, Muir was born on April 21, 1838 in Dunbar, Scotland. His family immigrated to the United States in 1849, settling near Portage, Wisconsin. Muir developed an early interest in nature and following three years at the University of Wisconsin, he left, preferring instead to enter what he called the "University of the Wilderness."

Muir traveled extensively around the world, including a 1,000-mile walk from Indianapolis to the Gulf of Mexico, always spending time alone and contemplating nature and man. In 1868, he walked across the San Joaquin Valley, later writing: "Then it seemed to me the Sierra should be called not the Nevada, or Snowy Range, but the Range of Light...the most divinely beautiful of all the mountain chains I have ever seen." This love affair with the Sierra would never waver and he returned there often.

His prolific writings and unbound love of nature helped create Yosemite National Park in 1890. In 1892, Muir and others founded the Sierra Club to "do something for wilderness and make the mountains glad." Muir's reputation also attracted the attention of President Theodore Roosevelt. Muir and Roosevelt traveled to Yosemite in 1903 and lay beneath the trees where they discussed and planned the essentials of many of Roosevelt's future conservation programs. Muir also helped in the creation of Mount Rainier, Sequoia, and Grand Canyon national parks. Muir remained an active conservationist and president of the Sierra Club until his death in 1914.

John Muir

MUIR WOODS NATIONAL MONUMENT

This relatively small, 560-acre park is very popular with summer tourists, especially those driving from San Francisco who want to experience a redwood forest. Anytime of the year is a good time to visit, with spring bringing its profusion of wildflowers, including the large, white blooms of the California buckeye (*Aesculus californica*). It's always nice to see the showy leaves of the bigleaf maple (*Acer macrophyllum*) open in spring because it is a reminder that in the fall, they will add wonderful splashes of brilliant yellow to the forest.

Coastal redwoods

What the park is best known for is its redwoods. The largest trees, both in height and diameter, grow in the **Cathedral** and **Bohemian groves**. At 14 feet across, 250 feet tall, and 1,000 years old, they are impressive, but are only teenagers when compared with their cousins in the redwood groves farther north in Humboldt County.

In April 1945, several months prior to the end of World War II, Muir Woods hosted 500 visiting delegates representing 50 nations of the newly formed United Nations for a special memorial honoring the late President Franklin D. Roosevelt. Held at Cathedral Grove, the delegates paid tribute to Roosevelt, who coined the term "United Nations" and was instrumental in the international group's creation. Unfortunately, the President passed away three weeks before the U.N.'s first meeting, held in San Francisco.

Although chipmunks and squirrels are most often seen, many different animals live among the coast redwoods (*Sequoia sempervirens*), Douglas fir (*Pseudotsuga menziesii*), and other trees. Black-tailed deer (*Odocoileus hemionus* spp.) and spotted owls (*Strix occidentalis*) are rarely seen, while numerous species of butterflies—including migrating monarchs (*Danaus plexippus*) and the acmon blue butterfly (*Plebejus acmon)*—are much more numerous and visible.

The national monument was created in 1905, when Congressman William Kent and his wife Elizabeth purchased the property because it contained some of the last remaining uncut old-growth redwoods in the Bay Area. They paid $45,000

Mendocino / Sonoma / Marin

for the original 295 acres, then donated the land to the federal government in order to assure its continued protection from logging. In 1908, President Theodore Roosevelt declared the property a national monument and wanted to name it after Kent. Kent had another idea, preferring that it bear the name of one of the country's leading preservationists of the time—John Muir.

On summer weekends, when up to 10,000 people may visit the park in a single day, it's good to arrive early because the small parking lot and the roadside shoulders fill quickly. There are no picnicking or camping facilities in the park. Also, vehicles more than 35 feet long are prohibited.

Activities: Hiking, bird watching
Facilities: Visitor center, paved walking trail
Dates: Open daily
Fees: There is an entry fee.
Closest town: Mill Valley
Info: Muir Woods National Monument, Mill Valley, CA 94941, 415.388.2595 or www.nps.gov

SAUSALITO

Sausalito is one of several small towns often overlooked by travelers, whose focus is generally on San Francisco. It is a wonderfully quaint town filled with shops and restaurants along its main street, which parallels the waterfront.

Dig more than a few inches below today's sidewalks, paved roads, and parking lots to find Indian middens—ancient mounds of buried shells and artifacts that are reminders of the Coast Miwok who first inhabited this region. The Indians' name for this area was *Lewan Helowah*, or West Wind. When the Spanish arrived in 1775,

they saw the abundance of clams, abalone, shrimp, and salmon, along with deer, elk, and bear, and immediately considered this to be a paradise. The Spanish called the area *Saucito* (Little Willow) because of all the small willows that grew along the nearby streams. The name was slowly Americanized to Sausalito.

Sausalito Harbor and the Golden Gate Bridge

126

William Richardson, an English seaman, married the daughter of the Commandante of Mexico's San Francisco Presidio. It was common for English and American men to marry Mexican women during Mexico's control of California. As a result of his marriage, Richardson was given a 20,000-acre land grant in today's Marin County, where he built his home near Sausalito's present downtown. He lost his land holdings in poor business deals, helped along by dishonest lawyers. In 1868, the land was sold to the Sausalito Land & Ferry Company, which laid out streets and subdivided the central waterfront into view lots. The ferry service was soon replaced by a rail line that attracted even more people to what had become a major transportation hub.

Even at this early date, Sausalito was becoming a community for San Francisco's rich and elite who built beautiful summer homes on the hillsides and moored their yachts in one of the harbor's yacht clubs. Their elegant lifestyles contrasted sharply with the working class who lived on the town's outskirts or in the cheap boarding houses. But it was the Portuguese boat builders and fisherman, Italian and German merchants, and Chinese railroad workers who made Sausalito a vibrant, lively town.

When the Golden Gate Bridge was finished in 1937, causing the town's train and ferry services to fold, Sausalito's importance as a transportation hub for goods and people moved to San Francisco. Seemingly doomed to obscurity, Sausalito bounced back to life with World War II's need for construction of Liberty Ships—its Marin shipyard closed on September 18, 1945, having launched 93 vessels.

The World War II Liberty Ship *SS Jeremiah O'Brien* is docked in San Francisco.

With world peace declared, the town returned to its pre-war size. As the 1950s descended upon Sausalito, the creative element of society—the writers, artists, and philosophers—discovered this retreat, with its low rent and warm climate. Some people claim there remains a bohemian aura among the small colony of artists and writers. Today, those creative intellects who call Sausalito home have been joined by urban escapees, software developers, bankers, and Hollywood stars.

Bridgeway, the town's main street, follows the shoreline of the bay as it winds along the base of the high bluff on the west. Driving, or better yet, walking its several blocks is the best way to enjoy most of what Sausalito has to offer. At the south end of the marina, near **Plaza Viña del Mar** there is a small visitor center where information and maps can be obtained, including a printed walking tour guide that is worth purchasing.

The **Sausalito Yacht Harbor** is one of the most intriguing such facilities anywhere. Tied here are watercraft ranging from ocean-going yachts worth millions to remarkably luxurious houseboats that serve as permanent homes for their owners.

Enjoying the view

Ark Row is a half-block west from the yacht harbor and a short walk down a wooden footpath. The small, flat-bottomed bungalows along the shore, some dating from the 19th century, were used as floating, year-round homes by artists and writers. Others, generally more elaborate than these that remain today, were used as floating summer vacation homes and winter duck hunting blinds by the rich. When not in use, especially during winter, they were dragged onto shore.

In 1893, the **Walhalla**, a German beer garden, was located at the south end of town, near the corner of Bridgeway and Second Street. During Prohibition, it was rumored that bootleg whiskey was smuggled up from under its pier supports through a trap door behind the bar. In 1950, well-known San Francisco madam Sally Stanford, looking for a more acceptable line of work, transformed the old edifice into an elaborate Victorian structure she renamed the **Valhalla**. It soon became a well-respected restaurant and bar for the Bay area elite. The site has since been occupied by different restaurants that have come and gone.

Info: Sausalito Chamber of Commerce, 1913 Bridgeway, Sausalito, CA 94966, 415.331.7262 or www.sausalito.org

BAY MODEL VISITOR CENTER

The streams and rivers that merge and finally empty into San Francisco Bay drain 40 percent of all California's fresh water. The intricate web of wetlands, estuaries, deltas, bays, tidal, and river flow rates are intimately connected, so much so that a single change in one area can have significant effects elsewhere, and not always for the best.

In an effort to better understand how this massive water system interacts, the U.S. Army Corps of Engineers constructed a scale model. It's not your typical model because this one covers a full 1.5 acres, all inside a World War II-era building used during the Liberty Ship construction. Also, it is the only model of this size in the world that can track river flows, tidal differences, and visually show how changes—such as water diversions, bottom dredging, or wetland fill projects—can affect other parts of the system.

Even though most of this geographic area is commonly referred to as San Francisco Bay, it's actually a collection of three bays and the Golden Gate, and at 72,000 acres, the largest remaining tidal wetland in California. As large of an area as the bays cover—350 square miles total—only about 20 percent is more than 30 feet deep. The deepest—at 110 feet—is the **Carquinez Strait** that connects San Pablo and Suisun bays. Much of the delta is less than 15 feet deep, with the shallowness created during the late 19th century when hydraulic gold mining in the Sierra washed millions of cubic yards of silt down the rivers, filling about 30 percent

San Francisco Bay from the Presidio

of the bay. Each tidal cycle brings approximately 1.5 million acre-feet of saltwater in and out of the Golden Gate, while 50,000 acre-feet of fresh water flows in from rivers. An acre-foot is equal to 43,560 cubic feet or the amount of water it takes to fill an acre to a depth of one foot.

The facility tour is self-guided, with a short introduction video available at the start of the tour. Walkways allow easy viewing of the different parts of the model, which is constructed in a horizontal scale of 1 foot = 1,000 feet and a vertical scale of 1 foot = 100 feet. During water-flow experiments, the difference between the vertical and horizontal scales is compensated for with small copper tabs strategically placed to slow the water's movement. It's a fascinating look at a very complex natural system.

Dates: Open Tuesdays through Saturdays
Fees: None
Closest town: Sausalito
Info: Bay Model Visitor Center, 2100 Bridgeway, Sausalito, CA 94965, 415.332.3871 or www.spn.usace.army.mil

SAN PABLO BAY NATIONAL WILDLIFE REFUGE

San Pablo Bay shares much of the same history with its more glamorous neighbor, San Francisco Bay, but also has its own stories to tell. Its rich waters, surrounding wetlands, and feeding rivers once provided refuge for untold millions of waterfowl, fish, and mammals, many of which are no longer found here. The original wetlands, drained for agricultural uses more than a century ago, have now been converted back to seasonal or tidal wetlands, both critical habitat for resident and migratory birds.

Today, the refuge and adjoining San Pablo Bay support the largest wintering population of canvasbacks (*Aythya valisineria*) on the West Coast. It also protects

Male canvasback

endangered species including the salt marsh harvest mouse (*Reithrodontomys raviventris*) and the California clapper rail (*Rallus longirostris obsoletus*).

For bird-watchers, the refuge is a paradise. Brewer's (*Euphagus cyanocphalus*) and red-winged blackbirds (*Agelaius phoeniceus*) fly in and out of the thick rows of tules that line the highway. Northern harriers (*Circus cyaneus*) fly low over the open lands, searching for squirrels, mice, rabbits, or small birds. They compete with go-pher snakes (*Pituophis melanoleucus*) for many of the same live prey, while turkey vultures (*Cathartes aura*) soar high overhead looking for the same animals, but only when they are dead. Cinnamon teal (*Anas cyanoptera*), mallards (*Anas platy-rhynchos*), northern pintail (*Anas acuta*), and northern shovelers (*Anas clypeata*) are only a few of the migrating waterfowl that spend time feeding and resting in the refuge.

Activities: Bird-watching, photography, seasonal waterfowl hunting
Facilities: None
Dates: Open year-round—check website for nesting related closures
Fees: None
Info: San Pablo Bay National Wildlife Refuge, 2100 California Street, Vallejo, CA 94592, 707.769.4200 or www.fws.gov

Example of Chinese nets at China Camp State Park

CHINA CAMP STATE PARK

This is one of those out-of-the-way places that few people except Bay Area locals ever get far enough off the U.S. 101 freeway to see. The park sits on the southwest edge of **San Pablo Bay** and in addition to its fascinating and sad his-tory, it features more than 1,600 acres of undeveloped hills, one of which offers a 360-degree view of the bay and several north bay counties. On clear days—and there are many because of the protecting hills that generally keep out the fog that invades neighboring San Francisco Bay—**Mount Diablo**, Angel Island, and Mount Tamalpais are also visible.

There are 15 miles of trails in the park and many offer short walks to salt marshes, mud flats, meadows, and up the hills into oak woodlands and a small redwood grove. The park protects the largest, undisturbed watershed in this very developed portion of Marin County. It also provides protected habitat for two endangered species—the salt marsh harvest mouse (*Reithrodontomys raviventris*) and the California clapper rail (*Rallus longirostris obsoletus*).

Fishing boat at China Camp

China Camp State Park is home to numerous animals. Squirrels, deer, and fox live and feed on the hillsides, while large populations of shorebirds search the wetlands for food. The park is also popular for fishing. Striped bass (*Morone saxatilis*) and white sturgeon (*Acipenser transmontanus*) can both be caught when the tide is in.

This land passed from the hands of the Coast Miwok Indians when the Spanish established their missions here in the 19th century. Timoteo Murphy acquired *Rancho San Pedro, Santa Margarita y las Gallinas* as a land grant. Following his death, the property was subdivided, and in 1868, John and George McNear purchased the land now occupied by the park. The McNears grazed cattle, manufactured bricks, and quarried basalt, shipping their products by barge throughout the area.

The park gained its name from the Chinese fishermen who settled here, creating more than 20 villages along the bay. They came to California from the maritime city of Guangzhou (Canton), China, looking for the golden riches that every immigrant expected during the mid-19th century. By the 1880s, there were nearly 500 people living in China Camp, most fishermen, netting grass shrimp. They were catching three million pounds each year then drying and exporting the shrimp to China. Business became so successful and profitable that non-Chinese fishermen pushed for passage of protective legislation. The Chinese Exclusion Act of 1882, which forbid any new Chinese laborers from immigrating to the U.S., marked the decline of China Camp. But a new law in 1911 that outlawed both shrimp exports and the special nets used by the Chinese was the final blow to a very successful fishing industry.

At the park's China Camp Village, remnants of some of the early buildings remain and a small museum exhibit explains the history of the Chinese here.

Activities: Fishing, swimming, hiking, picnicking, 30 walk-in campsites
Dates: Open daily
Fees: There are camping and day-use fees.
Info: Friends of China Camp, 101 Peacock Gap Trail, San Rafael, CA 94901, 415.488.5161, www.FriendsOfChinaCamp.org or www.parks.ca.gov

GOLDEN GATE NATIONAL RECREATION AREA

Golden Gate National Recreation Area is a unique combination of historic military sites, ships, and museums, combined with remote towering cliffs and open bluffs, redwood forests, islands, and sandy beaches. And while much of the recreation area is in and around San Francisco—one of California's most densely populated and popular cities—a large portion also lies in the wilds of Marin County, north of the Golden Gate Bridge. Within its boundary is Muir Woods, Stinson Beach, Marin Headlands, Alcatraz, and the Presidio of San Francisco, along with several historic forts. The national recreation area protects more than 76,000 acres, 1,250 historic structures, and 27 rare and endangered species, while serving 20 million visitors each year. With the Golden Gate Bridge connecting its northern and southern regions, anyone can hike a remote trail in the morning, view migrating hawks and grazing elk in the afternoon, and come evening, dine in some of the world's finest restaurants.

Mendocino / Sonoma / Marin

HAWK HILL

Like many bird species, raptors also migrate when changing weather reduces their food supplies below acceptable limits. Each fall, as temperatures drop and the days grow shorter in the higher mountains to the east and north and smaller prey animals slip into hibernation, thousands of raptors begin their southerly migrations to warmer climates.

Osprey with a fish in its talons

Most raptors are terrestrial hunters and prefer not to fly over large bodies of water. Therefore, as they migrate down California's coast, the Pacific Ocean forces them to stay inland. As they approach Marin, they are squeezed to the west by the sprawling open waters and wetlands of San Pablo Bay. The result is that thousands of hawks, turkey vultures, and a few eagles are funneled over the Marin Headlands before they cross San Francisco Bay at its narrowest opening, the Golden Gate.

The migration season runs roughly from September through November and during those three months, more than 20,000 birds of prey will pass through this very narrow corridor. Red-tailed hawks (*Buteo jamaicensis*) make up the largest number of birds, with an average of nearly 7,000 passing overhead. Sharp-shinned hawks (*Accipiter striatus*), Cooper's hawks (*Accipiter cooperii*), and turkey vultures (*Cathartes aura*) also pass over in large numbers. American kestrels (*Falco sparverius*), prairie falcons (*Falco mexicanus*), red-shouldered hawks (*Buteo lineagtus*), broad-winged hawks (*Buteo platypterus*), and a few ferruginous hawks (*Buteo regalis*) also are seen.

Sightings of golden eagles (*Aquila chrysaetos*) are rarer, with only an occasional bald eagle (*Haliaeetus leucocephalus*) crossing at the Golden Gate.

During September and October, **Golden Gate Raptor Observatory** docents offer free public programs on weekend afternoons at the summit of Hawk Hill. To reach Hawk Hill from the north end of the Golden Gate Bridge, drive west on Conzelman Road for 1.8 miles and look for the brown and white "Hawk Hill" sign. Park on the side of the road before it becomes a one-way road, and then walk the few hundred feet up the ocean side of Hawk Hill to the flat summit.

Closest town: San Francisco or Sausalito

Info: Golden Gate Raptor Observatory, Building 201, Fort Mason, San Francisco, CA 94123, 415.331.0730 or www.parksconservancy.org. Raptor hotline recording: 415.561.3030, ext. 2500

MARIN HEADLANDS

From a distance, the Marin Headlands and the lands behind them appear as reddish-brown hills, essentially devoid of plant life except for a few small pockets of green. Nothing could be farther from the truth. The headlands' geology is laid open for inspection and that story helps explain its modern appearance. The Marin Headlands block began its existence 100 million years ago in the depths of the Pacific Ocean far to the south, and it has slowly moved to its present location, sliding along the San Andreas fault.

Marin Headlands

At the north end of the Golden Gate Bridge from San Francisco, take the first exit, which swings under the freeway and back onto the west side of the bridge and Conzieman Road. There's a pullout at Battery Spencer and additional pullouts farther down the road that offer spectacular views and great photo opportunities looking back across the Golden Gate toward San Francisco, at least on clear, fogless days.

Check the rocks in the road cuts or hike down to **Rodeo Cove** or **Tennessee Cove** and look closely at the reddish rock formations. Through a hand lens or strong magnifier, the remnants of small, one-celled organisms that lived in the ancient ocean are visible. These radiolarians—now transformed into radiolarian chert— were originally laid down with layers

Indian paintbrush

of equally ancient mud, but over millions of years have been severely contorted by tremendous pressures and movement. Over the past several thousand years, the chert cliffs have been broken, eroded, and constantly reformed by the unending crash of waves. One road cut along Conzieman Road, west from the **Battery Spencer** overlook, has a wonderful example of relatively rare ribbon chert, easily recognized by its thin, ribbon-like strands of twisted and contorted rock.

Conzieman Road, from near the long-abandoned **Battery 129** (an artillery site), becomes a one-way road. Continue ahead and the road winds past both **Battery Wallace** and **Battery Mendell**, which are also long-abandoned coastal defenses. The road finally leads to the historic **Fort Barry Chapel**, which has been transformed into a visitor center. It's the perfect place to get maps and books about the area's natural and cultural history, along with ranger- and docent-led hike information.

An interesting leftover from the early days of the Cold War is the closed **Nike missile site**. It's only one of the many visual reminders of the Army's long presence on the headlands and the evolution of weapons, from 19th century smooth-bore cannons to World War II's 16-inch guns and anti-aircraft weapons, and finally to the underground Nike missiles of the Cold War. Each weapon system significantly extended the range that attacking enemy ships or aircraft could be engaged and destroyed. Today, guided tours of the site are available, including a demonstration alert that rolls and lifts one of the disarmed and unfueled missiles into firing position.

Over many years, ranchers and the Army built small dams in headland stream-beds, which created lagoons by joining small natural pools and ponds. The lagoons have become important habitat for numerous species of animals. Near the visitor center, **Rodeo Lagoon** is the largest of the water impoundments. There's a trail around the lagoon, which is mostly fresh water, except when high waves occasionally wash over the sand barrier that separates it from the ocean. Within Rodeo Lagoon's slightly saline waters lives the endangered tidewater goby (*Eucyclogobius newberryi*), which is only about 1 inch long. During spring and summer, most of the ponds are impossible to get close to because of the heavy growth of alders (*Alnus rhombifolia*), arroyo willows (*Salix lasiolepis*), and the ever-present cattails (*Typha latifolia*) and sedges (*Carex* sp.).

Nike missile site and Rodeo Lagoon

Some of the best hiking is along the trails that follow the main waterways—**Tennessee Creek** and **Rodeo Creek**. Here, the presence of water in a relatively dry land, especially during California's rainless summers, supports a large variety of plant life. The profusion of vegetation along the creeks and on the surrounding hillsides provides cover and food for dozens of animal and insect species. Butterflies are a bright addition to the spring wildflowers that cover the landscape. Orange sulfers (*Colias eurytheme*) are attracted to yellow mustard, swallowtails favor lupine and fennel, and the endangered mission blue butterfly (*Icaricia icarioides missionensis*) searches for lupine.

Brewer's blackbirds (*Euphaus cyanocephalus*) and sparrows favor the thick creekside vegetation, while brown towhees (*Pipilo fuscus*) and wrentits (*Chamaea fasciata*) are more likely to be seen in the coastal scrub. Hawks almost always soar overhead or sit on fences or power poles, especially during the fall migration. The always-present and seemingly ominous (but environmentally important) turkey vulture (*Cathartes aura*) uses its 6-foot wingspan to soar effortlessly on the thermals, depending upon its keen eyesight to locate dead animals on which to feed.

The Marin Headlands lie on the north side of the Golden Gate Bridge, west of U.S. 101. The easiest access is from Conzeiman Road, the first exit after crossing the

Golden Gate Bridge, from San Francisco and heading north. Leaving the park is another matter, as you can't reverse your course. To exit the park, from the visitor center at Fort Barry, pick up Bunker Road. The road winds through more of the open country, finally reaching a one-way tunnel controlled by a signal light that allows alternating traffic to pass.

Activities: Hiking, camping, picnicking, fishing
Facilities: Visitor center
Dates: Fort Barry Visitor Center is open daily.
Fees: None
Closest town: Sausalito
Info: National Park Service, Fort Mason Building 201, San Francisco, CA 94129, 415.561.4700 or www.nps.gov

Mendocino / Sonoma / Marin

TRAILS

There are dozens of miles of trails that lace the Marin Headlands and offer spectacular views of San Francisco Bay, the city beyond, and the Pacific Ocean. They also provide opportunities to explore deep canyons and hidden ponds. It is best to pick up a trail map from any of the visitor centers and dress for quickly changing weather conditions during any month of the year.

Approximately 0.75-mile of the **Miwok Trail** follows the north shore of **Rodeo Lagoon**, beginning on the north side of Rodeo Creek, near the visitor center at Fort Barry. It connects with another trail that continues around the sand barrier separating the Pacific Ocean from Rodeo Lagoon, passing the old Nike missile site, and finally returning to near the visitor center. The Miwok Trail actually meanders north about 15 miles, ending in Mount Tamalpais State Park and connects with the Redwood Creek Trail near Muir Woods Road.

The **Bobcat Trail** picks up from the east end of the Miwok Trail, about 0.3

miles northeast of the Fort Barry Visitor Center and continues on the south side of **Rodeo Creek** approximately 3.2 miles, heading up into the hills. It connects with several other trails, including the **Oakwood Trail, S.C.A. Trail**, and a 1.5-mile spur trail to the **Hawk Backpack Camping Area**.

From the parking area near Battery Wallace, it's about 1 mile out to the Point Bonita Lighthouse via the **Point Bonita Trail**. The lighthouse is open Saturday through Monday from 12:30 P.M. to 3:30 P.M.

California red-legged frog

MARINE MAMMAL CENTER

For a close-up view of marine mammals, the Marine Mammal Center is a must-see destination. Located on the Marin Headlands in the Golden Gate National Recreation Area, the center's focus is rescuing and rehabbing sick and injured marine mammals. The center's staff and more than 600 volunteers closely monitor 600 miles of northern and central coast shoreline, safely capturing injured mammals for rehabilitation and release. Since 1975, the center has rescued more than 18,000 animals.

When visiting, it's recommended you take advantage of one of the docent-led tours where you will learn much more about the center's work. If that's not possible, a self-guided tour can be almost as informative, where you will see exhibits and many interesting areas of the center. If you're lucky, there may be a patient—from a sea lion to an elephant seal to a sea otter—being cared for. Take a peek in the fish kitchen to see food being prepared for the patients, visit the chart room and the lab, and if you promise to be very, very, very quiet, you may be allowed to visit the upper viewing deck that overlooks the pools where the recovering animals are kept. There are usually docents around to answer questions.

Activities: tours, exhibits, special programs
Facilities: visitor information center
Dates: Open daily, 10 A.M. to 5 P.M., closed Thanksgiving, Christmas, and New Year's Day.
Fees: Free self-guided tours, fee for audio and docent-led tours
Closest town: Sausalito
Info: The Marine Mammal Center, 2000 Bunker Road, Fort Cronkhite, Sausalito, CA 94965, 415.289.7325 or www.marinemammalcenter.org

Harbor seals

138

California Coastal Trail

The vision for a trail that followed California's entire coastline was made official in 1972 when California voters passed Proposition 20. This proposition recommended that a system of trails—from Oregon to Mexico—be created along the entire coast. The California Coastal Conservancy adopted the project as part of their responsibility for enhancing coastal resources.

In 1987, a dedicated group of trail enthusiasts created the nonprofit group Coastwalk California (www.CoastWalk.org) and, working with the California Coastal Conservancy and the Coastal Commission, took on the role of actively promoting and identifying sections of what will ultimately become a 1,200-mile long trail. Today, about 600 miles of the trail have been identified or constructed.

The California Coastal Trail is unique for a long distance trail. It will never be a single contiguous trail, but instead, a series of trails. These trails will cross public beaches and meander around parcels of private property and restricted government properties, such air force and naval bases. Depending on the trail's city or county location, the trail can be a paved street, roadway, sidewalk, accessible walkway or paved bike trail. It could also be a pedestrian trail, sandy beach, equestrian trail and a hiking or mountain biking trail of dirt and rock.

In addition to exploring portions of the Coastal Trail on your own, there are dozens of organized one-day and multiple-day hikes available each year. For updated maps and directions: www.CaliforniaCoastalTrail.info

San Francisco and San Mateo Counties

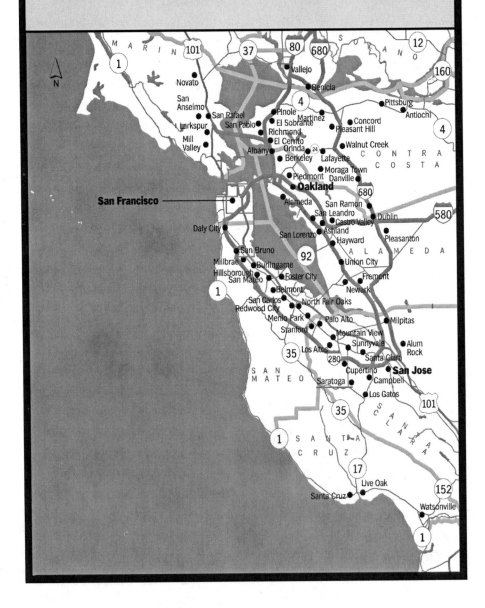

San Francisco and San Mateo Counties

The pastoral setting that marks most lands north of San Francisco Bay disappears as you cross over the Golden Gate and pass through the tollbooths at the south end of the bridge. Among the museums, skyscrapers, shops, and restaurants that help define the city, there are parks filled with gardens and forests and miles of open beaches. San Francisco's streets that traverse breathtakingly steep hills are legendary, as are the streetcars and Fisherman's Wharf.

Continue driving on Highway 1 as it heads south out of San Francisco, and the businesses and homes that crowd to the edges of the freeway soon give way to open mountains and craggy cliffs that drop directly into the Pacific Ocean. Highway 1 follows the coastline very closely here, with only a few small towns to mark the open lands used mostly for cattle grazing—when it is usable at all.

141

City and County of San Francisco

THE PRESIDIO OF SAN FRANCISCO

For more than 200 years, the Presidio of San Francisco has stood as a sentry under three national flags, guarding the entrance into San Francisco Bay. The Spanish built the first protective outpost here, a modest adobe-walled compound, in 1776. They added a larger adobe fort in 1779, overlooking the bay's entrance. Under Spanish and Mexican rule, several bronze cannons were added to the fort's defense arsenal. Many are still on the Presidio grounds, including the oldest known cannons in North America, cast in 1679 and 1693.

When Mexico gained its independence from Spain in 1821, the new government occupied the Presidio, considering it an important defensive point. Mexico abandoned the Presidio in July 1846 when the U.S. sloop *Portsmouth* landed a contingent of marines and occupied both San Francisco and the Presidio. The U.S. military officially established a full-time military reservation here in 1850.

In 1883, Major William A. Jones proposed changing the Presidio's barren hillsides into forests that would "crown the ridges…and cover the areas of sand and marsh." Over the next 20 years, the military planted 400,000 tree seedlings of pine, cypress, and eucalyptus, often in orderly, military-like rows. As the Army transformed the landscape and constructed buildings to meet its ever-increasing

The Presidio is home to a regional NPS visitor center and dozens of historic buildings.

needs, it was generally the officers who were the first to benefit from the improvements: "I went to the Presidio…where the soldiers live in barracks and tents. There are beautiful residences where the officers live and a wide cement drive where automobiles and carriages go, with dirt roads for the cavalry," wrote author Laura Ingalls Wilder in 1915.

San Francisco Bay

In spite of its name and a widespread belief, San Francisco Bay is not a true bay, but rather California's largest estuary. Its waters are very shallow, with 70 percent being less than 18 feet deep at low tide. Sixteen rivers, the two largest being the Sacramento and San Joaquin, drain more than 60,000 square miles and run into the estuary to mix and dilute the sea water that is washed in and out by strong tides and winds.

Hydraulic gold mining operations during the late 19th century began filling San Francisco Bay's original 720 square miles of open water. Hydraulic mining was outlawed in 1884 because its sediment waste was filling waterways and causing catastrophic flooding of towns and farmlands that bordered the rivers. Yet developers continued filling the bay well into modern times in order to create new land for development of businesses, airports, and freeways. Adding to the loss of wildlife habitat were the large portions of the shallow south bay that were diked and used as salt ponds. Today, the bay is just 480 square miles of open water and wetlands.

San Francisco Bay attracts 70 percent of the millions of waterfowl and shorebirds that migrate up and down the Pacific Flyway annually. For millions of other birds, the bay's mud flats, sloughs, and salt marshes serve as homes year-round. Brown pelicans (*Pelecanus occidentalis*), greater scaups (*Aythya marila*), mallards (*Anas platyrhynchos*), northern shovelers (*Anas clypeata*), great blue herons (*Ardea herodias*), and numerous species of gulls are common during different times of the year. Explore the waters of the tidal sloughs and, besides the all-important cordgrass (*Spartina foliosa*), mussels, snails, shrimp, bat rays (*Myliobatis californica*), leopard sharks (*Triakis semifasciata*), and harbor seals (*Phoca vitulina*) create a rich and productive milieu. Dig out just two handfuls of mud from the bay's mud flats and 40,000 microscopic organisms, the building blocks of this entire ecosystem, are present.

Mussels are found along the California coast, including San Francisco Bay.

San Francisco National Military Cemetery

As the Presidio became more vital to the defense of the West Coast, barracks replaced tents for the enlisted men and comfortable and lavish Victorian homes were soon added for higher-ranking officers. Many other buildings were added, including a hospital and fire station.

Today, the Presidio of San Francisco is a national park, with tree-lined streets and many of the historic structures restored. There is a 1-mile, self-guided trail that leads past a dozen stops on the main Presidio grounds. The **Presidio Visitor Center** has guide pamphlets available and is located on Montgomery Street, across from the main parade ground.

Within the Presidio's 1,480 acres lie many historic buildings and other sites: **Crissy Field** (the first airfield on the West Coast), **Fort Point,** the **San Francisco National Military Cemetery**, and the historic cavalry stables. The Presidio grounds are a favorite place for bicyclists, in-line skaters, walkers, and joggers.

Activities: Hiking, biking, in-line skating, sight-seeing, fishing
Facilities: Historic buildings, visitor center, the Walt Disney Family Museum
Dates: Historic grounds open year-round; visitor center open Thursday-Sunday, 10 A.M. to 4 P.M.
Fees: NPS facilities are free; parking meters, Walt Disney Family Museum charges an admission fee
Info: Golden Gate National Recreation Area, Presidio, Fort Mason, Building 201, San Francisco, CA 94123, 415.561.4323 or www.nps.gov

FORT POINT

Although the fort never came under attack, the Pacific Command saw Fort Point as the key to western defenses. But as smooth-bore cannons were replaced by more powerful and accurate breach-loading rifled guns, it became apparent that masonry fortresses could not stand up to modern artillery attacks. Over the next few years, the old guns were removed from the fort, and other uses—from barracks to a World War II anti-submarine net guard unit—were found.

With waves crashing into the granite seawall at its base, the old, three-story brick fort is an architectural delight. Visitors can wander throughout the structure, up dark staircases all the way to the top deck that once held some of the 69 artillery pieces that were placed in the fort. The fort never mounted all of its planned 141 guns, but it did acquire several 10-inch Rodman guns for the lower casemates. They could fire a 128-pound solid steel shot up to 2 miles. To give you an idea of how far this is, with approaches, the length of the Golden Gate Bridge is 1.7 miles.

Today, most of the cannons are gone, but several similar guns are displayed on the ground floor inside the fort. There's a great view of the bay from the top of the fort's walls—known as the barbette tier—where the old, rusting gun mounts remain. The fort's three spiral stairways are intriguing. They don't have central columns for support; instead, they rely on the weight of the 1,000 pound, hand-cut granite steps sitting on top of one another to hold the stairway structure in place.

Ft. Point beneath the Golden Gate Bridge

Activities: Tours, including audio tours
Facilities: Small visitor center, bookstore, theater
Dates: Open Thursday through Tuesday (closed Wednesday)
Fees: None
Closest town: San Francisco
Info: Golden Gate National Recreation Area, Fort Mason, Building 201, San Francisco, CA 94123, 415.556.1693 or www.nps.gov

SAN FRANCISCO BAY'S ISLANDS

The changing level of the ocean, strong tidal flows, two great rivers that drain much of the Sierra Nevada, and 300,000 years of shifting tectonic plates created the islands that jut skyward from San Francisco Bay and others located a few miles outside of the bay. The advance of the rising ocean through the relatively narrow gorge—named the "Golden Gate" by John Fremont—flooded the lower valleys and hills eastward to the straits of Carquinez, leaving only the tops of the highest

San Francisco / San Mateo

145

eroded hills visible. Two of these remnant hilltops are prominent, with Alcatraz Island being the most well known, although Angel Island certainly has played a much more important role in California's history. Alcatraz is part of the Golden Gate National Recreation Area, while Angel Island is a California State Park.

ALCATRAZ ISLAND

The Spanish named this place *Isla de los Alcatraces* (Island of the Pelicans), but had no use for it. Native Americans probably first visited Angel Island and Alcatraz Island as early as 10,000 to 20,000 years ago, but only Angel Island offered any sheltering trees or freshwater. The Ohlone Indians (Ohlone was a Miwok Indian word meaning "western people"), who inhabited much of the area around and to the south of San Francisco Bay, probably gathered bird eggs from the desolate rock, but there was never any attempt to establish a permanent settlement.

Permanent settlement of the island didn't occur until the U.S. Army began building gun emplacements in the mid-19th century. The U.S. military saw the island as crucial to the overall defense of San Francisco Bay and thus, California. The Army hauled dirt from Angel Island during the construction of its initial gun emplacements, but their attempts to grow grass and clover on the island's poor soil failed.

The Army continued adding soil, and within a few years, better-adapted native plants, such as coyote brush (*Baccharis pilularis*), California poppies (*Eschscholzia californica*), and blackberries (*Rubus ursinus*) finally gained footholds in the soil. During the 1860s, workers blasted pits in the rock and filled them with soil, getting

Alcatraz Island

trees and other larger vegetation to grow, with beautiful formal gardens finally being maintained by the 1880s. By the early 1900s, the land around the island's military buildings had been transformed into a multicolored garden.

San Francisco's importance to the Union was aptly illustrated by the platforms for 155 guns that were constructed on the island, including 6- , 8-, and 10-inch Solumbiad cannons mounted on wooden carriages. The Army also placed some of the Civil War's largest guns on the island, including the 15-inch Rodman that could fire its 440-pound shot 3 miles. The island's guns fired only one shot during the Civil War and that was at a British ship that had initially failed to identify itself.

The Civil War started what would become Alcatraz's most well-known use—it served as a prison for

The "C-block" inside Alcatraz

Army and Navy officers who refused to swear allegiance to the Union. They were followed by Southern sympathizers in California who unwisely spoke too loudly about their loyalties to the Confederate States. Something as simple as a drunken toast to Jefferson Davis, President of the Confederate States of America, landed people in what was quickly gaining a reputation as a harsh prison. Military prisoners broke rock all day while dragging around 24-pound iron balls chained to their legs, which were meant to discourage escape attempts. Civil War prisoners were followed by Spanish American War prisoners in 1898. The growing use of Alcatraz as a prison prompted additional construction of concrete cellblocks and other facilities.

The military finally abandoned Alcatraz as a prison in 1933, no longer willing to pay the high costs of maintaining and supplying the island. It was then that FBI Director J. Edgar Hoover agreed to take over the prison. It met his need for a "super prison," capable of handling the most dangerous and infamous criminals that his agents were capturing. The following year it was formally named "United States Penitentiary, Alcatraz."

Some of its first "super-prisoners" included Al "Scarface" Capone and "Machine Gun" Kelly, although it was always the prison administration's policy to never announce, confirm, or deny which prisoners were on the "Rock." Such secrecy, coupled with horror stories from released prisoners (one called it the "island of the living dead"), added both mystery and a sense of fear, further enhancing Alcatraz's reputation as the harshest prison in the country. Others, including both guards and prisoners, disagreed with that assessment.

Alcatraz cellblock and guard tower

Attorney General Robert Kennedy closed the facility on March 21, 1963, ending its 29 years as a federal prison. Kennedy closed it for the same reason as the Army—the aged and crumbling facility was much too costly to maintain. Plans to transform the abandoned prison into a national park were interrupted by the Native American Indian occupation that began in November 1969 and didn't end until June 1971. While the occupation brought much needed attention to Native American issues, portions of the old prison's historic fabric were damaged or destroyed during the occupation.

The National Park Service assumed control of the island soon after the Indian occupation, and it became part of the new **Golden Gate National Recreation Area**. The first public tours began in 1973.

Alcatraz isn't all military and prison history. The island is a refuge for a wide variety of plants and wildlife. Its tide pools are man-made, established on jagged piles of rock, granite, brick, concrete, and other debris that has been dumped on the island's shore for more than 100 years. Anemones, sea stars, and other common tide pool animals thrive in the waters around the island. On land, animals range from California slender salamanders (*Batrachoseps attenuatus*) and deer mice (*Peromyscus maniculatus*) to about two dozen bird species. They include brown pelicans (*Pelecanus occidentalis*), peregrine falcons (*Falco peregrinus*), barn swallows (*Hirundo rustica*), black-crowned night herons (*Nycticorax nycticorax*), and red-throated loons (*Gavia stellata*).

The views of San Francisco are wonderful from Alcatraz, but walking the island is work. The island is not flat, so wear comfortable walking shoes. It's a quarter-mile walk from the island's dock to the prison and the elevation gain (130 feet) is equivelant to climbing to the top of a 13-story building. Even inside the prison, there are additional sets of stairs. For information regarding accessibility, contact the ferry company or National Park Service office. The only way to get to Alcatraz is by ferry via Fisherman's Wharf, Pier 33. Private vessels may not dock at Alcatraz Island.

Activities: Hiking, tours
Facilities: Museum, gift shop
Dates: Open daily, times and frequency of tours vary seasonally

Fees: There is a fee for the ferry crossing, which includes entry onto Alcatraz Island. From April through October, it is advisable to purchase tickets at least three weeks in advance (415.981-ROCK or www.alcatrazcruises.com). During summer and on weekends, allot extra time to find parking in the Fisherman's Wharf area.

Closest town: San Francisco

Info: Golden Gate National Recreation Area Headquarters, Fort Mason, Building 201, San Francisco, CA 94123, 415.561.4323 or www.nps.gov

ANGEL ISLAND STATE PARK

Coast Miwok Indians were the first inhabitants of Angel Island, paddling their tule reed boats across the short channel from the Tiburon mainland and establishing villages near today's **Ayala Cove**. The island's deer, harbor seals, and sea lions, along with ducks, quail, and sea birds, provided plenty of food, especially when combined with acorns and various wild roots and bulbs.

In 1775, Spanish lieutenant Juan Manuel de Ayala sailed into San Francisco Bay and mapped its islands and shoreline, naming the island *Isla de Los Angeles*. Little was done with the island, but the Indians were soon pulled off and moved into the nearby mission. In 1837, the governor of Mexican-controlled California

San Francisco / San Mateo

Ayala Cove is the ferry destination on Angel Island.

149

granted most of Angel Island to Antonio Maria Osio for a cattle ranch, with a portion retained for a potential coastal defense post. In 1846, with the United States in control of California, Osio lost most of his land.

Often known as the "Ellis Island of the West," Angel Island has served the United States as a strategic military post for every conflict since the Civil War. In 1864, the Army began constructing Camp Reynolds and its defensive cannon emplacements. As the military build-up continued through the end of the 19th century, a quarantine station was also established at Ayala Cove. The station fumigated foreign ships entering the port and served as an isolation center for immigrants thought to be carrying contagious diseases.

In 1899, the Army maintained a detention camp for U.S. veterans who had either contracted or had been exposed to contagious diseases. As the Spanish-American War wound down, troops returning from the Philippines during 1901 passed through the island's facilities during their transition from soldier to civilian life.

The **Immigration Station** in today's North Garrison was in operation from 1910 until 1940, and handled primarily Asian immigrants. It carried out one of the island's most historical roles. With the Chinese Exclusion Act of 1882 still in force, Chinese desiring entry into the U.S. were detained here anywhere from a few weeks to two years—the time it took authorities to fully scrutinize and process their applications for entry. Chinese were generally required to have relatives already in the U.S. in order to be admitted—and even that was no guarantee. Prejudice ruled and their stays were full of harassment and stress. During the restoration of the station in 1970, the names of many who passed through the facility an33d the heartfelt poems they wrote were uncovered, written and carved on the inside walls of some of the buildings. Those are visible today.

The early 1900s marked the island's development as a major Army recruit receiving and processing center, primarily in the East Garrison. It included a 600-man barracks and other support facilities. At the beginning of World War

I, the island added a detention center for "enemy aliens," mostly German citizens who were unfortunate enough to be in U.S. ports when the war broke out.

Angel Island was the country's only overseas processing and training

Fog-shrouded Angel Island in the distance

facility prior to the beginning of World War II. It served the only U.S. overseas bases at the time, which were located in the Philippines, Hawaii, and in the Panama Canal Zone. During World War II, portions of Angel Island served as POW camps for Japanese prisoners. It also was as a major defense post, with anti-aircraft guns and searchlights positioned

Sailing around Angel Island

on the top of the mountain. The U.S. military ended most of its uses for the island following the processing of returning GIs after Japan's surrender. Then, in the mid-1950s, the island was identified as an ideal Nike missile site and silos were built on the island. But the defense system was deemed obsolete by 1962 and the silos, deactivated. This was the same time that efforts were underway to make the island a public park.

Today, many of the original military and immigration buildings remain, and the island is ringed by a paved trail that is great for bike riding. Bikes can be brought over on the ferries or rented from an island concessionaire. For the less adventurous, a tram provides tours of the island—or rent a Segway or scooter. There is also a trail to the top of **Mount Livermore**. With the summit 750 feet above the bay, the mountaintop views of the Golden Gate Bridge, San Francisco Bay, and the Bay Bridges—not to mention San Francisco—are awe-inspiring on clear, fogless days. Even on days when fog layers itself across parts of the bay, the view is worth the hike.

Ferry service is the most common way to get to Angel Island. There are numerous daily ferry departures from San Francisco's Pier 39 and Pier 41, located on The Embarcadero near Fisherman's Wharf. Ferry service is also available from Tiburon. But anyone with a boat can use the park's docks and slips. Overnight boat mooring is allowed, but passengers must remain on their boats after the park's day-use hours end.

Activities: Sight-seeing, hiking, biking, bird watching

Facilities: Visitor center, bookstore, restaurant, historic buildings, bike, Segway and scooter rentals

Dates: Open daily

Fees: There is a ferry crossing fee, which includes entry onto Angel Island.

Closest town: San Francisco and Tiburon

Info: Angel Island State Park, PO Box 318, Tiburon, CA 94920, 415.435.5390 or www.parks.ca.gov. Ferry schedules: www.aiisf.org

San Francisco / San Mateo

FARALLON NATIONAL WILDLIFE REFUGE

The refuge is the largest seabird rookery along the eastern Pacific Ocean south of Alaska. Each spring and summer, a quarter million seabirds visit the Farallon Islands' steep cliffs and rocky outcroppings, located 27 miles west of the Golden Gate. Pigeon guillemots (*Cepphus columba*), rhinoceros auklets (*Cerohinca monocerata*), tufted puffins (*Lunda cirrhata*), common murres (*Uria aalge*), cormorants (*Phalacrocorax* sp.), and oystercatchers (*Haematopus* sp.) are some of the more common birds seen. Jaegers (*Stercorarius* sp.), shearwaters (*Puffinus* sp.), and albatross (*Diomedea* sp.) join birds that can be seen during boat trips around the islands. California sea lions (*Zalophus californicus*), northern elephant seals (*Mirounga angustirostris*), Steller's sea lions (*Eumetopias jubatus*), and harbor seals (*Phoca vitulina*) haul out on the narrow beaches and lower rocks or swim in the area, as do several species of marine turtles.

Many trips to the islands include whale sightings, with blue whales and humpbacks being the most commonly observed during spring and summer. It's also a thrill when pods of Dall's (*Phocoenoides dalli*), Risso's (*Grampus griseus*), or Pacific white-sided dolphins (*Lagenorhynchus obliquidens*) begin riding the boat's wake.

The islands are off limits to visitors. The only way to view the islands' wildlife is offshore from a charter tour boat or a private boat.

Info: NOAA Gulf of the Farallones National Marine Sanctuary, 991 Marine Drive, The Presidio of San Francisco, CA 94129, 415.561.6622 or www.farallones.noaa.gov

Research center at Marine Terrace on South East Farallon Island

The Golden Gate Bridge, with San Francisco in the distance

THE CITY OF SAN FRANCISCO

San Francisco is one of the few cities in the world that captures the essence of everything a great city should be: sophisticated, beautiful, eclectic, enchanting, and certainly memorable. Five-star restaurants vie with tiny corner cafés featuring a wide variety of ethnic foods, while 100-year-old Victorian B&Bs compete with elegant suites in the city's finest hotels. Cable cars climbing steep hills and cars maneuvering Lombard Street—claimed to be the crookedest street in the world—add to the enchanting hustle and bustle of fishing boats at the wharf and the sounds and smells of freshly boiled crabs being cracked for eager diners.

The United States took possession from Mexico of what were mostly the pastoral hills of San Francisco, then called *Yerba Buena* (good herb), on July 9, 1846. While the U.S. Army saw the strategic importance of the old Spanish and Mexican presidio for protecting the entry to the bay, at the time there was only a trickle of American settlers coming to California. Two years later, in 1848, the cry of "Gold!" caused San Francisco to burst with new and vibrant life from its humble beginnings as a primitive military outpost. Within a year, San Francisco became the primary entry port for tens of thousands of hopeful "49ers," and as gold poured out of the rivers and mines, the city quickly became the center of commerce and banking that supported the gigantic economic boom.

One of many intriguing results of California's Gold Rush was the deluge of sailing ships that landed in San Francisco Bay to unload supplies, passengers, and, far too often, their entire crews. Unable to lure crews back from the gold fields, many of the ships were turned into floating hotels, offices, warehouses, and one even became a jail. During those early days, ships such as the *Niantic, Euphemia, Bryan,* and *Galen* changed careers from sailing ships to land-locked structures such as docks with soil fill dumped around them, burying their hulls. Fires often raged throughout this floating wooden city during those early years, with the May 4, 1851 fire devastating much of San Francisco and many of the anchored ships. The hulls of some of these maritime relics are occasionally rediscovered during city redevelopment projects.

GOLDEN GATE BRIDGE

Summer fog, strong winds, and unpredictable currents kept Europeans from discovering the narrow entrance into this perfect harbor until 1769, when Spanish explorers first reached it overland. The discovery was actually an accident. Sergeant José de Ortega was looking for the "lost bay" of Monterey to the south. When he found San Francisco Bay, the Spanish called the gateway *La Boca del Puerto de San Francisco.* It was American John C. Frémont who used the name *Chrysopylae,* or

Golden Gate, for "the form of the entrance into the bay of San Francisco." Frémont's choice was the name that stuck.

Many naysayers insisted that constructing the Golden Gate Bridge was folly and that such a bridge could never be built, yet it was opened on May 27, 1937, only four years after construction began. The engineering marvel possesses a long list of statistical information: the suspended main span stretches 4,200 feet; the length of one cable is 7,650 feet and is 36 inches in diameter; there are 27,572 individual wires in each cable, totaling 80,000 miles and 24,500 tons; and the towers rise 746 feet

Golden Gate Bridge

above the bay and descend 110 feet below the water's surface.

Walking across the Golden Gate Bridge is an extremely popular activity for the more adventurous, although most people only go part way before returning, unwilling to walk the nearly 18,000 feet (3.2 miles) round-trip. Choosing a warm, sunny day helps. When fog or cold winds are present, it's often best to view the bay from inside a car. Parking areas are available on both ends of the bridge, although on summer weekends, an empty parking space can be difficult to find. On the San Francisco side of the bay, parking is not far from Fort Point and can be reached either by coming in from Fort Mason on Lincoln Boulevard or by taking the last turnoff (Lincoln Boulevard) before the bridge. Don't miss it or you'll have to drive all the way across the bridge and pay the toll to come back south into the city. On the Marin side of the bridge, the parking lot is just off the east side of U.S. 101.

Activities: There is a pedestrian walkway on the east side of the bridge.
Dates: The walkway is open daily.
Fees: There is no fee to use the walkway. There is a vehicle toll for all southbound vehicles. Do not stop at the toll booth. For those without "FastPasses," the vehicle license is automatically read and a bill for the toll is mailed to you.
Closest town: San Francisco
Info: San Francisco Travel Association, 900 Market Street, San Francisco, CA 94102, 415.391.2000 or www.SanFrancisco.travel

Coit Tower and Telegraph Hill

COIT TOWER AND TELEGRAPH HILL

Coit Tower sits on Telegraph Hill—a hill that rises abruptly 275 feet above San Francisco Bay. The tower rises another 210 feet, its shape designed to resemble a giant fire hose nozzle. In 1851, Lillie Hitchcock Coit was a child when she became an honorary member of a SF volunteer fire company. She never forgot this and in the early 1930s, she donated $125,000 to construct the tower. Inside the tower are 30 murals painted by local artists depicting the Great Depression. The hill and the tower are located in Pioneer Park and offer breathtaking views of the city and bay.

San Francisco / San Mateo

155

The steep hillside leading up to the tower has seen many uses. On October 29, 1850, the people of San Francisco used it to build a huge celebration fire when they found out that California had been admitted into the Union. Over the years that followed, Telegraph Hill has provided home sites for Chileans, Italians, Irish, and in the 1890s, an artist colony. Today, expensive homes cover the hillside, sharing its coveted views of the city and bay.

Activities: Viewing the city and bay
Dates: Open daily
Fees: Yes, to ride the elevator to the observation deck
Info: San Francisco Travel Association, 900 Market Street, San Francisco, CA 94102, 415.391.2000 or www.SanFrancisco.travel

GOLDEN GATE PARK

What was once wind-swept dunes has been transformed into the world's largest ornamental park. The park was so impressive that it served as host for the California Mid-Winter International Exposition of 1894, a world's fair that operated between January and July. Today, the park boasts a dozen small lakes and ponds scattered throughout where fly casters practice, model boat builders run their newest creations, and romantics row along in row boats. A polo field, walking trails, an archery field, and a small golf course add to the opportunities for recreation. Golden Gate Park also features beautiful gardens and some of San Francisco's best art and natural history museums.

Located in the western portion of Golden Gate Park are two sentinels of a bygone era: the **Dutch**

Dutch Windmill

Windmill and the **Murphy Windmill** (www.Golden-Gate-Park.com). Built in the early 1900s to pump approximately 1.5 million gallons of water into the park per day for irrigation, both windmills were replaced by electric water pumps in 1913.

The mills fell into disrepair until the citizens of San Francisco rallied to bring back the windmills' former glory. The Dutch Windmill, which stands 75-feet tall, was restored in 1981 and the famed **Queen Wilhelmina Tulip Garden** was established nearby. The Murphy Windmill took longer to restore, reopening in 2012. Its sails are the longest in the world and turn clockwise, opposed to the normal counterclockwise motion.

The **Japanese Tea Garden** (www.Golden-Gate-Park.com), the oldest Japanese garden in the United States, began as part of the California Mid-Winter International Exposition of 1894. Thanks to Makoto Hagiwara, what was to have been a temporary exhibit for the fair was turned into a permanent part of Golden Gate Park. Hagiwara maintained the garden from 1895 until his death in 1925. His family lived here and continued managing the gardens until they were forced to relocate to a Japanese internment camp at the beginning of World War II.

Today, the Tea Garden is a popular fixture in the park, with paths that wind through its groves of bamboo, koi ponds, and beautiful pagodas. Be sure to visit the Japanese Tea House and enjoy a cup of tea. And when you open that fortune cookie, think of Makoto Hagiwara—he introduced them to America. There is an entry fee.

San Francisco Botanical Garden (415.661.1316 or www.Golden-Gate-Park. com) covers 55 acres within Golden Gate Park and features more than 7,500 plants from around the world. Plants range from those in a Mexican cloud forest to the succulents that survive in the world's deserts. Other themed specimen areas include a fragrance garden, a Biblical garden, and a California redwood grove. The Botanical Gardens are open daily and admission is free for San Francisco residents; there is a fee for nonresidents.

Swallowtail butterfly

Dates: Golden Gate Park is open daily.
Fees: The park is free. There are fees for entry into various attractions.
Info: www.Golden-Gate-Park.com

CALIFORNIA ACADEMY OF SCIENCES

The California Academy of Sciences was formed in 1853 by a group of naturalists concerned about what the Gold Rush was doing to California's natural resources. The naturalists used the academy as a forum for exchanging, documenting, and storing scientific information as they collected, identified, and classified plant and animal specimens. The 1906 earthquake destroyed all of their work, but they immediately started over. The academy moved to its current location in 1916, where they opened the first of several buildings to the public.

Steinhart Aquarium and Natural History Museum

Today within their 400,000-square-foot home, the academy maintains a natural history museum, the Steinhart Aquarium, and the Morrison Planetarium in a single complex. The natural history museum is one of the largest in the world. The academy's collections are worldwide in scope, as their nearly 1.5 million yearly visitors quickly discover.

The **Natural History Museum's** 140 million-year-old, 30-foot dinosaur may dominate many imaginations, but the exhibits that fill the remainder of the museum are equally commanding. Visit an African waterhole and see a mountain gorilla, zebra, and giraffe in re-creations of their natural habitats. In another hall, a 1,350-pound quartz crystal and a 465-pound amethyst-lined geode highlight more than 1,000 gem and mineral specimens. Exhibits on giant bugs, plate tectonics, earthquakes, birds, and butterflies fill other rooms of the museum.

The **Steinhart Aquarium** allows visitors to explore the underwater realm of the world's rivers, lakes, and oceans. Nearly 900 species of fish, invertebrates, reptiles, amphibians, and a few penguins fill the exhibits at the aquarium. Learn how fish have adapted to waters as different as San Francisco Bay and an African lake, a Himalayan stream and California's kelp forests. The Philippine Coral Reef Gallery showcases more than 2,000 brilliant-colored fish that inhabit tropical ocean waters. At a depth of 25 feet, the 212,000-gallon tank is one of the largest and deepest exhibits of coral reefs in existence.

The **Morrison Planetarium** features sky shows that realistically simulate the night sky. The shows can re-create views of the different stars and constellations observed from the Northern and Southern hemispheres, giving everyone an opportunity to see planets, stars, and celestial events, such as eclipses, that are rarely visible. The shows, which are presented inside the world's largest digitally-projected dome, are changed periodically, often featuring upcoming, popular heavenly events.

Facilities: Museums, gift shop, café, exhibits, public programs
Dates: Open daily
Fees: There is an admission fee, plus an additional fee for the Morrison Planetarium's Sky Shows.
Info: California Academy of Sciences, 55 Music Concourse Drive, Golden Gate Park, San Francisco, CA 94118, 415.379.8000 or www.calacademy.org

SAN FRANCISCO CABLE CAR MUSEUM

Every tourist who comes to San Francisco likely takes at least one ride on the city's famous cable cars. The San Francisco Cable Car Museum, located in the historic Washington/Mason cable car barn and powerhouse, offers a first-hand look at what drives all those bell-ringing cable cars. And you can ride a cable car to the museum—there is a stop at the corner of Washington and Mason streets, directly in front of the museum.

The San Francisco Cable Car Museum is a working museum—the observation deck overlooks many 510-horsepower electric motors and huge winding wheels that pull miles of heavy steel cable at a constant 9.5 miles per hour beneath

Cable car passing the Cable Car Museum

San Francisco's streets. Each cable is labeled to show which cable line is currently at work. The lower observation level offers a great view of how the pulleys work underground to redirect the cables as they operate beneath the city streets.

In addition to showing what powers the cable cars, this free museum features numerous exhibits, including the only car that remains from the very first cable car company in San Francisco—the Clay Street Hill Railroad. Andrew Smith Hallidie founded the company in 1873. It was his British father who invented and had the patent for "wire rope" cable. His success enticed others to start their own cable car companies in other parts of the city, signaling an end to the horse-drawn wagons.

The 1880s were the cable car's glory days. Eight separate companies operated in the city over many more streets than currently are served by cable cars today. As cheaper and more efficient electric streetcars were developed, there was an effort by the mayor in the 1940s to eliminate the old cable car systems. Fortunately, he lost, and the cable cars remain today, an historic vestige of early San Francisco.

Facilities: Gift shop, exhibits
Dates: Open daily
Fees: There is a fee.
Info: San Francisco Cable Car Museum, 1201 Mason Street, San Francisco, CA 94108, 415.474.1887 or www.cablecarmuseum.org

Winding wheels in action, powering the city's cable cars

The Great Earthquake

At 5:12 A.M. on April 18, 1906, a minor earthquake occurred in San Francisco. About 20 seconds later, the big one struck. Lasting between 45 to 60 seconds, the earthquake was felt north to Oregon, south to Los Angeles and east into central Nevada.

The quake brought one of the most vibrant, elegant and busiest cities in the world to its knees in less than a minute. Havoc ensued. Buildings toppled, fires followed, and 28,000 structures were destroyed, with the estimated property damage totaling $400 million—in 1906 dollars. More than 225,000 of the city's 400,000 residents were left homeless and 3,000 people lost their lives.

According to the USGS, gauging the size of the earthquake using moment-magnitude (based on slippage) made it a 7.7, and using the Richter scale, it was estimated at 8.3. The rupture, which occurred on the San Andres Fault, began in San Juan Bautista to the south and ended 296 miles north at Shelter Cove. As a comparison, the rupture line for the 1989 Loma Prieta earthquake was only 25 miles.

The infamous event is remembered each year at **Lotta's Fountain**, the city's oldest surviving monument. Located at the intersection of Geary and Kearney at Market Street, the fountain—which was donated to the city in 1875 by singer/dancer Lotta Crabtree—survived the earthquake and was a meeting place for many on that fateful day. A ceremony is held at the fountain at 5:12 A.M. on April 18th of each year.

Lotta's Fountain

CHINATOWN

Chinatown, overlooking the Golden Gate Bridge

San Francisco's Chinatown is one of the most fascinating and colorful areas of the city, and also one of the most popular with visitors. Besides being the oldest Chinatown in all of North America, it is also the largest Chinatown outside of Asia.

A wonderful and eclectic collection of shops and restaurants sit side-by-side in San Francisco's historic Chinatown, with merchandise spilling out onto the sidewalks and the aroma of wonderful food wafting through the air. Street-level shops often have narrow interior stairways leading downstairs to cluttered rooms filled with boxes and shelves stocked with everything from fine china to silk neckties. Some of the small restaurants feature street-side windows that allow passers-by to view the food being prepared and roasted, which often includes such things as plucked chickens with their heads still intact.

Numerous Chinese communities popped up throughout California as the Chinese began coming here in 1848; 20,000 arrived during the following four years. Most initially headed out for the gold fields, while others returned to the city to set up businesses, often more profitable than searching for gold. The Chinese generally lived in small communities that excluded outsiders, primarily for protection against the severe discrimination that existed during this time.

Discrimination was real back then. California congressmen rallied for passage of an 1882 federal law banning Chinese immigration because the low-paid coolies (the name then used for Chinese laborers) were seen as a threat to American workers. It was the first time such a law had been passed, and it wasn't repealed until 1943. Similar local laws kept the Chinese out of many of the prime gold-mining areas in California's Mother Lode. Local citizens harassed, beat, and murdered the hard-working and entrepreneurial Chinese, often viewing them as unfair competition.

In 1885, about 25,000 people called San Francisco's Chinatown home, but much of the community was destroyed in the 1906 earthquake and the fires that followed. The area was rebuilt and today is one of San Francisco's great places to wander and explore. Chinatown is easy to spot, with its pagoda-style roofs, lantern-shaped lampposts, and the joss houses (Chinese temples).

For the more adventurous, explore Chinatown's alleys, such as **Ross Alley**. It is the oldest alley in San Francisco, once known for its infamous brothels and gambling parlors. Today, one will find murals depicting the Chinese-American community, as well as the home of the **Golden Gate Fortune Cookie Factory**. In business since 1962, the factory workers create fortune cookies in full view of visitors. Be sure to make a purchase to help keep this time-honored tradition of handmade history alive.

Activities: Sight-seeing, shopping, restaurants
Facilities: Shops, restaurants, churches, fortune cookie factory
Dates: Open year-round
Info: San Francisco Travel Association, 900 Market Street, San Francisco, CA 94102, 415.391.2000, www.SanFranciscoChinatown.com or www.SanFrancisco.travel

MISSION DOLORES

Father Junipero Serra established *Misión San Francisco de Asis*, better known today as Mission Dolores, on June 27, 1776. It was the sixth mission in what would ultimately be 21 missions built in California. The church was completed in 1791, making it the oldest intact mission of the original 21 (others were either moved to new locations or have undergone significant restoration or reconstruction). The Mission Dolores chapel was San Francisco's first building, and since it survived the 1906 earthquake, it remains the city's oldest building.

Following the mission's secularization by the Mexican government in 1834, mission operations declined rapidly. In 1845, the mission was sold to a private owner, but, like many of the other missions, it was returned to the Catholic Church in the mid-1800s by U.S. presidential proclamation.

Mission Dolores and the Basilica

San Francisco / San Mateo

163

Today, Mission Dolores, which means "sorrow," is one of San Francisco's favorite historical attractions. Inside the chapel, the gold and red color scheme adds life to an otherwise dark and somber interior. The ceiling beams are original redwood tied together with rawhide, although following the 1906 earthquake, steel beams were added to strengthen the roof. Under the outside covered walkway between the chapel and the basilica next door, a large diorama shows what the mission and its surrounding lands were like more than 200 years ago.

The mission's garden and cemetery are located adjacent to the chapel. The garden includes native plants from the 1791-era. And the cemetery is the final resting place for 5,000 Ohlone, Miwok, and other early Californians, including the first Mexican governor—Luis Antonia Arguello—and Lieutenant Moraga, the first commandant of the Presidio.

Next door to the mission is the basilica. It was originally a Gothic church that was destroyed in the 1906 earthquake and rebuilt between 1913 and 1918. In 1952, Pope Pius XII changed its name to the "Basilica of Mission San Francisco de Asi" (Mission Dolores).

Activities: Tours
Facilities: Historic mission, museum, gift shop
Dates: Open year-round, except major holidays
Fees: Donations are requested
Info: Mission Dolores, 3321 Sixteenth Street, San Francisco, CA 94114, 415.621.8203 or www.MissionDolores.org

FISHERMAN'S WHARF

There is so much to see and do along the City-by-the-Bay's waterfront—known as Fisherman's Wharf (www.fishermanswharf.org)—that a single day will not suffice, especially if eating is on the agenda. The wharf area is actually about seven blocks long, with many of its attractions located near the end of The Embarcadero, on both sides of connecting Jefferson Street, and throughout much of Beach Street

Visitors love the sea lions found at the wharf.

Balclutha

San Francisco / San Mateo

between Powell Street and Van Ness Avenue.

There are several piers that jut into the bay, with **Pier 39** (www.pier39.com) being the biggest tourist attraction. It supports dozens of shops and restaurants, as well as the **California Welcome Center**, which is an area-wide visitor center. There's always something interesting going on at Pier 39. If a painter or juggler isn't amusing passers-by, then there's usually an impromptu theatrical performance or musicians entertaining the ever-changing crowds of people. Besides the **Aquarium of the Bay** (www.aquariumofthebay.org), the **Sea Lion Center** is open daily (www.sealioncenter.org).

The grand **San Francisco Carousel** is on Pier 39. Handcrafted in Italy, the carousel features 32 carved animals to ride—from dolphins to dragons. A closer look at the painting and handiwork on the carousel reveals famous San Francisco landmarks such as Coit Tour, Lombard Street, and the Golden Gate Bridge.

A few blocks away, the **Hyde Street Pier** (415.447.5000 or www.nps.gov) is part of the **San Francisco Maritime National Historic Park** and features one of the largest collections of floating historic ships in the country. The 1886, three-masted, square-rigged *Balclutha,* the 1895 schooner *C.A. Thayer,* the 1891 scow schooner *Alma,* and the 1890 steam ferryboat *Eureka* provide a broad-spectrum look at the types of ships that sailed into San Francisco Bay during the 19th century. There is a fee to see the vessels.

Adjacent to the Hyde Street Pier and the cable car turn-around point is the **Aquatic Park Bathhouse Building/Maritime Museum** (415.447.5000 or www. nps.gov). The museum was built in 1939 in the Streamline Moderne style, part of the Art Deco period—from outside, the building looks like a white ocean liner. It houses ship models, paintings, photos, figureheads, and a major permanent exhibit on the history of communications at sea. The museum is free and open daily.

DON EDWARDS SAN FRANCISCO BAY NATIONAL WILDLIFE REFUGE

San Francisco Bay was formed only 10,000 years ago when the rising Pacific Ocean entered through the Golden Gate as the last Ice Age was ending. The water filled the shallow valley and flooded into the flats that ran up to the base of the surrounding hills. The refuge, which was originally created in 1974 and later expanded to a total of 30,000 acres, includes not only wetlands, but some of those now dry hills, known today as **Coyote Hills**.

During the Ice Age, the surrounding hills were formed as portions of the Pacific and North American plates, shifted, uplifted, and folded the earth's crust. Spend much time around the refuge and you can find sedimentary, igneous, and metamorphic rocks. Red chert and shale make up most of the sedimentary rocks. Greenstone, formed from lava that solidified underwater, is a soft igneous rock. The metamorphic, green-colored serpentine is California's official state rock.

Co-author holding a sedimentary rock.

The visitor center is the best place to pick up information and maps to the refuge. It sits atop a hill that rises well above the surrounding wetlands, offering excellent views of the marsh and wetlands that extend nearly as far as you can see to the north and west. Inside the visitor center, exhibits explain the natural history of the area, and there is a good selection of books and other nature-related items. Outside the visitor center, a trail drops down to the wetland.

Activities: Hiking, bird watching, kayaking, fishing, hunting, canoeing
Facilities: Visitor center, bookstore, trails
Dates: Trails open year-round. Visitor center closed on Mondays and federal holidays.
Fees: None
Info: Don Edwards San Francisco Bay National Wildlife Refuge, 1 Marshlands Road, Fremont, CA 94555, 510.792.0222 or www.fws.gov

TRAILS

There are more than 30 miles of hiking and biking trails in the refuge. Many are on levies that are periodically closed for repairs. Check with the refuge to verify the status of any trails before hiking. Leashed dogs are allowed on some trails.

The **Tidelands Trail** is a 1-mile loop that leaves from the visitor center. It's a raised and level boardwalk that heads out into the wetlands and mud flats. The trail is very popular, especially with school groups and people with younger children not yet ready for more strenuous hiking.

The **Newark Slough Loop Trail** is another trail leaving from the visitor center, but it covers 5 miles, all of which is a level walk well out into the refuge. It's a good hike, especially during fall and spring when the refuge is filled with migrating birds.

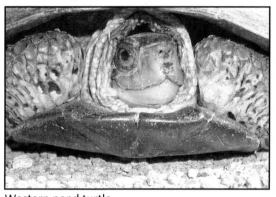

Western pond turtle

MORE TO EXPLORE

An expansive regional park system lies on the eastern side of San Francisco and San Pablo bays. East Bay Regional Park District includes 65 parks on 114,000 acres, with 1,200-plus miles of trails. With more than 4 million people living in the surrounding five counties, these regional parks are tremendously popular.

San Francisco / San Mateo

Point Pinole Regional Shoreline is a 2,315-acre park on the east shore of San Pablo Bay. It boasts numerous trails with great views of Mt. Tamalpais. The park opened in 1973, the property purchased from Bethlehem Steel Corporation, America's largest ship builder. It includes a 1,250-foot fishing pier. There is a weekend and holiday parking fee.

Carquinez Strait Regional Shoreline features 1,415 acres of bluffs, shoreline, oak woodlands, and open grasslands. One steep trail leads to an overlook 750 above the Carquinez Strait for a spectacular view. The park is home to a wide variety of wildlife including western bluebirds (*Sialia mexicana*), horned larks (*Eremophila alpestris*), American kestrels (*Falco sparverius*), golden eagles (*Aquila chrysaetos*), gray foxes (*Urocyon cinereoargenteus*), and mule deer (*Odocoileus* sp).

Tilden Regional Park is 2,000-plus acres and, in addition to its wildlands and wildlife, provides more kinds of experiences than the other East Bay Regional Parks. There are carousel rides, group picnic areas, scaled-down steam train rides, a golf course, and a regional botanical garden. It also includes several miles of

Coyote

hiking trails and swimming and fishing at Lake Anza. There is an equestrian campground and an environmental education center.

Coyote Hills is bordered on its west and south sides by the Don Edwards San Francisco Bay National Wildlife Refuge. Trails lead from Coyote Hills to the adjacent refuge, including the 12-mile Alameda Creek Trail. There are 2,000-year-old Tuibun Ohlone Indian shell-mound sites in the park, along with a reconstructed family house, sweat house, and tule reed boat. There's also a marsh boardwalk, paved bike trail, and a visitor center at the 978-acre park. There is a fee.

Info for East Bay Regional Parks: 888.327.2757 or www.ebparks.org

OAKLAND MUSEUM OF CALIFORNIA

The 300,000-square-foot Oakland Museum of California is one of the best museums in the Bay Area and on the West Coast. Over its 40-year history, the museum has collected more than 1.9 million artifacts and objects that focus on art, California history, and the natural sciences. Thus the reason that even though the museum is located in Alameda County, we just had to include it in the book.

What makes this museum so great is that you can practically touch the exhibits. With the majority of the collection not displayed in glass cases, visitors can build a sense of intimacy with the items. Of course the museum does not want you to touch the collections, but to appreciate their nearness—a trust the museum instills in their patrons.

The museum's collection of historic artifacts far exceeds what can be displayed at any one time, so some exhibits are periodically changed, allowing many different items to be enjoyed. One gallery of note is the Gallery of California History that includes Native American artifacts—including many of the museum's 2,500 baskets—the Spanish arrival, and the great Gold Rush. Another gallery focuses on the Golden State's natural sciences, recreating many eco zones, from ocean to tide pools to redwood forests. Here you come face to face with a life-size faux elephant seal, view a colorful coral reef up close, and are encouraged to feel the bones and pelts of sea otters and other marine mammals. This section also presents the issues of land uses, the need for conservation, and the environmental conflicts the California coast is continually undergoing.

Facilities: Museum, gift shop, café
Dates: Open daily Wednesday through Thursday, closed on Monday and Tuesday
Fees: There is an admission fee.
Nearest town: Oakland
Info: Oakland Museum of California, 1000 Oak Street, Oakland, CA 94607, 510.318.8400 or www.museumca.org

San Mateo County

Drive south on Highway 1 from the always enjoyable and exciting entrapments of San Francisco and civilization quickly melts away, once again showcasing the power and beauty of nature. San Mateo County stretches for 55 miles down the coast, where it connects with Santa Cruz County. There are numerous public beach access areas along Highway 1. While it's a beautiful drive, beware: summer can bring fog, obscuring many of the vistas and making sunbathing uncomfortably cold. And heavy winter rains can cause mudslides that close the highway for days.

Fog sets in fast along the coast.

San Francisco / San Mateo

HALF MOON BAY STATE BEACH

This state beach has one of the more developed coastal access parks along this stretch of the San Mateo County coast. The park, adjacent to Highway 1, actually has several beaches and access points, including **Francis Beach** at the end of Kelly Avenue in the city of Half Moon Bay, **Venice Beach** at the end of Venice Boulevard, and **Dunes Beach** at the end of Young Avenue. Francis Beach also has a campground with 52 sites, but no hookups.

Horses are permitted on some of the trails, such as between Dunes Beach and Francis Beach, but are not allowed on the state beach. There is a nearby private stable where horses can be rented (inquire at the park). The **Coastside Trail** runs

the length of Half Moon Bay State Beach, from Kelly Avenue on the north end to Miranda Avenue on the south. The trail gets plenty of use from bicyclists, joggers, and walkers.

Although not affiliated with the state beach, you can join fishing or whale-watching trips out of the **Pillar Point Harbor** on the north end of Half Moon Bay. The marina also offers boat berths and launching facilities.

Half Moon Bay is famous for its annual **Art and Pumpkin Festival**. Held every October for more than 40 years, the event celebrates everything pumpkin, from music to world-renown pumpkin carvers to terrific pumpkin food and vendors of every kind. But the main reason that so many visit this World Pumpkin Capital each year is to witness the weigh-in for the giant pumpkins, some of which can grow to the size of a small car and tip the scales at 1,200 pounds.

Activities: Hiking, biking, horseback riding, sunbathing, surfing
Facilities: Campgrounds, picnic facilities
Dates: Open year-round
Fees: There are camping and day-use fees.
Info: Half Moon Bay State Park, San Mateo Coast Sector Office, 95 Kelly Avenue, Half Moon Bay, CA 94019, 650.726.8819 or www.parks.ca.gov

MORE TO EXPLORE

Montara State Beach offers 2 miles of public beach popular with anglers, beachcombers, and, on sunny days, sunbathers. There are two access points that will get you down from the bluff to the beach. The first is off Highway 1, about 0.5 mile north of the Chart House restaurant in the community of Montara. The second is located across from Second Street, south of the Chart House restaurant. Info: 650.726.8819 or www.parks.ca.gov

The **Point Montara Lighthouse Hostel** is a historic lighthouse still operated by the U.S. Coast Guard. The surrounding grounds and several of the buildings have been transformed into a very popular hostel. Operated by Hostelling International, there are sleeping facilities, along with a kitchen, laundry, and plenty of bicycle racks for those peddling California's coast. The light station and hostel are located on Highway 1 between the small communities of Montara and Moss Beach. Info: 650.726.8819, www.parks.ca.gov or www.norcalhostels.org

The **James Fitzgerald Marine Reserve** offers 3 miles of coastline with tide pools and sandy beaches. It's a popular scuba diving area, although it's illegal to remove or disturb any of the marine life or surrounding habitat. Its shale reefs provide protection for a wide variety of marine life, including giant green anemones (*Anthpleura xanthogrammica*), purple sea urchins (*Strongylocentrotus purpuratus*), and several species of small crabs. There is a hiking trail along the bluff to the south and picnic tables in the sheltered cypress grove. The reserve is part of the Monterey Bay National Marine Sanctuary. Info: 650.726.8819 or www.parks.ca.gov

McNee Ranch—also known as **Montara Mountain**—has nearly 700 acres available for hikers, mountain bikers, and equestrians. There are great views from the old ranch's hills, which are now part of the California State Park System. Info: 650.726.8819 or wwparks.ca.gov

California sea lion

PESCADERO STATE BEACH

This is a favorite place for school group field trips because the area provides access to both a 1-mile-long sandy beach and to a marsh and wetlands area. On the east side of Highway 1, Pescadero Creek and Butano Creek join, forming a delta marsh rich with plants and wildlife. A few hundred yards away is the **North Marsh**, another part of the park. There are trails into both areas, none of which take more than 30 minutes to walk. The trail around North Marsh is one of the longest and is only 0.75 mile. On the ocean side of Highway 1 is a wooden walkway through part of the dunes, allowing disabled access across the sand.

The marsh areas found on the east side of Highway 1 are included within the 500-acre **Pescadero Marsh Natural Preserve**. Autumn brings thousands of

Marsh and dunes at Pescadero State Beach

waterfowl and other migrating birds into the marsh's brackish waters, while at least 60 species of birds nest in the marsh or on the beach. Great blue herons (*Ardea herodias*), marbled godwits (*Limosa fedoa*), American avocets (*Recurvirostra americana*), sanderlings (*Calidris alba*), brown pelicans (*Pelecanus occidentalis*), surf scoters (*Melanitta perspicillata*), and the endangered snowy plover (*Charadrius alexandrinus*) are common in the area. There are also long-tailed weasels (*Mustela frenata*), red-legged frogs (*Rana aurora*), the endangered salt marsh harvest mouse (*Reithrodontomys raviventris*), and numerous species of waterfowl.

Activities: Hiking, beachcombing, fishing, nature study, bird watching
Facilities: None
Dates: Open year-round
Fees: There is a day-use fee.
Closest town: Half Moon Bay
Info: 650.726.8819 or www.parks.ca.gov

AÑO NUEVO STATE PARK

The sight of a 2.5-ton northern elephant seals (*Mirounga angustirostris*) bellowing, charging, and battling across open dunes only a few dozen yards away from you is an unforgettable experience. Such is the way winter tours often go at Año Nuevo State Park. While the park's natural preserve is open all year, late December is when the females begin arriving in large numbers, and so do human park visitors. Within a week of their arrival, each of the pregnant females—themselves 10-feet-long and weighing about 1,600 pounds—give birth most often to a single 75-pound pup.

While all this is happening, the big bulls are battling each other, attempting to establish private harems for mating purposes. The battles can get very bloody at times, but more often the smaller, younger, and less-determined males wisely give up quickly and move away from the alpha bulls. While defending their harems, the alpha bulls are also attempting to mate with the females that are nearing the end of the 25 to 28 days they spend nursing their pups. If they've managed to escape being crushed by fighting bulls or by an alpha bull attempting to mate with their mothers, the pups grow rapidly on their mothers' rich milk, reaching up to 300 pounds during their three- to four-week nursing period.

Two bull elephant seals

The adult females and males begin leaving Año Nuevo in March, deserting the young pups that must remain to spend time learning to swim. Those pups will finally leave land in late April. The elephant seals generally swim north and feed off the coasts of Washington and British Columbia before returning to land for short

Adult elephant seal

San Francisco / San Mateo

The winter elephant seal birthing season may provide lucky visitors the opportunity to see an actual birth.

periods to molt. The adult females return to Año Nuevo during April and May, the sub-adult males from May to June, and the adult males during July and August in order to shed their old fur.

While northern elephant seals are the primary attraction for most people who visit Año Nuevo, the geology, general scenery, and the historic dairy buildings are also big attractions. A walk along **Cove Beach** reveals cliffs that run parallel with the underlying Año Nuevo thrust fault, part of the larger San Gregorio fault zone. The rock formations that make up most of the coastal range in this area are more than 12 million years old. The Monterey Formation, as it is known, is made up of the silica from skeletons of ancient, one-celled sea animals that were pressed between layers of silt and clay. Before it was uplifted to the surface, high temperatures and tremendous pressures over 12 million years transformed the original materials into light gray-colored mudstone that is very resistant to wind and wave action.

Grizzly bears once roamed the woods and hillsides of Año Nuevo. While grizzlies have been extinct here since the 1880s, many other species of wildlife are common throughout the reserve. On the coastal terrace above Cove Beach, a small pond teems with waterfowl such as pintail (*Anas acuta*), America widgeon (*Anas americana*), cinnamon teal (*Anas cyanoptera*), and mallards (*Anas platyrhynchos*). Warblers, thrushes, hummingbirds, vireos, and many more birds migrate through the park each year. Raptors, such as American kestrels (*Falco sparverius*) and northern harriers or marsh hawks (*Circus cyaneus*), are often seen flying a few feet above the open fields. Along the shoreline, marbled godwits (*Limosa fedoa*) and black-bellied plovers (*Pluvialis squatarola*) arrive during the fall migration.

During the mid-December through March elephant seal birthing and mating season, the reserve is open only for tours led by the park's docents. This policy is designed to protect both the animals and the visitors. It's amazing how quickly a 2-ton elephant seal can cover short distances, even across the loose sand. The docents are extremely well-versed in the elephant seals' natural history.

The tours cover about 3 miles, much of it over open sand, and take approximately 2.5 hours. The trail changes daily, depending upon where the mostly immature and non-mating male elephant seals have decided to take their frequent naps. The winter tours are extremely popular, so it's best to make reservations in advance, although unfilled tour slots are available first-come, first-served. Reservations can be made up to 56 days in advance. The tours occur rain or shine. Dress for rain and wind (umbrellas are not allowed), but hope for a warm, clear winter day. Pets are not allowed anywhere in the park, including inside parked vehicles.

Activities: Hiking, bird watching, elephant seal tours
Facilities: Visitor center, bookstore
Dates: Open year-round. During mid-December through March, the public must be part of a docent-led tour in order to enter the beach and dunes area where the elephant seals haul out. During other times of the year, a permit is required, obtainable at the park entrance.
Fees: There is a vehicle entry fee and a per-person tour fee. Reservations are almost always needed for the docent-led tours, 800.444.7275.
Closest town: Santa Cruz
Info: Año Nuevo State Park, 1 New Years Creek Road, Pescadero, CA 94060, 650.879-0227, www.parks.ca.gov or 650.879.2025 for recorded info

San Francisco / San Mateo

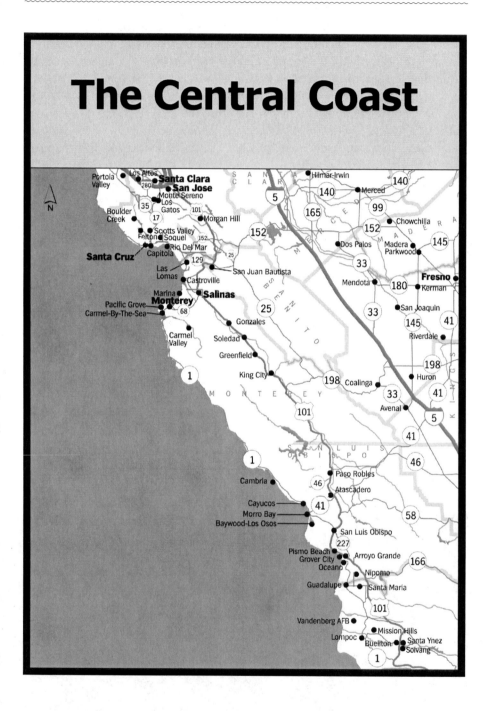

The Central Coast

The Central Coast

T he boundaries of California's central coast vary depending upon who is drawing the lines on a map, but essentially it's more than 225 miles long, encompassing Santa Cruz, Monterey, and San Luis Obispo counties. With the exception of three moderately sized cities—each taking its name from its respective county—the communities along this portion of the California coast are relatively small. Or, as in the case of the Big Sur coast, they consist of not much more than a number of isolated homes and a few small tourist-related businesses.

It's difficult to identify any one section of California's 1,100-mile-long coast as being more spectacular than another, but the Central Coast would certainly be high on anyone's list. From towering redwoods to surfing beaches, from spectacular ocean-bluff cliffs to migrating whales, it attracts millions of visitors each year, each searching for his or her own paradise—and generally finding it.

The Central Coast certainly has its share of iconic sites; the Santa Cruz Boardwalk, the Monterey Bay Aquarium, the Lone Cypress and golf courses at Pebble Beach, and the Big Sur coast's Bixby Bridge, star of dozens of car commercials. But there is much more to see and do here than can be accomplished during a long weekend. Whether it's dining at world-class restaurants, joining a fishing or whale-watching cruise, scuba diving in Monterey Bay, or walking among its historic homes, California's Central Coast will beckon your return, over and over again.

Central Coast

Santa Cruz County

BIG BASIN REDWOODS STATE PARK

Deep in the Santa Cruz Mountains you'll find giant coast redwoods (*Sequoia sempervirens*). While the ancient trees are found still farther south in a few protected canyons along the Big Sur coast, Big Basin Redwoods State Park is where extensive stands of 2,000-year-old trees still remain.

Efforts to save the trees began in earnest in 1900, when photographer Andrew

P. Hill and other early conservationists founded the Sempervirens Club, which led to the creation of the 3,900-acre Big Basin Redwoods State Park two years later. Since its inauguration as California's first state park (if Yosemite's temporary late 19th century state ownership is disregarded), Big Basin has grown extensively, now approaching 20,000 acres. Sempervirens Fund, the modern successor to the Sempervirens Club, along with numerous other private individuals and public benefit organizations have added property over the past 100 years.

What all of these people have seen worthy to protect is the result of the Pacific and North American plates' movement that created a complex assortment of geologic actions. The oldest rocks in Big Basin are found only in the eastern portion of the park. Its 70-million-

Coastal redwoods

to 90-million-year-old quartz diorite originated a few thousand miles to the south and moved north with the shifting plates. Sandstone, mudstone, siltstone, and shale—all of which range in age from 50 million years old to as young as 8 million years old—are the other rock types found within most of the park's Waddell Creek watershed.

Some 60 million years ago, a surge of uplifting began along the Zayante fault that lies within the park. The park's mountains rose in elevation from sea level to 2,000 feet. South of the fault, erosion slowly cut the deep gorge that follows Waddell and other creeks, while to the north, eroded sedimentary deposits accumulated behind the rising rock dam. The result was a flat valley floor where park headquarters is now located.

The deep alluvial soils that lie beneath park headquarters, combined with rainfall that averages 3 feet a year or more in the park, provide an ideal growing medium for coast redwoods. Some of the largest trees in the park are located here, alongside the turbid waters of meandering Opal Creek. But the towering redwoods aren't the only attraction in Big Basin. Wildlife abounds, although many of the animals are more secretive than most visitors would like.

One of the most interesting creatures is the 6-inch long, slimy banana slug (*Ariolimax columbianus*). These greenish yellow mollusks are common, especially where the ground is wet. Once actively fed by park employees and visitors, the black-tailed deer (*Odocoileus hemionus columbianus*) has become less common in the heavy-use areas of the park, but it is still seen. Fortunately for the deer, such harmful feeding practices have long since ended. Several species of chipmunks (*Tamias* spp.), raccoons (*Procyon lotor*), and chickarees or Douglas squirrels (*Tamiasciurus douglasii*) are relatively common.

It's not unusual to see California quail (*Callipepla californica*) running across trails and disappearing into shrubs such as salmon berry (*Rubus spectabilis*) and huckleberry (*Vaccinium* spp.). It's less common, but much more exciting, to see a pileated woodpecker (*Dryocopus pileatus*) and hear its jackhammer-sounding pecking near the tops of trees, which are loud enough to echo throughout the forest. This largest of the woodpeckers is easily identified by its size—up to 19 inches tall with a flaming red crest. Then there's the ever-present camp robber—the common Steller's jay (*Cyanocditta stelleri*). In fact, anywhere people linger with food, a raucous crowd of squawking Steller's jays is likely to appear suddenly. And along the creeks, the American dipper or water ouzel (*Cinclus mexicanus*) is a fascinating bird to watch as it dives underwater and swims,

Black-tailed fawn

Central Coast

Madrones have peeling bark

searching for small fish or invertebrates.

The park's visitor center is located in a 1936-era, Civilian Conservation Corps-constructed log lodge that also serves as the park headquarters and campground registration office. Exhibits tell the story of the area's early history, including the threat of logging that pushed so many people into creating the park and saving the ancient trees. Gunpowder was also part of the Big Basin story. The very hard wood of the madrone (*Arbutus menziesii*)—a tree common on the warmer ridges in the park and surrounding mountains and easy to identify by its peeling, reddish-brown bark—made excellent charcoal that was required for the manufacture of gunpowder. A large diorama shows the early days of the park when cottages and other structures, such as a barber shop, a post office, tennis courts, and a dance floor, were available for visitors' use. It also was a time when campsites cost $.50 per night. Park brochures, trail maps (the park has 80-plus miles of hiking trails), and a few nature books are available for sale. There are chairs set around the old stone fireplace, offering a comfortable place to sit and read or take a break. And don't overlook the park's museum, which is across from the visitor center.

In 2011, **Little Basin**—once a retreat for Hewlett-Packard—officially became part of the state park system. The 534-acre campground has 12 cabins, 38 campsites, RV sites, and a large group campground. There are no day-use facilities at Little Basin. Info: www.littlebasin.org

Activities: Camping, hiking, picnicking
Facilities: Campground, tent cabins (open-sided cabins with stoves), camp store, gift shop, visitor center, museum
Dates: Open year-round
Fees: There are camping and day-use fees.
Closest town: Boulder Creek
Info: Big Basin Redwoods State Park, 21600 Big Basin Way, Boulder Creek, CA 95006, 831.338.8860 or www.parks.ca.gov

TRAILS

There are 80 miles of trails in Big Basin Redwoods State Park, ranging from short, level walks to strenuous, multiday hikes. Many of the trails can be reached from trailheads that begin near park headquarters. Others are accessed from different areas within the park, and a few can be reached from trailheads that begin outside the park. Dozens of combinations of loop and one-way trails are possible, depending upon the time available and the level of adventure desired.

The **Redwood Trail** is a short, 0.5-mile, self-guided nature trail and is a great hike for families. Pick up a trail guide at the visitor center before you go, as it offers brief explanations about what will be found on the walk. For example, there's a large and very obvious redwood circle at post number one, which is a group of new trees growing from the original roots and in a circle around the slowly decaying stump of its old-growth parent tree. The remainder of the trail holds marked examples of tanbark oak (*Lithocarpus densiflorus*), chimney trees (redwoods hollowed by lightning-caused fires that can smolder inside the trees for months), and other wonders of natural history. On this trail, you'll see the **Mother-of-the-Forest**—estimated at 2,000 years of age, it is the oldest tree in the park. And it's also the tallest tree in the park, standing at 329 feet.

The **Skyline to the Sea Trail** begins in nearby **Castle Rock State Park**, and the 30-mile trail meanders into Big Basin near **China Grade Crossing** at the northwest corner of the park. It then heads southwest and 5 miles later, passes above **Opal Creek** near Big Basin park headquarters. It continues southwest some 12 miles on a mostly downhill trail, finally reaching the Pacific Ocean at the **Rancho del Oso Nature and History Center.** There are several trail camps along the way for those wishing to spend a little more time enjoying the backcountry trails.

The **Sunset Trail to Berry Creek Falls** is not for the weak of heart or lungs or legs. This 11.5-mile hike begins on an easy uphill slope from a trailhead located just off the Redwood Trail near park

Chimney tree

Sempervirens Falls

headquarters, reaches the top of a ridge, then plunges about 1,200 feet down a steep canyon trail. At the bottom, the trail passes three wonderful waterfalls, the highest of which, **Berry Creek Falls**, plunges 60 feet. The tough part is climbing back up the ridge to the top, at Hihn Ahammond Road, before the final short hike back to the beginning of the trail at park headquarters.

While the 4-mile-long **Sequoia Trail** can simply be bypassed and some of its destinations reached more quickly by driving, hiking is a much more enjoyable way to go. The trail picks up near park headquarters and loops south and east then north past the **Wastahi Campground**, finally reaching **Sempervirens Falls**. The small, but beautiful, waterfall tumbles into a pool, surrounded by redwoods and a cliff face covered with ferns. A few hundred yards north of the falls is **Slippery Rock** and the **Founders Monument**, the latter memorializing the founding of the Sempervirens Club in 1900. The trail continues north and connects with the **Skyline to the Sea Trail** that then leads south, returning to park headquarters.

MORE TO EXPLORE

The **Rancho del Oso Nature and History Center** is located on the inland side of Highway 1 and is the terminus of the **Skyline to the Sea Trail**. It is open weekends and by special arrangement. There is also a wetland on the inland side that is home to numerous water birds. **Waddell Creek Beach** is about 1 mile south of the San Mateo County line and is part of Big Basin Redwoods State Park. Info: 831.427.2288 or www.ranchodeloso.org

Davenport is 8 miles south of the San Mateo County line on Highway 1. The small, historic community has its roots in the 19th century whaling industry and the early shipping industry. The original town was actually built about 1.5 miles farther north, but it was moved in 1906. There's an overlook on the ocean side of Highway 1, and it is a good place to view migrating gray whales during winter.

Henry Cowell Redwoods State Park is an easy place to wander through a magnificent grove of coast redwoods, or, if you're more adventurous, hike or ride along 15 miles of trail. The park has a small visitor center, a gift shop, and camping and picnicking opportunities. There's also a beautiful meadow that fills with wildflowers and butterflies each spring. Info: 831.335.4598 or www.parks.ca.gov

The Forest of Nisene Marks State Park is located north of Aptos, off Highway 1. The park is named after Nisene Marks, who owned the property. Her children donated the 9,700 acres to the state in 1963. There are 30 miles of trails in the park, one of which is the **Loma Prieta Grade Trail.** The infamous October 17, 1989 Loma Prieta earthquake was named after this grade because the quake's epicenter was located here. The GPS coordinates for the actual epicenter are 37.03°N, 121.88°W. Info: 831.763.7062 or www.parks.ca.gov

WILDER RANCH STATE PARK

A great fertile crescent, beginning north of Santa Cruz and wrapping around to the Monterey Peninsula, has served farmers and ranchers quite well since 1791 when the missions began farming here. Even today, the rich soil and mild climate allows such difficult-to-grow crops as artichokes and Brussels sprouts to thrive. The area in which the park sits was originally the rancho that supplied food to Mission Santa Cruz in the 1790s. Between 1830 and 1871, the land exchanged hands several times until dairyman Delos D. Wilder took possession, turning the land into a successful dairy operation which lasted until 1969.

The entrance and parking lot to Wilder Ranch are off the ocean side of Highway 1, and then it's a short walk to the old Victorian farmhouse, the barns, and a small visitor center. A group of volunteers helps with the extensive flower and vegetable gardens, and maintains the farm animals that range from chickens to horses. A large shed shelters a wide assortment of antique farm implements and other equipment. (**NOTE:** Because of the animals, absolutely no pets are allowed in the park.)

A dirt road runs through the park, crosses under Highway 1, and leads

Many surprises await around the main farmhouse.

Wilder Ranch coastline

to a large corral area and reconstructed cowboy bunkhouse complex. The original bunkhouse was built by the Wilders for their ranch hands, but it served quite often as a gathering place for parties and practices for the annual rodeos in which many of the area's young cowboys competed.

Beyond the bunkhouse, a maze of dirt roads offers 34 miles of trails for hiking, horseback riding, and mountain biking. Being in shape certainly helps if a mountain bike is your chosen mode of outdoor transportation, because the trails get steep in a hurry. But once at the top, the views of the Pacific Ocean on fogless days are spectacular. In 1996, the state purchased **Gray Whale Ranch**, which is adjacent to Wilder Ranch. The acquisition of the additional 2,305 acres brought the park to a total of 7,000 acres.

Activities: Hiking, mountain biking, picnicking, living history events
Facilities: Visitor center, gift shop, trails, farmhouse, barns, bunkhouse, corral
Dates: Open daily
Fees: There is a day-use fee.
Closest town: Santa Cruz
Info: Friends of Santa Cruz State Parks, 831.429.1840, www.parks.ca.gov or www. thatsmypark.org

SANTA CRUZ

What began as home for the Ohlone Indians and was changed into a mission by the Spanish has been transformed into a summer recreation hot spot, mostly for tens of thousands of San Francisco Bay and Central Valley residents each year. Seems folks living in San Francisco are searching for a slightly less foggy and warmer weekend getaway and those living in the Central Valley are looking for an escape from summer's heat.

SANTA CRUZ BEACH BOARDWALK

The colorful and popular boardwalk is one of those places that kids of all ages enjoy. It's loaded with the kinds of fun food that most people probably shouldn't eat more than once or twice a year, and stomach-wrenching roller-coaster thrills that can make most people wish that food hadn't been a first priority upon arrival. The boardwalk stretches for nearly 1 mile right at the edge of the city's main beach, itself a vast stretch of sand that attracts thousands of people on warm summer days. The boardwalk itself can be as crowded as the beach on weekends and lines can be long for some of the more popular rides carrying such ominous names as **Tsunami, Crazy Surf,** and **Cliff Hanger**. For a great overview of what's here, there's a monorail that circles around and above the boardwalk at a leisurely pace. For those interested in nostalgia, the traditional wooden roller coaster—the **Giant Dipper**—that was built in 1924 remains one of the best and most historic roller coasters in the country. Updated over the years, the Giant Dipper continues to deliver beautiful views of the bay and the screams that partner with 55-mph speeds. For those with weaker stomachs, or parents with smaller kids, there is the equally classic **Looff Carousel**. With its 73 carved horses and its late 19th century, 342-pipe band organ, this National Historic Landmark has thrilled 50 million people since 1911. It is also one of the few remaining carousels that still has an operating ring dispenser. Riders on the outside horses can grab the rings and attempt to toss them into a large clown's open mouth.

Facilities: Rides, games, food
Dates: Open daily from Memorial Day to Labor Day. Off-season hours vary.
Fees: The boardwalk is free, but there is a fee for the rides.
Info: Santa Cruz Beach Boardwalk, 400 Beach Street, Santa Cruz, CA 95060, 831.423.5590 or www.beachboardwalk.com

Central Coast

SANTA CRUZ WHARF

Wherever there is a wharf, there are people. The Santa Cruz Wharf is no exception, and it has the added attraction of being the longest wharf on the West Coast to allow vehicle traffic. Built in 1914, the 2,745-foot-long wharf is loaded with shops and restaurants, and fishing can be remarkably good from the wharf if you'd prefer to catch your own. Halibut, striped bass, jacksmelt, and surf perch aren't opposed to taking live bait. The more adventurous can rent wooden skiffs with small outboard motors and head out a bit farther to the offshore rocky reefs where rockfish and larger lingcod are occasionally hooked.

Activities: Dining, fishing, shopping
Facilities: Restaurants, bait shop, gift shops, boat and kayak rentals
Dates: Open daily
Fees: There is a fee for vehicles, but no fee for pedestrians.
Info: Santa Cruz Wharf, Beach Street, Santa Cruz, CA 95060, 831.420.6025 or www.santacruzwharf.com

MORE TO EXPLORE

Drive along West Cliff Drive and Beach Street, both of which follow the cliffs at the edge of the city of Santa Cruz, and numerous surprises await. **Natural Bridges State Beach** is north of the main part of town and has a great beach. It gets its name from the offshore rocks, although the longest wave-carved rock bridge collapsed years ago. The park's eucalyptus grove hosts thousands of wintering monarch butterflies, sometimes more than 100,000 of them. Mid-October to mid-February are the best viewing times, but call ahead for migration updates. Info: 831.423.4609 or www.parks.ca.gov

Natural Bridges State Beach

LIGHTHOUSE FIELD STATE BEACH
AND THE SANTA CRUZ SURFING MUSEUM

Where **Point Santa Cruz** juts out to mark Monterey Bay's northern boundary, you'll find Lighthouse Field State Beach. The original lighthouse was built here in 1869, as an aid to navigation for the constantly increasing numbers of ships that passed by, heading to and from San Francisco. Within 10 years of its construction, the crashing waves had eroded so much of the cliff face that the structure was moved farther inland where it continued in operation until 1941. The lighthouse structure was replaced by an automatic beacon-topped wooden tower and the original wooden lighthouse was sold for scrap.

Today's lighthouse that stands near the cliffs was a gift to the people of Santa Cruz. Photographers Chuck and Esther Abbot sponsored the construction of the new lighthouse in memory of their son Mark, who was killed in a surfing accident. Today, the lighthouse—which overlooks **Steamer Lane**, an internationally renowned surfing destination—hosts the **Santa Cruz Surfing Museum**, which has been dedicated to the area's long history of surfing.

Activities: Surfing, fishing, biking, jogging, bird watching
Dates: Beach open daily; museum open summer, 10 A.M. to 5 P.M. (closed Wednesday); winter, noon to 4 P.M. (closed Tuesday and Wednesday)
Fees: None
Info: Lighthouse Field State Beach, 831.429.2850, www.parks.ca.gov, www.santacruzsurfingmuseum.org or www.thatsmypark.org

Santa Cruz Surfing Museum

Central Coast

SANTA CRUZ CIRCLE TRAIL

There are actually two loop trails that make up the Santa Cruz Circle Trail. Either can be picked up in any number of places and both trails meander through some of Santa Cruz's most interesting spots, including Natural Bridges State Park, where eucalyptus trees attract thousands of wintering monarch butterflies. Each trail can take three to four hours to walk, longer if any time is spent enjoying such things as Antonelli Pond, the natural history museum, or the wonderful University of California at Santa Cruz Arboretum. Bicycles are allowed on portions of the trail.

The western loop on the west side of the San Lorenzo River is about 12 miles long, and the eastern loop on the east side of the river is 11 miles long. When completed, the trail will pass through the **University of California at Santa Cruz** campus and total about 27 miles. For an interactive trail map with all landmarks shown, including info on each destination, visit www.ecotopia.org/trail.

Monarch Butterflies

During winter, several areas along California's Central Coast become overwintering grounds for more than 100,000 monarch butterflies (*Danaus plexippus*). These large, showy butterflies—that have wingspans of 4 inches or more—seek shelter in the eucalyptus groves. On late winter afternoons, when temperatures begin to drop, the butterflies return to their small section of trees by the thousands and cling to the branches and leaves, creating a shimmering wall of flickering orange and black wings. Each morning, when the ambient temperature rises enough, the butterflies leave in a swirling mass of color and seeming confusion, abandoning the security of their nighttime perches in search of nectar.

There are several places in the Golden State to view monarchs during winter, including at Natural Bridges State Beach in Santa Cruz; the City of Pacific Grove, which dubs itself "Butterfly Town U.S.A."; and in the eucalyptus grove at Pismo State Beach's North Beach Campground, which hosts the largest overwintering monarch butterfly population in California.

Check out this website for kids—and adults—where the lifecycle of these amazing butterflies is explained: www.monarch-butterfly.com

Brown pelican

ELKHORN SLOUGH

California's coastal estuaries and marshes are some of the most prolific producers and supporters of wildlife in the world. The 1,700 acres of vital marsh and tidal flats and the 7 miles of main water channel that comprise much of **Elkhorn Slough National Estuarine Research Reserve** and the adjacent **Moss Landing Wildlife Area** are home—either permanently or as a seasonal sanctuary—to more than 400 species of invertebrates and 80 species of fish. Not to be outdone are the 340 species of birds on the estuary's birder list. Yet, the unfortunate fact is that during the past century, nearly 90 percent of these same rich wetlands in California have been filled, drained, or in other ways destroyed. Even Elkhorn Slough has seen extensive commercial operations, such as the 200 acres of commercial salt ponds that were in production from the early 1900s until 1974. Today, the ponds have been reclaimed and serve a much more valuable role as rich feeding grounds for dozens of bird species and a summer resting ground for the endangered brown pelican.

The salt flats aren't the only areas of the slough that have been restored. Much of the marshland was diked and drained during the earlier part of the 20th century and used as grazing land for the **Elkhorn Dairy** operation. Two of the old barns remain on the property and are now homes to bats, barn owls, and other wildlife. Most of the dikes are gone, at least those that restricted the ebb and flow of seawater and fresh water. The land that has been reflooded today serves as a valuable research area where the success of such wetland restorations can be studied and new and better techniques developed.

Five miles of trails wind through the estuary, most starting near the **Elkhorn Slough Visitor Center**. The visitor center also provides free bird lists that include the seasons when the different birds are most likely to be seen. Summer brings large numbers of brown pelicans (*Pelecanus occidentalis*) to the mud flats,

Central Coast

189

Co-author's son fishing at the slough.

along with numerous species of shorebirds searching the wet mud for food. The prominent great egrets (*Casmerodius albus*) are here year-round, as are great blue herons (*Ardea herodias*). As an important winter stopover along the Pacific Flyway, Elkhorn Slough provides refuge for Canada geese (*Branta canadensis*), green-winged teal (*Anas crecca*), pintails (*Anas acuta*), gadwalls (*Anas strepera*), American widgeon (*Anas americana*), common goldeneyes (*Bucephala clangula*), and ruddy ducks (*Oxyura jamaicensis*). Jaegers (*Stercorarius pomarinus*), gulls (*Larus* sp.), terns (*Sterna* sp.), and a plethora of terrestrial birds are commonly seen by bird watchers. (**NOTE:** Pets are not allowed, even if left in vehicles.)

Activities: Hiking, bird watching
Facilities: Visitor center, gift shop, trails
Dates: Open daily, Wednesday through Sunday
Fees: None for anyone with a valid California hunting or fishing license, otherwise a small fee for those age 16 and over.
Closest town: Moss Landing
Info: Elkhorn Slough Office, 1700 Elkhorn Road, Watsonville, CA 95076, 831.728.2822, 831.728.2822 or www.elkhornslough.org

TRAILS

The **Long Valley Loop Trail** is an 0.8-mile loop that starts from the visitor center, passes through an area of oak woodland, and then drops down a short hill and follows along one of the fingers of a waterway known appropriately as **Five Fingers**. Most of the **Five Fingers Loop Trail** stays on the hillside, offering great views of Monterey Bay. The trail can be picked up from the Long Valley Loop or directly via the short, paved trail that connects with the visitor center. While anywhere within the estuary is great for bird watching, there is a wonderful blind that has been constructed in the tree line at about the halfway point in the loop. It overlooks the old salt mining area and provides cover for photographers and their equipment. It's also large enough to handle several people. The entire loop is about 1.8 miles.

The **South Marsh Loop** is a great trail (about 3.3 miles) that quickly drops down from the visitor center, passes the old Elkhorn Farm barns, and meanders around the south marsh area. Most of the walking is relatively level. The **Wheelchair Trail** is a wheelchair accessible slough-style trail that heads west for maybe 100 yards from the visitor center (the same trail that connects with all the other dirt trails), and ends in a paved circular area with two spotting scopes that overlook the majority of the estuary.

Kayaking the Estuary

For a different view of the waterways and their wildlife, kayaking in the Elkhorn Slough is extremely popular. Most of the estuary's channels are only accessible by small boat or kayak, as are many of the small side channels, at least during high tide. It's always important to be aware of the tides. Being caught on the wrong side of a shallow area that quickly becomes a mud flat as the tide races out is not only embarrassing, but a major pain—try towing a kayak across deep mud that is attempting to suck your feet off your ankles! Best thing is to time your trip with the tide movements in mind and with the afternoon winds at your back.

It's equally important to remember that tidal flows around the harbor can create problems when trying to negotiate under the Highway 1 bridge. Besides that, don't forget you'll have to maneuver around the commercial and private boat traffic that moves in and out of the Moss Landing Marina.

There are only two places to launch kayaks in the actual estuary. Kirby Park, located north of the Elkhorn Slough Visitor Center on Elkhorn Road, has a small launch ramp. The second launching facility is the Moss Landing Harbor District launch ramp.

While kayaking is a great way to experience the wildlife, it's also important to stay back at least 200 feet from harbor seals, California sea lions, and otters that are common to the slough. If the animals you see begin to appear nervous, then you're getting too close.

Dedicated co-author doing onsite research

Central Coast

Monterey County

MOSS LANDING

About halfway around Monterey Bay, at the mouth of Elkhorn Slough, is the small fishing village of Moss Landing. The harbor is home to dozens of boats, both pleasure and commercial fishing vessels. The small, quaint community is mostly comprised of small restaurants and an interesting collection of antique shops that are always fun to wander through and explore.

Zmudowski State Beach (831.649.2836 or www.parks.ca.gov) is another few miles south. Its long and wide beach is similar to its nearby neighbors, Salinas River and Moss Landing state beaches. Again, no pets are allowed on the beach.

At the north end of town is **Moss Landing State Beach** (831.649.2836 or www.parks.ca.gov). The park is a popular destination for surfing, windsurfing and bird watching. Pets are not allowed in the park, camping area, or on the beach.

Salinas River State Beach (831.649.2836 or www.parks.ca.gov) is located at the southern end of the community of Moss Landing and less than a mile off Highway 1. It offers a long stretch of open beach that is a favorite with anglers and beach explorers. There's usually a great deal of driftwood along the beaches. All of these waters are dangerous for swimmers. No pets are allowed on the beach.

MORE TO EXPLORE

Closer to Monterey, **Marina State Beach**, located at the Highway 1 exit at Reservation Road, is a fun place to stop. In addition to having a public beach similar to others around Monterey Bay, Marina has a concessionaire that provides hang-gliding supplies and lessons. It's a popular place for such activities, and even if hanging about in midair doesn't sound fun, watching the graceful flyers can be quite enjoyable. There's also a boardwalk into the dunes that passes by numerous

Marina State Beach

threatened and endangered dune plants that are doing very well in the rehabilitated dune habitat. This is a great place to sit in the evening and look across at the lights of Monterey and Pacific Grove. Marina State Beach is also an active nesting area for the endangered snowy plover. No pets are allowed. Info: 831.649.2836 or www.parks.ca.gov

Located south of Marina State Beach, **Fort Ord Dunes State Park** offers sand, history, and fun. One of California's newest state parks, the facility features miles of beach and coastline. There is also boardwalk access from the parking lot to a bluff-top viewing platform. The park is cellphone friendly: call 831.998.9458 during your visit and take a self-guided tour through the Army-facility-turned-state-park. Signs posted at the different places in the park list three-digit numbers you can enter into your phone to learn more about what you are looking at, such as the firing range, army bunkers, or target fields. Pets are allowed in the parking lot and on the paved road only. Info: 831.649.2836 or www.parks.ca.gov

Monterey Bay National Marine Sanctuary

Established in 1992, the Monterey Bay National Marine Sanctuary encompasses 4,601-square nautical miles of ocean, making it the country's largest marine sanctuary. It also has the distinction of claiming 276 miles of the nation's most beautiful and rugged shoreline. Ocean researchers come from around the world to conduct research on the sanctuary's rich underwater resources, which include not only the plants, geologic features, and the strange creatures found in depths that reach 2 miles, but also the extensive kelp beds that stretch along its entire length.

The sanctuary is operated by the National Oceanic and Atmospheric Administration. NOAA and numerous research institutes are committed to continuing research and education. Knowing what effects changing water temperatures will have on phytoplankton, the marine food chain's base organism, and what effect those changes have on the other animals, will help scientists make decisions about what marine resource protections might be added to or reduced.

The sanctuary stretches from Rocky Point—7 miles north of the Golden Gate—to Cambria Rock in San Luis Obispo County. While not prohibiting such things as commercial fishing, the sanctuary's status still provides significant protection for its 34 species of marine mammals, 180 species of shorebirds and seabirds, and 525 fish species. There are also four turtle species, 31 phyla of invertebrates, and more than 450 species of marine algae, kelp being the most prominent. Info: NOAA, 99 Pacific Street, Bldg. 455A, Monterey, CA 93940, 831.647.4201 or www.montereybay.noaa.gov

Central Coast

Monterey
Harbor,
with the
commercial
fishing wharf
in the distance

MONTEREY PENINSULA

While the younger, wilder, college set tends to favor Santa Cruz across the bay, the Monterey Peninsula attracts more of the mellower and slightly older generation who prefer quieter hotels, excellent restaurants, and numerous golf courses. But there are plenty of young people and families who also prefer Monterey. Daytime temperatures are often a few degrees cooler on the Monterey side of the bay and summer fog more common. The Monterey Peninsula includes the cities of Monterey, Pacific Grove, Seaside, Marina, Carmel, and the gated community of Pebble Beach with its famous golf courses and 17-Mile Drive.

The Monterey Peninsula is known for many things, not the least of which is long sandy beaches and incredible tide pools. Beaches circle around from the mouth of the Salinas River, across land that once was part of the U.S. Army's **Fort Ord**, but is now a California state beach. Sand continues until the granite outcroppings begin to appear near Fisherman's Wharf and continue around past the peninsula's protruding point at Pacific Grove's **Point Pinos**.

The waters of the bay are much too cold and dangerous for swimming, although a few hardier souls, such as youngsters, like to chase waves in the more protected coves during summer. Wet-suit clad surfers have several favorite spots, depending on the direction and size of the waves. **Lovers Point Park** and **Asilomar State Beach** are two favorite surfing locations, especially during winter when the waves are big. For those less inclined to brave the cold waters, exploring the many rock-bound tide pools is a popular pastime. The entire area is part of a **National Marine Sanctuary**, state parks, and a marine preserve, so everything in the tide pools must be left where they are. Look at the sea stars and urchins, the sculpins and crabs, but don't take them home. The animals won't live, and they stink when dead, especially in your car.

If you have a bicycle, bring it. There's a great bicycle trail that runs from Lovers Point in Pacific Grove to Monterey's Fisherman's Wharf—it is very level and kid-accessible. Actually, the bike trail continues northeast around the bay another 10 miles or so to the town of Marina. It's a nice ride, although there are several short, steep portions, as the trail must climb over freeway overpasses.

MONTEREY STATE HISTORIC PARK

Founded in 1770, Monterey is the second oldest city in California. While San Diego is a year older, it was Monterey that served as Spain's and then Mexico's center of government for their respective California empires. Monterey was also the center for trade back then, and for many years had the only customhouse—a government office that cleared incoming vessels and collected custom fees. Called the **Custom House**, the Monterey building was constructed of adobe bricks, molded from a combination of clay and straw, dried, then stacked into walls, and finally covered with plaster to protect them from the rain.

Unlike most parks with obvious entrances, Monterey State Historic Park is a collection of 18th- and 19th-century adobe buildings spread throughout several blocks of old Monterey. Start by visiting the **Pacific House**. Originally a government storage building during the 1800s, it now serves as a museum and orientation center for the state historic park. Be sure to ask for cellphone tour information so you can guide yourself through all of the historic buildings, keying in codes on your phone to learn more about the park's history.

In 1879, Robert Louis Stevenson moved to Monterey, mostly living off the good graces of friends, since he had not yet become the famous writer that he would in the years that followed. The rooming house where he stayed has been restored, and many of his later possessions have been donated and are exhibited in what has become known as the **Stevenson House**. Nearby, the **Cooper-Molera Adobe** complex offers a look at a fully furnished adobe home with its beautiful

The interior of the historic Custom House is filled with typical goods that would have been unloaded from early 19th century trading ships.

gardens. Several of the historic homes in Monterey have extensive flower gardens, and during summer docents lead special garden tours. Many of the historic adobes are featured on the different tours, as are city-owned historic buildings such as **Colton Hall** where California's Constitution was written (in both English and Spanish) and signed in 1849.

Activities: House and walking tours, periodic living history events, many weekend ethnic celebrations on the plaza during summer

Facilities: Museums, historic buildings, Custom House Plaza

Dates: Open daily

Fees: There's a fee for guided walking tours and house tours. Visitors may go on a free, self-guided walking tour by following the gold tiles in the walkways or via the cellphone tour.

Info: Monterey State Historic Park, 20 Custom House Plaza, Monterey, CA 93940, 831.649.7118 or www.parks.ca.gov

MONTEREY BAY AQUARIUM

Concealed inside the reconstructed facade of an old cannery building at the end of historic Cannery Row, the Monterey Bay Aquarium features one spectacular live exhibit after another.

Huge tanks are a given at any aquarium, but here, they reign supreme. For

Leopard shark

example, an entire kelp forest undulates to the rhythm of artificially produced waves behind the 7-inch thick acrylic windows of one floor-to-ceiling tank. Within the forest of giant kelp (*Macrocystis pyrifera*) swim dozens of species of fish: leopard sharks (*Triakis semifasciata*), schools of Pacific sardines (*Sardinops sagix*), and blue rockfish (*Sebastes mystinus*). One of the most interesting fish in the kelp forest is the sheephead (*Semicossyphus pulcher*). All sheepheads begin life as females. Once they grow to a foot or more in length, they change colors—developing broad stripes of red, white, and black—but more interestingly, they change sex, too. Several benches can be found in front of the tank where people sit mesmerized by this scuba-diver's perspective of the underwater world.

Nearby, numerous smaller live exhibits provide up-close looks at many species of octopi. A curious looking cousin—the cuttlefish (*Sepia officinalio*)—lies on the sandy bottom of its tank. It watches for prey and when dinner happens by, the cuttlefish shoots out two tentacles to capture its meal. When something bigger comes looking to make a meal of the cuttlefish, it changes color to better match its surroundings then disappears in a cloud of ink.

Around the corner, sharks greet the shredded fish their feeders drop in the tank; this is a fun feeding to watch, so be sure to check posted feeding times. Within this large tank, with its remarkably realistic shale reef reproduction, you'll find jack mackerel (*Trachurus symmetricus*), a beautiful seven-gill shark (*Notorynchus cepedianus*), chinook or king salmon (*Onochynchus tshawytscha*) that will have any angler's attention, striped bass (*Morone saxatilis*), and vermillion rockfish (*Sebaste miuiatus*), which are sometimes mistakenly called "rockcod" or "red snapper." Anemones and sea stars, some incredibly large, live on the bottom of the pool, thus adding to its realistic appearance.

Near the aquarium's main entrance, sea otters (*Enhydra lutris*) frolic in a large tank. The aquarium manages a marine mammal rescue and rehab program that has rescued more than 500 baby sea otters during the past 27-plus years. The aquarium otters on view are rescues that are unable to return to the wild. So how do otters stay warm in the cold Pacific waters? They have the world's densest fur with up to 1-million hairs per square inch. Humans have 100,000 hairs on their entire head! That rich fur is what made otters so attractive to early Russian, English, and American trappers, nearly bringing the species to extinction.

Main entrance to the Monterey Bay Aquarium

Head upstairs to the **Splash Zone** because not everything in the aquarium is devoted to only creatures that live underwater. The touch tanks are for kids of all ages. Here, a large assortment of live sea creatures spend time in saltwater pools, and aquarium volunteers make the creatures available for the public to handle. Equally exciting and fun is the large pool that houses a number of harmless bat rays (*Myliobatis californica*), some 2 feet or more across. Dozens of hands reach into the pool, and with patience, successfully pet these amazing creatures.

Nearby, the aviary is a wonderful refuge for examples of many of the shore-birds found outside. In a reproduced wet-land and beach area, with waves slapping gently on its sandy shoreline, are avo-cets (*Recurvirostra americana*), western sandpipers (*Calidris mauri*), sanderlings (*Calidris alba*), and willits (*Catoptropho-rus semipalmatus*). And for anyone in-terested in seeing the

Sea lions in Monterey Bay

endangered snowy plover (*Charadrius alexandrinus*) up close, there's usually one bobbing its way over the sand.

Most people associate penguins with snow and ice, but some, such as the aquarium's African black-footed penguins (*Spheniscus demersus*), do just fine in the ocean waters around South Africa—and at the Monterey Bay Aquarium. The waters in which they live are cold, but not icy, and the birds have a double layer of insulating feathers and down. The best time to see the dozen or so penguins that live here is during the two daily feeding sessions in the Splash Zone.

Swimming in a huge circular tank above the entrance to the jelly fish ex-hibits are thousands of anchovies. Passing through the anchovies, the lights dim, reminiscent of the deeper waters found farther offshore in Monterey Bay. This is the jellyfish exhibit. Windows illuminated by dramatic colored lights offer a look at some of the most extraordinarily delicate and beautiful creatures in the ocean. Visitors can see jellyfish ranging in size from basketballs to thimbles. Anyone who has swum into the floating stream of the orange-brown sea nettle's (*Chrysaura fuscescens*) tentacles might not agree that it is a delicate and beautiful creature. The sea nettle paralyzes its prey before eating it. It also causes severe stinging pain to swimmers who inadvertently cross its drifting path. At the **Open Sea** exhibit, tuna, sharks, a giant turtle, and swarms of sardines share the aquarium's largest tank. All is visible as you stand behind this 90-foot-wide window on the ocean depths.

Plan to spend at least two hours in the aquarium and much longer if you are especially fascinated by the ocean. Also, check the feeding times for the otters in the otter tank, one of the most popular attractions. Additional programs are shown in the outside viewing areas and in the aquarium's theaters.

Activities: Self-guided tours, special talks, movies, events
Facilities: Gift shop, snack bar, outside seating and viewing areas
Dates: Open daily, extended hours during summer
Fees: There is an entrance fee for adults and a lesser fee for children.
Info: Monterey Bay Aquarium, 886 Cannery Row, Monterey, CA 93940, 831. 648.4800 or www.montereybayaquarium.org

FISHERMAN'S WHARF

Monterey actually enjoys two wharves. The Fisherman's Wharf that draws most people's attention juts into the bay from near the front of the historic Custom House and the adjacent **Custom House Plaza**. It's a sensual jumble of sights, smells, and sounds that greet hundreds of people each day, especially during summer. Food is one of the real attractions here. In front of many of the small stands, proprietors offer free samples of their delicious clam chowders, while fresh fish and crab lie atop mounds of ice, and slabs of salmon smoke slowly on open smoke pits. There are many restaurants, all offering good food and great views of the harbor. Many people who wander onto the wharf simply pick and choose samplings of shrimp and crab cocktails, fried calamari, or the plethora of other seafood that tempts the palate. And there's always the many gift shops filled with T-shirts, postcards, and jewelry, and more stores selling ice cream, taffy, and chocolate-covered frozen bananas.

You can also charter a fishing boat at the wharf or join a scheduled trip. Fish that frequent these waters include cod, halibut, salmon, sea bass, and plenty of other species of game fish. It's always enjoyable to watch the gulls

Monterey's Fisherman's Wharf

and brown pelicans (*Pelecanus occidentalis*) swoop in, looking for free handouts around the fish-cleaning dock. They're often joined by one or more California sea lions (*Zalophus californicus*) also willing to fight for chunks of discarded fish entrails.

For those more interested in watching whales than catching fish, boats also depart several times each day on whale-watching trips. The peak months are January and February when gray whales (*Eschrichtius robustus*) are migrating south. Summer brings the giant blue whales (*Balanenoptera musculus*) into the bay, along with huge schools of dolphins (*Delphinus delphis*) and occasional pods of orcas or killer whales (*Orcinus orca*). Whale-watching boats, often for reasons of time, seldom venture out beyond the relatively sheltered waters of the bay. But even here, anyone prone to motion sickness should take appropriate precautions.

Activities: Fishing, shopping, eating, whale watching, charter fishing

Facilities: Restaurants, gift shops, fresh fish sales

Dates: Open daily

Fees: Hourly parking fees, but pedestrian access is free

Info: www.MontereyWharf.com or Monterey's Lake El Estero Visitors Center, 401 Camino El Estero, Monterey, CA 93940, 888.221.1010 or www.SeeMonterey.com

CANNERY ROW

The stench of sardines that permeated the heart and soul of this corner of Monterey and extended into neighboring Pacific Grove 50 years ago has long since disappeared. A read of John Steinbeck's famed *Cannery Row* can quickly bring it back to life, at least in one's imagination. Also gone are the canneries that began appearing here in 1902—those first canneries processed salmon and abalone for the San Francisco market. As those markets faded, the sardine fishery slowly began to take its place. Within a few years, improved technology and work practices allowed fishing boats to unload their holds more efficiently and quickly and fac-

Gray whale

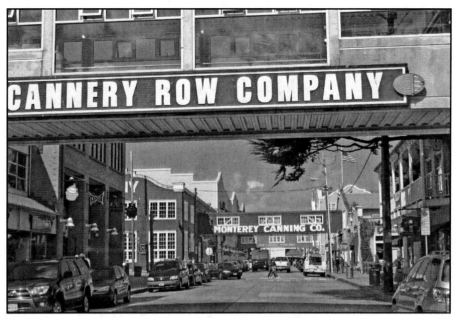

Cannery Row's sardines have been replaced by dozens of shops, restaurants, and the Monterey Bay Aquarium, which is located at the end of the street.

tories significantly increased the speed and efficiency of their canning processes.

As World War II raged, sardines became the mainstay of the Monterey fishing industry. Following a night of fishing, the boats—mostly large purse seiners—would return to unload as much as 70 tons of sardines into the factories, which processed most of the fish into fishmeal and fertilizer. On the first night of the sardine fishing season in 1949, some 52 purse seiners and 16 smaller boats returned to Monterey's canneries with more than 2,500 tons of sardines.

By the early 1950s, the sardine industry was in serious trouble. An entire season would see no more than what had been a slow night's catch during the 1940s. Overfishing, water temperature changes, pollution, and any number of other contributing factors brought the sardine industry to its knees and sent its owners into bankruptcy. The years that followed were not any kinder to the Cannery Row waterfront. The abandoned canneries fell into disrepair, and the entire area became a blight on the edge of Monterey Bay. Urban redevelopment and an increasing tourist industry finally started bringing the Row back to life. Some of the remaining canneries were transformed into shops, restaurants, and amusement centers. The opening of Monterey Bay Aquarium in 1984 brought a huge increase in tourism to the area. It also spurred further enhancements to the surrounding areas.

Wandering around Cannery Row's several blocks can be an adventure in itself. The interior of the old structures are a maze of corridors and walkways, stairs,

Central Coast

and passages that lead from one unique shop to another and from myriad restaurants to winetasting rooms. There are carousels and jewelry stores, kayak rentals, and bicycle rentals.

Info: Lake El Estero Visitors Center, 401 Camino El Estero, Monterey, CA 93940, 888.221.1010, www.SeeMonterey.com or www.canneryrow.com

THE NATIONAL STEINBECK CENTER

For those who can't get enough of the great John Steinbeck, especially after visiting Cannery Row, take a quick side trip to Salinas, located about 20 minutes inland from Monterey. Salinas was the birthplace of Steinbeck, whose novels and short stories have entertained millions of people. His Pulitzer Prize-winning novel, *The Grapes of Wrath*, also angered many of those who lived and worked in the Salinas Valley. Apparently, Steinbeck hit a little too close to home with his descriptions of the lives of farm workers and how the farm owners treated them. Some of Steinbeck's other books, such as *Cannery Row* and *Tortilla Flat*, brought to life the more colorful characters that lived and worked in 1930's Monterey.

Today, Salinas is home to the National Steinbeck Center, a multimedia experience of the famous author's life. Themed galleries feature exhibits related to his

Steinbeck's Rocinate

many novels and theaters show clips of the many films based on his writings. One of the center's prized possessions is "Rocinante." It's the GMC pick-up truck with a custom camper that Steinbeck drove across the country with his dog Charley while doing research for *Travels with Charley*. For the more academically inclined, the center houses more than 30,000 pieces of oral histories, photographs, original manuscripts, and first-edition books.

Facilities: Museum galleries, theater, gift shop
Dates: Open daily
Fees: There is an entrance fee with discounts for children and seniors.
Info: The National Steinbeck Center, 1 Main Street, Salinas, CA 93901, 831.796.3833 or www.steinbeck.org

MONTEREY BAY COASTAL RECREATION TRAIL

From tracks to trail, discover the 18 miles of pure joy when utilizing one of Monterey Bay's family-friendly bike trails. For example, the Monterey Bay Coastal Recreation Trail begins in **Castroville** to the north, ending in Pacific Grove to the south. Much of the route was once the track line for the Southern Pacific Railroad.

This trail slices right through many popular tourist attractions in Monterey. The trail is open to pedestrians and in-line skaters, although in some areas, pedestrians are directed by signs to walk on the dirt walkway adjacent to the paved trail while bicyclists and in-line skaters use the paved trail. But beware—pedestrians don't always do so. If you're a cyclist and speed is your need, staying away from the Pacific Grove/Cannery Row/Fisherman's Wharf area should be your priority during summer, unless biking early in the morning. By afternoon, the trail is much too crowded for fast-peddling bicyclists. Many bike rental operators offer a variety of bikes for rent, including the old-fashioned four-seater peddle buggies.

The best place to park and unload bicycles is either at the **Lovers Point Park** parking lot in Pacific Grove or in the parking lot off Del Monte Avenue, east of Sloat Avenue and across the street from the gate into the **Naval Post Graduate School**. The Fisherman's Wharf parking lot off Del Monte Avenue also offers easy access to the recreation trail.

Activities: The bike trail is open to walkers, runners, bicyclists, and in-line skaters. Skateboards are prohibited.

Facilities: Except at Lovers Point Park and Fisherman's Wharf, there are no stand-alone restrooms along the trail.

Dates: Open daily, not lighted for night use

Info: Monterey's Lake El Estero Visitors Center, 401 Camino El Estero, Monterey, CA 93940, 888.221.1010 or www.SeeMonterey.com

Bicycling around Pacific Grove's Lovers Point Park

Central Coast

MORE TO EXPLORE

Central coast beach waters are generally too cold and dangerous for swimming. One of the most popular—and relatively safe—swimming areas, especially for parents with children, is the protected cove at **Lovers Point Park** in Pacific Grove. The slope is gentle, the waves small, and the area is reasonably well protected from the afternoon breezes. Outside the cove, surfers often catch some pretty good-sized waves off the point. The park has a kayak and bike rental shop and snack bar open during summer. Info: 831.648.3100

For a closer look at the local commercial fishing boats unloading their catches, **Monterey's Commercial Wharf** is located a few hundred yards northeast of the tourists' Fisherman's Wharf, near the marina's boat launch area. Gulls, pelicans, and sea lions shadow the fishing boats as they motor into the wharf and tie-off. Their fish cargoes are sorted and packed with ice into large transport containers. Unknown to most people, this is also the best place for the public to purchase whole fish by the pound. The prices are generally the lowest you'll find anywhere around, and the fish come really fresh, sometimes still wriggling. The sellers will clean and fillet the fish for you for a small additional fee. Or, if you have a fishing pole and tackle, you can try your luck from the commercial wharf, as many people do. It's not a bad way to spend a few hours.

For anyone with their own kayak, **Monterey State Beach** has a long and gentle sandy beach that offers easy kayak launching. The beach is across from **Lake El Estero**. Info: 831.649.2836 or www.parks.ca.gov

At the east end of Cannery Row, adjacent to the U.S. Coast Guard pier entrance, scuba divers have discovered **San Carlos Beach**. Actually the city of Monterey developed the park, including plenty of parking (metered), and added a restroom and outside showers specifically to accommodate the large number of scuba divers who come here. It's a very popular place for beginning divers. The large grassy area offers plenty of space for picnics and for relaxing after a day of diving.

Monterey's commercial fishing wharf

Warning!

All of these beaches can be dangerous, especially during winter when even colder water and higher waves can and do sweep unsuspecting beach-goers and tide pool explorers offshore. Sleeper waves—a single wave or set of waves much larger than those that may have washed ashore for quite some time—strike suddenly and without warning. Unfortunately, they sweep people to their deaths every year in this region.

Large waves near Pfeiffer Beach

PACIFIC GROVE

Pacific Grove—the self-proclaimed "Last Hometown"—is a quaint and beautiful small community that sits on the point of land separating Monterey Bay from the open waters of the Pacific Ocean. While its neighbor Monterey enjoys afternoon sunshine, Pacific Grove is generally draped in fog during summer. The town's main street—**Lighthouse Avenue**—provides a short few blocks of wonderful antique shops, restaurants, and more; during the Christmas season, the trees and buildings are brilliantly illuminated in white and multicolored lights.

From where it begins near the Monterey Bay Aquarium, Pacific Grove's **Ocean View Boulevard** meanders along the coast. Continue on Ocean View Boulevard where several parking areas on the low, coastal bluff offer great opportunities to explore the rocky tide pools that the town is so well known for. Near **Point Pinos**, the same road turns into Sunset Avenue and continues around the point.

Central Coast

If you look closely at Pacific Grove's older Victorian and other quaintly designed homes, you'll notice that many have small wooden plaques near their front doors indicating the late 19th and early 20th century dates of their construction. Not many know this, but Pacific Grove was originally founded as a Christian retreat. An

Asilomar's registration building is one of many in the park designed by Juila Morgan.

example of the town's early beginnings can be found at **Asilomar State Beach and Conference Grounds** (831.372.8016 or www.parks.ca.gov), constructed in 1914 as a Young Women's Christian Association (YWCA) summer camp. Many of its original buildings were designed by Julia Morgan, the famed California architect who designed Hearst Castle. Today, Asilomar is a world-renowned conference center owned by California State Parks. Asilomar also accepts non-conference guests in its moderately priced accommodations.

Asilomar State Beach easily is the peninsula's most popular spot for sunset watching. While summer's fog somtimes obscures the sun behind a thick gray curtain, during much of the year cars begin parking along the road an hour or more before sunset in order to guarantee the perfect viewing spot. Here, the open ocean's crashing waves, especially during winter, offer ample opportunities for great memories and beautiful photographs.

Sunset Avenue circles around Pacific Grove crossing 17-Mile Drive, which offers access to one of several gates into Pebble Beach. Actually, 17-Mile Drive begins (or ends) in Pacific Grove, crossing Lighthouse Avenue a few blocks west of the town's business district.

One of the favorite trips for bicyclists in Pacific Grove is the Sunset Drive to Ocean

Watch out for the Enforcer!

View Avenue coastal route. While Ocean View is reasonably level with gentle hills, Sunset Drive has a fairly long and steep descent from its beginning at Highway 68, above 17-Mile Drive. There is also lots of traffic, most of which travels slowly, and that is good, since many of the drivers are more likely looking at the ocean and not for bicyclists.

PACIFIC GROVE MUSEUM OF NATURAL HISTORY

This is one of those hidden treasures that will remain undiscovered unless you happen to be traveling slightly off the main tourist route of popular Lighthouse Avenue. Outside the museum is a concrete replica of a gray whale, which kids can't help but climb on. Sometimes the tough part is getting them inside. But once inside, anyone interested in the Central Coast's natural history is in for a surprise. The museum, which opened in 1883, houses one of the most extensive bird collections on the West Coast; more than 400 birds are mounted and on display, representing 290 different species. Additional exhibits on geology (don't miss the 2,400-pound Big Sur jade boulder), mammals, insects, and more fill the small museum. And for those who drop in occasionally, there is always a major exhibit in the museum's large exhibit hall. Special guest lectures are also a feature. It's a good place to spend time becoming oriented to the area's diverse natural history.

Activities: Lectures, occasional children's programs
Facilities: Museum, natural history exhibits, gift shop
Dates: Open daily except Mondays and holidays
Fees: There is an admission fee.
Info: Pacific Grove Museum of Natural History, 165 Forest Avenue, Pacific Grove, CA 93950, 831.648.5716 or www.pgmuseum.org

White pelicans

Point Pinos Lighthouse

POINT PINOS LIGHTHOUSE

Located in Pacific Grove, this lighthouse is the oldest in continuous operation on the West Coast. With a beacon range of 17 miles out to sea, the Point Pinos Lighthouse has been lit nearly every night since 1855. The only exception was for the mandatory blackouts during World War II.

The lighthouse still has its original third-order Fresnel lens. Fourteen lighthouse keepers—including two women, which was unheard of during that time—took care of the light until 1914. Like most lighthouses, this beacon was originally lit with whale oil, and as the years went on, the lighting fuel was changed to lard oil, kerosene, an incandescent vapor flame, and then, in 1919, the lighthouse beacon started using electricity.

Today, the lighthouse—which is on the National Register of Historic Places—is staffed and maintained by dedicated volunteers and docents. It is owned by the city of Pacific Grove and operated in conjunction with the U.S. Coast Guard.

Activities: Docent-led and self-guided tours
Facilities: Lighthouse, lighthouse keeper residence
Dates: Open from 1 P.M. to 4 P.M. Thursday through Monday
Fees: Suggested donation
Closest town: Pacific Grove
Info: Point Pinos Lighthouse, 90 Asilomar Avenue, Pacific Grove, CA 93950, www.pointpinos.org

PEBBLE BEACH AND 17-MILE DRIVE

A must-do tour while on the Monterey Peninsula is the famous 17-Mile Drive. The original 17-Mile Drive began in Monterey, from the Victorian-style **Hotel Del Monte**, which, when constructed in 1880, was the "Queen of American Watering Places" and considered the most elegant seaside resort in the world. Fire destroyed the hotel, but another was rebuilt, serving today as the home of the **Naval Post Graduate School** headquarters in Monterey. The original tours from the hotel used horse-drawn wagons; today's tours begin at the private gates into Pebble Beach, with visitors using their own cars or bicycles.

Pebble Beach evolved from properties, including the coastline and the **Del Monte Forest**, originally consolidated into Del Monte Properties by railroad magnate Charles Crocker. Crocker began developing portions of the property, including a beach bathhouse and a racetrack, but the economics of the time took a downturn. Subsequently a young Samuel F. B. Morse—a very, very distant relative of Samuel F. B. Morse, who was best known for his invention of the telegraph—and a group of investors purchased the property in 1915. Soon afterward, Morse began developing Pebble Beach into what it is today.

The views today along 17-Mile Drive remain as memorable as those seen by visitors a century ago. From the Pacific Grove gate into Pebble Beach, 17-Mile Drive leads past the Inn at Spanish Bay and down to **Spanish Bay** where

Spanish Bay

Central Coast

209

Mariposa lily...and friend

many people come for the long, sandy beach. The tour road continues weaving between the many golf links. There almost always is a large population of feeding deer on the fairways. There are several popular stops along this stretch of 17-Mile Drive, including **Point Joe**, where the ocean's currents cross paths with currents from Monterey Bay, creating constantly crashing waves and ocean mist just offshore. The sounds of barking sea lions coming from **Bird Rock**, also a favorite resting place for seabirds, can easily be heard over the ocean waves. **China Rock** memorializes the Chinese who established fishing villages, not only here, but in other areas between Monterey and Point Lobos. Wind your way up to **Cypress Point Lookout,** and on clear days Point Sur Lighthouse, located 20 miles down the Big Sur coast, is visible.

Why has 17-Mile Drive remained so popular for so long? It certainly has something to do with the spectacular views of the coast. There are also the incredible homes tucked into the coastal cliffs and partially hidden in the Del Monte Forest, homes with prices that generally fall into the seven- and eight-figure range. If traffic and crowds are any gauge, the most popular site along 17-Mile Drive is the famed **Lone Cypress** that is perched rather precariously near the end of a rocky point surrounded by the swirling surf. The Lone Cypress is estimated to be somewhere between 200 and 300 years old, which is remarkable considering its extremely inhospitable home, surrounded by sea, wind, and non-fertile rock.

17-Mile Drive is popular for bicycle touring, but this is not a place for beginning or infrequent riders. There are several steep hills, and often there isn't much space between passing cars and bicyclists. Also, some parts of Pebble Beach are off limits to bicyclists, and motorcycles are not allowed anywhere on 17-Mile Drive.

Activities: Scenic driving with numerous stops, golfing, beach exploring, horseback riding, picnicking, fine dining
Facilities: Hotels, restaurants, golf courses
Dates: Open daily
Fees: There is a fee for nonresident vehicles to enter Pebble Beach and 17-Mile Drive. Bicyclists must sign a release form located near the entry gate

then enter at no cost. Motorcycles are not allowed. Hotels, most restaurants, and golf courses are expensive.

Closest town: Pacific Grove and Carmel

Info: 17-Mile Drive Association, Pebble Beach, CA 93953, 800.654.9300 or www.pebblebeach.com

CARMEL MISSION

One of California's better-known missions is *San Carlos Borromeo*, better known as the Carmel Mission. On June 3, 1770, Father Junipero Serra arrived in Monterey and founded his second mission, the first having been San Diego the previous year. Feeling that he had located his Monterey mission too close to the newly established Monterey Presidio (fort), the following year Serra moved it to where it remains today in Carmel. The mission's primary goal was to convert local Indians to Christianity and, ultimately, into Spanish citizens. Unfortunately, Spain's plans were implemented at the expense of the Indians' native cultures.

There is a certain charm that attracts people from all over the world to the Carmel Mission. Its place in California's history certainly plays a part in that attraction, but there is much more. Wander through the restored, yet remarkably

Carmel Mission

211

old-appearing complex, and enjoy its beautiful gardens, the awe-inspiring church, and the rooms filled with the history of this two century-old house of worship. Artists often try to capture its physical beauty on canvas, and photographers, amateur and professional alike, have taken untold millions of photographs.

Maybe part of the attraction is the fact that Father Serra died here in 1784. As Padre Presidentes of California's missions, Serra wished to spend his last years at the Carmel Mission. When he passed away, he was buried with his friend and fellow padre Father Crespi before the mission's main altar.

It was more than a decade after Serra's death that one of his successors began construction of the present-day stone church, but it fell into disrepair following Mexico's secularization of the missions in 1834. With the church's lands divided and gone, the buildings disintegrated, many into nothing more than partial walls. In 1931, local residents began a major effort to restore the mission to what it is today. And in 1961, Pope John Paul XXIII designated the Carmel Mission as a Minor Basilica.

Facilities: Gardens, courtyard, church, small gift shop, museum
Dates: Open daily
Fees: There is an admission fee.
Info: Carmel Mission Gift Shop, 3880 Rio Road, Carmel, CA 93921, 831.624.1271, x210 or www.carmelmission.org

MORE TO EXPLORE

Carmel City Beach, located at the end of Ocean Street in Carmel and managed by the city of **Carmel-by-the-Sea**, is another open, sandy beach, which is especially popular with dog owners. It's one of the few public beaches where dogs can run free without such hindrances as leashes. Info: 831.624.3543

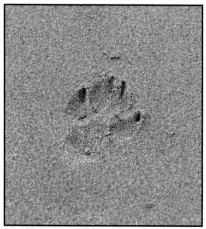

Carmel River State Beach, with its lagoon and wetland, is located about 1 mile south of Carmel on Highway 1. There's a small beach with pull-out parking along the highway, and it's a short walk to the water. The beach, or at least the small section closest to Highway 1, is better known locally as "**Monastery Beach**" or "**San Jose Creek Beach**," and is a spot frequented by scuba divers. It's also a dangerous beach, with sleeper waves, cold water, and a fairly steep drop-off. Stay back and don't allow children to play close to the water. Info: 831.649.2836 or www.parks.ca.gov

Dogs *love* Carmel City Beach

For antique luxury car enthusiasts, the Monterey Peninsula is the place to be in mid-August each year for the world-famous **Pebble Beach Concours d'Elegance**. Here, you will find nearly 200 exquisite cars from around the world. Be it a Ferrari or a Bentley, the cars are exhibited on the fairway of the famed 18th hole at the Pebble Beach Golf Course. The luxury cars' combined value is often in excess of $200 million. Info: www.carmelcalifornia.com or 831.624.2522

Co-author's son at a sandcastle event

For more than 50 years, sand artists have been showing up at Carmel-by-the-Sea for the city's annual **Sandcastle Contest**. Held in mid-October, the event draws dozens of sand architects and hundreds of encouraging visitors. And anyone can enter and possibly win the coveted Golden Shovel award—or the Sour Grapes award. Info: www.carmelCalifornia.com or 831.620.2020

Poet Robinson Jeffers and his wife Una first came to Carmel in 1914 and decided it was the place to spend the rest of their lives. On a rocky point overlooking the Pacific Ocean, Jeffers built their home, creating what he named the "**Tor House**." Four years later, he completed **Hawk Tower**, a special stone castle for his wife and sons. It was his refuge and the place where he wrote nearly all of his works, including the 1947 adaption of *Medea* for Broadway. The home was completed in 1919, but it was another three decades before electricity was added. Over the years, Jeffers hosted many guests including Charles Lindbergh, George Gershwin, Charlie Chaplain, and Edward Abbey. Jeffers died in 1962, and now his home is open to the public for tours on Fridays and Saturdays only. Info: www.torhouse.org or 831.624.1813

POINT LOBOS NATURAL STATE RESERVE

Point Lobos is one of those jewels that has attracted people since the earliest of times. Although permanent Native American villages were never possible because fresh water was not available year around, Indians did live along San Jose Creek, a half-mile or so to the northeast.

Point Lobos has seen many changes during the past 170 years. It was used as a whaling processing site, an abalone processing and canning plant, and a shipping point for coal that was mined from the nearby mountains. At the end of the 19th century, the land was even subdivided by a developer who envisioned making a

Central Coast

Sea lions enjoying the sunshine

fortune selling home sites. Fortunately, with a combination of private donations and funds from Save the Redwoods League, the property became a state park in 1933.

While the surface lands of Point Lobos may have been changed—at least superficially by those wanting to exploit its natural resources—what hasn't changed much in millions of years is the underlying geology. The relatively coarse-grained Santa Lucia granite that formed deep below the surface some 110 million years ago was uplifted to form the jagged headlands along the reserve's northern shore. Near the center of the reserve, by **Sea Lion Point**, the Carmelo Formation—a sedimentary conglomerate—is most prevalent. Only 60 million years old, the more easily erodible conglomerate is composed of smaller stones in what appears as a yellowish-colored concrete. Throughout the reserve, the conglomerate has eroded to form jagged cliffs and graceful arches. Yet scattered in a few protected coves, several sandy beaches await exploration, while others remain inaccessible.

Besides the obvious terrestrial beauty, 750 underwater acres are also part of the reserve. Point Lobos is an incredibly popular scuba-diving spot, generally requiring reservations weeks in advance. One of the reasons it remains such a treasure for divers is that the number of divers is limited each day and everything is protected. Any spearfishing has to be done outside the reserve's boundaries.

Many people first coming to the reserve are surprised by the numbers and varieties of wildlife that live here. The seemingly ubiquitous sea otters frolic in the cold waters, and during spring and early summer, they can be seen caring for their young offspring. The most vocally boisterous animals are the sea lions. Aptly named, **Sea Lion Rock** offers a small sanctuary from the crashing waves for large numbers of California sea lions (*Zalophus californianus*) at almost any time of the year. The adult males, which can weigh up to 800 pounds, leave the local waters during the first months of summer and swim to rookeries farther south. During the time of year when they are at Point Lobos in greater numbers, it is impossible to miss their loud, incessant barking or their antics on the offshore rocks. Their loud and persistent barking is what caused the early Spanish explorers to name the area *Punta de los Lobos Marino*: Point of the Sea Wolves.

Birds are another major attraction of Point Lobos. On almost any day, dozens of different species can be seen in the reserve. For Brandt's cormorants (*Phalacrocorax penicillatus*) and black oystercatchers (*Haematopus bachmani*), western gulls (*Larus occidentalis*) and great blue herons (*Ardea herodias*), the sea, and the lands around it, provide rich feeding grounds. It's not at all unusual, especially late in the afternoon, for deer to wander out into the open forest or meadows amidst grasses and wildflowers to graze, while coyotes and—even more rarely, a mountain lion—cross the reserve's several miles of trails.

Cabin at Whaler's Cove

In the wind-protected **Whalers' Cove**, there is a small wood cottage that has been around since the 1850s when Chinese fishermen and their families moved to Point Lobos. The museum houses numerous exhibits and whaling-era artifacts such as harpoons. A short walk down the road from the museum is where scuba divers park and enter the cove. There's also a restroom and a picnic table or two. Over its history, the area occupied by today's parking lot has served as a whale rendering area, held an abalone cannery, and been home to a quarry that supposedly provided stone for part of the San Francisco Mint. (**NOTE**: Pets are not allowed in the park, even if they are left in a car.)

Activities: Hiking, bird watching, whale watching, scuba diving, wildlife-watching, picnics in designated picnic areas only
Facilities: Trails, a small outdoor gift and book-sales cart
Dates: Opens daily
Fees: Day-use fee if driving in, walk-ins are free
Closest town: Carmel
Info: Point Lobos State Reserve, 831.624.4909, www.parks.ca.gov or www. pointlobos.org

Central Coast

TRAILS

The **North Shore Trail** is recommended for strong walkers and hikers. It begins at **Whalers' Cove** and immediately heads uphill. Spring and summer wildflowers highlight the trail and deer are not uncommon sights. The jagged cliffs of the shoreline and the small, near shore islands are homes to numerous nesting birds, including cormorants (*Phalacrocorax* spp.), western gulls (*Larus occidentalis*), and pigeon guillemots (*Cepphus columba*). The trail winds for 1.4 miles through the forest and ends at the information station at the Sea Lion Point parking lot.

The **Sea Lion Point Trail** begins at the Sea Lion Point parking lot and is about 0.5 miles long. It ends in an open bluff area that offers a great look at a part of the park's geology. The pounding waves and rain have sculpted the 60-million-year-old Carmelo Formation conglomerate into wonderful shapes. Harbor seals (*Phoca vitulina*) often lie balanced and sleeping on some of the smaller rocks offshore, while barking California sea lions generally cover the large rock known as Sea Lion Rock, farther offshore. Between shore and Sea Lion Rock, an area called **Devil's Cauldron** turns the approaching ocean waves into crashing, churning, spectacular white geysers of water.

Bird Island ADA Trail is a fully-accessible trail designed for physically-challenged visitors. It begins at the far southern parking lot and passes through the coastal scrub, finally ending on a bluff that overlooks Bird Island. On the way, the .08-mile-long trail passes two sandy beaches, one of which can be accessed via a staircase. While birds abound and otters play in the kelp offshore, it is the hundreds of Brandt's cormorants (*Phalacrocorax penicillatus*) that cover **Bird Island** during spring and summer that make this short hike unforgettable. Note that access to China Cove may be restricted due to erosion damage.

Hikers on a trail at Point Lobos Natural State Reserve

Ticks and Lyme Disease

Ticks are a fact of life throughout much of the country, including most of California. While there are several species, it's only the western black-legged tick (*Ixodes pacificus*) that transmits the infectious Lyme disease. The disease was first recognized in Old Lyme, Connecticut in 1975, and in California, three years later. While the disease can be both serious and difficult to diagnose, it is also easy to avoid.

Adult female ticks climb to the ends of branches and grasses and wait to attach themselves to any passing mammal, including humans. Once attached, ticks crawl to bare skin where their harpoon-like mouthparts are used to penetrate the skin. After a meal of blood, they drop off, molt, and climb onto another host, repeating the process until they are fully grown.

Wearing light-colored clothing makes seeing ticks easier, and a strong insect repellent sprayed on clothing generally helps convince the ticks not to stick around. Check yourself, your kids, and pets often, especially if hiking along brushy trails.

Removing ticks is relatively easy. Simply grasp the tick, preferably with tweezers or a tissue and gently pull it straight out. If all of the mouthpart comes out, wash the affected area with soap and water and apply an antiseptic. If a portion remains, drop the tick into a small container for later identification and seek medical care.

If you have been bitten by a tick, watch yourself. Anywhere from 3 days to 30 days following the bite, if a red, blotchy, circular rash develops anywhere on your body, possibly accompanied by flu-like symptoms, seek medical attention immediately. Also be aware that the symptoms may appear and reappear intermittently for several weeks.

Western black-legged tick

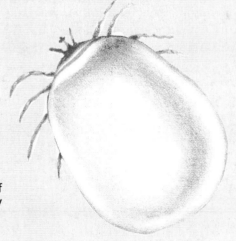

Actual size

Oversized for purpose of illustration...thankfully they're not really this big!

Central Coast

217

The Big Sur Coast's Bixby Bridge, seen in the distance, has been a favorite spot for automobile commercials for decades.

BIG SUR COAST

Highway 1, where it meanders along the Big Sur coast, is designated as both a National Scenic Highway and an All-American Highway. Heading south from Carmel, it is about 26 miles to Big Sur, yet when visitors ask the Big Sur locals exactly where Big Sur is, they are generally answered with a shrug. Big Sur is thought of more as a state of mind than a specific place. It's the sheer rugged terrain and the fog-shrouded cliffs that tower above the highway. It's the waves that crash into the rocky shore and the wildflowers that cast their colorful hues on the mosaic of mountainside vegetation. It's the remoteness, the quiet, the night skies bright with stars, and the daytime skies even more blue than the Pacific's vast waters. It is a state of mind. But, the Big Sur coast does not end at the community of Big Sur. It continues south, unofficially ending somewhere near San Simeon.

GARRAPATA STATE PARK

This park possesses nothing in the way of human creature comforts, but it does offer public access points to miles of rugged Big Sur coast and several more miles of trails that climb the steep mountains that immediately rise to the east.

In Spanish, *garrapata* means "tick." And ticks abound in the area, especially during spring and early summer. But in spring, the sight of entire mountainsides carpeted with the rich yellows and reds and purples of wildflowers is worth taking a few simple precautions, such as applying repellent to protect yourself.

There's a fence that parallels much of the park along the west side of Highway 1, with several numbered gates located at the trailheads. These trailheads lead to trails or stairways that offer relatively safe access from the ocean terrace down the steep cliff face to the beaches. Generally, look for other cars parked along the highway to find the most popular access points. An old barn on the east side of the highway marks one of the more popular starting points for hikers. From here there is access to one of several trails leading out to **Soberanes Point** (Gate #8). There is also access inland via the **Soberanes Canyon Trail**, which heads up the canyon and connects with the **Rocky Ridge Trail**.

The ocean here can be extremely hazardous, even during summer. Sleeper waves are common, sweeping people off beaches and rocks every year. Never turn your back on the ocean. And this is one of the few state beaches where you can take your pets, but they must be on a maximum 6-foot leash at all times.

Activities: Hiking, fishing, beach exploring
Facilities: None
Dates: Open daily
Fees: None
Info: Monterey District State Parks, 2211 Garden Road, Monterey, CA 93940, 831.649.2836 or www.parks.ca.gov

Fisherman at Garrapata State Park

Central Coast

POINT SUR STATE HISTORIC PARK

California's coast was a dilemma for the maritime traders who followed in the footsteps of the early European explorers. Fog, jagged offshore rocks, jutting headlands, unpredictable winds, surging tides, and storm-driven waves caused many captains to lose their ships, their cargoes, and their lives. As maritime shipping became more common along California's coast, the number of lighthouses slowly increased. The Point Sur Light Station was first lit in the summer of 1889 and has been in continuous operation since. The light actually sits lower than the top of the "**Rock**"—the name for the rock promontory which juts nearly 400 feet above the park's long shoreline beach—placed so that it would shine below where the fog most often settled.

The "Rock" (above) and the lighthouse (right)

The light was originally a first-order Fresnel lens that could be seen from 23 miles out to sea. While the lens certainly aided navigation safety, it didn't insure that ships and rocks still wouldn't meet. The *Los Angeles* was lost in 1894, the *Majestic* in 1909, and several more vessels, including the *Howard Olson* in 1956, went down near Point Sur. Each time a ship broke apart, its cargo was scattered along the coast, bringing out the locals who were quite happy to help cleanup the beaches.

Perhaps the most famous shipwreck

near the Rock was the crash of the *U.S.S. Macon*, a helium-filled rigid airship that went down on February 12, 1935. The 785-foot-long, lighter-than-air ship served as a flying aircraft carrier, able to launch and retrieve small, single-engine airplanes. The *Macon* crashed into the Pacific with its 83 crew members, all of whom survived but two; the crash was the result of operator error during a storm. The small visitor center at the top of the Rock includes exhibits on the *Macon*.

Today, while the Coast Guard still maintains an automated light at Point Sur, the remainder of the Rock is part of Point Sur State Historic Park. Several buildings are part of the light station, including a barn, blacksmith shop, two-story headkeeper's house, and the triplex where three assistant keepers and their families lived. There is an ongoing restoration program.

Point Sur State Historic Park is located 19 miles south of Carmel on Highway 1. The entrance is at a farm gate adjacent to Highway 1, about 0.25 miles north of the abandoned Point Sur Naval Facility, a casualty of the Cold War's end. All visitors must be part of a guided tour. But beware: the walk to the light station is strenuous and steep, with a very quick elevation change of 360-feet up the Rock. Visitors are also required to climb two staircases, one of which has 61 steps. No baby strollers or carriages are allowed. Visitors with disabilities who can transfer easily to a state park vehicle may ride to a drop-off point near the lighthouse. Call the park in advance for information.

Warning: Occasionally there are warm, sunny, beautiful days on the Rock. But often it is cold, foggy, and extremely windy. Wear or at bring with you several layers of clothing, even during summer, and wear good walking shoes. Pets are not allowed. Also, there is no smoking or picnicking anywhere in the park.

Activities: Tours of the lighthouse, headkeeper's house, the small museum, and other buildings as they are restored. This is a great winter whale watching site.

Facilities: Visitor center and small gift shop

Dates: Tours are held on a first-come first-served basis and take about three hours. Parking is limited and private vehicles are not allowed to drive up the narrow road to the top—all visitors are required to walk (see description of walk in story). Docents give tours on weekends and sometimes during midweek. Tour times and days may change, so call ahead. During the winter months, it's a good idea to call because tours will be canceled if rain or bad weather is likely.

Fees: There is tour fee.

Closest town: Carmel

Info: The park is not staffed. Call the park's tour information line, 831.625.4419 or visit www.pointsur.org, or Monterey District State Park Office, 2211 Garden Road, Monterey, CA 92940, 831.649.2836 or www.parks.ca.gov

ANDREW MOLERA STATE PARK

The Esselen Indians were the first to live in this area of Big Sur. Their home was eventually invaded by the Spanish, then taken over by the Mexicans, who were then soon overwhelmed by the Americans. The pioneers who settled the Big Sur area during the Mexican and the early American eras were a hardy and independent bunch. Andrew Molera State Park originally was part of a nearly 9,000-acre Mexican land grant known as Rancho El Sur, much of which remains intact today.

Captain John Rogers Cooper, born in England but living in America, sailed around the Horn, landing in California where his skills as a seafaring captain provided the money to purchase property. In 1840, he traded his Salinas Valley property for Rancho El Sur, which passed to his children following his death. Over the years, the property transferred down the line of heirs, finally ending in the hands of Frances Molera. The Coopers, and later through marriage, the Moleras, operated their land as a cattle and dairy ranch. Andrew Molera became well known locally for the wagonloads of Monterey Jack cheese he regularly hauled to Monterey. In 1968, Frances Molera sold what was to become Andrew Molera State Park to The Nature Conservancy, with the provision that it not be developed. The park was named for her gracious and well-liked brother, Andrew.

Today, Andrew Molera State Park provides public access to hills and meadows and to the Big Sur River where it meanders through Creamery Meadow and empties into the Pacific Ocean. The park offers a number of recreation opportunities, including rental horses during summer and a hike-in campground, access to more than 2 miles of beach, and many miles of trails that allow exploration of

The Big Sur River empties into the Pacific Ocean a short distance from here.

222

coastal chaparral, oaks, and redwoods. There are exceptional views from the park's bluff and ridge trails.

The old Molera ranch house, located a short walk from the park's entrance kiosk, has been restored and is now called the "**Discovery Center**." Managed by the **Ventana Wildlife Society**, volunteers can answer questions and provide information about the trails and the park's history. Besides the center's onsite ornithology lab (study of birds), a key exhibit is called "Bringing the Condors Home." Visitors will learn about the nonprofit's efforts to restore the California condor (*Gymnogyps californianus*) to the Big Sur Coast. These birds, which are nearly extinct, have wingspans of up to 10 feet.

California condor

There are 24 identified campsites in the park, and camping is on a first-come first-served basis, and only four people are allowed per site. Campers must walk their equipment into the site; it's a short walk of about 0.25 miles from the parking lot to the campground and it is not unusual to see people hauling equipment in backpacks or little red wagons. It's also very important to remember that some of the wiliest raccoons around thrive in the campground, sometimes shredding tents and opening ice chests to get to food. Keep all food well secured and remember that food inside a tent or in a backpack is not secure. Pets are not allowed anywhere in the park, including the campground and the beach.

As soon as the trails dry from winter's rain, the horseback riding concessionaire in the park opens for business. It provides an opportunity to ride many of the trails, including out to the beach. It's a great way to introduce the younger set to trail riding. Info: 831.625.5486

Activities: Hiking, fishing, horseback riding, camping, bicycling
Facilities: Visitor center and horse rentals during summer, campground
Dates: Open daily; Discovery Center is open 10 A.M. to 4 P.M. Saturday and Sunday during the summer months
Fees: There are fees for day-use vehicle entry and hike-in campground.
Closest town: Carmel, about 20 miles north, is the closest to offer full services. Limited public services are available 6 miles south in the community of Big Sur.
Info: Big Sur Station, 0.25 mile south of the Pfeiffer Big Sur State Park entrance, 831.667.2315, www.parks.ca.gov or www.ventanaws.org

Central Coast

223

TRAILS

The **Big Sur River Trail** is easily the most traveled because it leads from the parking lot at Andrew Molera State Park on the northwest side of the river, through the hike-in campground, and ends at the mouth of the **Big Sur River**. The trail passes the old **Cooper Cabin**, which is nestled in a grove of eucalyptus trees. The trees, in turn, attract thousands of monarch butterflies during winter. Hike up a short spur trail

Hundreds of monarch butterflies

from near the mouth of the Big Sur River to the promontory at the head of Molera Point, which is a great place to sit and contemplate life or watch for whales. During summer, there's usually a seasonal bridge in place near the mouth of the river, but if not, most people simply wade across, although the water can be nearly waist deep. It's best to ask at the entrance gate about the river's level.

Also leaving from the parking lot, the **Creamery Meadow Trail** parallels the river on the southeast side, loops through the meadow and after about 0.75 miles, meets several other trails as it nears the beach. It's quite level and many people like to ride bicycles. The only problem with this trail is that the seasonal bridge that crosses the Big Sur River at the parking lot is removed in the fall and isn't reinstalled until late spring or early summer, when the river's water level drops.

While the **Molera Beach Trail** is not an actual trail, the beach stretches south from the Big Sur River mouth more than 2 miles. There are a few rocky outcroppings that block passage at high tides, but at very low tides there is access to some lonely and very beautiful stretches of beach. Don't forget to pay attention to the tide tables or getting back will be impossible, at least until the next low tide. The bluff above the beach is difficult, if not impossible, to scale in most places.

PFEIFFER BIG SUR STATE PARK

If you spend much time wandering along the Big Sur River, through the redwood groves, or along the trails to the park's mountain promontories, it becomes immediately apparent why the early settlers fell in love with this land. Michael Pfeiffer and his wife Mary became the first European settlers in the area when they built their home in nearby **Sycamore Canyon** in 1869. To make a living, they cut redwood trees for lumber, farmed the land, and kept bees that feasted on the flower-covered hillsides, making plenty of honey. Their son John homesteaded a 160-acre parcel near the Big Sur River and moved to where the park's historic **Homestead Cabin** is located today.

By the turn of the century, Big Sur's redwoods and its rugged coast were drawing the more adventurous hunters and fishermen who were willing to travel the rugged coastal trail from Monterey. Seeing an opportunity for additional income, John Pfeiffer's wife Florence started **Pfeiffer's Ranch Resort**, built where today's Big Sur Lodge is located. During those early years, the Pfeiffers operated a small lumber mill in addition to several private guest cabins. In 1933, John Pfeiffer sold 680 acres to the California State Park System. That original acreage, and another 300-plus acres that have been acquired over the years, is now Pfeiffer Big Sur State Park.

Even though the park lies near the southernmost limit of the coast redwoods' range, and most of its old-growth trees were cut during the Pfeiffers' ownership, the groves that remain are quite impressive. The park's largest tree is located near the group picnic area. Named the "**Colonial Tree**," it measures 27 feet in circumference. Not far from the lodge, a grove of 800- to 1,200-year-old redwoods make up the **Proboscis Grove**.

Most of the redwoods grow on the flat that follows the Big Sur River as it runs the length of the park. Sycamores (*Platanus racemosa*), willows (*Salix* spp.), black cottonwoods (*Populus trichocarpa*), and alders (*Alnus* spp.) create a thick forest of riparian growth, which in turn provides food and homes for animals. Hiking up one of the trails, the moist riparian vegetation quickly changes to species better adapted to surviving the hot, dry summers on the mountainsides, especially along the south-facing slopes. The chaparral plants grow so densely that going off trail is nearly impossible. Chamise (*Adenostoma fasciculatum*), toyon (*Heteromeles arbutifolia*), manzanita (*Arctostaphylos* spp.), ceanothus (*Ceanothus* spp.) and California coffeeberry (*Rhamnus californica*), are some of the more common chaparral shrubs.

Pfeiffer Big Sur State Park is easily the most popular park in the Big Sur area. Its large campground is full all summer, mostly with families and the sounds of kids having fun. The **Big Sur River** is the main

The Pfeiffer family removed most of the old-growth coastal redwoods.

225

attraction, with people swimming or wading, especially during the warmest days. There's a trail that meanders up the north side of the river, officially ending perhaps 0.25 miles upriver from the **Whalen Bridge**. From there, most people continue, sometimes scrambling over the monster-sized boulders, sometimes wading in the river or swimming across the small, deeper pools, exploring an area called the "**Narrows**" or the "**Gorge**."

The historic **Big Sur Lodge** offers onsite lodging inside the park. They have many levels of rooms, from large cottage-style offerings that sleep up to six people to kitchenette rooms to standard hotel rooms. Note that there is no air conditioning, TVs, radios or even alarm clocks in any of the rooms. But there is a swimming pool for lodge guests only. Info: 831.667.3100 or www.bigsurlodge.com

Activities: Camping, hiking, picnicking, nature study, onsite lodging

Facilities: The park has two group camps, each with a 35-person capacity and 215 developed campsites, but none with RV hook-ups. Since riding the coast on bicycles is such a popular way to experience Big Sur, there are 10 bicycle environmental campsites. Camping reservations are almost always required during summer and spring holiday weekends.

Dates: Open daily

Fees: There are camping and day-use fees.

Closest town: The local Big Sur community has minimal services. The nearest major community is Carmel, 26 miles north on Highway 1.

Info: Pfeiffer Big Sur State Park, 47555 Hwy. 1, Big Sur, CA 93920, 831.667.2315 or www.parks.ca.gov

LOS PADRES NATIONAL FOREST

Stretching for more than 200 miles, the Los Padres National Forest covers nearly 2 million acres of California's Central Coast. It's a rugged and beautiful country, much of it accessible only on foot via 1,257 miles of trails. Within these forest- and chaparral-covered lands, there is a 19.5-mile stretch of the Big Sur River and 33-mile stretch of the **Sisquoc Creek**, both of which have been designated as Wild Rivers under the Wild and Scenic Rivers Act.

Hiking within either Los Padres National Forest or the contiguous **Ventana Wilderness** provides ample opportunities to experience the real Big Sur; rugged, steep-sided mountains that seem to climb higher and higher offering still more spectacular views, the cascading rivers and creeks that fight their way through narrow,

Mosquito

rocky gorges, and unimaginable views of spring wildflowers that stretch to the distant ocean. The only things missing are the discordant sounds of modern civilization, which quickly become a distant memory.

Many plants grow in their own little niches. Small, isolated groves of redwoods thrive in narrow, protected river canyons, while Ponderosa pine (*Pinus ponderosa*) and bristlecone fir, also known as the Santa Lucia fir (*Abies bracata*), grow on the drier slopes. Valley oaks (*Quercus lobata*) replace the shorter coast live oaks (*Quercus agrifolia*), and cottonwoods (*Populus* spp.) join willows (*Salix* spp.) in the riparian areas. Coastal wildflowers cover the open fields, with the purple hues of lupine (*Lupinus* sp.) and the golden yellow of California poppies

Backpacking in Big Sur

(*Eschscholtzia californica*) being prominent.

The Ventana Wilderness, along with nine other designated wilderness areas, lies within the Los Padres National Forest. Its 167,000 acres are a great reason to explore this part of the Santa Lucia Mountain Range. In Spanish, *ventana* means "window." Legend has it that the **Ventana Double Cone**— two large rock croppings found in the area at an elevation of 4,853 feet—once supported a natural rock bridge or arch. Thus, the name "The Window."

While there are many trailheads popular with both day-hikers and backpackers, the **Pine Ridge Trail** entrance at the Big Sur Station, located 0.25-miles south of Pfeiffer Big Sur State Park, is one of the most used access points. Wilderness permits and maps are available, as is parking in a lot that is patrolled. One of the real reasons this is such a popular jumping-off point is that it's an 11-mile hike from here to the hot spring near **Sykes Campground**. The hot spring is about 0.25 miles downriver from the campground area, on the south side of the Big Sur River. Its waters hover around 100 degrees Fahrenheit, but the area can occasionally become a bit overused because it is so popular.

Activities: Camping, hiking
Facilities: None inside the forest or wilderness area
Fees: There is a daily parking fee in the Big Sur Station parking lot.
Closest town: Carmel
Info: U.S. Forest Service, 805.968.6640 or www.fs.usda.gov; Ventana Wilderness Alliance, 831.423.3191 or www.ventanawild.org

Central Coast

Rocks off Pfeiffer Beach

PFEIFFER BEACH

Most of Los Padres National Forest is located on the inland side of Highway 1, but there are several areas within its boundaries where access to the Pacific Ocean is possible. About 0.25 mile south of the Big Sur Station, a narrow, barely marked road turns off Highway 1 and leads through Sycamore Canyon to Pfeiffer Beach. It's easy to miss the turnoff and once on the steep and twisty 2-mile, one-lane access road to the beach, meeting an RV creates problems. The road is not recommended for large RVs, cars pulling trailers, and any other large vehicle—besides possibly blocking the narrow road, turning around at the parking lot is nearly impossible. Also, please take care while driving, as the area has residential sections.

During summer weekends, the parking lot fills up. That's when the "full" sign at Highway 1 is posted, warning beach goers in any sized vehicle to not attempt the drive. And this is a walk-in beach, so you will need to hike all your things in and back out. There are no facilities at the beach.

Activities: Picnicking, beachcombing, fishing
Facilities: None
Dates: Open daily
Fees: There is a day-use fee.
Info: U.S. Forest Service, 805.968.6640 or www.fs.usda.gov; Big Sur Chamber of Commerce, 831.667.2100 or www.bigsurcalifornia.org; Big Sur Station, 831.667.2315 or www.parks.ca.gov

JULIA PFEIFFER BURNS STATE PARK

Spring and early summer are the best times to visit Julia Pfeiffer Burns State Park. The hillsides are covered with brightly colored wildflowers and the creek that feeds McWay falls is usually running full.

The steep canyon walls that rise from the parking lot make this appear to be a small park, yet it covers 3,600 acres, with 1,680 of its acres offshore and underwater. Most visitors seldom get beyond the short trail that passes under Highway 1 and leads to an overlook above **McWay Falls**; at one time, the 80-foot-tall falls dropped directly into the ocean, but now it drops onto an inaccessible stretch of beach.

The park's underwater reserve is open to very experienced divers only and diving permits are required. The inland portion of the park extends from the rocky shore to nearly 3,000 feet in elevation into the mountains immediately to the east. **McWay Creek Canyon** supports small groves of coast redwoods. Scattered among the redwoods, tanoak (*Lithocarpus densiflorus*), madrone (*Arbutus menziesii*), and California laurel (*Umbellularia californica*) are the dominant trees, with trillium (*Trillium ovatum*), redwood sorrel (*Oxalis oregana*), and columbine (*Aquilegia formosa*) thriving beneath their shading branches. Farther up the hillsides, the Central Coast's common chaparral species dominate. Wildflowers include sticky monkey-flower (*Mimulus aurantiacus*) and morning glory (*Ipomoea purpurea*), which are joined by shrubs such as the ubiquitous poison oak (*Toxicodendron diversilobum*).

Christopher McWay and his son Christopher Jr. originally settled this area of the Big Sur coast in 1874, when they began their ranching operation. Over

the next two decades, they filed land claims for what became known as **Saddle Rock Ranch**. Today, many of the area's landmarks still retain the McWay name.

In 1921, former New York State Congressman Lathrop Brown and his wife, Helen Hooper of Boston, began traveling extensively around the world, following 10 years of active social, political, and business activities. The two instantly fell in love with Big Sur and within a few years, had acquired much of the original McWay property. Although not extravagant by the standards set by William Randolph Hearst's home farther south, the home the couple built had a much more spectacular

McWay Falls—there is no access to the beach below

Central Coast

229

view. Their "**Waterfall House**" was perched on the cliff overlooking **McWay Cove** and the waterfall. They also had electricity in their home long before power lines stretched along the Big Sur coast, the power created by a small Pelton wheel generator set on nearby **McWay Creek**.

This remote home allowed for few neighbors, but Mrs. Brown became especially good friends with Julia Pfeiffer Burns, the daughter of Michael Pfeiffer, head of Big Sur's best known pioneer family. The Browns did enjoy entertaining, and following the completion of Highway 1, access to the retreat became much easier. While a list of their guests isn't known, Lathrop Brown, in his college years, roomed with Franklin Delano Roosevelt at Harvard and was also best man at Roosevelt's wedding. It's likely the Browns' guests included many well-known socialites of the day.

Mrs. Brown insisted that their house be demolished when she gave Saddle Back Ranch to the California State Park System in 1962. She also required that the new state park be named after a "true pioneer"—her good friend Julia Pfeiffer Burns, who had died 35 years earlier. Today, all that remains of the Brown's home is a stone terrace and the surviving exotic plants that the Browns had imported for

Walkway to the stone terrace

their gardens. During January through March, the terrace is a great place to watch migrating gray whales.

Activities: Hiking, whale watching, camping, picnicking
Facilities: Picnic tables at the parking lot and two environmental campsites on the ocean bluff
Dates: Open daily
Fees: There are camping and day-use fees.
Closest town: Big Sur
Info: Big Sur Station, 831.667.2315 or www.parks.ca.gov

TRAILS

From the parking lot at Julia Pfeiffer Burns State Park, the **Waterfall Trail** is a short walk through a tunnel that passes under Highway 1 then continues along the bluff overlooking McWay Falls. While the waterfall that cascades over the cliff once splashed directly into swirling ocean waves, during the El Niño winter of 1983-84, a massive landslide from the steep cliffs above raised the beach several feet. The waterfall now crashes onto the beach very near the waves that wash across the shore. The trail continues on another 100 yards or so, offering ever-changing views of the falls. The short trail ends at a promontory that was the site of the Brown's house, the last private owners of the lands here. Because of the high amount of danger, there is no access to the beach below and the state has posted it as such. If you decide to forgo the posted warnings, be prepared to bear the financial costs of being rescued.

The **Ewoldson Trail** begins at the eastern end of the parking lot at McWay Canyon and meanders up the canyon and out across the mountainside. It's about a 4.5-mile round-trip and offers spectacular views back into the mountains and of the ocean.

The **Partington Cove Trail** is located near the north boundary of Julia Pfeiffer Burns State Park, along Highway 1. On the ocean side of the highway, there's a wide, dirt pull-off at Partington Cove. Often there are other cars parked here. There are two trails, one on each side of the highway. On the ocean side, it's a quick and steep 0.4 mile walk down a wooden tunnel that leads to a small, rocky cove where Partington Creek runs into the ocean.

At the same Partington Cove parking area, but on the inland side of the highway, the

Wooden tunnel found on Partington Cove Trail

Tan Bark Trail meanders up the canyon and into the mountains for about 3 miles and an elevation change of 1,600 feet. You'll come across the "**Tin House**," which was built by Lathrop Brown. He used scraps from an old gas station to build the cabin, but after sleeping in it the first night, the Browns preferred their Waterfall House. They never returned to the structure. There's an optional route back, but unfortunately, it returns to Highway 1 about 1.5 miles south of Partington Cove, so it's a bit of a hike back to the parking area.

Info: Big Sur Trails, 831.667.2315 or www.hikinginbigsur.com

Central Coast

MORE TO EXPLORE

The **Henry Miller Memorial Library** in Big Sur was once the home of Emil White, author Henry Miller's best friend. When White died in 1989, he bequeathed the library to the Big Sur Land Trust in memory of Miller who lived in Big Sur from 1944 to 1962. Several of Miller's books, such as the *Tropic of Cancer* (1934), were banned in the U.S. as pornographic. It wasn't until 1961 that the Supreme Court ended the ban, claiming Miller's books to be literature. Miller died in 1980. The library is on Highway 1, 0.25-miles south of **Nepenthe Restaurant**, about 30 minutes from Carmel. Info: 831.667.2574 or www.henrymiller.org

In addition to having a small campground, **Limekiln State Park** provides easy access to both the ocean and beach along this sec-tion of the Big Sur coast. A 15-minute hike up the can-yon to a break in the second-growth redwoods reveals the remnants of

This trail bridge leads to the historic lime kilns.

the old kilns used for cooking limestone into lime, which was used for making concrete and mortar. In the 1870s there was a landing at the beach that was used to haul barrels of lime to waiting ships and on to San Francisco. Camping reserva-tions should be made during summer. The park is located is 2 miles south of Lucia off Highway 1. Info: 805.434.1996 or www.parks.ca.gov

Kirk Creek Campground is part of Los Padres National Forest and is 2 miles south of Limekiln State Park on Highway 1. The campground is filled with an introduced weed—pampas grass—along with eucalyptus trees. There has been a major effort to eliminate pampas grass along the Big Sur coast because native plants can't compete with it. The bluff along the campground has a steep trail lead-ing anglers, surfers, and coastal explorers to the narrow beach. There is no water in the park, so bring your own. Info: 831.434-1996 or www.campone.com

Three miles south of Plaskett Creek on Highway 1, you will find **Jade Cove**. Here, you can search for small pieces of jade along the beach, as long as the stones are found below the mean high-tide line; the idea is to keep people from digging in the serpentine cliff. Divers offshore have found huge pieces of jade. The beach is also a designated hang-glider site.

San Luis Obispo County

PIEDRAS BLANCAS LIGHT STATION

Piedras Blancas Light Station is one of only three tall, East Coast-style lighthouses constructed in California during the 19th century. Much of the East Coast lacked California's high coastal terraces, forcing the Lighthouse Service to construct exceptionally tall towers so that the signal light's height needs could be met, significantly increasing their usefulness.

A first-order Fresnel lens originally graced the top of this tower that rose 115-feet above the sea, providing a point of reference for passing ships. As with all the original lighthouses on California's coast, technology has long since replaced the Fresnel lenses. Piedras Blancas is one of many California lighthouses that had its original lens removed. The nearby town of Cambria now has the lens on exhibit. The light station is owned by the U.S. Bureau of Land Management and limited public tours are available, with the entrance fee going toward restoration efforts.

About 1 mile south of Piedras Blancas is an elephant seal rookery viewing area that is part of the **Piedras Blancas State Marine Reserve**, and what an area it is. During summer, there may be fewer than 100 northern elephant seals (*Mirounga augustirostris*) snoozing along the beaches, but come winter, several thousand cover the surrounding beaches, sleeping, fighting, mating, and giving birth to their young. Bull elephant seals can weigh 2 tons and often appear slow and lethargic. But they can move very quickly over short distances, so stay at least 50 feet away. The elephant seals are protected by law and getting closer could bring legal problems. There is a large parking area adjacent to Highway 1.

Reserve's elephant seal observation point

Activities: Guided tours of the light station, elephant-seal viewing
Facilities: None
Dates: Light station tours are offered
Fees: There is a tour fee for the light station.
Closest town: San Simeon
Info: 805.927.7361 or www.piedrasblancas.org

Central Coast

SAN SIMEON

Little remains of the town of San Simeon, located 4 miles south of Piedras Blancas Light Station. The town was founded as a whaling station in the 1860s. It later became part of George Hearst's extensive ranch holdings that included a wharf where Hearst shipped hides and tallow

Sebastian Store

from his ranching operations and quicksilver from his cinnabar mine. Today, only a few buildings remain, the oldest of which is a fun place to visit. The **Sebastian Store** is the oldest building along San Luis Obispo County's north coast. Originally built in 1852 at a location a half-mile farther west, the building was moved to its present location in 1878. The Sebastian family has operated the store since 1914. It is California Registered Historical Landmark No. 726; the marker sits outside the small, but busy store, which also serves as the town's post office, a gift shop and small grocery store, winetasting bar, restaurant, and museum.

Directly across Highway 1 from the Hearst San Simeon State Historical Monument visitor center (entry to Hearst Castle), a beach, wharf, and picnic area are part of **William Randolph Hearst Memorial Beach**. The sandy beach sits in a protected cove and is popular for swimming and kayaking. The pier allows fishing (no licensed required) and a fishing charter boat is also available. There are picnic tables and BBQs, along with seasonal rentals of kayaks and boogie boards.

At the end of the parking lot is a brightly painted trailer—the **Coastal Discovery Center.** Its interactive nature exhibits are especially fun for kids.

The beach is surrounded by coastal and inland land parcels that combine to make up **Hearst San Simeon State Park**. The park includes two inland campgrounds with **San Simeon Creek Campground** being the largest with 115 sites for tents and trailers. Nearby **Washburn Primitive Campground** has 68 sites. The park's **Washburn Loop Trail** and the **Moonstone Bluff Trail's** 1-mile-long beach boardwalk are

Coastal Discovery Center

ADA accessible.

HEARST SAN SIMEON STATE HISTORICAL MONUMENT

As William Randolph Hearst's publishing fortune accumulated to levels most people could only dream about, his growing collection of primarily European art and art treasures also grew. While creating a repository for his art collection was certainly one of the reasons for beginning construction of what was to become commonly known as "**Hearst Castle**," he also wanted to upgrade "camp hill" where his father had brought his family and friends on outings. After William Randolph Hearst's mother died in 1919, he began the complete transformation of "camp hill" with a simple message to his San Francisco architect: "...Miss Morgan, we are tired of camping out in the open at the ranch in San Simeon and I would like to build a little something..." What followed was 30 years of almost continuous construction and improvements to "camp hill," which Hearst renamed *La Cuesta Encantada*, The Enchanted Hill.

The castle's isolation and its grand elegance required a huge army of very skilled craftsmen and workers. Ocean steamers delivered the tons of necessary construction materials, including concrete, steel, and lumber, to the pier at San Simeon where strong backs and the underpowered trucks of the day hauled everything to the top of the 1,600-foot-high construction site, 5 miles away.

Spectacular views of the ocean and the surrounding mountains greeted Hearst's guests as they enjoyed the 137-foot-tall, 130-room Hispano-Moresque main mansion he named "Casa Grande" and the three guests' houses—Casa del Mar, Casa del Monte, and Casa del Sol. Hearst's guests were nearly always the rich and famous, especially Hollywood stars. They weren't restricted to the hilltop. Hearst encouraged horseback riding excursions to the distant parts of the 75,000 acres of his ranch, a portion of the 250,000 acres that his father, George Hearst, originally owned.

Hearst Memorial Beach

235

Some of what Hearst used to decorate his 137-acre hilltop home—the paintings and tapestries, the furniture, the vases and lamps—are originals purchased over a lifetime of collecting from around the world. Others, such as many of the sculptures, are pieces that he recruited the best sculptors of the day to create for him.

Hearst Castle is one of those places that is impossible to adequately describe in a few paragraphs. Its elaborately tiled outdoor and indoor swimming pools, the multilevel gardens filled with thousands of flowers, the eclectic collection of art pieces such as the beautiful French Gothic mantel, Spanish choir stalls, Flemish tapestries, bronze, gold, and silver sculptures, and fantasy beds require more than words. They must be seen. And don't be surprised when you see exotic animals, such as zebras, grazing with cattle in the park's grasslands. Hearst once had the largest private collection of zoo animals in the world, all located at "Animal Hill" near the main house. In 1937, Hearst donated much of his collection of exotic animals to public zoos. The effort lasted 15 years, but was never completed. Thus, zebras and other animals still roam the grounds.

Highway 1 motorists regulary pull over to take photos of the Hearst zebras.

The only way to see Hearst Castle is on a scheduled tour. The tours meet at the **Hearst Castle Visitor Center** and commence with a 15-minute, 5-mile bus ride to the top of the hill where the castle is located. All tours require stair climbing and lots of walking and standing. No pets are allowed on the tours. ADA tours are available; call to find out more.

Facilities: The tour staging area has food service, a large gift shop, theater, and a visitor center. The visitor center provides a glimpse into the history of the castle and the man who built it. It also provides a close-up look at many of the artifacts, the research that went into developing the exhibits, and some of the work required to restore many of Hearst's treasures.

Dates: Open daily, except Thanksgiving, Christmas, and New Year's Day
Fees: No fee for the visitor center, a moderate fee for the different tours.
Closest town: Cambria
Info: Reservations are usually required, 800.444.4445, www.parks.ca.gov or www.hearstcastle.org

MORRO BAY REGION

Not many people have heard of Estero Bay. It is one of those indentations in the California coast that offers little or no protection from ocean storms, but still it is called a bay. There are three small communities along Estero Bay: **Cayucos, Morro Bay,** and **Los Osos.**

Cayucos lies at the northern end of the bay. Turn off Highway 1, which actually runs east and west here, and head south to the **Cayucos Pier,** for what is generally very good ocean fishing. Like anywhere, the fish bite when they're ready to bite, but here, there's a better-than-even chance of hooking something besides kelp. It also helps to check one of the nearby bait shops or ask another fisherman on the pier about what's being caught and what everyone is using for bait.

In close, near the breaking surf, anglers regularly catch barred surfperch (*Amphistichus argenteus*). Out a bit farther, brocaccio (*Sebastes pancispinis*) and walleye surfperch (*Hyperprosopon argenteum*) are commonly landed, and the deeper water at the end of the pier produces catches of small (8-inch) shiner perch (*Cymatogaster aggregata*), which are then used as bait for much larger and tastier Pacific halibut (*Hippoglossus stenolepis*).

Morro Strand State Beach (805.772.2560 or www.parks.ca.gov) is also in the town of Cayucos. The 3-mile stretch of sandy beach is popular for fishing, beachcombing, picnicking, windsurfing, and kite flying.

Info: Cayucos Visitor Center, 41 South Ocean Avenue, Cayucos, CA, 93430, 805.995.1200 or www.cayucoschamber.com

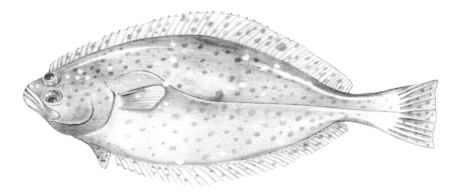

Pacific halibut

Morro Rock (background) is off limits to people, partly as a result of too many folks getting stuck climbing its steep slopes and needing to be rescued. Plus, birds nest on the rock.

MORRO BAY STATE PARK

Besides being the largest town on Estero Bay, the water portion of Morro Bay has the distinction of being a bay that lies within a bay. Morro Bay lies within Estero Bay and is nearly landlocked by a long sand spit that ends near **Morro Rock**. This rock is the area's most prominent landmark. It is one of several ancient, volcanic plugs that rose in a southeastward line beginning inland and extending into the ocean. These andesitic plugs—of which Morro Rock is the most spectacular—are composed of primarily dacite porphyry with crystallized quartz, black hexagonal plates of biotite, and white orthoclase.

Even on clear days, a shroud of fog can cling to the top of Morro Rock. Since its discovery in 1542 by Juan Cabrillo, the 23-million-year-old Morro Rock has been a maritime milepost. Cabrillo named the 580-foot-tall andesite outcropping "Morro" because he thought it resembled a Moorish turban. Today, Morro Rock is a protected State Historic Landmark, but such reverence for this special geologic landmark has not always been popular. Beginning in about 1880, tons of rock were blasted away from Morro Rock and transported by boat to nearby Avila Bay for construction of its breakwater. The quarry operation continued until the late 1960s, when conservationists, concerned for Morro Rock's protection, finally helped get the operation shut down, and the rock transferred to State Parks.

There is a reason why such a large variety of minerals is common in the area, including the iron-stained dunes, volcanic rhyolite tuff, and the sedimentary chert. From 100 to 140 million years ago, the area now occupied by Morro Bay was a shallow depression that subsequently filled with seawater, which was followed by rocks, sand, and other detritus. With the nearly constant moving of California's tectonic plates, the pressures created deep beneath the surface formed cracks in the overlying rock that lay beneath the sea. Ultimately, molten rock was forced upward as the faulting and folding continued and the sea retreated. Then, 20 million years ago (middle Miocene) the subsurface pressures became so great that volcanoes erupted, again pushing molten rock to the surface.

From 1 million to 4 million years ago, strong compressive forces folded and elevated all of the older rock formations during what became the Central Coast's most intensive mountain-building period. The seas that had flooded the area once again withdrew, and many of the southern coastal ranges were formed.

As much as the changing geology, the fluctuating sea level has had significant impacts on the Morro Bay region. Beginning 20,000 years ago, melting ice caps and glaciers began to cause the ocean to rise. At that time, the beach was about 4 miles farther offshore. Twelve thousand years later—about 8,000 years ago—the ocean water was about 5 feet to 10 feet shallower than it is in today's estuary.

Morro Bay's estuary covers 2,300 acres of mud flats, tidal wetlands, and open water, all of which serves as a repository and mixing bowl for the fresh water that flows from the nearly 50,000 acres of surrounding watershed. It also holds one of the least human-disturbed saltwater marshes in California, providing a rich mix of habitats that support one of the most diverse collections of bird species in the country. Because of its key position within the Pacific Flyway and its habitat offerings, some

Snowy plover

250 species of birds have been observed here. They include those that make the area their permanent home and many more that migrate through, often including threatened and endangered bird species, such as the peregrine falcon (*Falco peregrinus*), black brant (*Branta bernicla*), brown pelican (*Pelecanus occidentalis*), and snowy plover (*Charadruis alexandrinus*).

In addition to having a very popular campground and one of the very few golf courses owned by California State Parks, Morro Bay State Park is home to a wonderful museum that sits at the edge of an uplifted segment of sedimentary

Central Coast

chert overlooking the bay's shoreline—the **Museum of Natural History**. The museum also offers a view across the tidal flats that reach the harbor, its boats, and beyond to Morro Rock. Inside the museum is a vast collection of both natural and cultural history exhibits that provide a thorough introduction to the area. There are numerous birds and fish (all stuffed), along with a small gift shop featuring primarily nature-related publications. Docents at the museum also lead tours and offer other interpretive programs.

A short walk from Morro Bay State Park's natural history museum is a grove of eucalyptus trees that has been adopted by great blue herons as their primary nesting site in the area. Some of the nests are 4 feet across, added to each year by the returning herons. While great blue herons are year-round residents at Morro Bay, the best time to see them in their rookery is in February—when their courtship rituals begin—and throughout spring and summer when the surviving broods finally leave their nests.

Activities: Bird-watching, golf, boating, fishing, camping, picnicking
Facilities: Museum, golf course, campground, picnic area, marina
Dates: The park and museum are open daily
Fees: Day use is free, but there is a small admission fee at the museum.
Closest town: Morro Bay
Info: Morro Bay State Park, State Park Road, Morro Bay, CA 93442, 805.772.2560, 805.772.2694 for the museum, or www.parks.ca.gov

Inside the Museum of Natural History

LOS OSOS OAKS STATE NATURE RESERVE

If a single tree had to be identified with California's central coast, the coast live oak (*Quercus agrifolia*) would be at the top of any list. It lacks the grand size and graceful symmetry of some of its cousins, such as the valley oak (*Quercus lobata*). Instead, as if serving as inspiration to the many artists and other creative minds who have settled California's coast, the multi-trunked coast live oaks appear to grow in conformance to the whims and wishes of the coastal winds and the contours of the rolling hills they inhabit. Let the fog blow through this oak woodland and walking the trails of this small but important reserve can become a surreal adventure. Even on clear days, it's an extraordinary experience.

In the late 1760s, members of Don Gaspar de Portolá's expedition came across this area and named it after the many grizzly bears that were found here; *osos* is "bears" in Spanish. Later, when the Carmel Mission was in dire need of food, a hunting party was sent here and killed many bears, returning to the mission with the meat.

Grizzly bears disappeared from California in the 1920s

There is a figure-eight-shaped trail—the 2-mile round-trip **Oak Trail**—in the preserve that begins at a small parking lot. From the grasslands there, the trail crosses a bridge over a small stream and leads directly into a grove of coast live oaks, which are estimated to be 600 to 800 years old. Going left quickly leads to the riparian habitat along perennial **Los Osos Creek**. Since this 85-acre site sees few people and offers several different biotic communities, wildlife is almost always present. Whether or not it will allow itself to be seen is another matter. Fortunately, western rattlesnakes (*Crotalus viridis*) tend to shy away from people, and southern alligator lizards (*Gerrhonotus multicarinatus*) also prefer to escape from humans. The seemingly ever-present western fence lizard (*Sceloporous occidentalis*), with its blue sides and belly, will likely be the most visible reptile.

The most obvious residents here are birds. Nuttall's woodpeckers (*Picoides nuttallii*) and California thrashers (*Toxostoma redivivum*) are generally around, with many smaller birds keeping to the underbrush. The occasional tall pile of sticks is home to the 12- to 18-inch-long dusky-footed wood rat (*Neotoma fuscipes*). Gray foxes (*Urocyon cinereoargenteus*) and bobcats (*Felis rufus*) occasionally slip-up and get caught in plain view near the trail.

The trail passes through 30-foot-tall oaks, many contorted by the salt air and winds that kill new buds, creating the limbs' stubby, twisted shapes. Continue up a small hill and the trees are still as old as those first encountered, but now they are only from 6 feet to perhaps 10 feet tall. These dwarf trees simply occupy an environment that offers poorer soil with fewer nutrients, less water, and more wind, all of which combine to significantly stunt their growth. Also, the reserve is home to several species of lichen found nowhere else. Look for it hanging from the oak trees.

Continue beyond the oaks whose acidic leaves create soil conditions that most understory plants cannot endure and the woodland is replaced by the drier chaparral. Here is where black sage (*Salvia mellifera*) and bush monkey flower (*Mimulus* sp.) are joined by splashes of spring wildflowers such as mock heather and western peony (*Paeonia brownii*). Even more prevelent is poison oak (*Toxicodendron diversilobum*), so be cautious.

Activities: Hiking, bird watching
Facilities: None
Dates: Open daily
Fees: None
Closest town: Los Osos
Info: Los Osos Oaks State Nature Reserve, 805.772.7434 or www.parks.ca.gov

MONTAÑA DE ORO STATE PARK

It takes a bit of out-of-the-way driving to get here, but the rewards are worth the effort. It's also quickly evident that those people who would like to eliminate the tall and aromatic eucalyptus trees that some enterprising souls introduced into California from Australia in the 19th century have far to go. The narrow road passes through several groves of the trees, which emit a toxin from their leaves that has eliminated most of the understory native plants that might provide any competition. Unfortunately, with all the native plants go all the native animals that depend on them for food and

Montaña de Oro State Park

shelter. What results is a relatively open forest filled with a single plant species.

As you emerge from the eucalyptus groves, the park opens onto a marine terrace rich with native coastal scrub. During spring, wildflowers, such as sticky monkey flower and California poppies, splash the hillsides with gold, helping the park live up to its translated name: Mountain of Gold. To the west, often not more than a few hundred yards from the entry road, waves crash against the rocky cliffs and wash across the intermittent sandy beaches tucked between the extended fingers of land. While the road that leads into the park winds about 7 miles and finally dead-ends near the south boundary, there's an intricate system of trails, many of which are open to equestrians. The trails pass along cliff tops, across coastal dunes, and to the tops of nearby peaks, such as 1,649-foot-high **Alan Peak**.

It is estimated that as many as 30,000 Chumash Indians lived in small villages spread from Morro Bay to as far south as Malibu. In 1769, Don Gaspar de Portolá's expedition to establish Spain's missions and presidios marked the end for the Chumash and their traditional way of life. They had the ability to survive nature for thousands of years, but European diseases decimated their numbers.

By the late 19th century, dairy operations were the economic mainstay for the Americans who now controlled the land. One of those owners, Alexander Hazard, in a failed experiment to meet the lumber needs of the nearby growing communities, planted eucalyptus trees. His dairy operations proved much more successful. Most of the early dairy buildings were destroyed in 1947, when a grass fire swept up the coast from Diablo Canyon.

Exploring the park offers an opportunity to see firsthand the power of nature. Following millions of years of uplifting, tilting, and periodic seawater inundations, much of the park's geology is quite visible. The popular beach at **Spooner's Cove** is surrounded by rocky cliffs that show the power and

The park's ancient rock formations

stresses created by two great tectonic plates moving against one another. Tremendous pressures raised the area's predominant rock—Monterey shale—from its more humble beginnings as mudstone from the ancient sea floor to the surface. The mudstone, a mixture of mud and sand, combined with the leftovers of dead ocean organisms, solidified into thick layers of diatomite, clay porcellanite, dolomite, and chert. The cliffs both north and south of Spooner's Cover offer excellent examples of Monterey shale. The evidence of the receding ocean and the uplifted landmass can be seen along the trail to the top of **Valencia Peak** (1,347 feet). From points along the trail, the marine terraces to the south that once served as ancient beaches also become visible.

When the park's 8,000 acres and its 7 miles of shore became a state park in 1965, the name that its last private owner gave to it—*Montaña de Oro*—stayed. One of the few remaining structures, the **Spooner Ranch House** (another early owner), is now a visitor center that's operated primarily by volunteers. It's located about 4 miles into the park.

Activities: Hiking, horseback riding, mountain biking, fishing, beachcombing, camping, picnicking

Facilities: Visitor center, 47 primitive campsites plus an equestrian camp area, which has two group sites and three individual sites.

Dates: The park is open daily, the visitor center periodically

Fees: Camping fee

Closest town: Los Osos

Info: Montaña de Oro State Park, Pecho Valley Road, Los Osos, CA 93402, 805.772.9723 or www.parks.ca.gov

AVILA BEACH

Choosing to depart the main highway for a little side road exploration can generally reveal wonderful surprises. Such is the case with Avila Beach, tucked into the hills along the coast at the end of Avila Beach Drive, not far from Highway 1.

This small coastal town, situated at the tip of the upside-down fishhook-shaped San Luis Obispo Bay, provides a sheltered cove for a popular pier and swimming beach. The sand beach is a very busy place, as is **Port San Luis**, which is located at the end of the road. In addition to having a restaurant, the pier offers an opportunity to board a sport fishing boat and see whales from December through March, or during summer, fishing enthusiasts regularly catch rock cod, halibut, and albacore. For those not willing to fish for their fish, freshly caught fish can be purchased at the pier. There are a few restaurants, a bait shop, and a boat launch.

San Luis Lighthouse (805.540.5771 or www.sanluislighthouse.org) is the last of the Prairie Victorian style lighthouses on the West Coast. It took more than 20 years of politics and the accidental sinking of the *Queen of the Pacific* in 1888 in shallow water near the city pier before Congress approved money for the construction of the light. Finally, on June 30, 1890, it was lit and the 4th order Fresnel lens cast its alternating red and white flashing light 17 miles out to sea.

In 1969, the Fresnel lens was replaced by an automated electric light. The Coast Guard decommissioned the lighthouse in 1974, and it is now operated by the Point San Luis Lighthouse Keepers, a nonprofit group dedicated to maintaining and managing the lighthouse. Access is limited to docent-led fee tours because access to the lighthouse requires crossing private property. Private vehicles are not allowed, so visitors are transported via trolley. Kayakers can stop at **Whaler's Cove Beach** and climb the stairs up to the lighthouse, although the building interiors won't be open. Tours are offered on Saturdays and Wednesdays and fill quickly during summer, so reservations are suggested.

Info: Avila Beach Tourism Alliance, www.visitavilabeach.com

PISMO STATE BEACH

The town of **Pismo Beach** is a popular destination. Besides the hustle and bustle of people moving in and out of restaurants, surf shops, motels, and tourist gift shops in the city of **Pismo Beach**, the adjacent Pismo State Beach offers a unique experience for California's millions of beach-goers. The long stretch of beach has sand firm enough to support

Sea lions soaking up the sunshine

motor vehicles, so thousands of people each year drive their street-legal cars onto the beach. On nearly any given day, there are hundreds of passenger cars, motorcycles, truck-towed mobile homes, and RVs driving up and down the beach, all 8 miles of it. The experience can be a little disconcerting at first, especially when driving in something other than a four-wheel drive vehicle past the park entrance kiosk then down the ramp and onto the sand.

It's always wise to drive on the wet sand above the breaking waves, especially

Central Coast

during high tide when vehicles are forced higher up the beach toward what is generally the looser sand. Get too high up the beach and two-wheel drive vehicles are more likely to get stuck. The speed limit is 15 mph along the beach, and there's at least one place where a small stream—**Arroyo Grande Creek**—runs down the beach and into the ocean. During summer when the stream isn't particularly high, its easy enough to cross, but winter storms can create a much different scenario.

The beach provides great surf fishing and good sand castle-building opportunities for kids, but digging for the famed Pismo clam has been a favorite pastime for generations of beachgoers. The only problem is that today, the clam population is nowhere near what it was in past decades. Check the current fishing regulations for the open season and license needs. There's a minimum size limit of 4.5 inches, and it can often be challenging to find clams large enough to keep. For those not interested in digging in the sand searching for dinner, it's only a short drive off the beach and back into town where a plethora of restaurants awaits.

Pismo State Beach is also known for having one of the largest monarch butterfly wintering colonies in the world. **Monarch Butterfly Grove** is located at the **North Beach Campground**. Between November to February of each year, 20,000 to 200,000 butterflies call this area home.

Activities: Fishing, surfing, swimming, clamming, camping

Facilities: Open camping on the beach, two other nearby state park campgrounds away from the beach offer less primitive campsites. **Oceano Campground**, located at 555 Pier Avenue in nearby Oceano, offers 80 campsites, while **North Beach Campground** (a primary monarch butterfly wintering site), off Highway 1 in Pismo Beach has more than 100 campsites. Reservations are generally required during summer.

Fees: There is a day-use fee and a moderate camping fee per vehicle.

Closest town: Pismo Beach and Grover City

Info: Pismo State Beach, 555 Pier Avenue, Oceano, CA 93445, 805.473.7220 or www.parks.ca.gov

OCEANO DUNES STATE VEHICULAR RECREATION AREA

Oceano Dunes sits at the center of a stretch of dunes that begins near the town of Pismo Beach, includes Pismo State Beach, and continues south to near **Point Sal**. Don Gaspar de Portolá's expedition came across the dunes here in 1769. It wasn't until the 1930s and 1940s that the "Dunites" took over the dunes—this group of nudists, artists, writers, hermits and other free-spirits believed the dunes had mystic powers and creative energy.

The dune sand, originally washed down from the mountains via the nearby **Santa Maria River** and other smaller creeks and waterways, is pushed ashore by wave action then blown inland into the high dunes by the often strong prevailing winds. But these particular dunes are a wide-open playground for off-road enthusiasts. Here, dune buggies, quadrunners, and a few vehicles that don't look like anything that would ever be seen on a city street blast their way over the high dunes and across the open beach.

This is also the place to come for beach camping (reservations are required). Summer weekends can bring several hundred tents, RVs, and trailers set up just above the expected high tide line. The owners of the trailers and RVs set up cardboard and push sand up to the bottoms of their vehicles to keep the wind from blowing through. Barbecues and beach fires are everywhere. The only problem is expecting that the quiet slap of waves and the occasional squawks of birds will be the only nighttime sounds; the noise from revving engines is often more noticeable.

Like dunes along several other areas of California's coast, the sand here also serve as nesting areas for the threatened snowy plover and the endangered California least tern.

Teenagers will do anything to get on camera, like flips off the dunes—not recommended. But he *did* get in the book!

Surprisingly, their nesting success has been extremely good in the off-highway vehicle area. During the March-through-September breeding and fledging season, their nesting sites are fenced for protection from beach goers and sand-thrashing OHV tires.

Other areas of Oceano Dunes are set aside as preserves where native dune plants such as arroyo willow (*Salix lasiolepis*) and California sagebrush (*Artemisia californica*) thrive in the seemingly hostile dune environment. A few rare dune plants—surf thistle (*Cirsium rhothophilum*) and giant coreopsis (*Coreopsis gigantea*)—also grow here.

Activities: OHV use, fishing, camping, picnicking, swimming, surfing
Facilities: Seasonal quadrunner rental in the park. In town, full facilities.
Dates: Open daily
Fees: Vehicle fee for day-use and camping.
Closest town: Pismo Beach and Grover Beach
Info: Oceano Dunes State Vehicular Recreation Area, 928 Pacific Blvd., Oceano, CA 93445, 805.773.7170, www.parks.ca.gov or www.dunescenter.org

Central Coast

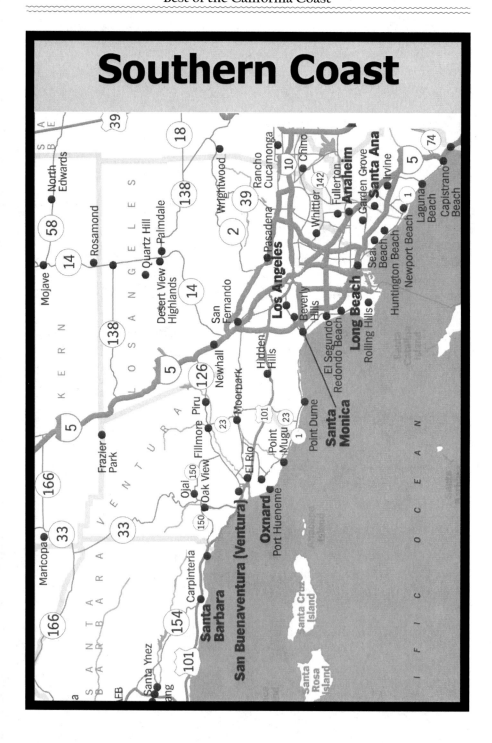

Southern Coast

The Southern Coast

race California's coastline from north to south, and there is a very obvious eastward shift in its orientation that begins at Point Conception, near the Santa Barbara County line. This shift in coastal orientation has many consequences, at least regarding weather. With few exceptions, winter storms are less violent here and the beaches tend to retain more of their sand than beaches farther north. The climate is generally warmer as high-pressure ridges hold back all but the strongest cold, wet storms that regularly swirl down from the Arctic and crash into Washington, Oregon, and Northern California.

The idyllic combination of warm sun, white sand beaches, and the blue Pacific Ocean is the image that comes to mind when most people are asked to describe California. From young, live-on-the-fly surfers, to established, well-to-do movie stars, and everyone else in between, California's southern beaches offer excitement, relaxation, and, more than anything, a retreat from an often hectic life in a very fast-paced world.

The Hollywood film industry has done more than any direct advertising campaign to promote the Southern California image. Frolicking beach movies of the 1950s and 1960s—such as *Beach Blanket Bingo* and continuing with television shows like *Bay Watch*—have encouraged the pursuit, or at least imitation, of the Southern California lifestyle.

Beyond the surfboards, sunscreen, and micro-bathing suits, there is a world of nature that still exists and flourishes along the beaches and in the mountains that rise, in some parts of the coast straight up from where the waves pound the shoreline. In many areas, coyotes, bobcats, and deer live only a few hundred feet away from shopping centers and crowded freeways. Miles of hiking, biking, and equestrian trails draw millions of recreationists each year to these wildlife islands.

Southern California also saw some of the state's earliest history, with Spain establishing the first Franciscan mission in San Diego in 1769, several years before the original 13 states had formed their union on the opposite side of the continent. From those years, and especially from the 19th century onward, land speculation, job opportunities, and mild weather have drawn millions of people to Southern California. This constant influx of new arrivals has created vibrant cities, incredible wealth, and a unique cultural blend that continues to lead the nation in popular trends. The growth and wealth has also resulted in the creation of some of the world's finest museums, restaurants, hotels, and other indicators of sophistication and refinement.

The counties covered in this chapter are Santa Barbara County, Ventura County, and Los Angeles County.

Santa Barbara County

LA PURÍSIMA MISSION STATE HISTORIC PARK

Unbeknownst to the Spanish missionaries, they chose some of California's most geologically active real estate on which to build their adobe missions. As a result, earthquakes took their toll on many of the early missions, including *Misión la Purísima Concepción de María Santísima*. In 1812, the original mission, which had been established in 1787, was destroyed by a strong quake. The mission's leaders decided to rebuild, but they moved the mission from its original location near today's town

California's most authentically restored mission

of Lompoc to its present location in *La Cañada de los Berros*, the "Canyon of the Watercress."

Following the U.S. takeover of California in 1846, many of the missions were abandoned and fell into disrepair. La Purísima was no different. By the early 1900s, little remained of the mission except a few adobe walls and foundations. Under President Roosevelt's WPA and CCC programs during the 1930s, restoration work began on the mission. The result is the most completely and authentically restored mission in California.

Spanish soldier barracks

There is a self-guided trail that begins near the parking lot at a small visitor center and museum. It will take about two hours to walk the 1-mile pathway that winds through and around all of the restored buildings. The first area the trail passes is a large corral with its sheep and cattle. It then crosses the historic *El Camino Real*, a stretch of dirt road that once was part of the **King's Highway** that connected all 21 missions. Ahead are the main buildings, including the church and cemetery. During the mission's reconstruction, archeologists discovered that hundreds of Indians and numerous Spaniards were buried here. It's likely that some of the Spanish soldiers were killed during a major Indian uprising in 1824.

You are free to wander inside the church, the shops, and the soldiers' quarters and residences. There is also the pottery shop, gristmill, blacksmith shop, and the site of the original Indian barracks. The Chumash Indians were coerced into abandoning their traditional cone-shaped thatched huts for two long adobe buildings that were divided into two-room apartments. There is also a mission garden that includes pomegranate, fig, and pear trees, grapevines, and other plants that were taken as cuttings from original plants still growing at other missions.

Activities: Walking tours, living histories
Facilities: Visitor center, museum, exhibits
Dates: Open daily
Fees: There is a day-use fee.
Closest town: Lompoc
Info: La Purísima State Historic Park, 2295 Purisima Road, Lompoc, CA 93436, 805.733.3713 or www.parks.ca.gov, 805.735.2174 for guided tours

SOLVANG

Solvang is a small, quaint town that has transformed itself from its original roots as a Danish farming community into a favorite stop for people traveling north and south along U.S. 101 through Santa Barbara County. Tucked into a small valley between the Santa Ynez and San Rafael mountain ranges, the town hosts about 12 blocks of gift and antique shops, restaurants, and bakeries, nearly all sporting a Danish theme. Solvang also has several full-size windmills, Hans Chris-

Solvang

tian Anderson and Little Mermaid statues, and a clock tower that plays seasonal tunes. Solvang is a great walking town, so park the car and enjoy a half-day or more wandering through the shops and sampling the many fine foods—you'll feel as if you're on the streets of Copenhagen.

Danish educators looking for the perfect site for a Danish-style folk school founded Solvang, meaning "sunny field," in 1911. The school was successful for many years, but when attendance declined, the school was closed and the structure demolished in 1970. While the school was the original reason for the settlers coming here, they also took up farming the rich land as a way to earn money.

The land around Solvang remains primarily undeveloped and is used for agriculture and ranching. The many Danish-Americans who live in the small community still practice Danish customs. One of the customs is *refsefilde*, which is a celebration held at the raising of the highest rafter on a new building. Many in the community also are members of the Royal Order of Dannebrog, an organization that recognizes the efforts of the town's citizens to strengthen linkages between Denmark and the United States.

Activities: Shopping, dining, sightseeing
Facilities: Shops, restaurants, historical structures
Closest town: Buellton
Info: Solvang Conference and Visitors Bureau, 1639 Copenhagen Dr., Solvang, CA 93463, 805.658.6144 or www.solvangusa.com

MISSION SANTA INES

On September 17, 1804, Father Estevan Tapis founded Mission Santa Ines, a long day's travel of 30 miles from Mission Santa Barbara. He named the mission after the 4th century Christian martyr and saint who was beheaded by the Romans; the English translation of her name is "Saint Agnes." To confuse matters, the nearby town was named "Santa Ynez" (now known as Solvang), which is the Americanized version of the same Spanish name.

This was one of several inland missions designed to reach the estimated 1,000 Chumush Indians who lived in the surrounding mountains and valleys. The mission became quite successful, with the mission Indians—called "neophytes"—harvesting wheat, corn, beans, and peas. The mission also had 7,000 head of cattle, 5,000 sheep, goats, pigs, mules, and horses.

Mission Santa Ines

Like its neighboring missions, Mission Santa Ines was severely damaged by the 1812 earthquake. It was also the center of a relatively large Indian uprising in 1824. The Spanish guards, who were mostly uneducated and paid meager wages, took out their unhappiness on the neophytes. After a soldier flogged one of the neophytes, the Indians revolted, burning several buildings, but not the church.

By 1834, the year Mexico gained its independence from Spain, the mission was already near collapse. Mexican Governor Manuel Micheltorena transferred 35,000 acres of mission land in 1843 to Alta California's first bishop, Francisco Garcia Diego y Moreno, who established a seminary there. The seminary relocated a year later and in 1846, the last Mexican governor of Alta California—Pio de Jesus Pico—illegally sold Mission Santa Ines for $7,000. Three weeks later, the U.S. military took control of Alta California and, in 1862, President Lincoln transferred the mission back to the church.

Today, the mission is an active parish. What is interesting about this mission is that you can take an audio tour, with the program describing everything from the musical instruments to the polychrome wood carvings and crosses. Inside the church, you'll find numerous paintings, many of which were collected from other missions and restored. One painting of particular interest shows Jesus wearing a hat, something not seen anywhere else. Don't miss the gardens, which are worth spending time exploring, even though they are only about one third their original size.

Mission graveyard

Activities: Self-guided tours
Facilities: Museum, gift shop
Dates: Open daily
Fees: Entrance fee, children 11 and under are free
Closest town: Solvang
Info: Mission Santa Ines, 1760 Mission Drive, Solvang, CA 93464, 805.688.4815 or www.missionsantaines.org

GAVIOTA STATE PARK

Gaviota State Park has nearly 3,000 acres of coastal mountains and 5.5 miles of ocean beaches and cliffs. During Spanish explorer Gaspar de Portolá's expedition in 1769, his soldiers named this part of California *gaviota*—"seagull." And while there are still plenty of gulls, there's much more here to see and do.

The park's main visual feature is an elevated Southern Pacific railroad trestle. Railroad tracks run much of the length of Southern California's coast, and trestles pass through many coastal parks, requiring cars or pedestrians to cross under them to reach the beaches. In addition to the old wooden trestle, there's also a small campground, a seasonally operated beach store, and several miles of trails.

Besides the beach—which during summer is always popular for swimming, fishing, and beachcombing—there's a marsh at the east end of the main parking lot. It's a good place to see great blue herons (*Ardea herodias*) and perhaps a red-tailed hawk (*Buteo jamaicensis*) swooping down low, hoping to grab a western harvest mouse (*Reithrodontomys megalotus*) or a pocket gopher (*Thomomys* sp.).

In the mountains above the beach, hikers will pass through woodlands of coast live oak, open grasslands, and the ever-present coastal chaparral.

Activities: Swimming, fishing, surfing, beachcombing, hiking, camping
Facilities: Campground, seasonal store, boat launch
Dates: Open daily
Fees: There are camping and day-use fees.
Closest town: Buellton
Info: Gaviota State Park, c/o Refugio State Beach, #10 Refugio Beach Road, Goleta, CA 93117, 805.968.1033 or www.parks.ca.gov

TRAILS

There are several trails at Gaviota State Park. The **Overlook Fire Road Trail** is a 3-mile round-trip to the top of a hill that is 925 feet above sea level and offers great views of the Pacific.

For those with more stamina, there is a 6-mile round-trip hike to the top of 2,458-foot-tall **Gaviota Peak**. If it is a fogless day, you should be able to see Point Conception, the Channel Islands, and the Lompoc Valley.

The **Gaviota Hot Springs Trail** is a popular 0.7-mile hike on the Gaviota Peak Fire Road from a parking lot located 2.5 miles north of the park entrance at the intersection of U.S. 101 and Highway 1. The reward is sulfur springs open to the public.

The hike up to Gaviota's **Wind Caves** will literally steal your breath away. Besides the dramatic caves, there are great views of the coast and Pacific Ocean. The ocean winds, over thousands of years, have carved dramatic caves into the soft sandstone mountain. They are well worth the effort to get there. After entering Gaviota State Park, follow the road to the right just before the kiosk. There is a trailhead (**Beach to Backcountry Trail**) and parking after the first big right-hand bend in the road. The trail to the caves is not well marked. It's about a 5-mile round-trip that includes a 700-foot elevation gain, and it tends to fork off toward other destinations, so it's wise to check with park staff for directions before you set out.

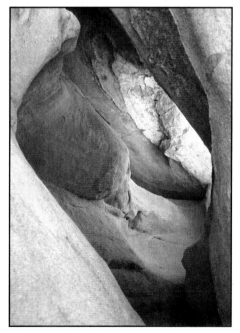

Wind cave

REFUGIO STATE BEACH

As with all the beaches along this stretch of California's coast, Refugio runs east to west, which means it faces south, where it is warmed by the sun and protected from northerly ocean swells. Here, where the Santa Ynez Mountains mark the westernmost end of the east-west orientation of the Transverse Range, ancient marine terraces stand against crashing ocean waves. At the cliff bases are sandy beaches and rocky tide pools, with a scattering of streams and canyons that cut through the cliffs to reach the ocean.

This land was originally inhabited by the Chumash Indians who lived on the mainland and on the Channel Islands offshore. Their culture depended on the sea for survival, with their villages situated close to the ocean where food was plentiful. Using crude stone tools, they were able to split wood planks from trees then lash them together with milkweed fiber to build their boats. They sealed the cracks with asphaltum, the naturally occurring tar found along this part of the coast.

The beach park is a good place to see a number of animals. Barn owls (*Tyto alba*), red-tailed hawks (*Buteo jamaicensis*), red-shouldered hawks (*Buteo lineatus*), and black-shouldered kites are found here. There are also the shoreline birds, including curlews (*Numenius americanus*), sandpipers (*Calidris minutilla*), and short-billed dowitchers (*Limnodroumus griseus*), that constantly follow the beach waves, probing the sand for insects and small animals.

A bike trail runs along the beach bluff and connects with **El Capitán State Beach** 2.5 miles to the east. The park has a campground that will accommodate tents and campers, and there's a seasonal snack shop and a large grass picnic area near the beach. There are also a lot of non-native palm trees in the park, which Southern Californians seem to enjoy growing. Extra offerings for an enjoyable beach outing include beach wheelchairs and summertime kayak tours led by state park lifeguards. Contact the park about reservations for both.

Fun at the beach

Activities: Swimming, fishing, camping, kayaking, bike riding, hiking
Facilities: Picnic tables, campground, seasonal snack bar
Dates: Open daily
Fees: There are camping and day-use fees.

Closest Town: Santa Barbara
Info: Refugio State Beach, #10 Refugio Beach Road, Goleta, CA 93117, 805.968.1033 or www.parks.ca.gov

EL CAPITÁN STATE BEACH

While this is a very popular summer swimming beach, it's equally popular year-round with the surfing crowd and fishermen, especially off **El Capitán Point**. Anglers catch kelp bass (*Paralabrax clathratus*) and Pacific halibut (*Hippoglossus stenolepis*) from the beach and rocky outcroppings.

California gull

This is a relatively small park of only 168 acres, made up of the sandy beach, a picnic area, and the popular campground. The park's name came from Captain Jose Franciso de Ortega, who first owned *Rancho Nuestro Senora del Refugio*, "Our Lady of Refuge Ranch." The ranch was larger than the beach park, extending up to 4 miles inland and west to **Cojo Canyon** near **Point Conception**.

In addition to the sandy beach and tide pools, El Capitán State Beach features stands of sycamores and oaks along **El Capitán Creek**. A paved ramp leads from the bluff parking lot to the beach, and a bike trail connects the park with Refugio State Beach, 3 miles away. Beach wheelchairs are available: contact the park for reservations.

Activities: Swimming, surfing, beachcombing, fishing, bike riding, camping
Facilities: Campground, picnic grounds, seasonal snack bar
Dates: Open daily
Fees: There are camping and day-use fees.
Closest town: Santa Barbara
Info: El Capitán State Beach c/o Refugio State Beach, #10 Refugio Beach Road, Goleta, CA 93117, 805.968.1033 or www.parks.ca.gov

SANTA BARBARA

The city of Santa Barbara's near-perfect weather—combined with its beach, wharf, and historic district—create a special ambiance that makes this a favorite vacation spot for thousands of people each year. Santa Barbara began as a Spanish presidio that was built in 1782 in an effort to stop Russia's threat of continued southerly expansion down the California coast. One hundred years later, the growing town had gained a reputation as a wonderful coastal resort, a reputation it retains today.

Southern Coast

Downtown Santa Barbara has managed to retain much of its Old World feeling with its combination of Mediterranean, Spanish Colonial, early Californian, Mexican, Moorish, and Islamic architecture. From restaurants to the city's court and government buildings, here you'll find no steel and glass high-rises, but attractive buildings with white plaster walls, arched windows, doorways, and facades, all complemented by their low-pitched tile roofs and decorative wrought iron work. Hidden patios and gardens are part of the overall design of many of Santa Barbara's buildings.

It wasn't always this way. A population boom in the late 19th century brought an eclectic assortment of architecture, much of it Victorian. Of the many Victorian structures built during that time, the **Upham Hotel** still remains, making it the oldest continually operating hotel in Southern California. In the 1880s, many prominent citizens of the growing city called for controls on the styles of architecture that could be added. Even today, ordinances help define architectural styles, allowing Santa Barbara to retain its Spanish-Mediterranean appearance.

Found within Santa Barbara, **El Presidio de Santa Bárbara State Historic Park** (805.965.0093 or www.parks.ca.gov) houses the only two original presidio adobe structures that have survived in the town. One of those original structures is **El Cuartel,** which is the oldest building in Santa Barbara and the second oldest in

California. What today is a museum and gift shop originally was built to house 42 Spanish soldiers and their wives and children soon after they arrived here in 1782. The presidio fell into disuse following the American takeover of California in 1846. Earthquakes and the frenzied development that followed as Santa Barbara's popularity increased resulted in many buildings being destroyed. The Santa Barbara Trust for Historic Preservation has been heading a restoration and reconstruction program since 1964. The chapel, padre's and comandante's quarters, and soldiers' quarters across Santa Barbara Street, are well worth a visit. The presidio's other surviving building is the **Canedo Adobe**, which houses museum exhibits.

El Cuartel

Santa Barbara and Stearns Wharf

Santa Barbara's top tourist spot—**Stearns Wharf** (805.564.5530 or www.stearnswharf.org)—extends from the end of State Street into the blue waters of the **Santa Barbara Channel**. John Peck Stearns built the wharf in 1872. It's been in continual operation since then, although it has changed owners over the years. During the 1940s, actor Jimmy Cagney and his brothers were part owners of the wharf enterprise. There's a fanciful dolphin fountain near the foot of the wharf, a favorite spot for photographs. The wharf offers the typical seafood market, a bait and tackle store, several restaurants, winetasting, and gift shops.

The **Santa Barbara Historical Museum** (805.966.1601 or www.santabarbaramuseum.com) is a historic adobe home that now exhibits a regional history collection that includes fine art, saddles, costumes, and antique toys. The museum also houses the **Gledhill Library** with its extensive holdings of books, photographs, maps, and manuscripts, making it a rich resource of information for history buffs. Two other 19th century adobes are adjacent to the museum and surround a tree-shaded courtyard. The museum is closed Mondays. Admission is free, but donations are appreciated.

The **Santa Barbara Museum of Natural History** (805.682.4711 or www.sbnature.org) is nationally renowned for its coverage of California and North American West Coast natural history. Highlights include a diorama of prehistoric Chumash Indian life in the Santa Barbara area and the skeleton of a giant blue whale. The museum, which is located behind Mission Santa Barbara, also has a planetarium. The museum is open daily except Thanksgiving, Christmas, and New Year's Day. There is an admission fee.

Info: Visit Santa Barbara, 500 E. Montecito Street, Santa Barbara, CA 93103, 805.966.9222, 800.676.1266 or www.santabarbaraca.com

MISSION SANTA BARBARA

Founded in 1786, Mission Santa Barbara—the "Queen of the Missions"—is one of the most recognizable of California's 21 missions. Its twin bell towers, the curious but beautiful Roman temple facade, and a large expanse of grass in front of where the mud huts of Indians once sat make it strikingly attractive. While the Roman influence came from the 27 BC renderings of Vitruvius Pollio, the mission's name came from the Christian Roman virgin whose head her less-than-understanding pagan father lopped off.

Father Junipero Serra initially founded the mission, or attempted to, in the spring of 1782, but the Spanish governor refused to allow the needed work to be done. It wasn't until two years after Serra's death—on the Feast of Santa Barbara in December 1786—that Father Fermin Francisco de Lasuen actually raised the cross that allowed the mission to become official. He placed Father Antonio Paterna

Mission Santa Barbara

in charge of the mission, and Paterna began construction. Three successive adobe churches were built, each larger than its predecessor, until the last was destroyed in the 1812 earthquake. Soon after, work began again on the church that exists today, but it wasn't completed until 1820. The foundation in front of the mission predates most of the present-day structures; it was completed in 1808.

Santa Barbara hosted the first bishop of California, and some of his personal belongings are part of the museum's collection. The museum is also the archive for many important Franciscan documents, including those created by Father Serra. A few of the paintings in the church are more than 200 years old. While inside the church, look for the carved skull and crossbones above the church's other door; it indicates the way to the cemetery. More than 4,000 Indians were buried here, alongside some of Santa Barbara's earliest settlers. Near the side of the church's cemetery are remnants of the original aqueduct that brought water from a small reservoir that the padres built about 2 miles away. Below the Moorish fountain, constructed in 1808, is the *lavandería*— "laundry"—where Indian women washed clothes.

Activities: Self-guided tours and occasional docent-led tours
Facilities: 10-room museum, mission, church, gift store
Dates: Open daily
Fees: There is an admission fee.
Closest town: Santa Barbara
Info: Old Mission Santa Barbara, 2201 Laguna Street, Santa Barbara, CA 93105, 805.682.4713 or www.santabarbaramission.org

DOUGLAS FAMILY PRESERVE

The 70-acre Douglas Family Preserve, which sits on a mesa above **Arroyo Burro Beach**, is an undeveloped city park. And the citizens of Santa Barbara wouldn't want it any other way.

This breathtaking slice of coastal waterfront was saved through a local grassroots movement. The property was originally owned by Roy Wilcox, who opened a plant nursery here in 1949. Referred to by locals as the "Wilcox Property," the nursery closed in 1972. That's when big development stepped in, vying for the property—plans included a housing development and luxury hotel. Locals raised $2 million to save the property, but that still wasn't enough to help the Trust for Public Land make the purchase. At the last minute, actor/director Michael Douglas contributed $600,000, saving the project. Thus, the honor of naming of the park was given to Douglas, who then named the park in honor of his father Kirk Douglas.

This park is the largest area of coastal open space in Santa Barbara. Here, you will find a mix of native plants and exotic vegetation, the latter the result of the area once having been a plant nursery. City staff and volunteers are working to restore the native habitat.

There are several entry points into the park—check the website for details if your GPS can't locate it. The preserve allows dogs to be off-leash in designated areas. Because this is an undeveloped city park, there are no restrooms or picnic facilities. Parking can be found on surrounding neighborhood streets.

Info: Douglas Family Preserve, Linda Road, Santa Barbara, CA 93101, 805.564.5418 or www.santabarbaraca.gov

SANTA BARBARA BOTANIC GARDEN

The Santa Barbara Botanic Garden is tucked into the hills above Santa Barbara and is California's oldest botanic garden dedicated to showcasing the state's native plants. The garden's 5.5 miles of trails wander through 78 acres with more than 1,000 indigenous and rare plants growing in organized plant communities. There are numerous garden sections and displays such as the desert, woodland habitats, a home demonstration garden, and an extensive manzanita grove with 60 different specimens. Also found here is the **ShinKanAn Teahouse and Garden**. Open from 12 P.M. to 2 P.M. the second Saturday of every month, teahouse volunteers, dressed in traditional Japanese garments, treat guests to a tea ceremony while explaining the country's rich heritage and culture. Teahouse volunteers also offer private lessons in the art form.

Santa Barbara Botanic Garden

The botanic garden also offers excellent views of the Pacific Ocean and several of the Channel Islands. If you're interested in obtaining native plants, the garden's nursery grows specimens that are available for purchase. Pets are allowed, but they must be leashed.

From downtown Santa Barbara, take Los Olivos northeast past the Santa Barbara Mission toward the mountains. At Foothill Road (Highway 192) turn right then take the first left onto Mission Canyon Road. Stay right at the fork. The garden is 0.5 mile on the left.

Activities: Docent-led walks, self-guided walks, picnicking
Facilities: Gift shop, nursery, teahouse
Dates: Open daily with extended seasonal hours
Fees: Admission fee, parking is free
Info: Santa Barbara Botanic Garden, 1212 Mission Canyon Road, Santa Barbara, CA 93105, 805.682.4726 or www.sbbg.org

MORE TO EXPLORE

For tourists and families, **East Beach**, which is adjacent to Stern's Wharf, is an easy destination to reach. With its expansive and pristine sandy coastline, long bike path, and volleyball courts where toned and tanned people play, this beach is iconic to everything Southern California.

Ledbetter Beach, located near the local city college, is also another easily accessible park and popular with those who want a quick fix of beach time. The park offers outdoor showers, a grassy picnic area, and even a seasonal café.

Where do the locals go? Two beaches: **Butterfly Beach** and **Arroyo Burro Beach** (also known as "**Hendry's Beach**"). Butterfly Beach is across from the Four Season Biltmore in the Montecito area, and the hotel is frequented by celebrities. But that's not the reason the locals love this beach—they go because the small beach is gorgeous, the view is amazing, and the beach area is not as "touristy" as East and Ledbetter. There are no facilities at this beach, so come prepared.

Arroyo Burro Beach is where the dogs can be found. This dog-friendly park has a designated off-leash area where dogs frolic in the surf. And if that isn't enough, there is a coin-operated doggy shower to rid your canine of unwanted sand before heading home. The beach also has a restaurant and snack bar, grassy picnic area, and free parking—until it fills up. The only negatives are during high tide the beach area shrinks and the seaweed that litters the beach attracts sand flies.

Info: Visit Santa Barbara, 500 E. Montecito Street, Santa Barbara, CA 93103, 805.966.9222, 800.676.1266 or www.santabarbaraca.com

CHUMASH PAINTED CAVE STATE HISTORIC PARK

Middens—Native American buried garbage sites filled with long-discarded shells and occasional stone tools—are often the only evidence that Chumash Indians lived along this portion of California's coast for thousands of years. There is a wonderful exception. The walls of a sandstone cave located high in the mountains above Santa Barbara are covered with exquisite examples of Chumash art. The colorful paintings depict the lives of the Indians, including images of coastal Native American fishermen. The paintings are estimated to have been created in the 1600s. Unfortunately, anthropologists cannot absolutely be sure of what the paintings mean or represent.

Looking inside the cave

The cave is located up a steep path from the road, with parts of the path having stairs. Its wide entrance to the relatively shallow cave is enclosed by a cage to protect the walls from graffiti and touching. But the brilliant-colored paintings are easily seen or photographed from outside the iron grillwork.

From Santa Barbara and U.S. 101, take Highway 154 east approximately 5.9 miles and turn right on Painted Cave Road, which is easily missed. Follow the very narrow, twisting, and steep Painted Cave Road about 1.9 miles. A sign on the left side of the road marks the site. There is parking space for only a few vehicles. Trailers and RVs should not attempt to drive up Painted Cave Road.

A peek inside at the native artwork

Activities: Viewing the cave—a flashlight is recommended
Facilities: None
Dates: Open daily
Fees: None
Closest town: Santa Barbara
Info: Chumash Painted Cave State Historic Park, c/o La Purísima SHP, 2295 Purisima Road, Lompoc, CA 93436, 805.733.3713 or www.parks.ca.gov

264

CARPINTERIA STATE BEACH

This mile-long beach is the primary attraction in the small town of Carpinteria. The beach has a reef offshore that softens the ocean's movement, essentially eliminating the rip currents that are found along most other Southern California beaches. As far back as 1602, the Spanish who first arrived here recognized the natural beach conditions and described this as *cosa segura de buen gente*, or "the safest beach on the coast." Near Carpinteria State Beach's popular sandy shore, which is favored by sunbathers, there are also tide pools containing their share of anemones, sea stars, crabs, snails, and sea urchins.

While wading at the edge of the surf or walking on the beach, it's not unusual to step on small blobs of gooey tar. The tar isn't the result of a major offshore oil tanker spill. The tar is continually washed ashore from naturally occurring seeps in the Santa Barbara Channel's sea floor. Geologically induced pressures beneath the surface force the thick oil through the porous sediment floor where it then floats to the surface, often attaching itself to kelp or simply washing ashore. Marine biologists have discovered that some species of shrimp, sand dabs, and bacteria have evolved so they can thrive near the seeps. Bacteria of the genus *Beggiatoa* are able to consume the oil's hydrogen sulfide and convert it into sugar.

The ample supply of tar is the reason the native Chumash Indians chose this spot to build their large seagoing canoes—they used the tar to seal the seams of the plank boats. The Spanish discovered the Indians' manufacturing endeavor and named the site *Carpenteria* or "carpentry shop." Archeological investigations discovered the remains of prehistoric animals, similar to those found in the more famous **La Brea Tar Pits** in Los Angeles that died in some of Carpinteria's tar pits. Tar from the Carpinteria pits also was used by the early settlers in the construction of piers and wharves.

Carpinteria State Beach has a 216-site campground, which is a good choice for anyone wanting to stay near the beach overnight. And in 2011, the **Tomol Intrepretive Play Area** was built here for kids. The playground mirrors a Chumush Indian village, complete with canoe, thatched houses, a "cloudburst" slide, a cave, and sandstone boulders to climb on.

Activities: Swimming, sunbathing, beachcombing, fishing, surfing
Facilities: Campground with RV hookups
Dates: Open daily
Fees: There are camping and day-use fees.
Closest town: Carpinteria
Info: Channel Coast District State Parks, 911 San Pedro Street, Ventura, CA 93001, 805.585.1850 or www.parks.ca.gov

Ventura County

CHANNEL ISLANDS NATIONAL PARK

Eight islands in all, the Channel Islands lie from 14 to 55 miles off the California coastline. The islands provide an effective barrier that deflects winter storm-produced waves from the mainland. Combined, the eight islands comprise 250,000 acres, with five of those islands (79,000 acres total) making up Channel Islands National Park.

The islands are part of the Transverse Range and were once a single large island that geologists call "Santarosea"—most of that island now lies beneath the Pacific Ocean. At one time, the islands were also connected with the mainland.

Anacapa Island, part of Channel Islands National Park

Rising oceans and moving landmasses separated the Channel Islands from their mainland mountain cousins thousands of years ago. That separation has resulted in many plant and animal species that once were identical to those on the mainland to evolve in size, color, and shape. The Santa Cruz Island scrub jay; six separate subspecies of the island fox found on six different islands and thought to be related to the mainland gray fox; and a subspecies of the spotted skunk, but with a broader face and shorter tail than its mainland cousins, are found only on the Channel Islands. Another endemic threatened species is the island night lizard, found on Santa Barbara Island and on San Nicolas and San Clemente islands outside of the national park's boundaries. While the rare Torrey pine grows on Santa Rosa Island and at Torrey Pines State Park on the mainland, the Santa Cruz Island pine is found nowhere else but on its Channel Island home.

The weather on the islands can be harsh, ranging from cold and very windy to hot and dry. There are many miles of trails and numerous beaches and tide pools available for exploration. Please remember that most of the islands and their surrounding waters are protected. This includes the animals in the tide pools, the plants on the islands, and even the remnants of shipwrecks that are accessible to scuba divers.

SAN MIGUEL ISLAND is the westernmost of the islands, lying directly south of Point Conception. Only 8 miles long and about 4 miles across at its widest point, its 9,325 acres—which includes offshore islands and rocks—provide a resting ground for California sea lions (*Zalophus californicus*), stellar sea lions (*Eumetopias jubatus*), northern elephant seals (*Mirounga angustirostris*), harbor seals (*Phoca vitulina*), Guadalupe fur seals (*Arctocephalus townsendi*), and northern fur seals (*Callorhinus ursinus*). **Point Bennett** hosts the largest pinniped rookery on California's coast.

One unique part of the island is the caliche forest. The "ghost forest" was created thousands of years ago when calcium carbonate sand, composed primarily of powdered lime skeletons of dead shellfish, blew inland and covered the vegetation. Organic chemicals from within the plants reacted with the sand and cemented it together. As the plants died and decayed, they left behind the eerie gray castings of their original forms. Winds continue to erode and bury some of the brittle castings while uncovering new ones. There is also a memorial at **Cuyler Harbor** that commemorates Juan Rodriques Cabrillo, the first European to land on the island. He is now buried on the island. Besides the Chumush people, other inhabitants raised sheep here from 1850 to the 1940s, when forced to leave due to fears raised from the Pearl Harbor attack. Access to the island has been off and on, mainly due

Northern elephant seal

Southern Coast

to the U.S. Navy's surveying for unexploded ordinances. When access is allowed, visitors must sometimes navigate 8-foot swells and rough landings. The National Park Service strongly advises visitors to take food and water with them in case they become stranded due to bad weather.

SANTA ROSA ISLAND is next in the east-west line of ancient mountaintops. It's the second largest in the island chain with its 84 square miles covered mostly by non-native grass introduced over more than a century of cattle and sheep grazing. There are 15 rare or endangered species, along with three endemic species; the tree poppy (*Dendromecon harfordii*), island manzanita (*Artostaphylos tomentosa insulicola*), and island oak (*Quercus tomentella*). There is also a remnant Torrey pine (*Pinus torreyana*) forest that has been here since the Pleistocene Era. In 1994, archeologists discovered the fossilized skeleton of a pygmy mammoth, which is on display at the **Robert J. Lagomarsino Channel Islands National Visitor Center (RLCIN-VC)** in Ventura. As on some of the other islands, many scattered Chumash burial and midden sites can be found here, too.

Pygmy mammoth dig

There is a campground at **Bechers Bay** with windbreaks and pit toilets. Boat landings are permitted on most of the beaches year-round, although there are exceptions. Contact the RLCINVC for specific closures and required camping reservations.

SANTA CRUZ ISLAND's 62,000 acres make it the largest of the Channel Islands chain, and with its highest peak at 2,450 feet, it also possesses the tallest of the islands' mountains. The western 76 percent of the island is owned by The Nature Conservancy, which allows public day use access. The remaining 24 percent that lies east of a line between **Chinese Harbor** on the north and **Sandborne Point** on the south belongs to the national park service. The 24-mile-long by 6-mile-wide island has some 650 species of plants and trees within its 10 different plant communities. Eight of the plants are endemic, found nowhere else in the world. Such varied habitat helps account for the more than 140 terrestrial bird species that have been recorded here. In 2006, the first bald eagle to hatch without human help occurred on the island. The last time this happened was in the mid-1960s.

This island is a perfect destination for a one-day adventure. The hour-long boat ride takes you to the Scorpion anchorage, and a trip to the island's visitor center—located inside the historic **Scorpion Ranch House**—is a must. Besides learning about the island's culture and environmental offerings, the visitor center shows an important orientation video designed

A display at the Scorpion Ranch Visitor Center

to keep both visitors and the island's flora and fauna safe. Camping is allowed.

ANACAPA ISLAND is actually three small islands (East, Middle, and West Anacapa) covering a total of only 700 acres, making it the smallest of the northern Channel Islands. This 5-mile-long island chain was once used to graze sheep, but the park service removed the animals when the island became a national monument in 1938. Anacapa is the West Coast's primary nesting site for brown pelicans (*Pelecanus occidentalis*). In order to protect the pelican rookery, West Anacapa is closed to the public. What is open to guests is the **Anacapa Visitor Center**, which offers information about both the cultural and environmental aspects of the area.

Anacapa's steep cliffs are punctuated by sea caves, and on the east end, **Arch Rock** is a natural 40-foot bridge. In 1912, the U.S. Coast Guard built a light beacon here, and then a light station 20 years later. The light station was the last to be built by the U.S. Lighthouse Service. The lighthouse is still in active use today.

Camping is allowed on East Anacapa and landing access is allowed at Landing Cove. Primitive camping reservations are required. Contact park headquarters for information before heading to the island.

Anacapa Visitor Center

SANTA BARBARA ISLAND is the smallest of the Channel Islands and lies off the coast of Ventura. Most of its 640 acres are comprised of an ancient marine terrace with two peaks, the highest being 634-foot **Signal Peak**. Park service rangers use a World War II Navy Quonset hut as an office, visitor center, and museum.

Several trails wind through a much-changed environment. Goats were introduced here in 1846, followed by heavy farm use, grazing, and intentional burning of the land. The introduc-

tion of rabbits completed the near total destruction of the native habitat, but the park service removed the non-native wildlife and instituted a very successful ongoing restoration program. Today, stands of giant coreopsis (*Coreopsis gigantea*)—sunflowers that can reach 10 feet high—thrive here. Western gulls (*Coreopsis gigantea*) use the island for nesting and one of

Scripp's murrelet chick

the world's largest breeding colonies of the rare seabird, Scripp's murrelets (*Synthliboramphus scrippsi*) can be found on the island.

A small and primitive campground is located near Landing Cove. No fee is charged, but reservations are required. As with most of the islands, there is no water, so it must be packed in.

Info: The Channel Islands can only be reached by boat, although there is very limited private air service available. Some areas on the islands are off-limits to the public or require a ranger guide. Pets and open fires are not allowed on any of the islands. Charter boat fees vary. Contact the RLCINVC for information and permits: National Park Service, Robert J. Lagomarsino Channel Islands National Visitor Center, 1901 Spinnaker Drive, Ventura, CA 93001, 805.658.5730 or www.nps.gov.

MORE TO EXPLORE

Drive along Highway 1—better known locally as the Pacific Coast Highway or PCH—and between the growing number of beachside houses and businesses, you can find dozens of public beaches. The best and safest way to reach these beaches is by using the well-marked public beach access points and parking areas.

But for the more adventurous, there are unmarked beach access points all along the coast that can usually be identified by several vehicles parked in wide pullouts along the road. Listed here are only those Ventura County and California State Park beaches with officially recognized and signed public beach access points. Also, pets are typically not allowed on the beaches.

Hobson Beach Park is a day-use beach with a campground. Because it is just feet away from the Pacific Ocean, it may close during strong storms. The park is adjacent to Highway 1, south of Sea Cliff and about 7 miles north of Ventura. Info: 805.654.3951 or www.ventura.org

Rincon Parkway North is a roadside parking area along the Pacific Coast Highway seawall, between Hobson County Park to the north and the Faria County Park to the south. There are 112 designated campsites available for self-contained RVs on a first-come, first-served basis. Info: 805.654.3951 or www.ventura.org

Faria County Park lies south of Rincon Parkway North and has stairs that allow access to its combination rocky shoreline and sandy beach. The park offers both tent and RV campsites next to the ocean. As with nearby Hobson County Park, Faria County Park may be closed during times of heavy surf. It's located off the old Pacific Coast Highway, which parallels Highway 1 on the ocean side at Pitas Point. Info: 805.654.3951 or www.ventura.org

Emma Wood State Beach is a great place to spend a day swimming, surfing, or fishing. Anglers regularly catch sea or shiner perch (*Cymatogaster aggregata*) and cabezon (*Scorpaenichthys marmoratus*). There's a freshwater marsh—the **Ventura River Estuary**—near the southwest end of the beach where resident and migrating songbirds can be seen and red-tailed hawks soar overhead. The ruins of a World

Sunset on a Southern California beach

271

War II coastal artillery site are also here. There is a small and primitive camp-ground for hikers and bikers only. The beach is located about 2 miles northwest of Ventura on U.S. 101. Info: 805.968.1033 or www.parks.ca.gov

San Buenaventura State Beach is long and wide with a 1,700-foot pier at its northwest end, complete with a restaurant, bait shop, and snack bar. On the beach, there are volleyball courts, picnic sites, beach equipment rentals, and dress-ing rooms. The main beach entrance is off San Pedro Street from Pierpont Boule-vard in Ventura. Info: 805.968.1033 or www.parks.ca.gov

McGrath State Beach is located in Oxnard, off U.S. 101 and Harbor Bou-levard. In addition to the park's nearly 300 acres, its rolling dunes, and 2 miles of beach, there's a marsh at the mouth of the **Santa Clara River**, which is protected within the **Santa Clara Estuary Natural Preserve**. The beach also has a camp-ground. While swimming and surfing are popular here, there are strong rip cur-rents along the shore, so extreme caution is advised. Info: 805.968.1033 or www. parks.ca.gov

SANTA MONICA MOUNTAINS NATIONAL RECREATION AREA

This is an island paradise that exists in the middle of a vast sea of humanity. It amazes most newcomers to the Los Angeles area—the second largest urban area in the United States—that in the middle of all these people, businesses, freeways, and homes is a vast mountain wilderness where the sounds and sights of civiliza-tion completely vanish.

Mountain biking fun!

The park, which at 153,075 acres is the world's largest urban national park, lies within the Santa Monica Mountains, a rug-ged stretch of terrain, much of which is accessible only on trails or the few roads that manage to navigate the steep, narrow, and winding canyons. The national recreation area is actually a co-operative effort by the National Park Service, state parks, various conservancies, and private land-owners who are working togeth-er to protect the land's resources while allowing and encouraging public access.

This part of Southern California enjoys a true Mediterranean climate. Summers are hot and dry, ranging from 80 to 100 degrees Fahrenheit, with cool, comfortable nights. Winters are relatively wet and cool, ranging from 40 to 70 degrees, although freezing nighttime temperatures in protected mountain valleys are not uncommon. The maritime influence generally keeps the ocean side of the mountains 10 to 15 degrees cooler than the inland side. During winter, the pattern is reversed with warmer temperatures more common along the coast.

The Chumash and Tongva/Gabrielino Indians originally inhabited this land. The Spanish arrival in the 1500s marked the beginning of the end for the Native Americans' way of life. When real colonization efforts began 200 years later, European diseases and the mission system soon decimated native populations. Following Spanish, Mexican, and finally in 1846, American control of California, much of what is now the national recreation area ended up in the hands of Frederick and May Rindge, who purchased the property for about $10 an acre. They called their acquisition *El Rancho Topanga Malibu Sequit*. If not for their efforts at keeping development and roads out of these mountains during those early years, it's unlikely there would be much public open space existing here today.

This is a land of sandy beaches and dry chaparral, lush streams and open meadows, all of which work together to support more than 1,000 plant species, 50 mammal species, and 400 bird species. And more than 50 threatened and endangered plants and animals can be found here, making the Santa Monica Mountains home to one of the highest concentrations of rare species in the United States.

While much of the recreation area use is centered on the popular beaches, there are ever-increasing demands for new trails. Most summer weekends bring steady streams of people using the more popular trails. Equestrians, mountain bikers, and hikers share some of these trails, but many are only available to hikers.

No matter your chosen mode of transportation, if using the trails, carry a map, plenty of water, sunscreen, and a couple of light layers of clothing, even on warm summer days because the fog can roll in quickly. A good first place to obtain maps, trail guides, and information about the Santa Mountains National Recreation Area is the **Anthony C. Beilenson Interagency Visitor Center** at the King Gillette Ranch, located in Calabasas.

The 588-acre **King Gillette Ranch** was founded by American businessman King Camp Gillette, the inventor of the Gillette Safety Razor. It was

Visitor Center at King Gillette Ranch

1903, and even though there were other men's razors on the market, Gillette's razor blade was made of thin disposable blade of stamped steel, opposed to his competitors' more expensive blades made from forged steel. His new product sold by the millions, thus making him a very rich man. In 1926, he bought land in the Santa Monica Mountains and hired famed architect Wallace Neff to design and build a Spanish Colonial Revival home for he and his family. Following Gillette's death in 1932, his wife sold the ranch and the property subsequently passed through many owners, including Academy Award nominated film director Clarence Brown, Bob Hope, three churches, and a private university. In 2005, the National Park Service, California State Parks and two major nonprofits purchased the ranch then opened it to the public.

For those who would like a slightly different experience in the Santa Monica National Recreation Area than the beaches and mountain hiking, visit the **Paramount Ranch**. This is a great place to see the history of Hollywood, and perhaps some current

Paramount Ranch

Hollywood action. The ranch originally consisted of 2,700 acres that Paramount Pictures purchased in 1927 to use as a movie-making area. It was an extremely active filming location with directors such as Cecil B. Demille and actors of the day like Gary Cooper and Claudette Colbert on the ranch regularly.

The varied terrain allowed movie directors the ability to recreate locales such as ancient China (*The Adventures of Marco Polo*), the South Seas (*Ebb Tide*), and San Francisco (*Wells Fargo*). Paramount finally sold the property in 1953 to film fan William Hertz, who created a permanent western town using old sets and prop storage sheds. The result was a resurgence of filming interest as television came on the scene. Westerns became the focus with the producers of *The Cisco Kid* and *Dick Powell's Zane Grey Theater* becoming regulars at the ranch. Hertz sold the ranch in 1955 and filming continued until finally the National Park Service purchased the area in 1980. Today, film crews still use the old sets. For example, *Dr. Quinn, Medicine Woman* was filmed here from 1991 to 1998. Visitors always have a good chance of running across a working film crew.

There are dozens of access points throughout the Santa Monica Mountains National Recreation Area, which, in general, is located west of Griffith Park in Los

Angeles County and to the east of the Oxnard Plain in Ventura County. U.S. 101 (Ventura Freeway) borders the mountains on the north, and Highway 1 (Pacific Coast Highway or PCH) and the Pacific Ocean form the southern boundary. Access to most park areas is available via the several roads that cross the mountains linking U.S. 101 and Highway 1. The national recreation area's primary interior access roads are Kanan Dume Road, Las Virgines Road, and Topanga Canyon Boulevard, each of which runs north-south through the national recreation area connecting U.S. 101 with Highway 1.

Activities: Hiking, camping, swimming, surfing, horseback riding, fishing, mountain biking, climbing, nature walks, picnicking, historic house tours

Facilities: Campgrounds, picnic areas, museums, visitor centers, gift shops

Dates: Public lands are open daily. There may be winter closures of some trails due to mudslides. Open hours at the museums and visitor centers vary.

Fees: There are camping and day-use fees at the state parks (Point Mugu, Malibu Creek, Topanga), which are within the boundaries of the national recreation area. With the exception of vehicle parking fees in some areas, there are no fees for using the beaches and trails.

Closest town: Malibu on the south (Highway 1) and Calabasas, Agoura Hills, and Thousand Oaks on the north along U.S. 101

Info: Anthony C. Beilenson Interagency Visitor Center, 26876 Mulholland Hwy., Calabasas, CA 91302, 805.370.2301 or www.nps.gov

TRAILS

The **Backbone Trail** meanders 67 miles across the rugged and beautiful Santa Monica Mountains, running through much of the national recreation area and several state parks. This is not a trail for the weak-of-heart. It's a sometimes torturous pathway that begins and ends near sea level, but it encompasses several major elevation gains and losses, with the trail ranging from less than 200 feet to nearly 3,000 feet above sea level. It can be hot, dry, wet, foggy, muddy, and dusty, sometimes on the very same day. The views, the rock formations, and the spring wildflower shows can take your breath away in a much more pleasant way than the steep climbs.

Hiking in the Santa Monica Mountains has many rewards.

Many people catch short portions of the Backbone Trail on day hikes that begin from any number of starting points along the trail. But for anyone wishing to do the entire trail, there are designated camping sites available.

The northwestern end of the trail is in Point Mugu State Park. In the south, the trailhead is in Will Rogers State Historic Park. The trail passes through the Circle X Ranch, crosses from Ventura County into Los Angeles County, meanders through Malibu Creek State Park, Trippet Ranch, and Topanga State Park, and finally ends in Will Rogers State Historic Park at its farthest point southeast.

The **Mishe Mokwa Trail to Split Rock** is a 3.5-mile round-trip that winds through riparian, coastal sage scrub, and chaparral plant communities. There are great views of **Balancing Rock** and a wonderful oak grove picnic site at Split Rock. Begin at the Backbone trailhead approximately 6 miles up Yerba Buena Road, which intersects with Highway 1 about 1.7 miles west of Leo Carrillo State Park.

Balancing Rock

Mishe Mokwa Trail to Sandstone Peak is a strenuous 7.1-mile round-trip that follows a portion of the Backbone Trail, beginning at a trailhead off Yerba Buena Road. After reaching Split Rock (1.75 miles), the trail loops about another 3 miles to Sandstone Peak at an elevation of 3,111 feet. The trail connects with and follows a portion of the much longer and more heavily used Backbone Trail. Along the Backbone Trail portion, hikers are likely to encounter mountain bikers and equestrians who are not allowed on most of the narrower connecting trails, so be on your guard.

The **Grotto Trail** is a moderate to strenuous 3.5-mile round-trip hike that begins at the **Circle X Ranch** ranger station. The trail heads downhill on some pretty rough terrain, following the hillside and the West Fork of the Arroyo Sequit. But once you get to the Grotto, you will be pleased. The last 200 yards is actually the streambed. Obviously, it's uphill on the way back, so be prepared. Circle X Ranch, which was a former Boy Scout camp, is located on Yerba Buena Road, about 5 miles north of Highway 1. On Highway 1, the Yerba Buena Road turnoff is located 1.7 miles west of Leo Carrillo State Park.

Paramount Ranch offers three short (less than 1 mile each), round-trip hikes. **Coyote Canyon Trail** takes hikers on an easy stroll through a chaparral-covered canyon. **Medea Creek Trail** is open to hikers and equestrians and loops through streamside riparian and oak woodland areas. The **Overlook Trail**, also open to hikers and equestrians, heads up from Coyote Canyon (leaving from the ranch's Western town) to a viewpoint of the western mountains. From U.S. 101 in Calabasas, take the Las Virgenes Road exit and drive south about 3 miles, turning right (west) on Mulholland Highway. Paramount Ranch is located off Mulholland Highway, about 3 miles west of Las Virgenes Road.

Zuma Loop Trail is an easy 2-mile trail that wanders through a rare (for California) riparian hardwood forest of oak, sycamore, willow, and black walnut trees. Zuma, a word derived from the Chumash language that means "abundance," aptly describes the diversity of habitat and the wildlife that live here. The trail begins at a parking area at the end of Bonsall Drive, which is 1.5 miles north on Kanan-Dume Road. Kanan-Dume Road intersects Highway 1 about 6.5 miles west of Malibu.

Satwiwa Loop Trail is another easy 1.5-mile trail that leads through the grasslands and chaparral of the **Satwiwa Native American Indian Natural Area**. The area has been set aside to preserve and celebrate Native American cultures. To reach the **Satwiwa Native American Indian Culture Center**, from U.S. 101 in Thousand Oaks, take the Lynn Road exit, drive south to Via Goleta and turn left into the park.

Peter Strauss Ranch Trail is a short, 0.6-mile loop through chaparral and oak woodlands. The old ranch, through which the trail meanders, was named after actor Peter Strauss who purchased the property after falling in love with it while filming *Rich Man, Poor Man* here in 1976. He sold the land to the Santa Monica Mountains Conservancy and, in 1987, the National Park Service took possession.

In the 1930s, long before Strauss purchased the property, the owners created "Shoson," a fairyland attraction for children and parents. It was later renamed "Lake Enchanto." There are still remnants of the 1935 amusement park here, including the terrazzo dance floor and a 650,000-gallon swimming pool, which

Southern Coast

Pacific Ocean view from the Santa Monica Mountains

in 1940 was the largest pool on the West Coast, able to accommodate 3,000 people. Take the Las Virgenes Road exit from U.S. 101 (Ventura Freeway) in Calabasas and drive south 3 miles, turning right (west) on Mulholland Highway. The parking entrance is located near the intersection of Troutdale Drive and Mulholland Highway, about 5.1 miles west of Las Virgenes Road.

Solstice Canyon Trail is only 2.1 miles long, but it traverses a relatively level canyon floor that was the site of several fascinating structures, including the **Keller House,** built about 1865 and thought to be the oldest stone building in Malibu. In 1952, the Roberts family built their home here. Only remnants remain of the landmark house's foundation, a fishpond, and the concrete bomb shelter, a sign of the times. The Roberts also leased part of their property as a testing site for satellite equipment, including *Pioneer 12*. The trail begins at the parking area located off Corral Canyon Road, which intersects with Highway 1, about 6 miles west of Malibu.

POINT MUGU STATE PARK

The Chumash Indians called this area Muwu, or "beach." Today, the area is a popular ocean beach, but the vast majority of the park lies inland as part of the Santa Monica Mountains. The state park extends about 7 miles inland from the beach and includes the 6,000-acre **Boney Mountain State Wilderness Area**. Within the park's total 15,000 acres, its highest point rises 3,010 feet above sea level.

Hiking Boney Mountain State Wilderness Area

Most of the visitation is focused along the 5 miles of beach and in Big Sycamore Canyon that runs northwest through the length of the park. From the campground near the coast there is a wide trail that leads east across the park. It ends near the Satwiwa Native American Indian Cultural Center, a visitor center that is part of the Santa Monica Mountains National Recreation Area and is operated by the National Park Service. Big Sycamore Canyon is home to the largest groves of sycamores (*Platanus racemosa*) protected within California State Parks. Both sycamores and coast live oaks (*Quercus agrifolia*) dominate the lower canyons, while chaparral covers the sides of the upper mountains. Blue elderberry, (*Sambucus cerulea*), wild rose (*Rosa* sp.), California bay (*Umbelluria californica*), and the ubiquitous poison oak

(*Toxicodendron diversilobum*) are very common. A side trail—the **La Jolla Valley Loop**—travels through a native tall-grass prairie, something very rare anymore in California.

With such a diversity of habits, from grasslands and oak woodlands to chaparral and the bedrock outcroppings of the Boney Mountains, wildlife within the park is equally diverse. Southern mule deer (*Odocoileus hemionus*), gray foxes (*Urocyon cinereoargenteus*), striped skunks (*Mephitis mephitis*) and spotted skunks (*Spilogale gracilis*), badgers (*Taxidea taxus*), bobcats (*Felis rufus*), and mountain lions (*Felis concolor*) live here, a few miles from several million people. Along the coast, California sea lions (*Zalophus californicus*) and harbor seals (*Phoca vitulina*) can often be seen playing along the surf line, while gray whales (*Eschrichtius robustus*) and large schools of dolphins often pass near to shore during their migrations. The monarch butterfly (*Danaus plexippus*) is a common and welcomed winter visitor.

> **Activities:** Camping, fishing, swimming, mountain biking, hiking, surfing, horseback riding, picnicking, beachcombing
>
> **Facilities:** Campground, picnic facilities
>
> **Dates:** Open daily.
>
> **Fees:** There are camping and day-use fees.
>
> **Closest town:** Oxnard
>
> **Info:** Point Mugu State Park, 9000 W. Pacific Coast Highway, Malibu, CA 90265, 310.457.8143 or www.parks.ca.gov

TRAILS

Point Mugu State Park has 70 miles of trails, many of which meander across relatively flat terrain, but others climb to peaks that rise to 1,600 feet above sea level. It is best to stop at the park's campground or one of the visitor centers and pick up a trail map. Without a map, becoming confused and lost on the many different trails

Poison oak

and loops can be relatively easy for those unfamiliar with the area.

Mountain bikes are restricted to the wider, designated fire roads and are not allowed on narrow, single-track trails or within the Boney Mountain State Wilderness Area. Be aware that summer temperatures can climb into the 90s in these mountains and within a few minutes fog can sweep in and drop temperature to the 60s. Carry plenty of water and dress in layers in anticipation of weather changes.

The 6.5-mile round-trip **Big Sycamore Canyon Trail** begins at the park's Big Sycamore Canyon Campground off Highway 1 and passes through some of California's best remaining examples of sycamores. The trail is relatively level, ending at Wood Canyon Junction, and then goes on to Deer Camp Junction. You can turn back or return via the **Overlook Trail**, which has a 700-foot elevation gain. If returning via Overlook, the round-trip is approximately 10 miles.

Big Sycamore Canyon

La Jolla Valley Loop Trail begins at the Ray Miller trailhead about 2 miles north of the Point Mugu State Park headquarters' entrance along Highway 1. While the trail passes near the top of 1,266-foot **Mugu Peak**, most of the approximately 5-mile loop is not uncomfortably steep. Part of it passes through a native tall-grass prairie. It's not too unusual to see a fox, bobcat, and coyote out hunting, even during the daytime here. The trail also leads to the La Jolla Valley walk-in campground, which is 2 miles from the Highway 1 parking area.

Coastal whiptail

Mountain Lions

Sighting a mountain lion or cougar (*Felis concolor*) in the wild can be both exciting and frightening. Mountain lions range throughout most of California, but the secretive cats are seldom seen by humans. Whenever hiking in mountain lion country—which includes most of California's undeveloped coast—it's best to travel with others. Always keep smaller children nearby and don't allow them to run down the trail by themselves.

Hiker Safety Tips

If you encounter a mountain lion, never run. They are likely to assume that you are fleeing prey and give chase. You can neither outrun nor hide from a mountain lion.

- Stand tall and wave your arms or a jacket, trying to appear as large as possible. Throw sticks or stones, but try to bend down as little as possible while picking them up.

- If the lion does not move away first, back away slowly while facing the lion.

- If you have small children with you, pick them up, bending over as little as possible.

- In the unlikely event that you are attacked, face the cat and fight back. Mountain lions will attempt to bite the back of your neck and head.

- Report any lion sightings to authorities immediately. Call 911.

Los Angeles County

LEO CARRILLO STATE PARK

This park, like several of Southern California's beaches and parks, has taken the name of a film celebrity. Although most people today may not recognize the name Leo Carrillo (1881-1961), as an actor he had a very successful film, Broadway, and television career. Perhaps his best-known part was that of Pancho, the Cisco Kid's sidekick in the 1950s television series. Leo Carrillo, the great grandson of one of California's last governors during Mexico's rule, was instrumental in the acquisition of several key state parks, including Hearst Castle and the one carrying his name.

Leo Carrillo State Park's 2,513 acres include not only more than 1.5 miles of beach, but also a large area of inland acreage that rises into the mountains northeast of the Pacific Coast Highway. It also connects with more than 1,000 acres of Santa Monica Mountains National Recreation Area lands, providing access to additional opportunities for hiking. All of this contiguous, diverse, and undeveloped land provides excellent wildlife habitat. Among the California bay (*Umbellularia californica*), black walnut (*Juglans californica*), and sycamore (*Platanus racemosa*) trees, scrub jays (*Aphelocoma coerulescens*), great horned owls (*Bubo virginianus*), and acorn woodpeckers (*Melanerpes formicivorus*) either rest, feed, or nest. California quail (*Lophortyx californicus*) and warblers hide in the chamise (*Adenostoma fasciculatum*), mountain mahogany (*Cercocarpus* sp.), and manzanita (*Arctostaphylos* sp.) that form the low, dense chaparral. Coyotes (*Canis latrans*), bobcats (*Felis rufus*), and gray foxes (*Urocyon cinereoargenteus*) spend their days and

Leo Carrillo State Park

nights hunting small mammals, while Pacific rattlesnakes (*Crotalus viridis*), gopher snakes (*Pituophis melanoleucus catenifer*), and common king snakes (*Lampropeltis getulus californiae*) search for many of the same small mammals, birds' eggs, and other small food sources.

Along the beach is plenty of sand for beachcombing and swimming. **Arroyo Sequit**, a small, seasonal creek that runs through the middle of the park, forms a low, rocky, intertidal area where it empties into the ocean. It's a great place to explore during low tides. Sea slugs, tube worms, turban snails, mussels, and sea urchins live on and among the rocks.

While most of the animals in the tide pools are protected, ocean fishing beyond

Riding a wave

the tide pools is allowed and is a popular activity. Below lifeguard towers numbers 2 and 3 are favorite fishing spots. Anyone with the equipment and a little luck can catch kelp bass (*Paralabrax clathratus*), surf or shiner perch (*Cymatogaster aggregata*), and an occasional Pacific halibut (*Hippoglossus stenolepis*) fishing from the beach. A little more exciting are the thresher sharks, shovelnose guitar fish, and California corbina that anglers also pull from the surf.

Scuba divers also like the beach at Leo Carrillo. Easy access to nearby kelp beds, the clear water, and the bounty of underwater plant and animal life gives divers great opportunities for exploration. Just remember not to dive alone.

The park has three campgrounds, one of which is for groups only. The others will handle tents, with some sites accommodating trailers and RVs. There are no hookups. The campground on the ocean side of Highway 1 does not allow RVs because the access tunnel that goes beneath Highway 1 allows only vehicles under 8 feet in height.

Activities: Swimming, diving, hiking, camping, surfing, fishing, picnicking
Facilities: Campgrounds, visitor center
Dates: Open daily
Fees: There are camping and day-use fees.
Closest town: Santa Monica
Info: Leo Carrillo State Park, 35000 Pacific Coast Highway, Malibu, CA 90265, 310.457.8143 or www.parks.ca.gov

TRAILS

Found within the park, **Yellow Hill Fire Road** is a trail that follows an abandoned fire road. Naturally, this is a favorite destination for a multitude of mountain bike riders in Southern California. While the descent is steep, it is not too difficult for hikers. The trail heads into the park's backcountry hills, offering panoramic views of the Pacific Ocean. On clear days, Anacapa and Santa Cruz islands, two of the closest of the Channel Island group, are visible offshore. The trail starts near the park entrance and winds for about 3 miles one way.

Nicholas Flat Trail is steeper than the Yellow Hill Trail, rising much more quickly into the inland mountains for about 2 miles. Besides spring wildflowers and great views, there's a pond at **Nicholas Flat**. The round-trip trail is 3.5 miles.

California quail

MORE TO EXPLORE

Study a map of Los Angeles County, which includes all of the Santa Monica Bay shoreline, and it's evident that probably 80 percent of the thin strand of beach is held in the public domain, either by national, state, county, or city parks.

Beginning at the northern end of Los Angeles County, the long series of public beaches offers swimming (with lifeguard service during summer and busy non-summer weekends), surfing, fishing, and beachcombing. Some feature concessions that rent bikes and skates for use along their paved bike trails, and several have piers for fishing and sitting. Most offer off-street parking for a small fee, but many people prefer to park along Highway 1 and pay nothing. Busy summer days can put the free roadside parking at a premium, and crossing busy Highway 1 can be very dangerous for pedestrians.

Santa Monica Beach, operated by the City of Santa Monica, is where the much of the Los Angeles beach-going population escapes during the summer respites. Their cars squirt out of the Los Angeles Basin from the end of Interstate 10, then spread both north and south, their numbers diminishing with distance. Santa Monica sees perhaps a quarter of the 15 million people who visit this stretch of California's southern coast each year. Info: 310.458.8310 or www.smgov.net

Santa Monica Municipal Pier has a wide assortment of restaurants, snack bars, and boat rentals. The pier was built in 1909, making it the first concrete pier on the West Coast. There is also an amusement park, designed and built by famed carousel carver Charles Looff in 1915. Of course, Looff included a one-of-a-kind carousel in the project, hand-carving the wooden horses. The carousel is still in operation to this day.

The pier and surrounding beach attract thousands of people on warm sunny days, so arriving early can make finding parking easier. The area was seriously considered as a major new harbor in 1889 when the U.S. Senate Committee of Commerce planned to develop a port either here or at San Pedro. San Pedro got the nod, and in 1899 construction began on the San Pedro Breakwater, which marked the beginning of the **Los Angeles/Long Beach Harbor Complex**. The Santa Monica pier is located at the foot of Colorado Avenue. Info: 310.458.8901 or www.santamonicapier.org

This stretch of blue water along **Malibu's** sandy beaches and rugged cliffs is where the rich and famous love to build their homes. Malibu is well known for its enclave of Hollywood actors, producers, and directors, many of whom own beach-front homes suspended on spindly piers and jutting out toward the bay. Many more prefer the bluffs and rugged mountains on the east side of the Pacific Coast Highway, which runs around the edge of the bay.

Along parts of the coast, the line of businesses and homes many times crowds against one another, forming an impenetrable wall between highway and beach.

Santa Monica Beach during the summer season

But there are plenty of public access points to the miles of beaches and tide pools. The beaches here are also popular Hollywood filming locations. It's not unusual to see a film production company's gaggle of trucks, trailers, and other support vehicles parked along the highway. Info: 310.456.2489 or www.malibucity.org

Zuma County Beach, located at the north end of Los Angeles County, is a very popular summer swimming, surfing, and sunbathing destination. An "arroyo" or ravine tumbles down through Trancas Canyon from the Santa Monica Mountains to the beach here. Canyons like Trancas bring much of the sediment to the ocean's edge, where littoral or near-shore currents transport and deposit it, helping to replenish sand on the beaches during summer. During winter, increased wave action tends to wash much of the sand away, reducing the width of the beaches. While the difference between summer and winter beach width often isn't dramatic, that's not always the case. A storm in the late 1950s removed 50 feet of Zuma Beach in a single 24-hour period. Info: 310.457.9701 or http://beaches.lacounty.gov

There are two marine terraces near **Point Dume State Beach**, with Point Dume itself rises 215 feet above the ocean. Some geologists believe that this erosion-resistant volcanic rock was once an island that was connected to the mainland by a tombolo. A tombolo formation is created when waves are diffracted around a rock or small island, which reduces their energy and causes them to drop out the sediments they are carrying. As the sediments continue piling up behind the island they ultimately create a link to other islands, or as here, with the mainland. This state beach is operated by Los Angeles County. Info: 310.457.8143, http://beaches.lacounty.gov or www.parks.ca.gov

Venice Beach is probably best known for its oceanfront walkway where on any given summer day, hundreds of uninhibited youth show their physical wares, most often just barely tucked inside scanty bathing suits, as they skate, bike, jog, lift weights, and walk along its length. There are numerous tourist shops, specialty

Venice Beach in the off-season

boutiques, and artists' booths here, making the sidewalk spectacle even more vibrant. **Muscle Beach** is a part of Venice Beach you don't want to miss, that is, if you like to see bodybuilders showing off their pects or other buffed body parts. Info: 310.578.0478 or http://beaches.lacounty.gov

MALIBU LAGOON STATE BEACH

This is a relatively small park covering only 22 acres, but the majority of the land is beach property. The most notable exception is where **Malibu Creek** passes into the park and opens into a large lagoon before finally emptying into the Pacific Ocean. The park's **Surfrider Beach** is very popular with surfers and sunbathers.

Frederick Rindge, the recipient of a $2 million inheritance, originally acquired the park's land in 1892. He purchased the 13,000-acre Rancho Malibu from Henry Keller and moved west from his Cambridge, Massachusetts home. He planned to create a farm or ranch in what he described as the "American Riviera." Initially, Rindge constructed a home in Malibu Canyon, but fire destroyed it in 1903. The following year, the ever-expanding Southern Pacific Railroad was attempting to extend its transportation empire by building track along the coast from Santa Barbara through the still roadless Malibu coast. To keep Southern Pacific out, Rindge built his own Hueneme, Malibu, and Port Los Angeles Railroad, designed to bring in supplies and to ship out his cowhides and grain.

When Frederick Rindge died in 1905, his wife Rhoda May continued working the ranch. She also continued her husband's opposition to allowing other avenues of public transportation to intrude on their private domain. Eventually, the county and state acquired a right-of-way and finally constructed a coastal highway in 1928.

In 1915, Rhoda Agatha Rindge—the daughter of Frederick and Rhoda May—married the ranch's superintendent Merritt Adamson. Besides being an attorney, Adamson was also an expert in farming; his family owned a sheep farm in Arizona. He began Adohr Stock Farms, one of the world's largest producing dairies. Merritt Adamson died in 1949 (*Adohr* is Rhoda spelled backwards).

Malibu Creek

Adamson House

What sets Malibu Lagoon State Beach apart from the many other similar Southern California beaches is the **Adamson House**. Twenty years before his death, Merritt Adamson and his wife hired well-known architect Stiles Clements to design a new house. It had a spectacular location on a low hill above the beach, and Clements designed the two-story home to include large amounts of a special tile being manufactured by Malibu Potteries, once located a half-mile down the coast.

Malibu tile is considered historically significant because of the secret formulas that were incorporated into the company's hundreds of design motifs that included Spanish, Mayan, Persian, neo-classical, and modern. The Malibu Tile plant went out of business in 1932, but not before seeing its tiles incorporated into numerous private residences in Los Angeles, Los Angeles City Hall, the Hollywood Roosevelt Hotel, and the Mayan Theatre, among many others.

Good soil from nearby mountain canyons was trucked in and used to cover the sand surrounding the house. Gardeners then planted mature olive trees, roses, Chinese magnolias, and many other shrubs, trees, and flowers around the grounds in the new soil, which was 5- to 10-feet deep.

The home's original seven-car garage has been transformed into the **Malibu Lagoon Museum** that features exhibits on the original Native Americans who inhabited this part of California. The museum is also a good place to see rare artifacts, photographs, and documents relating to the early history of Malibu, including the Malibu Railroad, the Malibu movie colony, and the Malibu Dam.

Malibu tile fills much of the Adamson House, including the kitchen.

Activities: Swimming, surfing, picnicking, fishing, beachcombing, house tours. Pets are not allowed in the park or on the tours.

Facilities: Museum, gift shop, picnic area. There is no parking on the Adamson House grounds. Parking is available along Highway 1 or in the adjacent county pay lot.

Dates: Beach open daily. The Adamson House grounds are open daily; tours of inside the house occur Wednesday through Saturday, 11 A.M. to 3 P.M., with the last tour beginning at 2 P.M.

Fees: There are no fees for using the beach unless you park in one of the county pay lots. There is a tour fee for the Adamson House.

Closest town: Malibu

Info: Malibu Lagoon State Beach, 23200 Pacific Coast Highway, Malibu, CA 90265, 310.457.8143 or www.parks.ca.gov. For Adamson House tour info, 310.456.8432

MALIBU CREEK STATE PARK

This park is for walkers, mountain bicyclists, and horseback riders. The trails are relatively level and surprises await you around every corner. There is a small campground not far from the entrance road parking lot, but nearly everything else, from the visitor center and creek to **Century Lake** and the old M*A*S*H* filming site takes walking or riding to reach.

Local businessmen acquired much of the original property during the early 1900s and formed the Crags Country Club. After the club folded in 1936, 20th Century Fox entered the picture, filming *How Green Was My Valley* in 1941. The company purchased the property in 1946 and made hundreds of movies in the surrounding hills, including such films as *The Defiant Ones, Butch Cassidy and the Sundance Kid, Planet of the Apes*, and the 1967 *Doctor Dolittle*. Both the movie and TV series M*A*S*H* were also filmed at Malibu Creek State Park.

The area became a park in 1976 following the state's purchase of the studio's property, along with

Malibu Creek State Park

the adjacent Bob Hope and Ronald Reagan ranches. Today, there are 8,215 acres to explore. Within the park are three natural preserves, which protect a rare and beautiful stand of valley oaks (*Quercus lobata*), a nesting area for golden eagles (*Aquila chrysaetos*), and volcanic formations, along with rare plants. Riparian plant communities abound within the park as sycamore (*Platanus racemosa*), cottonwood, willow (*Salix* sp.), and bay trees (*Umbellularia californica*) grow in profusion along Malibu Creek and some of the smaller feeder streams. California sagebrush, black sage (*Salvia mellifera*), purple sage (*Salvia leucophylla*), and wild buckwheat (*Eriogonum* sp.) cover many of the drier hillsides.

With such a variety of plant communities comes an equally wide range of wildlife. Red-tailed hawks (*Buteo jamaicensis*) and golden eagles are relatively common in the skies. The bizarre-looking regal horned lizard is occasionally seen, while more common lizards are usually sunning themselves on the rocks. Buffle-heads and mallards are frequent visitors along the creek, with rattlesnakes, gopher snakes, king snakes, bobcats, coyotes, and mule deer adding to the mix.

Activities: Hiking, camping, mountain biking, horseback riding, fishing, rock climbing, picnicking
Facilities: Campground, picnic area, visitor center, small gift shop
Dates: Open daily
Fees: There are camping and day-use fees.
Closest town: Calabasas
Info: Malibu Creek State Park, 1925 Las Virgenes Road, Calabasas, CA 91302, 818.880.0350, www.parks.ca.gov or www.malibucreekstatepark.org

TRAILS

The interesting **Malibu Creek State Park Visitor Center** is located in an old country club home about a mile from the parking lot. To reach the center, follow the trail down an unpaved service road. When you reach the small

Co-author and her son crossing Malibu Creek

bridge, you'll see the center on the other side. The walk is much shorter and faster if Malibu Creek is low enough to be crossed, but if you do, beware that the rocks in the creek are very slippery.

Rock Pool, part of Malibu Creek

The **Rock Pool** is a few hundred yards from the visitor center. Cross back over the bridge and turn left down a short trail—the **Malibu Creek Trail**—that passes through a small oak grove to the wide pool in Malibu Creek. During late summer there may not be much of the pool remaining; spring and winter are the best times to visit. There are some beautiful rock formations here. Although the pool looks inviting, especially on a hot summer day, diving or jumping into the water is prohibited. The round-trip is 3.5 miles from the parking lot.

The 20-acre **Century Lake**, named by 20th Century Fox studio heads, is a quick half-mile trek north of the Rock Pool. The lake, formed behind a dam built in 1903, is a popular fishing spot, although, after a century of siltation, it's mostly a tule- and willow-filled marsh now.

The **M*A*S*H* Film Site** is one of the more popular hiking and biking destinations. Found about 0.75-mile from Century Lake, the area was used for both the 1970 movie and the TV series, which ran from 1972 to 1983. There are a few old military vehicles used in the television series remaining on the site.

Little remains of the *M*A*S*H* film site.

291

Chaparral Fire Ecology

Southern California's chaparral has evolved over millions of years, making it a hardy survivor of this dry land's periodic wildfires. Lightning strikes most often start the devastating fires, which burn through the low, resinous chaparral plants, often sending flames more than 100 feet into the air and creating temperatures of 2,000 degrees Fahrenheit.

When the fire has cooled, all that remains is a layer of ash and the charred skeletal remains of the bushy chaparral plants. Most animals escape unharmed, either by running or flying away, or by remaining deep in their burrows. But within weeks, even during summer when rain is still months away, green sprouts begin showing. The dead plants "stump sprout," sending new shoots out from near their bases. The first late autumn rain provides life-giving moisture so that grasses, wildflowers, and other broad-leafed plants quickly begin to sprout, covering hillsides with their differing hues of green. And the wildlife returns, often in greater numbers, now that a tender, nutritious new food source is growing so profusely.

Today, many state and national parklands either allow wildfires to burn naturally, or they start what are termed "prescription burns." When temperature, wind, humidity, and fuel moisture content are all at acceptable levels, these fires are purposely started in control areas and closely monitored. Allowing fires to burn and starting controlled fires reduce dangerously high fuel levels, so that when wildfires do occur, they tend to burn cooler, causing less damage to plants and animals, while giving firefighters a better chance to protect human life and nearby developed properties.

Remnants of a fire in La Jolla Canyon

TOPANGA STATE PARK

In the Santa Monica Mountains, surprises await anyone willing to spend time looking. Topanga State Park is one of those surprises. The park's 11,000 acres lie entirely within the Los Angeles city limits and it is therefore considered the largest parcel of wild land located in a major city. Within the park's variety of habitats—ranging from oak woodlands to chaparral-covered mountains—its streams and ponds serve as water sources for the abundance of wildlife that lives here.

The steep mountains and weather-worn rock formations found in the park have evolved over the past 18 million years. The area began as mostly sub-

Oak woodland

merged sedimentary rocks with areas of intrusive volcanic basalt. About 3 million years ago, the Santa Monica Mountains began to rise, and as they did, streams carved narrow canyons through the soft sandstone and shale. More earthquakes and ongoing upward thrusting continued the geologic molding process, and with two fault lines within the park, the shaping continues even today.

The first European to see these mountains was Juan Rodriquez Cabrillo who sailed along the California coast in 1542. But humans had occupied this area for at least 7,000 years before he passed by. The Gabrieleno Indians lived in the mountains here and also in the San Fernando Valley to the east. The Chumash lived along the coast, a few miles away. It appears that for the most part they lived peacefully along an indistinguishable boundary. Topanga, or in early documents, "Topango," is a Gabrieleno word that is believed to mean something similar to "the place where the mountains meet the sea." It is the most westerly known landmark possessing a Gabrieleno name. Once the Spanish arrived in the late 18th century, the lives of the Indians changed quickly. Most either died of European diseases or were absorbed into the mission system as workers. Afterward, much of the land was given as Mexican land grants. Topanga State Park is part of what was once *Rancho San Vicente y Santa Monica*.

Trippet Ranch is named after federal court judge Oscar Trippet, who owned a 60-acre ranch during Woodrow Wilson's presidency. It was 1917 and the Great War was still going on. But the rich and powerful in Hollywood and Southern California preferred to play and relax—many did not carry the burdens that other American citizens were facing. Trippet purchased the land from a beekeeper, and

Southern Coast

Trippet's family used it as a quick get-away from Los Angeles. When Trippet died in 1923, his son, Oscar Jr., had a skeet lodge, superintendent's quarters, and stables built on the property. He also had a pond added, which was stocked with fish. The Trippets owned the land until 1963. The next year, a park bond passed and the property was purchased. It wasn't until 1974 that Topanga State Park was opened.

Hikers and equestrians sharing the trail through heavy chaparral

When spring wildflowers begin to bloom, the grasslands, intermittent streams, and scattered oaks around the ranch house support some the best viewing opportunities. Blue-eyed grass (*Sisyrinchium bellum*), goldenstars (*Bloomeria humilis*), wild onion (*Allium* sp.), and mariposa lilies (*Calochortus* sp.) paint patches of bright colors in the grasses. The park maintains a wildflower hotline (818.768.3533) that provides weekly updates about wildflower blooms throughout much of Southern California's mountains and deserts. In the cooler canyons where streams tend to run throughout the year, or at least much longer than they do on the open hillsides, coast live oak, willows, and western sycamores provide a canopy over maidenhair ferns and miner's lettuce.

Wildlife is abundant throughout the park with each species finding its own special niche and a few, such as bobcats, mule deer, and mountain lions, able to range over dozens of miles of mountains and valleys. Wrentits (*Chamaea fasciata*), scrub jays (*Aphelocoma coerulescens*), and California thrashers (*Toxostoma redivivum*) create their own cacophony in the trees and bushes. Red-tailed hawks and golden eagles fly overhead searching for a good meal of ground squirrel (*Spermophilus beecheyi*) or cottontail rabbit.

Musch Trail Camp is located about 1 mile from Trippet Ranch. It's available for hikers, mountain bikers, and equestrians.

Activities: Hiking, camping, picnicking, mountain biking, horseback riding
Facilities: Trail campground, picnic sites

Dates: Open daily
Fees: There are camping and day-use fees.
Closest town: Santa Monica
Info: Topanga State Park, 20825 Entrada Road, Topanga, CA 90290, 310.455.2465 or www.parks.ca.gov

TRAILS

Topanga State Park has 36 miles of trails. While all of the trails are open to hikers, only the fire roads are open for mountain bikes. Also, no pets are allowed on fire roads or trails.

Eagle Spring Loop Trail can be reached from Trippet Ranch by first hiking about 2 miles to **Eagle Junction**. From Eagle Junction, there is a 2.6-mile loop that passes by **Eagle Rock**, a 1,957-foot promontory made up of ancient volcanic rock. There are spectacular views from the boulder outcroppings. (**NOTE**: Some trail guides and maps list this as Eagle *Rock* Loop Trail.)

The trail to **Santa Ynez Canyon** and **Santa Ynez Falls** begins from Trippet Ranch. The 6-mile round-trip hike descends into the canyon where you will see wonderful weather-formed sandstone along the way; eroded pockets collect enough moisture that small plants grow, creating cliff gardens. At a fork in the trail near the bottom of the canyon, head left (north) to a beautiful waterfall that cascades over the rock formations. Continue south at the trail fork to reach the park boundary at Vereda Montura (a paved road). This road leads into the community of Palisades Highlands.

WILL ROGERS STATE HISTORIC PARK

Will Rogers, best known for his "cracker barrel" humor, made his Hollywood debut in 1919. He saw only moderate success in silent films under Samuel Goldwyn until the "talkies" made him a star. Most often seen spinning his rope, Rogers added a trademark drawl to make his point, one that was often aimed directly at lethargic, uncaring, and self-important politicians.

In 1935—when he was at the top of his show business career—Rogers died tragically in an Alaska plane crash along with his good friend, and famed aviator Wiley Post. Rogers had developed not only fame as a film star, but also as a radio commentator and newspaper

Inside the expansive ranch house

columnist. Some of his best known comments said a lot about the man: "I never met a man I didn't like," and "You must judge a man's greatness by how much he will be missed."

Several years before his death, Rogers moved his wife Betty and their three children to a 183-acre ranch in Pacific Palisades. His wife continued living in the 31-room ranch house until her death in 1944. Following her death, the ranch became a state park. Today, the park boasts a polo field where Hollywood stars such as Sylvester Stallone occasionally play on weekends and TV shows and movies use the field for on-location shots. There are also several miles of trails that loop through the hills behind the ranch house or connect with longer trails into the Santa Monica Mountains National Recreation Area.

In 2006, state parks and the Will Rogers Ranch Foundation completed a major restoration of the ranch, totaling $5 million. Today, docents offer tours of the ranch house.

Activities: Hiking, historic house tours, picnicking, horseback riding lessons via an onsite concessionaire
Facilities: Visitor center, polo field, equestrian stables, picnic area
Dates: Open daily; visitor center opened Thursday through Sunday
Fees: There is a day-use fee.
Closest town: Pacific Palisades
Info: Will Rogers State Historic Park, 1501 Will Rogers State Park Road, Pacific Palisades, CA 90272, 310.454.8212 or www.parks.ca.gov; Will Rogers Ranch Foundation, 866.988.9773 or www.willrogersranchfoundation.org

Will Rogers historic stables

Hollywood on Location

During the early 20th century, Southern California, which typically experiences nine months or more of dry weather, quickly became the fledgling film industry's favorite place to make movies. Legendary filmmakers Cecil B. Demille, Samuel Goldwyn, and Jesse Lasky Sr. made Hollywood's first film, *The Squaw Man*, in 1912-14. They shot their movie in a makeshift studio built inside a barn at the corner of Selma Avenue and Vine Street. The historic building was subsequently moved to the 2100 block of Highland Avenue and now serves as the Hollywood Studio Museum.

M*A*S*H* sign, Malibu Creek State Park

While Universal Studios is a great place to see how movies are made, many movies, or at least parts of them, are shot on location rather than inside soundstages. It's not at all unusual to run across movie sets while driving nearly anywhere in the greater Los Angeles area. Beaches, such as Leo Carrillo, Malibu, and Dan Blocker, are always popular shooting locations. Movies ranging from *Planet of the Apes* to *M*A*S*H* have been filmed in Malibu Creek State Park, which sometimes hosts dozens of film companies each year.

One thing that first-time observers quickly discover about filming a movie is that there is much more downtime, as lights, reflectors, and cameras are moved and reset, than there is action. But it's still fun to see the real thing.

LOS ANGELES

The City of the Angels began as a small and temporary camp on the edge of the Los Angeles River in 1769. Traveling with Spanish explorer Gaspar de Portolá, Father Crespi named the campsite *Nuestra Señora la Reina de los Angeles de la Porciúncula*, "Our Lady the Queen of the Angels of the Porciúncula." *Porciúncula* referred to a parcel of land near a church in Assisi, Italy where St. Francis received a revelation in 1206.

During their exploration, Portolá's party passed the La Brea tar pits and camped near today's La Cienega Boulevard, between Gregory Way and Olympic Boulevard in Beverly Hills. Over the next several months, they visited numerous other sites in and around present-day Los Angeles, including the Santa Monica Mountains and the San Fernando Valley. The Spanish, and later the successor Mexican government, expanded their settlements in the area, dividing the land into great ranchos and giving them as land grants to various deserving individuals. *Rancho Los Alamitos* later became the city of Long Beach, *Rancho Santa Gertrudes* is now Downey, *Rancho El Encino* is Encino, *Rancho El Escopión* is Calabasas, and *Rancho Rincón de San Pasqual* now includes Pasadena and Altadena. The only remnants of the original ranchos are a few adobe buildings, for the most part maintained in state and local parks.

Info: Los Angeles Visitor Information Center, 333 S. Hope Street, #1800, Los Angeles, CA 90071, 213.624.7300 or www.discoverlosangeles.com

El Pueblo De Los Angeles market

EL PUEBLO DE LOS ANGELES STATE HISTORICAL MONUMENT

The color, sounds, and smells are what make this historic center of Los Angeles a special place to spend an afternoon. During festivals, colorfully dressed dancers whirl to the sound of Mexican music, and excellent, flavorful food is always in abundance. The hustle and bustle of shoppers and shopkeepers as they deal for Mexican crafts and clothes adds to the wonderful feeling of being in Old Mexican California.

The Spanish officially founded *El Pueblo de Nuestra Señora la Reina de los Angeles*, the pueblo or town's full name, on September 4, 1781, making it the third of their Alta or upper California settlements. The current location of the historic pueblo is actually the last of three sites the Spanish attempted to build on. The first two were washed away when nearby dry streambeds swelled suddenly with seasonal rains.

Around the historic plaza that is here today, the **Church of Nuestra Señora la Reina de los Angeles**, which was completed and dedicated in 1822, remains the oldest building. It is located in the plaza at 535 North Main Street. Just south of the church is Los Angeles's first cemetery. The oldest house in Los Angeles is also here in the park. It was originally completed in about 1818 with additions in later years, and then removal of some portions, probably before 1920. Commodore Robert Stockton made his headquarters in this adobe for several days in 1847, following the U.S. takeover of California from Mexico.

Olivera Street is the central focus of the park, and that's what the locals call this area. Many shops and restaurants have been built in and around the old adobes. There's also a small museum with exhibits that include the story of water in the Los Angeles area, an often hotly contested issue historically and even today. The park, which is managed by the City of Los Angeles, is on the National Register of Historic Places, and 16 of its 27 historic buildings are listed separately.

Activities: Shopping, dining, cultural events, self-guided walking tours
Facilities: Shops, booths, restaurants, museum, historic buildings
Dates: Most facilities are open daily
Fees: None
Info: El Pueblo de Los Angeles Historical Monument, 125 Paseo de la Plaza, Suite 400, Los Angeles, CA 90012, 213.485.6855 or www.elpueblo.lacity.org

El Pueblo's historic area includes small museums and numerous outdoor vendors.

RANCHO LA BREA TAR PITS AND MUSEUM

For a look at the plant and animals that inhabited this portion of California from 40,000 to about 10,000 years ago, the tar pits, located in what is now downtown Los Angeles, provide the perfect window. Long-extinct dire wolves and the more famous saber-toothed cats are the most common animal bones found in the ancient tar. Less common, yet equally extinct, are native horses, camels, mammoths, and the long-horned bison.

As it has for thousands of years, crude oil oozes to the surface in this part of Southern California, and as the lighter oil evaporates, the remaining sticky asphalt accumulates in pools. Smaller mammals and birds—rabbits, mice, ducks,

The entrance to Rancho La Brea Tar Pits; George C. Page Museum in background

and hawks—still step or fly into the tar and become stuck. But prior to the development of the surrounding city, local carnivores descended on the free meals. Occasionally, bigger animals also became stuck and ultimately died, so many that more than 1 million individual specimens, representing 650 different species have been recovered from the tar pits. Only one human skeleton has ever been found in the pits—a 9,000-year-old Native American woman.

The tar served many useful purposes for the area's primitive peoples. The ancient Chumash used it to waterproof their canoes and to seal baskets. The early Spanish smeared tar on the roofs of their houses to keep out the seasonal rains.

Located in a park that is open and free to the public, the tar pits are fenced for safety reasons. There are 23 acres of observation pits, with replicas of some of the mammals that once roamed this area. The world-renowned **George C. Page Museum** is located within the park's boundaries and displays hundreds of examples of the animals recovered from their sticky burial grounds. The Page Museum is part of the Natural History Museum of Los Angeles County. The museum offers numerous exhibits, including hundreds of recovered dire wolf skulls mounted inside a dramatically lighted wall display. Visitors can also watch scientists working inside the "fishbowl" as they clean, identify, and label newly recovered animal bones. And depending on the museum staff's schedule, visitors may get the chance to see scientists and staff working in Pit 91; at 40 years and counting, it is the longest-running pit excavation project at Rancho La Brea.

Parking in this area can prove challenging, especially with all of the other museums and attractions found here. Look for the the museum's parking lot, at the corner of Curson Avenue and 6th Street directly behind the museum. The lot charges a flat daily rate. If that lot is full, there are other pay lots in the area. The museum strongly warns that street parking is confusing, so read the signs carefully and do not park along Wilshire Boulevard between the hours of 7 to 9 A.M. and 4 to 7 P.M. Monday through Friday, even if you parked and paid at a meter. Since these lanes are used for the morning and evening rush hour, your car will be ticketed and towed.

Activities: Self-guided tours, specialty packages of guided tours
Facilities: Exhibits, gift shop
Fees: There is an entry fee, free general admission on the first Tuesday of every month, except in July and August. California PreK-12 teachers are free, but must show a valid school I.D. or current pay stub.
Dates: Open daily, closed on Independence Day, Thanksgiving, Christmas, and New Year's Day.
Info: Rancho La Brea Tar Pits and the George C. Page Museum, 5801 Wilshire Blvd., Los Angeles, CA 90036, 213.763.3499 or www.tarpits.org

NATURAL HISTORY MUSEUM OF LOS ANGELES COUNTY

This museum is located in the University Park area of Los Angeles, inside Exposition Park. Also found here is the Los Angeles Memorial Coliseum, known to locals as "The Coliseum." The outdoor stadium is home to the University of Southern California Trojans football team and to two Olympic Games—in 1932 and 1984.

The Natural History Museum of Los Angeles County is filled with many truly rare treasures. It is also the third largest natural science and cultural history museum in the United States, holding more than 35 million artifacts and specimens dating back 4.5 billion years. The museum's newest exhibit is their Dinosaur Hall. With more than 300 fossils and 20 complete dinosaurs, the collection will take your breath away, that is, if you love dinosaurs! The star of **Dinosaur Hall** is the "T. rex Growth Series," where you can see the only trio of differently aged T. rex specimens in the world.

Natural History Museum

One of the rarest specimens to be seen here is a megamouth (*Megachasma pelagios*), an odd-looking and extremely rare shark with a huge bathtub-shaped mouth. Preserved in a large case, the shark is nearly 15 feet long and weighs 1,550 pounds. The megamouth was first discovered in 1976 off the coast of Hawaii, and the second specimen ever to be caught—off Catalina Island— is now displayed here.

It can take several hours to see everything in the museum's several floors of exhibits. On the main floor in several galleries there are life-zone dioramas filled with appropriate mammals, from grizzlies and wolves to bison and deer. For anyone interested in geology, or simply fascinated by rare and valuable gems, the mineral collection is superb. In addition to samples of hundreds of minerals and precious and semiprecious gems, there are exhibits that explain the geologic forces that create these wonders of nature. For example, it takes 50 kilobars of pressure— the equivalent of 150 adult elephants all standing on 1-square inch—to produce a diamond. And while all other gems are formed within 6 miles of the earth's surface, diamonds are formed from 90 to 200 miles down.

A rather interesting area is the hall of birds. It includes not only specimens in glass cases and in natural habitat exhibits, but also a few strange mechanical birds that move. There's a rain forest where visitors can view the plants and animals at ground level, and a walkway that leads to the canopy of the same jungle where completely different animals live.

There is much more to see here, from models of extinct dinosaurs to marine habitats featuring common, endangered, and extinct mollusks. There are also exhibits on historic Americana.

Activities: Self-guided and docent tours, lectures

Facilities: Museum, gift shop, restaurant

Dates: Open daily, closed on Independence Day, Thanksgiving, Christmas, and New Year's Day

Fees: There is an entry fee, free general admission on the first Tuesday of every month, except in July and August. California PreK-12 teachers are free, but must show a valid school I.D. or current pay stub.

Info: Natural History Museum of Los Angeles, 900 Exposition Boulevard, Los Angeles, CA 90007, 213.763.DINO or www.nhm.org

LOS ANGELES MARITIME MUSEUM

The Los Angeles Maritime Museum, located on Berth 84 at the Los Angeles-San Pedro Port, is truly a maritime historian's paradise with some of the best exhibits and artifact collections of any maritime museum in the country. Visitors have the opportunity not only to see large and beautiful models of historic ships, something found in nearly all maritime museums, but also to stand on the deck of the real thing.

The tug *Angels Gate* was originally built in Alabama for the military in 1944 as the ST 695 (small tug). It found its way to the Los Angeles Port of Embarkation where it continued its duties until after World War II. The military transferred title to the Los Angeles Harbor Department in 1947, where it continued to work until 1992 when it was given to the Los Angeles Maritime Museum. What is remarkable is that after more than a half-century of use, most of the original equipment is still onboard the old tug.

Inside the museum is the 22-foot-long, movie studio-built *SS Poseidon* constructed in great detail for the 1972 film *The Poseidon Adventure*. Another model,

the *HMAV Bounty*, is a replica of the ship used in the Clark Gable and Charles Laughton movie *Mutiny on the Bounty*, which was filmed here in San Pedro. And the museum features a very detailed 18-foot scaled model of the *HMS Titanic*.

Exhibits and artifacts cover the wide range of maritime history ranging from the early tall ships, the

SS Poseidon model used for the 1972 film

grand sailing vessels engaged in the 19th-century trade and whaling industries, to recreational sailing and the merchant marine. Naval history is also a theme, along with the commercial shipping industry, which is especially appropriate because the Los Angeles-San Pedro Port is the busiest in the world.

Activities: Tours, seminars, maritime festivals, visits by tall ships
Facilities: Museum, gift shop
Dates: Open Tuesdays through Sundays, closed Mondays
Fees: A donation is requested
Closest town: San Pedro
Info: Los Angeles Maritime Museum, Berth 84, 600 Sampson Way, San Pedro, CA 90731, 310.548.7618 or www.lamaritimemuseum.org

MORE TO EXPLORE

Point Fermin Lighthouse

The **Point Fermin Lighthouse**, located in San Pedro, is a stick-style Victorian house built in 1874 to light the entrance to the **Los Angeles Harbor**. Its first lighthouse keepers were sisters Mary and Ella Smith. The lighthouse was closed at the beginning of World War II, after 67 years of service. The building has been restored and is listed in the National Register of Historic Places. Info: 310.241.0684 or www.pfls.org

The **Cabrillo Marine Aquarium**, also in San Pedro, holds the largest collection of Southern California marine life in the world. It's located adjacent to **Cabrillo Beach Coastal Park** and near the **Port of Los Angeles**. The aquarium provides a look at the region's major marine habitats; kelp forests, rocky shores, mudflats, sandy beaches, and the open ocean, including a large collection of representative plant and animal species found in each. A portion of the facility is hands-on—great for kids! Info: 310.548.7562 or www.cabrillomarineaquarium.org

Rancho Palos Verdes' **Point Vincente Lighthouse** is one of the newer lighthouses, constructed in 1926. It was automated in 1971, but its 3rd order Fresnel lens is still present. The 67-foot-tall light tower is perched near the edge of a 130-foot cliff. It is still controlled by the U.S. Coast Guard, but open to the public usually on the second Saturday of each month, except March when it switches to the first Saturday. Adults are required to show a valid photo I.D. to tour the structure. Info: www.vicentelight.org

LONG BEACH

A vibrant waterfront city, Long Beach often disappears in the shadow of Los Angeles, which is unfortunate because it has so much to offer. Long Beach is the fifth largest city in California, and its harbor and neighboring Port of Los Angeles together form one of the busiest shipping centers in the world.

Unlike its larger cousin city to the north, Long Beach's business district lies at the water's edge where there is plenty of nearby shopping, sailing, bicycling, fishing, and beachcombing, along with a plethora of museums to explore. There's a great beach with a bike trail along the business district's entire 5.5-mile length, which then connects with another bike trail that heads still farther south.

The iconic **RMS Queen Mary** (562.435.3511 or www.queenmary.com), located in the harbor not far from downtown Long Beach, offers a unique dining, shopping, and lodging experience. Built in 1937, the retired cruise ship is now a floating museum of art deco luxury and undeniable class. A quick drive over the large Queensway Bridge, which crosses **Queensway Bay**, will take you to the ship.

Co-author's son on the bow of the *Queen Mary*

If you have the chance, spend at least one night at this floating hotel. A favorite overnight destination for people from all over the globe, the ship has a reputation for being haunted. And yes, some guests (namely, the McKowen family) have been known to run back and forth in the long cabin corridors at night with sheets over their heads, pretending to be ghosts. Regardless if you are a registered hotel guest or not, the *RMS Queen Mary* offers haunted and ghost tours for a fee—you're guaranteed a spooky and terrifying time!

Shoreline Village with the *Queen Mary* in the background

Across from the *RMS Queen Mary* is another tourist favorite—**Shoreline Village** (562.435.2688 or www.shorelinevillage.com). This intriguing cluster of waterfront businesses resembles a Cape Cod destination. Throughout this lovely quasi-island venue, you'll find different gift shops, food choices, and a wonderful restaurant for a romantic evening meal under the stars, with the the bay lit up in its showy elegance. Shoreline Village also offers fun activities, including a carousel, bike rentals, and sail- and power-boat rentals. You can even rent a yacht, which includes a captain and crew.

Long Beach has made getting around the downtown area easy. The bright red **Passport Shuttle** (562.591.2301 or www.lbtransit.com) is a complimentary bus service that has stops along most of Long Beach's main streets and in front of the city's main attractions. For a very small fee, the Passport will even take you up to **Belmont Shore** and **Naples Island**, seaside communities filled with shops and restaurants where Italian-style gondoliers cruise along the canals.

Info: Long Beach Area Convention and Visitors Bureau, 301 E. Ocean Blvd., Suite 1900, Long Beach, CA 90831, 562.436.3645 or www.visitlongbeach.com

LONG BEACH AQUARIUM OF THE PACIFIC

This beautifully designed aquarium sits near the water's edge in downtown Long Beach and features 11,000 ocean animals and fish representing nearly 500 different species. Besides the multitude of habitat and live exhibits, the aquarium also has an animal care center and hosts aquarium webcams.

The rocky intertidal exhibit contains strange-looking animals such as giant keyhole limpets (*Megathura crenulata*), warty sea cucumbers (*Parastichopus parvimensis*), and aggregating

Aquarium of the Pacific

anemones (*Anthopleura elegantissima*). For tropical fish fanatics, black and white Moorish idols (*Zanclus cornutus*), yellow and green scralled filefish (*Aluterus scriptus*), and the brilliant blue, yellow, and green king angelfish (*Holacanthus passer*) swim among nearly a dozen other species.

Other tropical fish galleries include species such as the harlequin tuskfish (*Choerodon fasciatus*), which is a yellow-and-turquoise-striped fish, the strange-looking humphead wrasse (*Chelinus undulatus*), and the zebra shark (*Stegastoma fasciatum*). You will also find blue-spotted stingrays (*Taeniura lymma*), porcupine fish (*Diodon hystirx*), and clown triggerfish (*Balistoides conspicillum*).

In addition to the many species of fish, there are harbor seals (*Phoca vitulina*) and California sea lions (*Zalophus californianus*). There's also an interactive penguin habitat, were South America Magellanic penguins (*Spheniscus magellanicus*) thrill visitors with their up-close antics.

Activities: Self-guided tours, special programs
Facilities: Café, kids' area, gift shop
Dates: Open daily, except Christmas day and during the annual Grand Prix of Long Beach, held for three days every April.

Fees: There is an entrance fee.

Nearest town: Long Beach

Info: Long Beach Aquarium of the Pacific, 100 Aquarium Way, Long Beach, CA 90802, 562.590.3100 or www.aquariumofpacific.org

SANTA CATALINA ISLAND

Once owned by chewing-gum magnate William Wrigley, Jr., today, nearly 90 percent of Santa Catalina Island is owned by the Santa Catalina Island Conservancy. The organization's mission is to restore the island to a more natural state, while providing for recreational opportunities.

Catalina is the most popular tourist island off the Southern California coast. Hundreds and sometimes thousands of people each day take boat trips across the open waters that separate Catalina from harbors at either San Pedro, Long Beach, Newport Beach, or Dana Point. The trip of about 20 miles takes from one to two hours, depending on the departure port and the type of passenger boat booked. Others visitors skip the boat trip and fly into the island's small airport.

What attracts most of these people are opportunities to tour the island, scuba dive, fish, hike, bicycle, or simply wander the quiet streets of **Avalon** and its quaint shops and restaurants. For anyone who has never seen bison—what most people refer to as buffalo—several hundred of the shaggy creatures now wander the island. The non-native beasts were originally brought here in 1924 for the film *The Vanishing American*, but the bison footage was cut from the film during editing. When the filming was completed, the original 14 buffalo were allowed to remain. Over the years, their numbers reached 600 animals augmented by births and by additional bulls introduced in order to strengthen the genetic line. Today, between 150 and 200 are allowed on the island in an actively managed program.

The harbor at Avalon

Catalina Casino

Easily the most famous and the most prominent building on the island is the **Catalina Casino**, which was built in 1929 by Wrigley for $2 million. The tall, white, circular structure is home to Avalon's movie theater, a local museum, an art gallery, and the world's largest circular ballroom, which in another era was famous for its Big Band dances. Famous theater and art deco artist John Gabriel designed and oversaw the painting of the marine-themed murals on the concrete walls. Other lavish and beautiful artwork is found throughout the building. And no, it is not an actual casino; in Italian, *casino* means "gathering place."

When the Spanish first discovered Santa Catalina Island the people living here called themselves "Pimungans" and their island home, "Pimu." For perhaps 7,000 years, they were traders who paddled their plank canoes across the channel to trade with other Indians. Spanish diseases and their mission system soon ended the Pimungans' ability to survive on the island, which by the 1800s also had been invaded by American, Russian, and Aleut sea otter hunters. The American era brought squatters, along with silver miners, and even the U.S. Army for a while.

When Wrigley came onto the scene in May 1929—just months before the stock-market crash, which triggered the Great Depression—Wrigley introduced controlled development, actually building and selling homes to residents at very reasonable prices. He also established various businesses to help the island's many inhabitants support themselves. Following his death in 1932, his son took over and continued his father's legacy, although with much less money available for investment. The interruption of World War II completely shut the island down to tourism, but after the war, tourism dramatically increased. By the 1970s, taxes forced Wrigley to deed the land to the newly formed Santa Catalina Island Conservancy in perpetuity, with 88 percent of the property planned as open space.

The geologic history of Catalina is as fascinating and dynamic as the cultural history. Near **Big Fisherman's Cove** on the leeward side of the isthmus, where the **University of Southern California's Marine Science Center** operates, diatomaceous earth cliffs are visible. They were formed mostly from the ancient "microfossils" of planktonic organisms. The cliffs also contain fossils of shellfish such as scallops.

On the opposite side of the island, **Ribbon Rock** provides an excellent example of metamorphosed sedimentary rocks. Its name comes from the alternating horizontal layers of light and dark rock. The light ribbons were originally sand that heat and pressure transformed into quartz feldspar, while the dark layers were mud and other fine sediments that were laid down. Closer to the center of the main part of the island, **Kennedy Rock**—an ancient volcanic plug—is evidence of the lava flows that periodically covered portions of this area millions of years ago.

One of the better things about the island is the obvious small number of cars. Visitors can't bring their own and so must depend on what's already on the island. There's usually plenty of transportation available, and for those not venturing too far, everything in the small community of Avalon is within easy walking distance.

Bicycling is a great way to enjoy the island. While you can pay a little extra to bring a bicycle over on one of the ferries, bikes can also be rented on the island. But you must become a member of the Catalina Island Conservancy if you wish to ride beyond Avalon's paved roadways to the many miles of dirt roads around the island.

Catalina Island Conservancy (310.510.1445 or www.catalinaconservancy. org) leads a wide variety of tours of Avalon and sight-seeing tours across the island. It also leads visitors in activities including biking, boating, diving, fishing, and hiking, the latter requiring a permit, which can be obtained for free via the conservancy's website. Several ferry companies depart the harbors at San Pedro, Long Beach, Newport Beach, and Dana Point. A list of companies can be found at www.visitcatalina.com.

Activities: Shopping, diving, fishing, boating, hiking, biking, camping
Facilities: Hotels, shops, restaurants, harbor
Fees: Cost of transportation to the island varies considerably
Info: Catalina Island Visitors Bureau, PO Box 217, Avalon, CA 90704, 310.510.1520 or www.catalinachamber.com

Orange and San Diego Counties

Orange and San Diego Counties

S an Diego holds an important place in California's history as the location where Spain's Father Serra chose to establish the first of 21 Catholic missions. Today, that early Spanish and Mexican influence is impossible to miss, from the names of towns, cities, and streets to the food, architecture, and historic sites. San Diego County serves as California's U.S. border with Mexico. Its San Ysidro Port of Entry is the busiest border crossing in the country with 25 million vehicles and 50 million people crossing each year, primarily for work.

Today, California's two most southern coastal counties are well known for their sandy beaches and comfortable year-round climate. This mild climate supports an incredible variety of plants, from annual wildflowers to cacti. In the near-desert climate, fresh water is at a premium, not only for the millions of people who make this region of California their home, but for the native plants that have adapted to the dry weather patterns. The rugged hillsides are covered with chaparral and seldom by large trees, unless they have been planted by residents willing to irrigate. San Diego's many parks are testaments to what a mild climate, adequate water, and 150 years or more of dedicated planting can bring to a land that sees only a few inches of rain each year.

Orange / San Diego

311

Orange County

While most of the county's namesake orange trees that were first planted here in the late 19th century have been swallowed by development, what remains are the cliffs, the beaches, and the warm climate that continue to attract people to this part of California. While surfers can be found riding the coastal waves at any time of the year, most of the beach use comes during summer, and usually later in the day after the rising sun has burned off any morning fog.

With miles of beautiful sandy beaches and thousands of people flocking here, there is lifeguard service in most areas during the beach-going season. While use of the beaches is free, parking seldom is. In most of the beach areas, there is a parking fee, which is sometimes collected at an entry gate, such as at Huntington and Bolsa Chica state beaches, or via parking meters in most of the city parking spaces.

Rip currents are prevalent along many of the beaches, so caution is always advised. Remember, anytime you find yourself being pulled out to sea by an outgoing current, don't fight it. Instead, swim parallel to the shore until you break free from the generally narrow current stream, and then swim back to shore.

Belted kingfisher

BOLSA CHICA ECOLOGICAL RESERVE

The reserve is one of an increasing number of successful wetland restoration efforts occurring along the length of California's 1,100 miles of coast. This area was originally a wetland that covered several thousand acres. For thousands of years, Native Americans found its waters and mud flats to be rich and dependable sources of food. In 1900, hunters hoping to improve their duck hunting prospects closed the tidal opening that fed the wetlands. Their attempts for improved waterfowl hunting failed, and the wetlands and surrounding upland areas were subsequently used for agriculture, cattle grazing, and World War II shore artillery defense. Following the discovery of oil here in 1920, it also became California's richest oil production area. Land developers have always eyed this valuable coastal land, but, fortunately, many of their efforts have been thwarted.

Today, most of the remaining 1,449 acres of surrounding wetlands are in public ownership controlled by the California Department of Fish and Wildlife. The Bolsa Chica Conservancy is very involved in the restoration and interpretation of the wetlands. Its members also continue raising funds to purchase the remaining undeveloped land that surrounds the current holdings. And since 2004, more than 500 acres of lowlands have been restored to their original condition, including removal and cleanup of the oil facilities.

A great place to start your visit is at the **Bolsa Chica Conservancy Interpretive Center**. The 1,400-square-foot facility is filled with examples of animals, birds, and marine life found throughout this region. There is a 1.5 mile trail that circles Inner Bolsa Bay and offers numerous opportunities to view many of the 320 bird species that have been seen here. Along the trail, evidence of the efforts to restore the wetland is prevalent. Numerous culverts, levees, and water control gates have been added, determining where and when both salt water and fresh water flows. From the parking lot there is a boardwalk that crosses the waterway, allowing views of some of the creatures that serve as food for the thousands of birds that live here year-round or migrate through annually. California horn snails (*Cerithidea californica*) are extremely abundant, as evidenced by their trails on the mud flats; the numerous shells of dead jackknife clams (*Tagelus californianus*) testify to their successful return to this restored wetland.

The wetland serves as a spawning area and nursery for many species of animals, including the translucent common jellyfish (*Aurelia aurita*), round stingrays (*Urolophus halleri*), anchovies (*Engraulis mordax*), and several species of sharks. During the summer nesting season, endangered California least terns (*Sterna antillarum*) and threatened snowy plovers (*Charadrius alexandrinus*) nest on South Island. During April and May, several species of terns begin their aerial courtship displays before nesting on North Island.

Orange / San Diego

The reserve's boardwalks offer easy wildlife viewing access.

There is a curious archaeological aspect to the wetlands or at least on the bluff where the spur trail leads. About 4,000 years ago, the local Indians made cogstones here. Cogstones are flat, round stones ranging in diameter from 3 to 5 inches and are about 1 inch thick. They have notches around their edges and many have holes in their centers, making them appear to be some type of ancient mechanical cog or gear. The only problem with this theory is that none of the cogstones found show any indication of wear and there is no apparent pattern of matching "teeth" among the cogs. Archaeologists assume they served as ceremonial or religious objects.

Activities: Bird-watching, photography, hiking
Facilities: Visitor center
Dates: Open daily
Fees: None
Closest town: Huntington Beach
Info: Bolsa Chica Conservancy, 3842 Warner Avenue, Huntington Beach, CA 92649, 714.846.1114 or www.bolsachica.org

HUNTINGTON BEACH

Huntington Beach is probably the best known of Southern California's

Huntington Beach Pier

towns, although most people probably think more about the activities that take place here on the beach rather than of the vibrant seaside town itself. Many people still remember the Jan and Dean hit song about Huntington Beach in the 1960s entitled *Surf City*. For Huntington Beach residents and business owners, the "Surf City USA" name is now legally theirs alone and being used by the community, much to the chagrin of Santa Cruz—that seaside town had begun using the name in 1927. Most of the old (and somewhat tacky) buildings and businesses in Huntington Beach have been replaced by new, more classy, and more expensive restaurants and shops. But, with 8.5 miles of white sandy beach along this section of coast, the focus is on the ocean and there's plenty of fun, sun, sand, and surf here for everyone.

The town is named after Henry E. Huntington who brought the Redline-Pacific Electric Railway to what was then a small seaside resort. With the railroad came more people, and the fledgling city was incorporated in 1909. After oil was discovered in the area in 1920, the population grew rapidly.

The Huntington Beach International Surfing Museum (714.960.3483 or www.surfingmuseum.org) exhibits photo displays showing the history of surfing in the area, including pictures of world championship surfing competitions

held here. There are also old surfboards, guitars, and other memorabilia. The museum is at 411 Olive Avenue, Huntington Beach. The **Surfing Walk of Fame** (714.698.5710 or www.surfing-walkoffame.com) located at 101 Main Street, honors the immortals of the surfing culture.

Huntington Beach International Surfing Museum

Most people come here for the surf and sand. A good way to begin any stay is to take a walk on the **Huntington Beach Pier** (714.969.3492 or www.surfcityusa.com). At 1,852 feet, it's the longest municipal concrete pier in California. The pier offers a different view of the surfers and body boarders working the breaking waves north and south of the structure. There are several shops and food vendors at the very end of the pier.

There are actually two beaches here, **Huntington City Beach** (714.969.3492 or www.surfcityusa.com) and **Huntington State Beach** (714.536.1454 or www.parks.ca.gov), although most would be hard pressed to tell the difference between the two. Both have the same sandy beach, volleyball nets, fire rings, and a connecting bike trail running along their lengths. There generally is plenty of parking between the day-use lots and street parking meters.

Info: Visit Huntington Beach, 301 Main Street, Ste. 212, Huntington Beach, CA 92648, 714.969.3492 or www.surfcityusa.com

NEWPORT BEACH

This picturesque town began as a shipping point built by Captain S.S. Dunnells and D.M. Dorman in 1872. Over the years, as new people entered the local scene, it was given different names: Newport Landing, McFadden's Landing, Port

Orange / San Diego

Orange, and the Old Landing. It finally became known as Newport Beach after the town's streets were laid out in 1892. This was the same year that the Santa Ana and Newport Railroad selected the original wharf, constructed here in 1888, as its terminus. The railroad and the port served as the primary movers of products and produce from Orange, San Bernardino, and Riverside counties.

Within Newport Beach is **Balboa Beach**, which is a long and narrow peninsula of sand that stretches for about 5 miles and protects Newport Harbor and the bay. On the bay side of Balboa Beach is the impressive **Balboa Pavilion**, a unique domed structure that the Newport Bay Investment Company built in 1905. It was designed to attract investors to the new town. The pavilion later became the southern terminus for the famous Red Cars of the Pacific Electric Railway.

The **Newport Pier** is a good place to begin a morning visit to the beach. Anglers line the pier and surfers ride the waves along the shoreline nearby. The Newport Dory Fishing Fleet, founded in 1891, returns to the north side of the pier at about 9:30 A.M. each day to sell its catch along the beach. There's also a restaurant at the end of the pier.

Boasting more than 9,000 boats, **Newport Harbor** is one of the largest small craft harbors in the world. Here, you will find watercraft from small sailboats to multimillion-dollar yachts.

Info: Newport Beach Visitor Center, 401 Newport Center Drive, Newport Beach, CA 92660, 855.569.7678 or www.visitnewportbeach.com

CRYSTAL COVE STATE PARK

Crystal Cove State Park has something for just about everyone, from hikers to scuba divers. Most of the park's 3,936 acres rise steeply from the beach and are located on the east side of Highway 1. Inland trails wind along deep and treacherous canyons and pass colorful spring wildflower shows. The trails also allow access to the park's hike-in campsites. **Moro Canyon** is one of the more popular destinations. During California's mission period, cattle from Mission San Juan Capistrano were grazed in the canyon. Today, it's popular with mountain bikers and hikers. It's a good idea to watch for either of the park's two rattlesnakes—the western diamondback (*Crotalus viridis*) or the red diamondback (*Crotalus* sp.), especially early in the morning or late evening. This is when they tend to stretch

Follow the signs!

The park's restored historic beach cottages are in high demand, so make reservations well in advance of your desired stay.

out on trails and roads, trying to soak up the warmth given off by the ground. Ticks, including the 1 percent that can cause Lyme disease, are also found in the park, so check yourself closely during and after hiking or bike riding.

Cross to the west side of Highway 1 and there are several beaches that welcome swimmers, sunbathers, divers, and surfers. The beaches, most of which are sand with occasional rocky tide pool areas, are at the base of a 50-to 80-foot-tall coastal bluff. These bluffs are the eroded remnants of an ancient marine terrace uplifted to its present level by tectonic plate movement and are primarily leftover sandstone and limestone scrapings from the top of the Pacific Plate as it dove into the subduction zone beneath the North American Plate.

The park, which is popular with scuba divers, extends into offshore waters out to a depth of 120 feet. Within this 1,240-acre ocean protection zone, the only fishing allowed is for game fish and lobsters when they're in season. The park's waters are also a favorite anchoring spot for fishing boat enthusiasts. Shore fishing is also very popular, with anglers tending to favor the beach near **Pelican Point**.

Those wishing to escape the crowds at the more popular swimming beaches to the north come to the broader, more southerly beach located at **Reef Point**. Near the north end of the park the beach tends to be much more narrow, often disappearing completely during high tides as the waves wash against the base of the coastal terrace cliff. While swimming in the 50-degree Fahrenheit waters during winter requires a wetsuit, in summer the water temperature generally reaches a much more comfortable 70 degrees Fahrenheit.

Within the park, you'll find the **Crystal Cover Historic District**. This part of the park features 46 vintage cottages, all restored to their original 1930 and 1940 character by state parks and the Crystal Cove Alliance (www.crystalcovebeachcottages.org). Some cottages serve as the park's visitor center and education venue, another is a restaurant, while 21 of the small homes can be rented through the state park reservation system.

Activities: Fishing, swimming, snorkeling, scuba diving, hiking, camping
Facilities: Primitive hike-in campsites, cottages
Dates: Open year round
Fees: There are camping, cottage, and day-use fees.
Closest town: Laguna Beach
Info: Crystal Cove State Park, 8471 North Coast Highway, Laguna Beach, CA 92651, 949.494.3539 or www.parks.ca.gov

MISSION SAN JUAN CAPISTRANO

The town of San Juan Capistrano, where this mission is prominently located, is best known for the swallows that return on St. Patrick's Day each spring. But less known is that the mission is a wonderful contrast between the old and the new; the old being the crumbling original mission, which is open for public viewing, and the new being the amazing reconstruction of the mission church that parishioners use today.

The mission was founded in 1775, but and Indian revolt at nearby Mission San Diego de Alcala caused the San Juan mission to be abandoned, but not before its new bells were hidden. The following year, Father Junipero Serra returned and reopened the seventh California mission on November 1, 1776—the Feast of All Saints Day. Thankfully, the hidden bells were still there, and a small adobe church was built in 1777. That small adobe church still stands and is the oldest continually used building in California, despite two centuries of earthquakes. It is best

Gardens and mission ruins

known as "Father Serra's church" because it is the only surviving original church where Father Serra celebrated Mass.

In 1796, work began on a new church that was finally completed in 1806. The church was massive, at 108-feet long and 40-feet wide, with a 120-foot-tall bell tower at its entrance. Unfortunately, its thick adobe walls were no match for the 1812 earthquake, commonly referred to as the "San Juan Capistrano earthquake"—geologists believe that the epicenter was very close to the mission. The magnitude-6 quake happened during Sunday Mass and the ceiling and walls of the mission collapsed, killing 40 parishioners. The ruins of the great stone church remain toady, providing a sense of how large the 19th-century adobe church had been and the devastation the earthquake caused. A few partial restoration efforts were attempted over the years, but most of the church remains in ruins. Among the crumbling walls and restored buildings are lovely gardens and fountains. The mission's museum collection contains Native American baskets, an original letter from President Lincoln returning control of the mission to the Catholic church, as well as building remains from the original church.

One of San Juan Capistrano's most famous attractions is the return of the swallows on St. Joseph's Day each year, marking the end of winter. It seems that swallows do indeed arrive each year, generally on the day they're scheduled—March 19. The swallows begin their annual migration to San Juan Capistrano from Santa Elena, a town of 15,000 located in Argentina's Entre Rios Province. San Juan Capistrano's Swallows Festival is celebrated each year in mid-March.

Nesting swallows at San Juan Capistrano

Activities: Tours
Facilities: Museum, gift shop
Fees: There is an entrance fee; visit the Mission's website to download a discount coupon
Dates: Open daily. Closed Thanksgiving, Christmas, Good Friday afternoon
Info: Mission San Juan Capistrano, 26801 Oretaga Highway, San Juan Capistrano, CA 92675, 949.234.1300 or www.missionsjc.com

MORE TO EXPLORE

Seal Beach is a long and sandy beach that stretches south beginning near the mouth of the San Gabriel River in the town of Seal Beach along Highway 1. A paved bike trail starts near the beach on the south side of the river and heads inland for several miles. There's a grassy area above much of the beach, along with restrooms, a jetty, and the Golden State's second longest wooden pier. Info: 562.431.2527 or www.sealbeachca.gov

Bolsa Chica State Beach is 6 miles of sand along the west side of Highway 1, starting at Warner Avenue in Huntington Beach. Its 50-site campground has electrical and water hook-ups for trailers and RVs only—no tent camping allowed. There is also a paved bike trail that runs from Bolsa Chica 8.5 miles south to Huntington State Beach. Info: 714.846.3460 or www.parks.ca.gov

Doheny State Beach was California's first official state beach. Edward Doheny donated the land to the state in 1931, but the beach wasn't named after the well-known oil tycoon until 1963. In addition to having a great beach and picnic area, it also has a large campground. The campground is so popular during the summer that reservations are almost always needed to get in. The beach park has a visitor center with exhibits and a touch tide pool. Info: 949.496.6172 or www. parks.ca.gov

San Clemente State Beach is another popular camping, hiking, picnicking, swimming, and surfing area. The state beach was once home to a 300-man California Conservation Camp during the Depression, and it was these CCC workers who built the park's campground. Nearly half of the 160 campsites have full hook-ups for RVs. The campground is on the coastal terrace, and there are trails down to the beach. Info: 949.492.3156 or www.parks.ca.gov

Father and kids checking out the waves

Grunion Runs

These strange little fish, which don't grow to much more than 6 inches in length during their three or four years of life, flop their way on shore to lay their eggs on Southern California's sandy beaches. They are quite predictable, coming ashore en masse in what are commonly called "grunion runs."

On those nights with the highest tides following full and new moons, the fish head toward shore. They time their spawning assaults so that when the females lay their 1,000 to 3,000 eggs each, the incoming high tide has just begun to ebb so the eggs won't be washed back out to sea. The females use their tails to drill into the wet sand up to their pectoral fins. Temporarily anchored in place, they lay their eggs as the males curl themselves around the females and release milt, which fertilizes the eggs.

The baby grunion develop inside a protective membrane and are ready to hatch within about nine days. A few days later, the next series of high tides arrives and the wave action triggers an enzyme that causes the eggs to hatch. The waves carry the newly hatched grunion out to sea where they grow for about a year before becoming mature enough to begin their own spawning cycles.

Grunion runs occur from March through August and each one usually lasts about three hours. The fish may be caught—generally June through March—but only with bare hands. For anyone age 16 and older, a valid California fishing license is required. Always check current fishing regulations for possible changes in open seasons.

Orange / San Diego

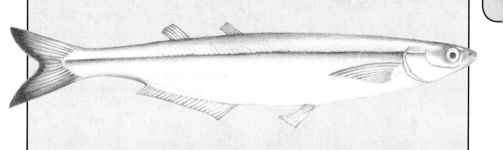

Grunion are noted for their ability to know when the highest tides will be accompanying full or new moons—the perfect time for the females to spawn on Southern California's sandy beaches.

San Diego County

With more than 70 miles of coastline and its warm year-round climate, San Diego County is a very popular place to be. And more than 3 million people agree, making it the second most populous county in the state and the city of San Diego, the seventh most populous city in the U.S.

Since the beginning of World War II, San Diego has been the focus of the military. Today, there are 16 naval and military installations ranging from the U.S. Coast Guard to the Marine Corps' Camp Pendleton and their Miramar Air Station, the Naval Air Station North Island, and a Navy SEAL training facility.

Today, the city is a delightful vacation refuge offering great beaches, museums, and parks that are unparalleled in the country. From miles of sandy beaches to Balboa Park and its world-class zoo to Old Town San Diego and the mission where it all began, there is always plenty to do.

SAN ONOFRE STATE BEACH

This 3,000-acre beach, which receives more than 2.5 million visitors a year, surrounds the now closed **San Onofre Nuclear Generating Station**. The state beach is comprised of three sections: San Onofre State Beach, which includes a campground; **San Onofre Surf Beach**, a day-use area; and **San Mateo Campground**, which is located on the inland side of Highway 1.

The majority of the state beach parallels Highway 1 for about 3.5 miles. The Marine Corps' Camp Pendleton is located across Highway 1, making it quite common to see tanks and helicopters being used in training exercises while driving either on the highway or in the park.

Beach is split by San Onofre Nuclear Generation Station

San Onofre State Beach's coastal campground is actually a series of parking spaces that parallel the bluff above the beach. Many are designed for RVs, while others allow space for tents. This beach is extremely popular with surfers. The area known as **Trestles Beach** is rumored to have some of the best breaking waves in California and in the nation. There are several paths leading from the sandstone bluff parking and campground areas to the beach. From the inland San Mateo Campground, you'll find a 1.5 mile trail to the ocean.

Activities: Camping, surfing, swimming, beachcombing, fishing, picnicking
Facilities: Campground
Dates: Open year round
Fees: There are camping and day-use fees.
Closest town: San Clemente
Info: Orange Coast State Parks District Office, 3030 Avenida del Presidente, San Clemente, CA 92672, 949.492.4872 or www.parks.ca.gov

MORE TO EXPLORE

Carlsbad State Beach is easily one of San Diego's most popular coastal beaches. An offshore reef creates smaller waves, perfect for the beginning surfer. There is also a swim-only section of beach and a generous promenade that stretches along much of the beach providing great views of nearby **Agua Hedionda Lagoon**. Info: 760.438.3143 or www.parks.ca.gov

South Carlsbad State Beach is often more of a cobble beach than sand, especially during winter as waves and water currents remove much of the sand. At the north end of the beach is a tall smoke stack that supports the local power plant. Back in the late 1960s, four smoke stacks lined the beach and the plant was fired by oil. Today, the plant has gone to one stack, and is fired by natural gas, producing very little carbon emissions. And San Diego County's first desalinization plant is currently being built next to the power plant. The park has 220 campsites. Info: 760.438.3143 or www.parks.ca.gov

Moonlight State Beach is located in the city of Encinitas, and surfing, swimming, and fishing are popular along its sandy shore. There is also a seasonal snack bar and equipment rentals. The beach got its name in the early 1900s as a popular place for midnight picnics. There are several other beaches in Encinitas including **Leucadia State Beach** (known by the locals

Co-author and son at South Carlsbad State Beach during winter

Orange / San Diego

as "**Beacon's Beach**"), **Stonesteps Beach, D Street Beach,** and **Swami's Beach**. Info: 760.633.2740 or www.ci.encinitas.ca.us

San Elijo State Beach and **Cardiff State Beach** are connected and offer more than 2 miles of shoreline. San Elijo is primarily a campground with 171 sites, while its southern partner Cardiff State Beach is focused on day-use. Cardiff State Beach is well known for its favorite surfing spots, with names like Pipes, Turtles, Georges, Cardiff Reef, and Seaside. Strong rip currents and near-shore holes can make this area dangerous for young or inexperienced swimmers. Check with the lifeguards about safe swimming areas, as they may change as conditions change. Info: 760.438.3143 or www.parks.ca.gov

Silver Strand State Beach is located on the 7-mile-long tombolo to San Diego Bay's Coronado Island. This is a great bicycle riding area with a paved bike trail paralleling the highway. There is easy parking adjacent to the ocean and a seasonal food concession, picnic tables, and dressing rooms. Self-contained RVs are allowed to stay the night. On the south side of the park entrance is **Silver Strand Natural Preserve**. Besides the rare coastal plants found here, it is also a nesting site for western snowy plovers. Info: 619.435.5184 or www.parks.ca.gov

Surf's up!

MISSION SAN LUIS REY DE FRANCIA

Father Antonio Peyri was placed in charge of Mission San Luis Rey de Grancia from the day it was founded in 1798, and he stayed for more than 30 years. Father Peyri created one of the largest and most successful missions, designing the original compound, an elaborate river- and spring-fed irrigation system that included charcoal-filtered water, a beautiful sunken garden, and a fanciful *lavanderia* where the Indians washed laundry from water that spewed from the mouths of carved stone gargoyle heads. The facilities sprawled across nearly 6 acres and included a large soldiers' barracks, a lime kiln, and an expansive cemetery. At its peak, the mission supported 3,000 mostly Luiseño Indians and 50,000 cattle, horses, and other livestock.

Mission San Luis Rey

Following Mexico's independence in 1821, Father Peyri returned home to Spain. Without the Father's leadership and guidance, the mission fell into ruin. In 1847, the U.S. Mormon Battalion occupied the mission for 10 years, and then in 1892, a small group of Franciscans from Mexico approached the bishop and requested that they be given refuge in California. He agreed and assigned them to Mission San Luis Rey de Francia, and Father Joseph O'Keefe was brought in to help them at the mission. What they found there were crumbling buildings and a nonexistent infrastructure. For the next 14 years, Father O'Keefe and his charges rebuilt the mission, including the church and the living quarters, on the foundations of the original buildings.

Significant restoration has taken place since that time. Some of the best finds occurred in the 1950s and 1960s when archaeologists discovered and uncovered the soldier barracks' foundation and the lavanderia, the latter a short walk across the mission grounds and down a long, elaborate set of stone steps.

The mission, which is located in what is today known as Oceanside, houses collections from the Spanish, Mexico, and U.S. military historical periods and many Indian baskets, and inside a walled enclosure on the east side of the church is a large cemetery. Inside the mission's main quadrangle, an expansive lawn and garden area are highlighted by what is likely the oldest pepper tree in California. Sailors actually brought the seeds from Peru in 1830, mistakenly thinking they were chili pepper seeds; the wrong type of pepper plant grew instead. The 170-plus-year-old tree has a trunk diameter exceeding 40 feet, and its longest limbs now require support so they don't break.

The famed pepper tree

Activities: Self-guided tours and Saturday tours by appointment

Facilities: Mission, church, gift shop

Orange / San Diego

Dates: Open daily
Fees: There is an admission fee.
Closest town: Oceanside
Info: Mission San Luis Rey, 4050 Mission Avenue, Oceanside, CA 92057, 760.757.3651 or www.sanluisrey.org

LEO CARRILLO RANCH HISTORIC PARK

It's likely that most people today have never heard of Leo Carrillo, but anyone old enough to have watched TV during the 1950s will remember seeing him play Pancho in the *Cisco Kid*. Carrillo was Cisco Kid's sidekick, and Pancho often got himself into trouble. The series was one of the first to be filmed in color, although it was broadcast in black and white. The park's visitor center has 200-plus of the series' programs available to watch, and one is usually playing for visitors.

Carrillo was descended from a long line of prominent early California families—his great grandfather was Carlos Antonio de Jesus Carrillo, one of California's governors under Mexican rule. Even though politics ran through his veins, he favored show business instead, launching his entertainment career in vaudeville during the 1920s. Later in life, he spent much of his time in Hollywood, but his life actually centered on the home he helped build in Carlsbad, the present location of the ranch. He purchased the 1,700-acre property in 1937 for $17 an acre and added 800 more acres later.

Carrillo's dream was to create a working cattle ranch, but he was going to do it in style. In 1939, construction began on the main wing of his hacienda; the architecture is a cross of Spanish, Southwestern, and some of his own creation. One thing to look for throughout the ranch is "LC"—Carrillo's initials can be found on everything from door knockers to fence posts. It was obvious that Carrillo wanted everyone to know that this was his place.

One thing that Carrillo loved most was hosting parties at his ranch. Many of his fellow Hollywood stars enjoyed horseback riding or sitting by the pool—which originally included a white sand beach. The big stone barbeque served up lots of ranch-raised meals to visitors such as Clarke Gable, Carol Lombard, and Will Rogers. There were so many parties that Carrillo's wife

Ranch house

Historic El Camino Real

While traveling U.S. 101, Highway 1, and other roads in Central and Southern California, watch for mission-style bells suspended from shepherds' crooks. These markers identify El Camino Real: The Royal Road. During Spain's control of Mexico and Alta California, any road under the jurisdiction of the Spanish Crown was called a camino real. In North America, that practice lasted only until 1821, the year Mexico won its independence from Spain. The new government quickly eliminated all road names that referenced the Spanish Crown.

Often called the King's Highway, this 600-mile long pathway was once traveled by Spanish missionaries

through Alta California as they established their 21 missions, the first being in San Diego in 1769. As much as they could, the padres traveled along the coast, but in several areas—such as the rugged mountains and steep cliffs along Big Sur—they were forced inland. The missions were spaced about 30 miles apart, which equated to a long-day's ride on mule or horseback. It is said that the padres spread mustard seed along the trail, so the yellow flowers would help fellow travelers identify the route.

In 1912, California began paving sections of the pathway, and by the 1920s portions of the original El Camino Real became U.S. Route 101. Today, the only remaining unpaved section of the original El Camino Real can be found along the San Andreas Fault scarp directly adjacent to Mission San Juan Bautista. The California state legislature identified the modern highways that follow as closely as possible the original King's Highway. They include sections of U.S. Route 101, SR 82, SR 37, SR 238, SR 123, and a half dozen more.

The bell placement program was begun by private citizens in 1892, picked up by the Automobile Club of Southern California from the mid-1920s to 1931, and finally taken over by the California Department of Transportation in 1933. Caltrans placed more than 500 new bells in 2005.

Orange / San Diego

Edith, who went by "Deedie," had another small house built up the hill from the hacienda so she could have some peace and quiet.

As the ranch matured, several head of cattle and a number of *vaqueros* (cowboys) lived here to keep it all running smoothly. Today, the cattle and vaqueros are gone and the city of Carlsbad oversees the rancho, preserving it as a last-

The old Cantina, where Carrillo and his vaqueros shared food and drink after a long day.

ing tribute to the man who believed in the importance of parks and open space. Always a conservationist, Carrillo served on the California State Park and Recreation Commission for 18 years and was instrumental in the state's acquisition of Hearst Castle in San Simeon. There is also a park named for him and listed in this book: **Leo Carrillo State Park** in Malibu, Los Angeles County (page 282).

The rancho is open to the public, but no pets are allowed. It is recommended that visitors wear comfortable walking shoes as the terrain is very uneven. Docents give free 90-minute tours on weekends—call the park for times.

Activities: Self-guided tours and free 90-minute docent-led tours
Facilities: Visitor center, museum
Dates: Open daily, closed on Monday
Fees: Donation
Closest town: Carlsbad
Info: Leo Carrillo Ranch Historic Park, 6200 Flying Leo Carrillo Lane, Carlsbad, CA 92009, 760.476.1042 or www.visitcarlsbad.com

SCRIPPS INSTITUTE OF OCEANOGRAPHY AND BIRCH AQUARIUM

The Birch Aquarium serves as the public education arm and interpretive center of the **University of California at San Diego's Scripps Institute of Oceanography.** Its outside entrance area is dramatic, with a large fountain sculpture of spy-hopping whales. While the Birch Aquarium may be smaller than some of California's other aquariums, its exhibits make up for its size and are a wonderful opportunity to experience underwater domains from around the world.

The aquarium's 60-plus habitat exhibits feature a variety of ocean life, from a giant Pacific octopus (*Octopus dofleini*) and wolf eels (*Anarrhicthys ocellatus*) to round stingrays (*Urolophus myliobatiformes*), and shiner seaperch (*Cymatogaster aggregata*). The giant kelp forest and its typical

California horn snail
(*Cerithideopsis californic*)

fish inhabitants are housed in a 70,000-gallon tank. Nearby, purple-striped jellies (*Pelagia colorata*) float with the currents in their tank and more than a dozen different sea horse species float about their own private home. There is also a beautiful and extensive coral reef exhibit.

The aquarium has many exciting interactive areas, including a tide-pool plaza featuring three living pools, where visitors are encouraged by docents and staff to get their hands wet. And in the "Boundless Energy" area, visitors can explore and learn about how nature can be used for generating power. Unlike most large aquariums, which are built near their water sources, the Birch Aquarium is located high on a hillside, so the aquarium's outside plaza offers a beautiful and expansive view of the Pacific Ocean.

Activities: Self-guided tours, demonstrations
Facilities: Gift shop, museum exhibits
Dates: Open daily, except Thanksgiving, Christmas, and New Year's Day.
Fees: There is a parking fee and an aquarium entrance fee.
Info: Birch Aquarium at Scripps, 2300 Expedition Way, La Jolla, CA 92037, 619.534.3474 or www.aquarium.ucsd.edu

Orange / San Diego

The Torrey Pine

The Torrey pine (*Pinus torreyana*) is one of the world's rarest pines, found only along the San Diego coastline and on Santa Rosa Island, one of the Channel Islands. The trees take the form of their environment—some are short and their canopies molded by the constant winds to the shape of the cliff edges they cling to. Others in protected canyons grow taller and more erect. An often day-long veil of fog helps them survive the dry summer months on their otherwise arid footholds.

Early Spanish sailors used the forested point they called Punto de Los Arboles or Point of Trees, as a navigational landmark as they sailed along the California coast. In 1850, Dr. Charles Parry identified the tree as a unique species and named it after his friend and fellow botanist John Torrey. Even at that early date—the year California was admitted to the Union—Dr. Parry was concerned for the trees' continued survival as they were being cut to create grassland for cattle grazing, as well as other uses. Finally, in 1885, San Diego officials offered a $100 reward for the apprehension of anyone vandalizing a Torrey pine tree. In 1889, the city council assured the protection of 369 acres of forest as a public park.

Popular use of the park was causing significant damage to the trees. Several leading citizens, including Ellen Browning Scripps, became involved in promoting the protection of the trees. Scripps—of the Scripps newspaper empire—donated much of her wealth to such endeavors as the Torrey Pines Natural Preserve, Scripps Institution of Oceanography, and the San Diego Zoo. She was instrumental in having botanist Guy Fleming appointed as the first custodian of the reserve in 1921. Today, Torrey Pines State Natural Reserve covers 2,000 acres and includes 300 endangered and protected native plant species.

Torrey pine cone

TORREY PINES STATE NATURAL RESERVE AND BEACH

This beautiful reserve protects the Torrey pine (*Pinus torreyana*), the rarest pine tree in the United States. These relatively small, often wind-sculpted pines live only in the park and on Santa Rosa Island. Disease, climate changes, and development have combined forces to reduce the once larger numbers and range of the tree to its remaining two small domains.

Torrey Pines Visitor Center

While the park's namesake is the Torrey pine, which grows primarily on the ancient terrace above the beach, there is also a major saltwater marsh area lying to the north. With saltwater marshes nearly extinct in Southern California, this area is a vital link in the Pacific Flyway for migrating birds. Surrounded by houses and other development on both sides, the marsh is an island paradise for wildlife.

From the park's entry gate at the beach level, it's a short, but steep, walk, bicycle ride, or drive to the top of the terrace where trailheads and a small visitor center are located. The **Torrey Pines Visitor Center** is inside the pueblo-style house that was originally built in 1923 as a restaurant. Today, it houses exhibits on the park's natural and cultural history, in addition to a small gift shop. There is also a garden of native plants, each identified with both common and scientific names, in front of the house. Wonderful easterly views can be seen from the bluff behind the visitor center.

The trails are relatively short and several drop down between the steeply carved gullies and lead to the beach along the face of the bluff. Look closely at the bluff and fossils of ancient marine creatures can occasionally be found imprinted in the soft rocks. The park is protected, so digging in the bluff is not allowed, but high tides and winter wave action often uncover new fossils.

Torrey Pines State Beach

Orange / San Diego

331

The reserve and the beach are open for day use only. There is no camping in either. When walking the trails, please do not take shortcuts up or down the switchbacks, which tends to increase erosion rates. Picnicking is not allowed in the reserve, but food may be taken down to the beach. Because of the high fire danger, smoking is not permitted in the reserve. For those who do not wish to hike the trails to the beach, there is a parking lot next to the reserve and at the beach entry kiosk, which is at sea level and only a few yards from the beach. Pets are not allowed in the natural reserve, park, or the beach and cannot be left in vehicles.

Activities: Hiking, swimming, fishing, surfing, beachcombing, beach picnics
Facilities: Visitor center, gift shop
Dates: Open daily
Fees: There is a day-use fee.
Info: San Diego Coast District Office, 4477 Pacific Hwy., San Diego, CA 92110, 619.688.3260 or www.parks.ca.gov

MISSION SAN DIEGO DE ALCALÁ

Mission San Diego de Alcalá was the first Spanish mission in Alta California. Founded by Father Junipero Serra in 1769, the last time Europeans had been in the area was in 1602, when Spanish explorers sailed through the bay. Thus, when the Franciscan missionaries arrived more than 150 years later, it was the first time these Indians had seen Europeans, and it was also the first time they had been exposed to Christianity.

The first mission was established near the coast and the presidio—founded by Captain Gaspar de Portola. After five years, the site was determined to be unsuitable, and Father Luis Jayme, the pastor, moved the mission to its current location. While most mission Indians were peaceful, there were attacks on the mission. In 1775, a few Indians hostile to the church attacked, burning the new mission and killing Father Jayme.

By 1780, a new mission and its support building had been constructed on the same site, this time of adobe and in a fort-like quadrangle around a central open patio. Over the next 20 years, the mission flourished, housing more than 1,400 Indians who tended to livestock, horses, and fields of barley, wheat, and corn on 50,000 acres. As was relatively common in California, an earthquake in 1803 severely damaged the church. Following the 1812 earthquake, which caused more damage, the padres built thick buttresses at the base of the church to protect it from future earthquakes.

The mission ceased being a profitable enterprise in 1833, after being secularized by the Mexican government. U.S. Army troops found the mission in disrepair, but made enough repairs to turn the mission into temporary quarters where they stayed until 1857. Even though President Lincoln returned the missions to the Catholic Church in 1862, the mission continued to be neglected. It wasn't until 1915 that the Sisters of Saint Joseph of Corondolet established an American Indian school at the mission, and then CCC crews came in during the Depression to do additional restoration. Finally, in 1941, the mission reopened its doors as an active parish, a role it continues to fulfill to this day.

The mission's museum is named for Father Jayme. The exhibits, housed in different buildings throughout the compound, feature hundreds of artifacts from firearms to tools and even an old gin jug. Apparently, the lonely outpost required a few of its citizens to partake in more than ceremonial wine and prayer. There is also an active archaeological dig site that contains remnants of the mission's original monastery. But the most

The mission's bell tower

prominent architectural feature here is the bell tower—its tall, triangular shape holds five bells. The largest weighs 1,200 pounds and was cast from five smaller bells sent to the mission in 1796.

Activities: Self-guided and guided tours
Facilities: Mission, church, visitor center, gift shop
Dates: Open daily
Fees: Suggested donation
Closest town: San Diego
Info: Mission San Diego de Alcalá, 10818 San Diego Mission Road, San Diego, CA 92108, 619.283.7319 or www.missionsandiego.com

OLD TOWN SAN DIEGO STATE HISTORIC PARK

Mexican artwork at Fiesta de Reyes

San Diego is California's oldest community. This is evident in Old Town San Diego State Historic Park, a restoration of life back to the 1820s through 1870s. Walking the roads of this vibrant park today, it takes a bit of work to imagine what it was like here so long ago.

Old Town's reformation from near ruin began when it became a state historic park in 1968. The historic adobes have been restored and the streets no longer turn to mud during San Diego's very infrequent rainy days. The result is an incredibly fun and informative place to spend several hours. For history buffs, there are nearly two dozen historic buildings, some of which have been restored and refurbished and serve as gift shops, restaurants, and antique shops. Others are now museums that exhibit hundreds of early San Diego artifacts.

Begin your visit at the **Robinson-Rose House Visitor Center**. Attorney James Robinson built the home in 1853 for his family. When he passed away in 1857, Louis Rose purchased the home. Fast forward to today and the home-turned-visitor center is full of helpful information, including a model display of Old Town as it looked in 1872. Guided tours—at 11 A.M. and 2 P.M. each day—start from here.

La Casa de Estudillo is the centerpiece of the park. Captain Jose Maria de Estudillo built this adobe in 1827-29, but only enjoyed his new home for a year. He died in 1830, and the home passed to his children, and then, unfortunately, to a caretaker who sold many of its fixtures. Building restoration began in 1910,

There are ample restaurants and shops to explore

along with efforts to refurnish the home. Today, it provides a wonderful look at how these early Spanish and Mexican settlers lived.

La Casa de Bandini was constructed in 1829 by Juan Bandini, Jose Estudillo's son-in-law. Bandini was always a step ahead politically, holding offices under the Mexican government's control then providing supplies and his home to the U.S. Navy's Commodore Stockton when the Americans took over. In 1850, Bandini sold his home to Albert Seeley, who added the second floor and turned it into the Cosmopolitan Hotel. Today it is a colorful Mexican restaurant with a beautiful outdoor garden seating area in addition to its indoor tables.

View of Seeley Stable from the upper level

The **Seeley Stable** belonged to Albert Seeley who owned the San Diego-Los Angeles Stage Line and ran his Concord stages over the 130-mile trip in less than 24 hours. The Southern Pacific Railroad ran Seeley out of business in 1887. Today, the stable and barn hold an extensive horse-drawn carriage collection and exhibits of Western memorabilia, including saddles and Indian artifacts.

La Casa de Machado y Stewart was built in 1835 by Jose Manuel Machado, a corporal at the presidio. His daughter Rose married Jack Stewart in 1845 and moved in with the family. Although remodeled in 1911, the house remained in the Machado family until sold in 1945. It is now a museum.

Fiesta de Reyes is where nearly everyone who comes to Old Town San Diego ends up. It's a large cluster of buildings in the corner of the historic park that greets everyone with its multitude of brightly-colored flowers. The walkways pass shops filled with treasures, from fine jewelry and clothes to china and paintings, mostly from Central and South America. There are also several restaurants serving a variety of foods, but Mexican cuisine is the specialty; it seems only appropriate while in this historic Spanish-Mexican town.

Activities: Shopping, dining, historic tours
Facilities: Visitor center, shops, restaurants, museums, historic buildings
Dates: Open daily, except Thanksgiving, Christmas, and New Year's Day.
Fees: There is an entrance fee for Seeley Stables and La Casa de Estudillo.
Info: Old Town San Diego Historic Park, 4002 Wallace Street, San Diego, CA 92110, 619.220.5422 or www.parks.ca.gov

Orange / San Diego

BALBOA PARK

Named one of the best urban parks in the United States, Balboa Park is home to 14 museums and art galleries, four theaters, and a world-renowned zoo. The 1,200-acre park attracts up to 15 million people each year. Although officially established in 1868 by the City of San Diego, the park began to establish its reputation in 1915 when it teamed with San Francisco in trying to be named the site of the 1915 California-Panama Exposition. Twenty years later, San Diego officially hosted the California Pacific International Exposition, adding new buildings to what was still simply known as "City Park."

The **San Diego Natural History Museum** (619.232.3821 or www.sdnhm. org) is one of the more interesting museums in Balboa Park. Originally founded in 1874 as the "San Diego Society of Natural History," the museum is the second oldest natural history museum west of the Mississippi. Although society members had explored and collected specimens since its founding, they developed the organization's first natural history exhibits in 1912, in the newly constructed Hotel Cecil. The society moved the museum to three different locations over the next few years until finally, in

The Botanical Building

1933, a permanent home was found in Balboa Park, where much of the existing building was constructed.

One of the best things about this natural history museum is that most of what would normally be static, permanent displays are neither permanent nor static. New exhibits—that can range from bugs to wildfires—bring freshness to the museum and often tell the bigger story than simply looking at bones or wildlife specimens. For example, one exhibit may show how humans interact with sharks and black bears, and, more importantly, how humans impact these animals' existence.

There are many museums and attractions here, all within easy walking distance. Some favorites include the **San Diego Air and Space Museum** (619. 234.8291 or www.sandiegoairandspace.org), the **San Diego Museum of Man** (619.239.2001 or www.museumofman.org), and the **San Diego History Center** (619.232.6203 or www.sandiegohistory.org). The **San Diego Zoo** (619.231.1515 or www.sandiegozoo.org) is also found in Balboa Park. Known for its conservationism, the zoo features more than 4,000 rare and endangered animals. And last, the **Botanical Building** is one of the most photographed sites in Balboa Park. Constructed for the 1915 Exposition, the garden includes more than 2,000 plants. Admission is free, hours are Friday through Wednesday, 10 A.M. to 4 P.M., closed Thursdays and holidays.

> **Activities:** Museum hopping, picnicking, bicycling, swimming, golf, jogging
> **Facilities:** Museums, zoo, visitor center, gardens
> **Dates:** The park is open daily, but some of its museums and other facilities may be closed on holidays or have different hours.
> **Fees:** The park is free. There are fees for the museums and zoo.
> **Info:** Balboa Park Visitors Center, 1549 El Prado, Balboa Park, San Diego 92101, 619.239.0512 or www.balboapark.org

CORONADO ISLAND

San Diego Bay's Coronado Island, which means "the crowned one" in Spanish, has seen many changes since it was controlled by the Spanish during the late 1700s. The land was purchased by three private citizens in 1885, their intention being to create a major resort community. Three years later, **Hotel del Coronado** was completed.

The Hotel del Coronado, which is a State Historic Landmark, offers high-end

Hotel del Coronado

337

luxury. It has served such guests as Charles Lindbergh, Muhammad Ali, Babe Ruth, Willy Mays, and a number of presidents, including Franklin D. Roosevelt, Ronald Reagan, Richard Nixon, Gerald Ford, Jimmy Carter, Bill Clinton, and George Bush.

For those unable to afford the hotel's high-priced luxury

Cyclists on the Silver Strand tombolo bike trail

during those early years, tents and cottages were available in the adjacent **Tent City**. The last of the cottages was removed near the beginning of World War II.

When the city of San Diego began expanding their public transit system in 1910, they added Coronado to the line. In 1969, the prominent **San Diego-Coronado Bridge** opened, allowing significantly easier access to the island. Today, driving over the bridge provides a spectacular view of the surrounding U.S. Navy shipyards. A shallow channel called "Spanish Bight" originally separated Coronado from **North Island**, but the advent of World War II saw the Navy filling the water passage to better meet their needs. The Navy still maintains several facilities on the island, including a Navy Seal training area.

Coronado's identity as an island is a little confusing since the Silver Strand tombolo connects the island to the mainland south of Coronado. A tombolo is a narrow strip of beach or a sand bar that links an island to its nearby mainland. Silver Strand tombolo provides a well-traveled roadway that connects with the Coronado Bridge. The strand also has a great beach and a paved bike trail along its length. **Coronado Central Beach** runs along Ocean Boulevard, offering easy access to swimming, fishing, and tide-pool exploring. **Glorietta Bay Beach** is south of Hotel del Coronado and offers a large grass area and a great view of the San Diego-Coronado Bridge. About 4.5 miles south is **Silver Strand State Beach**, which offers beaches on both the bay and ocean sides of the Silver Strand. Beachfront camping is available for fully self-contained RVs only.

There are many other great places to stay on Coronado Island, too, and the Coronado Visitor Center's website has a detailed list of vacation and overnight accommodations.

Info: Coronado Visitor Center, 619.435.7242 or www.coronadovisitorcenter.com; Hotel del Coronado, 619.435.6611 or www.hoteldel.com

MARITIME MUSEUM OF SAN DIEGO

This isn't a museum-in-a-building, but a museum of historic ships and boats on the waters of San Diego Bay. For many, the star of the museum is the *Star of India*, the oldest active sailing ship in the world. Built in the Ramsey Shipyard on the Isle of Man, located in the Irish Sea, her hull was made of iron, which was an experiment of sorts since wooden ships were still the norm at that time. When completed in 1863, she was named *Euterpe*, after the Greek muse of poetry and music. On two of her first voyages, she was nearly sunk by a collision and a typhoon. When she was purchased by new owners in 1906, they renamed her the *Star of India*. The ship is docked and visitors can both tour the ship and even sail on her during special voyages.

For Cold War buffs, the museum's B-39 is the last and largest of the Soviet Navy's diesel-electric submarines used in the Pacific to track U.S. and NATO warships. And one of the museum's newest additions is the PCF 816 Swift Boat used to patrol rivers and canals primarily in the Vietnam's Mekong Delta. These boats proved extremely successful at stopping one of North Vietnam's primary supply lines into Vietnam during the Vietnam war. Swift Boat tours around San Diego Bay are offered twice daily on weekends.

There are several additional ships in the collection including the *Berkeley*, an 1898 steam ferryboat that worked San Francisco Bay for 60 years. Today it serves as the museum's offices, library, workshop, and museum store. Not far away is the state of California's official tall ship, the *Californian*. It's a replica of the 1847 Revenue Cutter *C.W. Lawrence*, which enforced federal laws along the California coast during the Gold

View of the *Star of India* from the *HMS Surprise*

Rush. The *Californian* is used for at-sea educational programs and public adventure sails of varying lengths and distances. Also dockside is the *HMS Surprise*, a replica an 18th century Royal Navy frigate. Her primary claim to fame is having been refitted as a 24-gun frigate for the Academy Award winning film, *Master and Commander: The Far Side of the World*. It is now part of the museum and open to the public.

> **Activities**: Ship tours, rides on vessels
> **Facilities**: Exhibits, museum store
> **Dates**: Daily 9 A.M. to 8 P.M.
> **Fees**: Museum fee, addition fees for vessel rides
> **Closest town**: San Diego
> **Info**: 1492 Harbor Drive, San Diego, CA 92101, 619.234.9153 ext. #101 or www.sdmaritime.org

CABRILLO NATIONAL MONUMENT

The monument memorializes Juan Rodriquez Cabrillo, the first European to land on what would become 400 years later the West Coast of the United States. Cabrillo spent less than a week here before continuing his exploration north along the coast. Today, on the grounds of Cabrillo National Monument, rather than the isolation and the Native Americans that Cabrillo and his crew would have encountered, are the remains of **Fort Rosecrans**, the **Old Point Loma Lighthouse**, and the **Visitor Center at Cabrillo National Monument**. The monument is a popular daytime destination for thousands of people each year, partly because of the spectacular views of the city of San Diego and its sprawling harbor.

The Old Point Loma Lighthouse has an interesting—and somewhat sad—history. Point Loma was selected as the home of San Diego's new lighthouse because, at 422-feet above sea level, it would be a beacon to those at sea. But

View from the Old Point Loma Lighthouse; the park's visitor center is on the left and the city of San Diego in the distance on the right.

Old Point Loma Lighthouse

the lighthouse only served for 36 years—from 1855 to 1891—because it and Point Loma were routinely shrouded in fog and low clouds, which obscured the beam of light. Thus, a new structure, called the **"New Point Loma Lighthouse,"** was built at the bottom of Point Loma, 100-yards south of the original. Today, visitors can tour the old lighthouse and during special events, climb the stairs to the top of the historic structure.

On the closest weekend to September 28th—the day that Cabrillo landed—the annual Cabrillo Festival is held, with a re-enactment of his landing and plenty of food and cultural events to keep everyone active and satisfied. The third weekend in January is also Whale Watch Weekend, with lots of marine related programs, demonstrations, and whale watching at the peak of the gray whales' southern migration.

In addition to the films shown in the visitor center, rangers lead tours of the tide pools and coastal scrub plant community. There is also a self-guided trail with interpretive panels along the way that tell the natural and cultural history of Point Loma. While exploring the park, visitors are required to stay on established trails in order to protect the fragile coastal sage scrub ecosystem. The cliff edge is very unstable and crumbles easily, so visitors are advised to be vigilant.

Juan Rodriquez Cabrillo

Activities: Hiking, fishing, picnicking

Facilities: Visitor center, gift shop, museum, lighthouse

Dates: Open daily

Fees: Fees are charged to enter the park.

Closest town: San Diego

Info: Cabrillo National Monument, 1800 Cabrillo Memorial Drive, San Diego, CA 92106, 619.557.5450 or www.nps.gov

Orange / San Diego

TIJUANA RIVER NATIONAL ESTUARINE RESEARCH RESERVE

Within view of Mexico, the Tijuana River National Estuarine Research Reserve has brought together three partners—California State Parks, the U.S. Fish and Wildlife Service, and the National Oceanic and Atmospheric Administration (NOAA)—in order to protect 2,500 acres of wetlands found here. **Tijuana Slough National Wildlife Refuge, Border Field State Park,** and **Tijuana River Valley County Park** are included within the reserve's boundary.

With development having filled more than 90 percent of California's coastal wetlands, the reserve has become a critical resting and feeding stop for millions of migrating birds each year. Within the reserve, numerous trails meander among the tules and rushes and around the open and protected waters of the estuary that lie north of the border that separates the U.S. and Mexico's Baja, California.

Established in 1982, the Tijuana River Estuary is one of only 22 national estuarine research reserves in the nation. Border Field State Park lies in the far southwest corner of the estuary. There is a marker here that was placed on the site in 1851, following the treaty of Guadalupe Hidalgo, which identifies the international border.

At the Border Field park entrance, a dirt parking lot also serves as an equestrian staging area. If the gate is not locked, you can drive to a picnic area that is situated on a bluff overlooking the ocean. This area is directly adjacent to the **U.S./Mexican border**, where a fence separates the United States from its neighbor to the south. The border fence drops down into the ocean and a small town is visible on the other side, including a bullring arena.

Part of what makes the estuary and the neighboring state park so attractive is the diverse natural habitats that they encompass. But the reserve has not always

A fence extending into the surf zone marks the U.S./Mexican border

been so pristine. Walk the **McCoy Trail** from the **Tijuana Estuary Visitor Center** and you're walking on a dike built before World War II, when the area was divided into sections and used as sewage settling ponds. The dikes were breached in the 1980s in order to restore the natural tidal flow.

Riparian, coastal sage scrub, open beaches, salt marsh, and mud flats provide the diversity of food and safe havens for over 370 species of migratory and native birds. At least six endangered species are seen here: California least tern (*Sterna antillarum*), California brown pelican (*Pelecanus occidentalis*), the light-footed clapper rail (*Rallus longirostris levipes*), western snowy plover (*Charadrius alexandrinus*), least Bell's vireo (*Vireo bellii pusillus*), and Belding's savannah sparrow (*Passerculus sandwichensis beldingi).* In addition to the endangered species, plenty of non-endangered birds also can be seen throughout the two areas—peregrine

Snowy egret

falcons (*Falco peregrinus*), sandpipers (*Calidris minutilla*), black-necked stilts (*Himantopus mexicanus*), and snowy egrets (*Egretta thula*).

The animals here depend on the different plant habitats scattered around the reserve. Dunes, salt marsh, mud flat, vernal pool, brackish pond, and coastal sage scrub are the most common, with the presence or absence of saltwater significantly changing the types of plants that can inhabit any area. For example, in the upper marsh, salt marsh bird's beak (*Cordylanthus maritimus*)—a federally listed endangered plant—grows immediately above the high tide line. The reserve is one of the few places in the world where the plant is able to survive.

There are several miles of trail that cross the relatively flat terrain, offering access to prime bird-viewing areas and a path down to the mouth of the Tijuana River, where it empties into the Pacific Ocean. The river drains over 1,700 square miles of watershed along the California and Mexican border.

The visitor center features exhibits on the area's plants and animals, a research library, interpretive programs, special trips, and videos. Outside the visitor center is a garden filled with indigenous plants from the area.

Activities: Hiking, bird watching, beachcombing, horseback riding
Facilities: Visitor center, picnic facilities
Dates: Open daily; visitor center closed on Monday and Tuesday
Fees: None
Closest town: Imperial Beach
Info: Tijuana Estuary Visitor Center, 301 Caspian Way, Imperial Beach, CA 91932, 619.575.3613 or www.trnerr.org

Orange / San Diego

About the authors . . .

Together, Ken McKowen and Dahlynn McKowen have 60-plus years of professional writing, editing, publication, marketing, and public relations experience. The McKowens, who are married, have such a large body of freelance work that when they reached more than 2,000 articles, stories, and photographs published, they stopped counting.

The McKowens founded and own Publishing Syndicate LLC, a Northern California publishing house. Dahlynn is the CEO and publisher, and Ken serves as president and managing editor. Publishing Syndicate has many authors under contract for all types of genres, including the successful anthology series *Not Your Mother's Books* (www.PublishingSyndicate.com).

They are also prolific authors, travel writers, and well respected ghostwriters, having worked with CEOs and founders of some of the nation's biggest companies. They have even ghostwritten for a former President and a few California governors and elected officials.

From 1999 to 2009, Ken and Dahlynn were consultants, coauthors, and editors for *Chicken Soup for the Soul*, where they collaborated with series founders Jack Canfield and Mark Victor Hansen on several books, such as *Chicken Soup for*

Ken, video camera in hand and camera bag on his shoulder, doing research for this book, and Dahlynn at the beach in Crescent City, California

the Entrepreneur's Soul; *Chicken Soup for the Soul in Menopause*; *Chicken Soup for the Fisherman's Soul*; and *Chicken Soup for the Soul: Celebrating Brothers and Sisters.* They also edited and ghost-created many more Chicken titles during their tenure, with Dahlynn reading more than 100,000 story submissions.

For highly acclaimed outdoor publisher Wilderness Press, the McKowen's books include national award-winner *Best of California's Missions, Mansions and Museums; Best of Oregon and Washington's Mansions, Museums and More;* and *The Wine-Oh! Guide to California's Sierra Foothills.*

Under Publishing Syndicate LLC, the couple authored *Wine Wherever: In California's Mid-Coast & Inland Region,* and are actively researching wineries for *Wine Wherever: In California's Paso Robles Region,* the second book in the series. The couple also created a winery app; called "Wine Wherever," the mobile winery-destination journaling app is available for the iPhone (www.WineWherever.com).

If that's not enough on their plate already, the McKowens also created and host their "Places to Discover" website and blog, which features many travel destinations they have visited around the world (www.PlacesToDiscover.com).

Ken pointing to a whale (Big Sur Coast) and Dahlynn comes face-to-face with a lifesize replica of a bull elephant seal at the Mammal Marine Center in Sausalito (page 138)

Photo Credits

Of the 330-plus photos in this book, all but the following 80 were taken by the co-authors:

Page 6: fotosav/Shutterstock.com (freeway overpass)
Page 6: spirit of america/Shutterstock.com (fault line)
Page 10: wk1003mike/Shutterstock.com (fish)
Page 13: Courtesy of the National Park Service
Page 14: trubach/Shutterstock.com
Page 15: Courtesy of the National Park Service
Page 19: Ron Kacmarcik/Shutterstock.com
Page 22: cvalle/Shutterstock.com (common egret)
Page 31: littleny/Shutterstock.com
Page 44: Courtesy of the National Park Service
Page 52: Courtesy of the National Park Service
Page 57: Courtesy of the National Park Service
Page 60: Jonathan Lenz/Shutterstock.com (Douglas iris)
Page 78: James R.T. Bossert/Shutterstock.com
Page 93: Andreas Altenburger/Shutterstock.com
Page 95: Stephen B. Goodwin/Shutterstock.com
Page 100: Rich Carey/Shutterstock.com
Page 105: Mariusz S. Jurgielewicz/Shutterstock.com
Page 107: Mari Anuhea/Shutterstock.com
Page 112: Matt Tilghman/Shutterstock.com
Page 113: Tory Kallman/Shutterstock.com
Page 114: cdrin/Shutterstock.com
Page 116: Jerry Sanchez/Shutterstock.com
Page 119: cdrin/Shutterstock.com
Page 122: Phil McDonald/Shutterstock.com
Page 124: Courtesy of National Park Service
Page 126: cdrin/Shutterstock.com
Page 129: Radoslaw Lecyk/Shutterstock.com
Page 130: Paul Reeves Photography/Shutterstock.com
Page 132: Keith McIntryre/Shutterstock.com
Page 134: millerium arkay/Shutterstock.com
Page 137: Courtesy of the National Park Service
Page 139: cdrin/Shutterstock.com
Page 144: Arthit Kaeoratanapattama/Shutterstock.com
Page 145: Martin D. Vonka/Shutterstock.com
Page 155: M. Wassell/Shutterstock.com
Page 161: Michael Warwick/Shutterstock.com
Page 167: Courtesy of the National Park Service
Page 180: Anderl /Shutterstock.com
Page 196: Christophe Rouziou/Shutterstock.com
Page 208: Brandon Bourdages/Shutterstock.com
Page 209: Carrie Abrahamson/Shutterstock.com
Page 210: Courtesy of the National Park Service
Page 223: Courtesy of the National Park Service
Page 227: Juancat/Shutterstock.com
Page 231: Doug Meek/Shutterstock.com
Page 239: Gerald A. DeBoer/Shutterstock.com
Page 252: Dwight Smith/Shutterstock.com
Page 255: Bryan Brazil/Shutterstock.com
Page 258: Henrick Lehnerer/Shutterstock.com
Page 262: Ken Wolter/Shutterstock.com
Page 263: Susan Schmitz/Shutterstock.com
Page 266: Courtesy of the National Park Service

Index

This index identifies the first major reference point for each entry.

C

E

Index

Index

M

N

Nike Missile Site, 135
North Beach Campground, 246
North Humboldt Bay, 70
North Island, 338
North Marsh, 171
North Shore Trail, 216
Northern spotted owl, 74
Noyo River and Harbor, 92

O

Oak Trail, 241
Oakland Museum of California, 168
Oakwood Trail, 137
Ocean View Boulevard, 205
Oceano Campground, 246
Oceano Dunes State Vehicle Recreation
   Area, 246
Octopus Tree Trail, 62
Old Mine Trail, 123
Old Point Loma Lighthouse, 340
Old Town Eureka, 66
Old Town San Diego State Historic
   Park, 334
Olivera Street, 299
Opal Creek, 181
Open Sea Exhibit, 198
Orange County, 312
Orchard Creek, 84
Orick, 56
Overlook Fire Road Trail, 255
Overlook Trail, 277, 280

P

Pacific Grove, 205
Pacific Grove Museum of National
   History, 207
Pacific House, 195
Palomarin Trailhead, 114
Pantoll Campground, 122
Pantoll Mountain Theater Trail, 123
Pantoll to Old Mine Trail, 123
Pantoll Trail, 123
Paramount Ranch, 273
Partington Cove Trail, 231
Patrick's Point State Park, 59
Patrick's Point Visitor Center, 59
Pebble Beach, 118
Pebble Beach/17-Mile Drive, 209
Pebble Beach Concours d' Elegance, 213
Pebble Beach Drive, 42
Pelican Point, 317
Pelican State Beach, 42
Pescadero Marsh Natural Preserve, 171

Pescadero State Beach, 171
Peter Strauss Ranch Trail, 277
Pfeiffer Beach, 228
Pfeiffer Big Sur State Park, 224
Pfeiffer's Ranch Resort, 225
Piedras Blancas Light Station, 233
Piedras Blancas State Marine Reserve, 233
Pier 39: 165
Pierce Point Road, 112
Piercy, 79
Pillar Point Harbor, 170
Pine Ridge Trail, 227
Pismo Beach (city), 245
Pismo State Beach, 245
Plaza Viña del Mar, 128
Point Arena Lighthouse, 96
Point Bennett, 267
Point Bonita Trail, 137
Point Cabrillo Light Station State
   Historic Park, 95
Point Conception, 257
Point Dume State Beach, 286
Point Fermin Lighthouse, 304
Point Joe, 209
Point Lobos Natural State Reserve, 213
Point Magu State Park, 278
Point Montara Lighthouse Hostel, 171
Point Pinole Regional Shoreline, 167
Point Pinos, 194, 205
Point Pinos Lighthouse, 208
Point Reyes Beach (North and South), 115
Point Reyes Historic Lighthouse, 115
Point Reyes National Seashore, 112
Point Sal, 246
Point Santa Cruz, 187
Point Sur State Historic Park, 220
Point Vincente Lighthouse, 304
Port of Los Angeles, 304
Port San Luis, 244
Prairie Creek Redwoods State Park, 51
Prairie Creek Visitor Center, 52
Preston Island, 42
Proboscis Grove, 225
Punta Gorda Lighthouse, 83

Q

Queen Wilhelmina Tulip Garden, 157
Queensway Bay, 305

R

Railroad Creek, 84
Rancho del Oso Nature and History
   Center, 181, 182

Index

Abandoned boat, California coast